To my
Brother George!
good luck on the whole *house*!
& Happy B'Day '84
Willie

THE
HANDBOOK OF
DO-IT-YOURSELF
MATERIALS

Also by Max Alth

The Homeowner's Quick-Repair and Emergency Guide
Masonry and Concrete Work
Do-It-Yourself Plumbing
The Stain Removal Handbook
All About Bikes and Bicycling
All About Locks and Locksmithing

THE HANDBOOK OF DO-IT-YOURSELF MATERIALS

MAX ALTH

A STONESONG PRESS BOOK

CROWN PUBLISHERS, INC.
NEW YORK

Dedicated to

CHAR

MISCH

KIM

MIKE

DARCEY

MENDLE

ARABELLA and all

other building-crafts

people

Library of Congress Cataloging in
Publication Data

Alth, Max, 1917–
    The handbook of do-it-yourself materials.

    Includes index.
    1. Building materials—Amateurs'
manuals. 2. Dwellings—Maintenance and
repair—Amateurs' manuals.
I. Title.
TA403.4.A45 1982   643'.7'028   82-2378
ISBN: 0-517-543664   AACR2

Book Design by Deborah & Richard Waxberg
10 9 8 7 6 5 4 3 2 1
First Edition

CONTENTS

PREFACE

This book has been prepared with four goals in mind:

• to acquaint you with home construction, repair, and remodeling materials presently available;

• to help you select whatever is best for your purpose by describing the nature and qualities of the materials;

• to prepare you for the tools, skills, and labor that may be necessary to apply the various materials;

• to provide a handy reference volume in which you can find dimensions, weights, and other important data on common building materials, data you could not otherwise find without securing hundreds of brochures or visiting dozens of supply houses.

This book does not include everything in the field of construction, repair, and alterations. One hundred books this size would be insufficient.

What we have selected from this vast range of manufactured materials is that which you are most likely to use, and that which you will find without problem in most lumberyards, building supply houses, and other sources. We have chosen the known and dependable materials over what is new and untried. In a word, this is a practical book.

The application information furnished is sufficient in some instances, given a good dose of common sense, to enable you to accomplish whatever is necessary with the materials you select. At a minimum, this information will prepare you for what is required by way of time, labor, and skills so that you will not undertake a job that is too much for you or pass up a job that is relatively easy.

1 INTRODUCTION

The days when a nail was something the blacksmith hammered out on his anvil are now long gone. At present there are more than 1,400 different types and sizes of nails being manufactured. Some are so small and thin that a thousand are required to make one pound. Others—boat spikes—are two feet long and weigh several pounds each. In between there are box nails, spiral nails, split nails, painted nails, copper nails, aluminum nails, ribbed nails, steel nails. . . .

Years ago the same blacksmith who made nails and horseshoes also made building hardware—locks, latches, hinges—on the same forge. Today there are thousands of different types and sizes of metal and plastic parts that fall into the building hardware category.

Not too long ago trees were cut into rough timbers at a sawmill or by the hands of two sturdy sawyers. Carpenters then took the timbers and cut and shaped them into all the parts of the building by hand. The carpenters made the doors, windows, trim, and floor. They even cut shingles from short blocks of cedar logs. Today, all these things—and more—can be bought at the lumberyard in almost ready-to-use form. Wood is shaped at the mill and called millwork. Doors and windows come ready-made and assembled.

These changes have made it possible for both the professional carpenter and the novice to work that much more quickly. One no longer needs a great deal of experience. Much of the work is already done. In some instances, such as windows and doors, all the work is done. All you need do is install them. Windows come mounted in their frames. Doors too can be purchased prehung in their frames with all the hardware—hinges and locks in place.

You can even purchase window and door trim precut to size. Whereas an experienced carpenter with a suitable miter box may require twenty minutes or so to cut the trim, no time is needed for the task of accurately cutting the trim when it is purchased cut to size. Installation is the easiest part of this job.

Change in plumbing materials has also greatly reduced the time and skill necessary to cut and install pipe. For example, galvanized iron pipe can be replaced today with plastic pipe. Not only does the plastic pipe weigh one twentieth as much as the iron, but it doesn't rust or sweat and can be quickly cut with any saw. Plastic pipe does not need to be threaded. Instead it can be "welded" to its fittings with a daub of cement.

The old lead-caulked joints that were necessary with the old-fashioned cast-iron pipe have been replaced by rubber grommets and a bolted-in-place, No-hub fitting. There is no longer any need for the pot of molten lead, the leather gloves and pads, and the caulking irons. The joint that took a skilled man half an hour can now be accomplished by a novice in minutes.

The net result of all these changes is that while the need for skill has been reduced, the task of selection has been complicated. All doors do not come prehung; plastic pipe and No-hub joints cannot be used everywhere. Whereas early carpenters had to worry about only securing properly seasoned wood, today's carpenters have to know when to use solid wood or plywood or particle board or plastic. And whereas yesterday's mechanics had to choose only between shingles and clapboard, today there are fifty different sidings and roofing materials from which to make your selection. The problem today lies not in securing material, but in securing the material best suited to one's needs, and this is rarely simple. Going to the proper source of supply—lumberyard, masonry yard, or builder's hardware supply shop—and simply describing your needs won't work for a number of reasons.

Generally, the workers at the yards know where the material is stored and a little basic information but not much about the materials themselves. And even if they knew more, they would not give serious advice on materials, which might, after all, return to haunt them. If you push them, they will direct you to an architect or a carpenter or plumber, people who are paid to take responsibility for making decisions.

No yard or supply source ever displays even a small percentage of its wares. And no single supply source ever carries anything near the total number of items manufactured. Generally, on entering a commericial outlet for building materials you will be greeted by a man behind a desk or counter. He will ask you what you want. If you don't know exactly what you want and cannot describe it very clearly, it is unlikely he will make more than one or two fruitless forays into the stock room to accommodate you.

Most, if not all, of the supply sources will accept returns if the products are undamaged and accompanied by the sales slip. However, most, if not all, will charge you 10 to 15 percent for handling the returns. And if you return materials too often they will not sell you anything else. Lumberyards and masonry yards are not department stores.

Thus the selection of materials and assemblies best for your purpose can only be made by yourself. It's necessary for you to know exactly what you need before you go out to look for it. That is the basic aim for this book: to provide you with the information you need for selecting the best materials for your purpose.

GETTING THE MOST OUT OF THIS BOOK

No one, not even the author, argues that this handbook makes for exciting reading. On the other hand, it is more than just a reference book. It is, in a sense, a course in the materials of modern construction. And as such, a onetime, slow and careful read-through will more than repay you for your time and effort.

THE VALUE OF JUST KNOWING

Whether you are a longtime professional experienced in one or more of the construction skills or a rank beginner contemplating the building of your first birdhouse, just knowing what is available will save you time, money, and labor. For example, you want to erect a partition wall in your basement. Your first thought may be to build the wall of 2 × 4s and cover it with Sheetrock. But have you thought of building the wall of 4-inch concrete blocks set on edge and then plastering the block? Have you considered using metal studs in place of wood? Have you thought about using plywood panels, hardboard panels, or Masonite panels in place of the Sheetrock? Sheetrock over wood studs is not the only way to go. One of the other methods suggested may be less costly, faster, or better suited to the particular conditions and needs of this basement and its occupants. For example, if there is a possibility the basement may flood, the block partition is your best bet. If it is backed up to a furnace, metal studs are preferable to wood studs, and so on.

If you are a beginner, you may not know the terms or may be unaware of the alternatives. If you are on the other end of the learning scale, however, you may have forgotten there are alternatives to wood studs for a partition wall.

Just reading through will bring all the available materials to mind, and perhaps surprising to yourself, most of what you see and read will remain in your mind for later-day application.

AS A DESIGN AID

There are two steps to designing any-

thing and everything. The first is to envision the end product, be it doghouse or mansion. We cannot help you there. The second is to translate the vision into practical terms with a minimum of labor and costs. This is where this book can be of immeasurable help.

MODULAR DESIGNING

This simply means selecting finished dimensions that are even multiples of the materials available. For example, most plywood comes in 4- × -8-foot sheets. If you plan to wainscot a wall, which means to cover the lower portion of a wall with a layer of wood, and you want to use plywood, there would be a minimum of wasted wood if you make the wainscoting 4 feet high. If you wanted it 6 feet high, and did not want any patching, you would have to discard 2 feet of paneling.

Should you opt to use plywood for shelving, you could cut the panels into strips that are even multiples of its width or length, and waste no more than the width of the saw blade. This too would be an example of modular planning and construction.

Assume further that you want to construct a storage shed of concrete block, and you would like to make it 6 feet wide overall. If you select 16-inch-long blocks you will have to cut some of the blocks because 16 is not an even multiple of 72 inches (6 feet). Neither will 14- nor 16-inch blocks work out evenly. It would appear then that you have only two options: to alter the width of the building or cut some of the blocks (and thus waste some by breakage). But you would be making a mistake. If you check with this book you will find that blocks do come in half-lengths. Not all yards stock half-blocks, but many do.

The same holds true of windows. If you are building with 16-inch block you should choose windows that fit into openings that are even multiples of 16 inches. On the other hand, if the only window or door that you wanted or could use did not fit such an opening, you could consider the use of special blocks made to be used around window openings.

On a wood-frame building with studs 16 inches apart on their centers, you would be wise to select windows and doors that fitted between studs and included space for the jack studs (side braces often used with large windows).

Consider a flat roof for a garage or similar structure to be spanned by roof joists. If you select a building width that is an even multiple of 2 feet you can use joists as they come from the yard without waste. Joists and other timbers come in lengths of 8, 10, 12, 14, and 16 feet. This is common knowledge in the building trades but not to a professor of English designing his first do-it-yourself building.

We discussed earlier planning from the outside in. In many instances you should plan from the inside out. For example, you are planning to add a room to your home. The room will encompass a new kitchen that will consist of dishwasher, stove, refrigerator, and prefabricated kitchen cabinets. You should start with the dimensions of the equipment and cabinets and mark off the interior of the new room accordingly. Obviously, it is easier to vary the dimensions of the room to fit the enclosed

equipment than to alter the dimensions of the equipment.

We could carry these examples on indefinitely, but the reasoning behind them all remains the same. Modular design simply seeks to minimize cutting and patching and thus minimize construction labor and costs.

DESIGNING FOR MATERIAL EFFICIENCY

Some materials are more efficient—meaning that they accomplish their purpose or a number of purposes more efficiently than others. For example, when running (installing) water pipe you can run copper tubing one size smaller than galvanized iron pipe and still get the same rate of water flow. Under equal pressure a ¾-inch, internal diameter (ID) copper tube will pass as much water as a 1-inch, ID galvanized iron pipe. Copper tubing can be joined by soldering far more quickly and usually far more cheaply than can galvanized pipe when you have to cut thread and purchase fittings. Copper tubing can be bent around corners; galvanized cannot. Copper is also much lighter in weight and easier to handle and place. Is there also a financial savings? This depends on the relative prices of the two, which constantly keep changing. But if you place a dollar value on your time, which you should, bear in mind that it takes three to four times longer to run galvanized than copper.

STRENGTH OF MATERIALS

It is, of course, important to use enough material or reliably strong material to accomplish your purpose with a margin of safety. When you don't know just how much load a material can take, it is only natural to be extra cautious and go overboard on strength. When you know what can be safely used you can select that which is adequate and no more.

For example, poplar is a soft, relatively weak wood that is considerably less costly than fir. Poplar studs are more than strong enough, however, for any home, so it is a waste of money to use fir for studding. On the other hand, to span a roof opening, you must use thicker or wider timbers of poplar than you would of fir. Depending on the relative costs, one type of lumber may be less expensive than another.

By using the tables provided throughout this book you can select with confidence materials that are adequate for their loads and not waste money by overdesigning just to be safe. The same tables can, of course, prevent you from seriously underdesigning a structure.

THERMAL EFFICIENCY
Knowing how much insulation one material provides as compared to another will help you select the best material from both a cost and efficiency point of view.

So review the entire book just to become aware of what is currently available, then concentrate on the materials you believe you may use. Consider them for their dimensions, strength or load-bearing qualities, thermal ratings, weather resistance, and everything else that may be of importance to your project.

2 ADHESIVES

Adhesive is the generic term for any substance used to make things stick together. Glue, paste, cement, and tar are all examples of adhesives. The first strong adhesive was made by boiling animal parts until nothing was left but a thick, smelly brown muck. It is still used for joining wood to wood. And it is still called animal glue.

Today there are hundreds of different kinds of adhesives that not only produce stronger and more waterproof joints than is possible with animal glue, but make it possible to join materials unaffected by animal glue, for example glass and plastic.

The very qualities that make many of the modern adhesives so effective, however, often limit their effectiveness to just a few materials. For example, an acetone-based cement such as Duco or Ambroid works exceedingly well on wood or on cellulose acetate plastics but will leave such plastics as those used for eyeglass frames untouched. Upon hardening, these cements are easily peeled off.

TYPES

Adhesives can be divided into twelve general groups. Each group or type has its own characteristics, but within each general type there are some variations. If the work you are doing is important or extensive, it is wise to make a careful test of the adhesive you plan to use. Careful testing means following whatever instructions are provided, making certain the glued surfaces are clean, sufficient time has elapsed at the time of application, and that the temperature is correct.

Many of the manufacturers list the materials with which their adhesives may be used. Unfortunately some manufacturers do not make specific recommendations and others list everything in sight. While you can generally be confident that their adhesive will cause the listed materials to adhere, you have no way of knowing from a mere listing what the strength of the joint or its limitations may be. If it is important that you know, write the manufacturer and ask for technical data or test the adhesive yourself.

PAPER GLUES

You can make your own from wheat or rice flour and water or egg yolk. Wallpaper paste is a form of flour and water glue, as is that sour white paste we used in kindergarten. Mucilage is a form of watered-down hide glue. Rubber cement, which is the cleanest of the paper glues because you can rub off the excess glue, is made by dissolving uncured rubber in a solvent. If you apply the cement to one sheet of paper alone you can, with some difficulty, separate the two sheets afterward. If you apply the cement to both facing sheets, the bond is made more quickly and is virtually permanent. Rubber cement has one failing. It turns brown with time, and when it does, it also stains the papers it is joining. For example, if you use rubber cement to fasten photos in an album, in time the photos will develop brown spots where the cement has been applied.

On the other hand, rubber cement is simpler to use than mucilage. Rubber cement is easily redissovled by its solvent. This is not easily accomplished with paste or mucilage. To separate the two cemented papers, pull them apart as far as they will go. With the aid of a clean oilcan, squirt a little cement solvent on the joint. Wait a moment and pull the papers apart.

ANIMAL GLUE

This comes in two forms, solid and liquid. The solid is made in thin flat cakes, flakes, and granules. The best is made from hide and is the lightest in color. In order to be used the glue must be soaked in clean, cold water until it is completely dissolved. In this matter use no more or less than the quantity of water suggested by the manufacturer. The best glues generally are dissolved in twice their weight of water. When it is dissolved, heat the glue to no more than 150°F. Clamp the parts together with a pressure of about 25 pounds per square inch, more if the glue is chilled.

Liquid animal glue may be as strong as "solid" animal glue. The problem, however, is that it is difficult to tell what the glue was made of. It may have been made of fish heads or bones, in which case it will be comparatively weak. Very weak liquid animal glue is nothing more than mucilage. But liquid animal glue has the advantage of easy prep-aration and is therefore used when joint strength demands are not great. Liquid animal glue is much more expensive than solid animal glue.

Both are excellent for wood joints and joining other such fibrous materials. The glue tends to fill voids and is in itself strong, which makes it tolerant of moderately loose-fitting joints. While these glues are excellent for furniture, they are not waterproof and should never be used on anything that will be exposed to water or moisture. Both glues require a full twenty-four hours at average room temperature to cure completely (that is, to achieve full hardness).

WHITE LIQUID GLUE

Sold in plastic squeeze bottles, this glue looks like thin sweet cream and has the sour smell of coconut juice. Sometimes called PVA because it is a polyvinyl resin adhesive, it is to be found under various brand names including Elmer's Glue-All, Sears White Glue, Du Pont white glue, Titebond, Evertite, Duralite, and Franklin Concrete Adhesive.

It has good stress resistance, is slightly flexible, sets in four hours, cures in twenty-four, but cannot stand up to water and moisture. The glue should not be exposed to the air for more than fifteen minutes. It is flammable, and you can wash your hands free of it with soap and water.

PVA glue is excellent for furniture, as it dries almost clear. It can be used for other porous materials such as Styrofoam, unglazed ceramics, leather, and stone. It should not be used on photos, bare metals, or materials that are to be soaked or heated. To use with paper or cloth, spread it very thin and permit it to dry after pressure is applied.

YELLOW LIQUID GLUE

Very similar in its characteristics to white liquid glue, the yellow is aliphatic, meaning it is derived from fat. It costs a little more than the white but it sets in thirty minutes, which means you can proceed with your work much more quickly. But set time is not curing time. The yellow glue takes the same twenty-four hours to reach full hardness and strength. Yellow glue is more easily sanded and takes stain better than white. This means that glue lines are more easily hidden when they are made with the yellow glue.

RESORCINAL

This is a very strong, waterproof glue excellent for boatbuilding, outdoor furniture, and the like. It is not first choice for ordinary gluing because it is expensive and consists of two parts that must be mixed with care, as the proportions are critical. It should never be used where the joint will be visible, as it hardens to a dark brown color. Resorcinal glues require ten hours to set and twenty-four hours to cure. The joint must be kept under pressure for the first ten hours and above 70°F for the entire twenty-four hours.

Resorcinal glue is marketed as Craftsman plastic glue, Sears Waterproof Resorcinal glue, U.S. Plywood Waterproof glue, and Weldwood plastic resin glue.

FORMALDEHYDE GLUE

This is another very strong glue. Like Resorcinal it is rigid and nonflammable. It is easier to use because it is mixed with water instead of a resin. It has very low resistance to moisture and heat, however, and therefore is used mainly for furniture.

EPOXY GLUE (CEMENT)

This is possibly the best all-around glue (or, technically, cement) that we have. Its strength is very high, its weather resistance is good; it resists temperatures to 180°F, which makes it good for dishes that go into the dishwasher. It doesn't shrink, so it won't leave gaps in loose joints. It will adhere to wood, metal, glass (sandpapered first), and just about anything that has some tooth—not a perfectly smooth surface. It can also withstand a lot of different solvents.

The major problem with epoxy is its cost. Compared to animal glue or white glue, it is very expensive and there is no point to using it for ordinary wood-to-wood joints. It is a two-part glue, which means it must be mixed, and this has to be done thoroughly. Some people are allergic to it.

Setting and curing time can be accelerated by warming the epoxy above its minimum 70°F temperature. This, however, softens the glue, so you must be certain the pieces are clamped together. At 70°F, epoxy sets in as little as fifteen minutes, but it still requires a full twenty-four hours for full strength.

So-called instant epoxy formulations set and harden more quickly but they cost more and are not as strong. Filled epoxies are epoxies that have been extended with various fillers. (You can do the same with wood chips, metal scraps, etc.) Filled epoxies are not as strong, but they cost much less and are useful for joining ill-fitting parts. When fully hardened, filled epoxy can be filed, drilled, and screwed.

Some of the companies that market epoxy use the following brand names: Devcon, Kling Enterprises, Ruscoe, Wilhold Epoxy, Helor Quick-Set Epoxy 1177, Elmer's Epoxy.

CONTACT CEMENT
This is the glue to use when you have to bond large surface areas together, for example Mircarta, veneer, carpet to a tabletop or wall or whatever. Contact cement works fast and holds well, but is unforgiving. This glue develops a full 50 to 75 percent of its ultimate holding power upon contact. You must align the two parts perfectly before you bring them together, otherwise you may destroy what you are gluing when you try to pull it up and reposition it.

The recommended system of application consists of separating the two parts with a sheet of brown paper. Align both parts and pull the sheet partially out from between them. Apply pressure, then pull out more of the paper, apply more pressure, and so on. When the separating paper is out, the job is done.

Contact cement is made in two forms. The latex-based cement has little smell, won't burn, and can be cleaned up easily. But it is not as strong as the older, solvent-based contact cement. The solvent types produce noxious, flammable fumes and you must use a suitable solvent for cleanup. Nail polish remover works on some solvent cements.

Both types of cements must be brushed on to each of the materials to be joined. Both types are highly weather resistant, set immediately, cure in one to two days, and are fairly strong, flexible, and flammable. Don't leave the can open or the cement on the joint surface for more than thirty minutes.

Brand names include Pliobond, Devco rubber, Sears Miracle Pliobond, Weldwood, Duro, Craftsman, Duralite.

PLASTIC CEMENT
There are thousands of different plastic formulations and possibly dozens of different solvents that work on these plastics. To be effective a plastic cement must be based on a solvent that will, to some extent at least, dissolve the plastic. Plastic is not porous, so there is no possibility of the cement or the glue entering the pores and taking hold that way. Some plastics, for example those that are classified as duroplasts and elastomers, cannot be glued at all in the ordinary sense. Others, as for example the acrylics, are very easily and quickly "welded" with methylene chloride. Cellulose acetate is easily joined the same way with acetone or an acetone-based cement such as Duco. You can even make this cement yourself by dissolving the plastic in the solvent. Ambroid, long used by model airplane builders, is an acetone-based cement.

But that solves your problem for only two types of plastics. What about the others? In some cases, for example when working with PVC (polyvinyl chloride) or CPVC (chlorinated polyvinyl chloride) pipe, you simply purchase cleaners and cements made for these plastics. When you don't know the plastic and even when you may know it, you may not know if it can be cemented or what cement will work; your only sure bet is to run a test. (Remember, epoxy is a plastic cement, try that too.)

Note that all the plastic solvents are poisonous and flammable. Give yourself plenty of ventilation and don't smoke or use them near flame.

Plastic cements have, when hardened, all the qualities of the plastic they join, which means they are waterproof, long-lasting, heatproof to some degree, but not fireproof.

CYANOACRYLATES

These are the one-drop "super glues" that are touted as being capable of holding a ton or more. They can. The only problem is that the faying (mating) surfaces must be perfectly flat, and they cannot be porous. This glue is very brittle. It will not fill any gap; even a light film of dust will cause it to fail completely. But it will join your fingers together if you are not careful. Setting time is very short when the temperature is 80°F or more.

Despite the inherent danger of cyanoacrylate glue—sticking fingers, eye damage—and its very high cost, it is the best glue for certain limited applications, as for example mending china, holding nuts in place on threaded rods, making small metal objects without welding or bolts, and the like.

Brand names include Loctite, Krazy Glue, Eastman 910, and Permabond.

CONSTRUCTION ADHESIVES

Many professional and amateur builders are turning to construction adhesives to cut their labor and improve their results. Although some nailing is required in some instances, it is still faster to force a bead of glue out of a tube than to drive home a dozen nails or more. And whereas nailing forces a panel to follow the irregularities of the supporting surface, the flexibility of construction adhesive permits the panel to straighten itself out to a considerable degree. This does not weaken the joint because construction adhesive can bridge gaps of ⅜ of an inch and still hold firmly.

Generally the adhesive is applied to the panels only and remains plastic for twenty minutes or so, which gives you time to reposition it if necessary. The bond these adhesives form is stronger than the wood itself. For example, B. F. Goodrich Plastikon 200 forms a 354-pound bond per square inch of contacting surface. This amounts to 67 tons of holding power between a panel and its supporting studs.

Construction adhesives are manufactured by several companies in what may be classified as three general formulations: panel adhesives, a multipurpose panel and polystyrene foam adhesive; construction adhesive, and interior/exterior, general-purpose adhesive for light construction and remodeling; subfloor adhesive, made to bond plywood subfloor to wood or metal joists.

These adhesives can be used to bond:

foam insulation to wood studs
dry wall to steel studs

finished plywood to aluminum
   studs
unfinished plywood to dry walls
chipboard to subflooring
fiberboard to masonry
cork to foam insulation
hardboard to furring strips
furring strips to chipboard

MASTICS

Now called adhesives by many manufacturers, mastics differ from adhesives in that they are cheaper on a volume basis, have more "body," and retain some resiliency when hard.

When selecting a mastic you must choose one from among those designed for your purpose, which might be the application of floor covering, ceramic tile, or ceiling tile. Next you would need to make certain the general formulation is compatible with your materials. For example, you would require a different mastic when applying wood floor tiles than you would when applying resilient tiles. The same mastic would not be suitable for both a jute-backed carpet and a urethane foam-backed carpet. Always be sure to study the labels or the manufacturer's literature.

Just a few of the ways modern adhesives are used in building construction.
Courtesy B. F. Goodrich

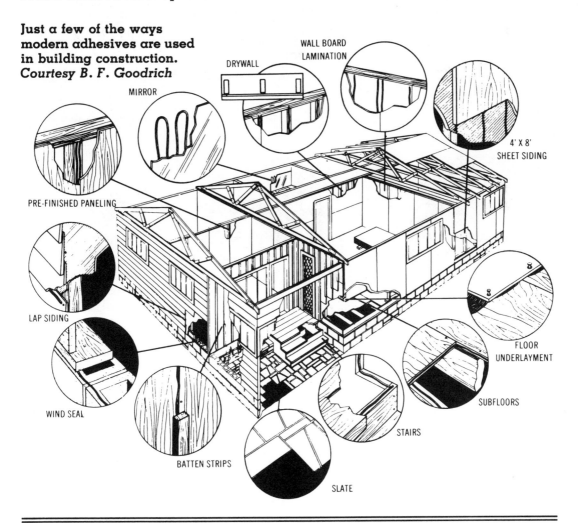

DRYWALL

WALL BOARD
LAMINATION

MIRROR

4' X 8'
SHEET SIDING

PRE-FINISHED PANELING

LAP SIDING

WIND SEAL

BATTEN STRIPS

SLATE

STAIRS

SUBFLOORS

FLOOR
UNDERLAYMENT

Flooring to joists   Furring to concrete

How construction adhesive may be used to bond furring strips to concrete block wall, and how the glue gun is used to spread a bead of construction adhesive atop a floor joist. *Courtesy H. B. Fuller Co.*

Bonding tongue-and-groove subflooring to floor joists with subfloor adhesive, in this case PL-400. *Courtesy B. F. Goodrich*

It is recommended that a single-ply floor system be used. Use ⅝″ or ¾″ T & G underlayment grade plywood or a high quality ¾″ particle-board.

1. Chalk line the joists at 4′ intervals. Apply PL-400 for one sheet at a time. Apply a ¼″ high bead to each joist where sheet will fall. (Two beads will be used on butt joint.)

2. Start at corner and lay a full course of decking to the next corner. Position sheet with a minimum of sideways slippage. Space panels ¹⁄₁₆″ at ends and edges to accommodate any expansion.

3. Nail each sheet as you go 12″ O.C. with 6d annular ring or spiral nails. (8d common can also be used.) For plywood thicker than ⅞″, use 8d deformed shank or 10d common shank. For stapling and nailing schedules see FHA Bulletin UM 25.

4. Apply a ³⁄₁₆″ bead in groove of plywood. Adhesive is to be applied to all contact areas.

5. Lay 2 x 4 on tongue side and, where necessary, use sledge to secure T&G fit. Be sure to stagger end joints.

6. Use putty knife or wood scrap to remove any adhesive squeeze-out.

General Applications

1. Apply adhesive as it comes. Do not dilute or otherwise modify.

2. Apply adhesive using quart cartridges, special extrusion equipment, or bulk loading caulking guns. When bonding very irregular surfaces, apply ⅜″ bead (all bead sizes referred to are round beads). A bead diameter of ¼″ is sufficient in most cases, as it provides 100% coverage on a stud or joist. A ½″ diameter bead will allow automatic shimming up to ⅜″ (adhesive bridging). In some applications, where contact is close, ⅛″ beads can be used.

However, experimentation is the best gauge in establishing proper adhesive coverage for necessary contact.

3. Position components within ten minutes after application of PL-400. (Five minutes if ⅛″ beads are used.)

4. Press components firmly in place to wet the contact area. Adhesive should spread to edges of desired contact area.

5. Use weight or supplemental fasteners to hold components in desired position for at least 48 hours.

Applying decorative brick with the aid of an adhesive mortar, a type of mastic containing acrylic resin. *Courtesy H. B. Fuller Co.*

Using an adhesive to bond a plastic cover to a wall-floor juncture. This is a soft, thick, dark brown paste containing a synthetic resin. Excess adhesive can be removed with alcohol. *Courtesy H. B. Fuller Co.*

Steps involved in bonding a plywood panel to a stud wall, using PL-200. *Courtesy B. F. Goodrich*

1. Start in corner, mark out-of-line ("low") studs using straight edge or chalk line. Draw plumb line down stud 4' from corner.

LOW STUD

PLUMB LINE →

FIT TO PLUMB LINE

2. Trim and fit panel so that butt edge will be even with plumb line on stud.

3. Apply 1/4" high bead down the center of in-line studs and 3/8" bead to out-of-line ("low") studs. On butt stud apply bead inside of plumb line to avoid adhesive "squeeze out."

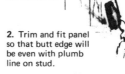

4. Pivot first panel from plumb line to corner. Align with plumb line. Fasten with three or four finishing nails along top and bottom (where molding goes).

PLUMB LINE

5. Press panel at all stud areas into PL-200, holding just a second. When released, panel will spring out from "low" studs and provide a straight finished wall. Press panel into PL-200 only ONCE.

Pivot subsequent panels away from butt stud in opposite direction, otherwise repeat same procedure.

6. TEMPORARY FASTENERS. To level any butt edges which bow out, use a small block of wood held with a finishing nail driven into the joint. Allow adhesive to set 24-48 hours before removing blocks.

BLOCK— CONCRETE

Concrete block is manufactured by placing concrete in a mold, then heating the block by steam to cure and harden it rapidly. There are possibly a thousand different shapes, types, and sizes of blocks manufactured today. Unfortunately, few yards carry more than a dozen or more basic types and sizes of block. If you do not want one of these blocks and opt for a special order, be prepared to pay an extra charge for hauling.

BASIC CHARACTERISTICS

Standard block is made of concrete using small stones. A standard block nominally 8 × 8 × 16 inches weighs between 40 and 50 pounds. That works out to roughly 60 pounds per cubic foot of block. Standard concrete block can carry a load of 80 psi (pounds per square inch), including the holes. Thus a block with an 8-×-16-inch surface could sustain a load of 10,240 pounds or a little better than 5 tons, despite the fact that the block may be 25 percent hollow because of the vertical holes.

Lightweight, or cinder, block is made of concrete using lightweight aggregates such as cinders and volcanic ash in place of stones. An 8-×-8-×-16-inch lightweight block

WEIGHT AND QUANTITIES OF MATERIALS NEEDED FOR CONSTRUCTION OF CONCRETE BLOCK WALLS

Nominal wall thickness, in.	Nominal size (width × height × length) of concrete masonry units, in.	Average weight of 100-sq. ft. wall area, lb.		Material quantities for 100-sq. ft. wall area		
		Units made with sand-gravel aggregate	Units made with light-weight aggregate	Number of units	Mortar, cu. ft.	Mortar for 100 units, cu. ft.
4	4 × 4 × 16	4,550	3,550	225	13.5	6.0
6	6 × 4 × 16	5,100	3,900	225	13.5	6.0
8	8 × 4 × 16	6,000	4,450	225	13.5	6.0
4	4 × 8 × 16	4,050	3,000	112.5	8.5	7.5
6	6 × 8 × 16	4,600	3,350	112.5	8.5	7.5
8	8 × 8 × 16	5,550	3,950	112.5	8.5	7.5
12	12 × 8 × 16	7,550	5,200	112.5	8.5	7.5

Courtesy Portland Cement Association

weighs between 25 and 35 pounds. This works out to between 15 and 21 pounds per cubic foot.

As you can readily see, the lightweight block is much easier to lay up (position in place). Lightweight blocks are not acceptable to many building departments, however, and acceptable or not they should never be used for foundation or where they will be constantly exposed to water. They are excellent for indoor partitions and the like.

DIMENSIONS, TYPES, SHAPES

Block dimensions are always given as if they are laid up in a ⅜-inch bed of mortar. A concrete block is always ⅜ of an inch less than its nominal size in each of its dimensions. A standard 8-×-8-×-16-inch block is actually 7⅝ × 7⅝ × 15⅝ inches in size. This and similar blocks are designed to be installed with the holes in a vertical position. Hence, if you build a wall using 8-inch block, the wall will only be 7⅝ inches thick, front to back. Height and length will remain 8 and 16 inches because you have used ⅜-inch-thick mortar to place the block.

BUILDING BLOCK

Ninety percent or more of all the block made to be used in building construction comprise just three basic shapes, which are made in a number of sizes. The shapes are stretcher, end, and solid. Stretcher blocks have indented ends and are used in the run of a wall. End blocks have smooth ends and are used to terminate a wall or frame an opening in a wall. Solid blocks do not have core holes as do the other two types.

The remaining block shapes run the gamut from chimney blocks, which are flat, square blocks with round holes in their centers—they are stacked to make chimneys—to coping blocks used on top of walls to door-jamb units used to frame a door. There is also a large variety of pierced block manufactured for use in making ornamental walls and the like.

SURFACES

Standard block has a surface similar to that of troweled concrete. But there are blocks with much smoother, denser surfaces. And there are blocks with rougher surfaces—some caused by actually breaking a block in half. And some blocks have molded surfaces: circles, diamonds, grooves, and more.

COLORS

Standard block is dull gray-brown in color. Lightweight block is a dark gray in color. But there are pale and dark brown blocks to be had on order.

LAYING BLOCK

Both standard and lightweight block are laid up in cement mortar containing a small percentage of lime. Generally the blocks can be laid up as they are. But following a heavy soaking they should be permitted to drain off and dry, but not completely. In desert country, the block should be soaked with a hose and then laid after the water has drained off. For proper adhesion, block must have some moisture content.

SURFACE BONDING

A commercially proved alternative to laying up block in mortar is a process known as surface bonding. The first course (row) of block is laid up in mortar. Following courses are laid up dry. The blocks are then moistened with a spray of water and a special bonding mortar is applied to both sides of the block wall. The special mortar contains ½-inch-long glass fibers and results in a waterproof shield.

Called surface-bonding mortar, and sold under various trade names, it is normally applied in a layer

RECOMMENDATIONS ON CONCRETE MASONRY PAVING UNITS

Application	Thickness of subbase, inches		Thickness of concrete masonry paving units, inches
	Well-drained dry areas	Low wet areas	
LIGHT DUTY Residential Driveways Patios Pool Decks Walkways Parking Bicycle Path Erosion Control Temporary Paving	0 to 3 inches	4 to 8 inches	2½ to 3 inches
MEDIUM DUTY Sidewalks Shopping Malls Residential Streets Public Parking Bus Stops Service Roads Cross Walks Parking Lots Camping Areas Mobile Home Parks Canal Lining Safety Zones Maintenance Areas Farm Equipment Storage	4 to 6 inches	10 inches	3 to 4 inches
HEAVY DUTY City Streets Intersections Gas Stations Loading Docks Loading Ramps Industrial Floors Stables	8 inches	12 inches	4 to 6 inches

NOTE: The sand base between the subbase and the concrete paving units is always made 2 inches thick.

Courtesy National Concrete Masonry Association

1/16 to ⅛ inch thick with a trowel or a spray gun. Surface-bonding mortar comes in several colors, and therefore no further wall treatment, such as painting, is required. The only problem that may come up is that the standard block used with surface-bonding mortar is ⅜ inch short of its nominal length. This means that three bonded blocks will not come out to 48 inches, as they would when mortar is used between them.

CONCRETE PAVING BLOCK

Concrete paving blocks are made in a number of colors and in two basic types: open and solid. The open paving blocks are usually 15 to 18 inches wide, 24 inches long, and 4½ to 6 inches thick. They can be laid directly on almost any flat surface whether level or sloped. Since the open paving blocks have spaces, grass will grow through them. The grass makes the open paving more attractive than the solid. On hillsides, the grass growing through the blocks acts to hold them in place.

The solid paving blocks range from 2½ to 6 inches in thickness. Typically, each block will cover from 15 to 64 square inches. Shapes include square, rectangular, hexagonal, even octagonal. Some types interlock, which, of course, helps hold them together and in place.

All paving blocks are made of very strong concrete. Typically, they have compression strengths ranging from 5,000 to 10,000 psi (pounds per square inch). They are also very dense with a water asorption rating of less than 5 pounds of water per cubic foot of block.

Solid paving blocks are usually laid down on a 2-inch layer of sand, which may or may not be atop a layer of crushed stone. The sand makes it easier to achieve a smooth surface. The sand and gravel provide drainage, which reduces frost heave in the winter.

MINIMUM RECOMMENDED BLOCK SIZE FOR SMALL CONCRETE BLOCK BUILDINGS

Overall wall height	Roof span	Block size
under 8 feet	under 10 feet	6 inches
8 to 20 feet	to 18 feet	8 inches
8 to 20 feet	to 25 feet	10 inches
20 to 25 feet	to 20 feet	10 inches
25 to 30 feet	to 25 feet	12 inches

A few examples of pierced or screen-wall units.
Courtesy Portland Cement Association

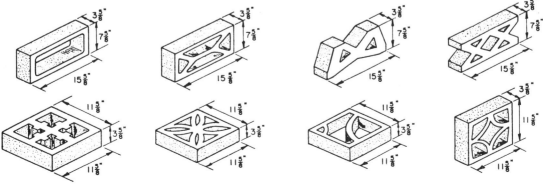

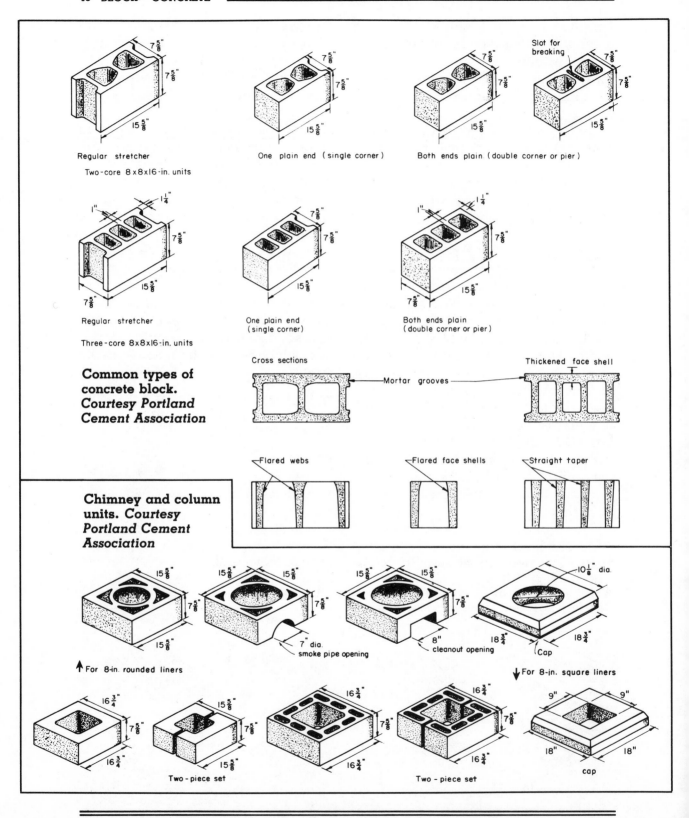

Regular stretcher

Two-core 8x8x16-in. units

One plain end (single corner)

Both ends plain (double corner or pier)

Slot for breaking

Regular stretcher

Three-core 8x8x16-in. units

One plain end (single corner)

Both ends plain (double corner or pier)

Common types of concrete block. *Courtesy Portland Cement Association*

Cross sections

Mortar grooves

Thickened face shell

Flared webs

Flared face shells

Straight taper

Chimney and column units. *Courtesy Portland Cement Association*

For 8-in. rounded liners

7" dia. smoke pipe opening

8" cleanout opening

10 1/8" dia.

Cap

For 8-in. square liners

Two-piece set

Two-piece set

cap

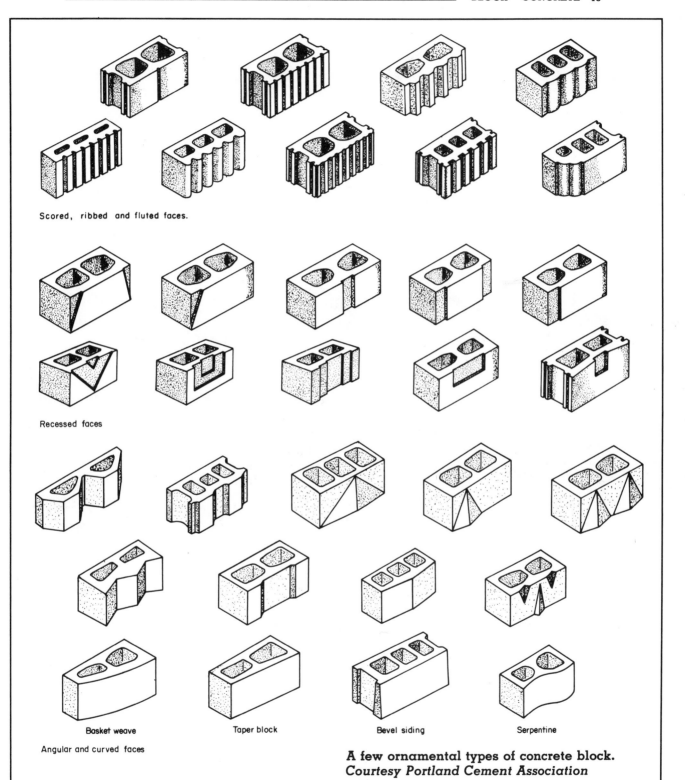

Scored, ribbed and fluted faces.

Recessed faces

Basket weave   Taper block   Bevel siding   Serpentine

Angular and curved faces

A few ornamental types of concrete block.
Courtesy Portland Cement Association

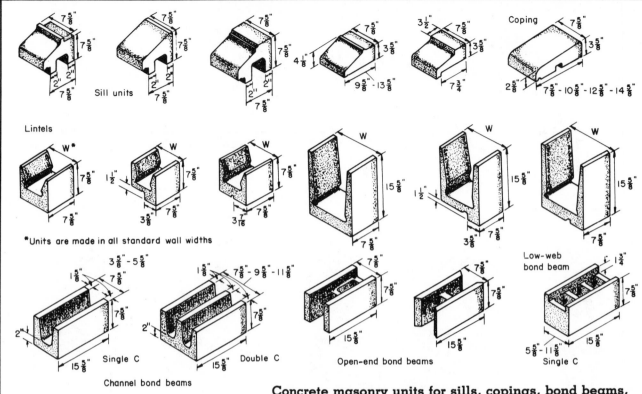

Sill units

Lintels

W*

*Units are made in all standard wall widths

Low-web bond beam

Single C
Channel bond beams

Double C

Open-end bond beams

Single C

Concrete masonry units for sills, copings, bond beams, and lintels. *Courtesy Portland Cement Association*

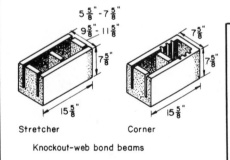

Stretcher

Corner

Knockout-web bond beams

Lintel made from bond beam or lintel blocks, provided with reinforcing bars and filled with concrete.

Ornamental garden wall made from pierced concrete block. *Courtesy National Concrete Masonry Association*

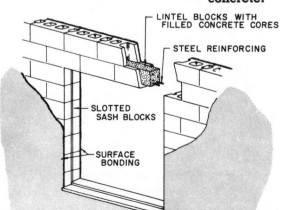

LINTEL BLOCKS WITH FILLED CONCRETE CORES

STEEL REINFORCING

SLOTTED SASH BLOCKS

SURFACE BONDING

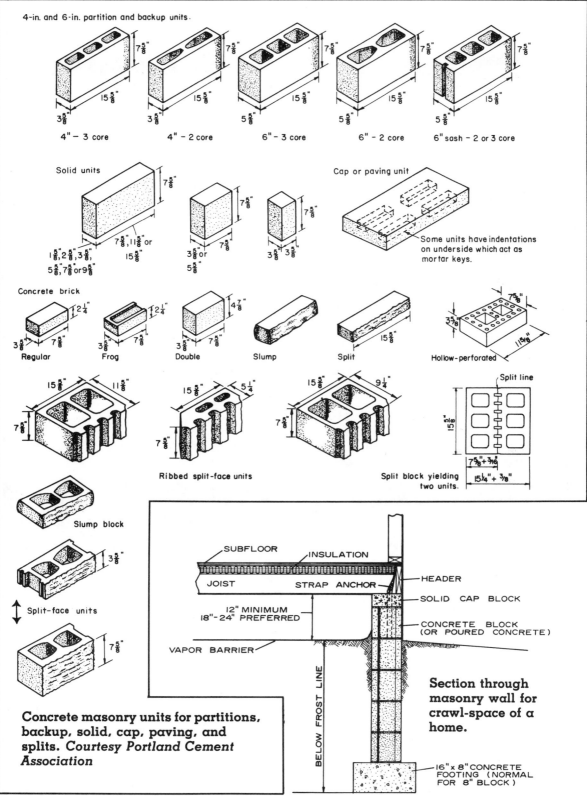

4-in. and 6-in. partition and backup units.

7⅝" 15⅝" 3⅝" 4" – 3 core

7⅝" 15⅝" 3⅝" 4" – 2 core

7⅝" 15⅝" 5⅝" 6" – 3 core

7⅝" 15⅝" 5⅝" 6" – 2 core

7⅝" 15⅝" 5⅝" 6" sash – 2 or 3 core

Solid units

7⅝" 7⅝", 11⅝" or 15⅝" 1⅝", 2⅝, 3⅝, 5⅝, 7⅝ or 9⅝"

7⅝" 3⅝" or 5⅝"

7⅝" 3⅝" 3⅝"

Cap or paving unit

Some units have indentations on underside which act as mortar keys.

Concrete brick

2¼" 3⅝" 7⅝" Regular

2¼" 3⅝" 7⅝" Frog

4⅞" 3⅝" 7⅝" Double

Slump

15⅝" Split

7⅝" 3⅛" 15⅛" Hollow-perforated

7⅝" 15⅝" 11⅝"

15⅝" 5¼" 7⅝"

15⅝" 9¼" 7⅝"

Ribbed split-face units

Split line

15⅝" 7⅝" + 3⁄8" 15¼" + 3⁄8"

Split block yielding two units.

Slump block

3⅝"

Split-face units

7⅝"

Concrete masonry units for partitions, backup, solid, cap, paving, and splits. *Courtesy Portland Cement Association*

Section through masonry wall for crawl-space of a home.

SUBFLOOR INSULATION HEADER STRAP ANCHOR SOLID CAP BLOCK JOIST CONCRETE BLOCK (OR POURED CONCRETE) 12" MINIMUM 18"-24" PREFERRED VAPOR BARRIER BELOW FROST LINE 16" x 8" CONCRETE FOOTING (NORMAL FOR 8" BLOCK)

Basic steps in laying concrete block.

A. A line is snapped or scratched on the concrete footing that will carry the block wall. Nail marks end of wall.

B. A bed of mortar is spread over the footing. An end block is positioned in line with scratch mark. Spirit level is used to make block perfectly level in both directions.

C. A second block is positioned at what will be the other end of the wall. With the aid of bricks, a mason's line is stretched between the two end blocks. Blocks are now aligned with the line.

D. Ends of a stretcher block is buttered with mortar.

E. More mortar is spread over the footing. The stretcher block is placed alongside the in-place end block.

F. The first course (row) of block is carried around the turn. Now the end block of the second course may be laid in position. Here it is being tapped with the mason's hammer to make it lie perfectly level.

G. If you have to cut a block, chip a groove across the width of the block along the desired line of cut. Make a second groove on the other side of the block in line with the first. The block will crack along the grooves.

H. As you lay block, remove excess mortar with the edge of the trowel. Go over joints with a joint tool as shown.

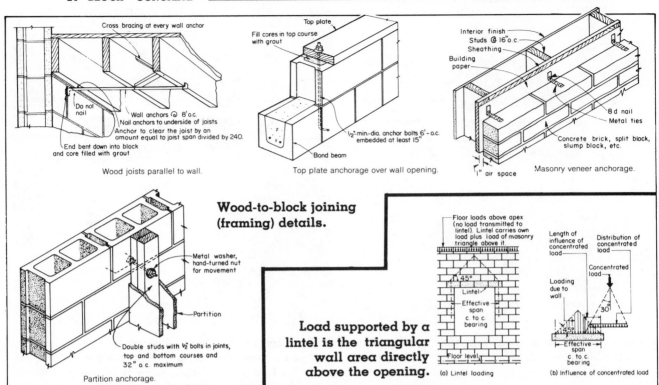

Wood-to-block joining (framing) details.

Wood joists parallel to wall.

Top plate anchorage over wall opening.

Masonry veneer anchorage.

Partition anchorage.

Load supported by a lintel is the triangular wall area directly above the opening.

(a) Lintel loading

(b) Influence of concentrated load

REQUIRED REINFORCEMENT FOR END-SUPPORTED CONCRETE MASONRY LINTLES.

Type of loading**	Nominal size, in., of lintel section	Reinforcing bars based on clear span							
		3 ft. 4 in.	4 ft. 0 in.	4 ft. 8 in.	5 ft. 4 in.	6 ft. 0 in.	6 ft. 8 in.	7 ft. 4 in.	8 ft. 0 in.
Wall load	6×8	1—No. 3	1—No. 4	1—No. 4	2—No. 4	2—No. 5	—	—	—
	6×16	—	—	—	—	1—No. 4	1—No. 4	1—No. 4	1—No. 4
Floor and roof load	6×16	1—No. 4	1—No. 4	2—No. 3	1—No. 5	2—No. 4	2—No. 4	2—No. 5	2—No. 5
Wall load	8×8	1—No. 3	2—No. 3	2—No. 3	2—No. 4	2—No. 4	2—No. 5	2—No. 6	—
	8×16	—	—	—	—	—	—	2—No. 5	2—No. 5
Floor and roof load	8×8	2—No. 4	—	—	—	—	—	—	—
	8×16	2—No. 3	2—No. 3	2—No. 3	2—No. 4	2—No. 4	2—No. 4	2—No. 5	2—No. 5

Required reinforcement for end-supported concrete masonry lintels.

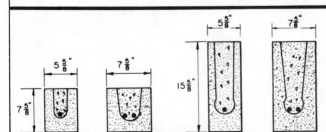

Dimensions of channel blocks used as reinforced lintels with required reinforcing bar data above.

An example of what can be done with interlocking paving blocks. *Courtesy National Concrete Masonry Association*

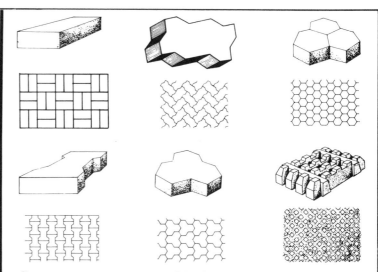

Some concrete paving blocks and the patterns they produce when assembled. *Courtesy National Concrete Masonry Association*

How solid concrete block can be laid directly on grass to form an interesting walk.

To make a level patio with concrete blocks, the blocks are laid atop leveled soil. High blocks can be pounded level as shown.

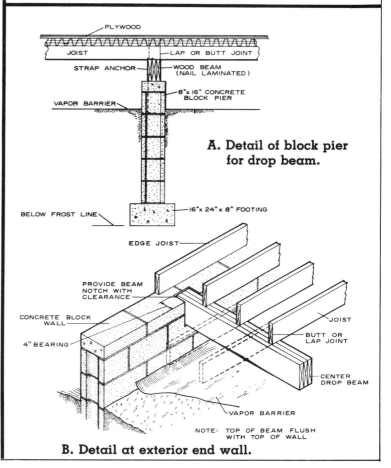

A. Detail of block pier for drop beam.

B. Detail at exterior end wall.

4 BRICK

Bricks are made by mixing clay, crushed shale (which is a type of stone), and water. The mixture is molded into shape, air-dried, and then kiln-fired, a process that can take as many as one hundred hours. This is the way bricks were made thousands of years ago and undoubtedly how they will continue to be made in the future. The only major change that has occurred in brickmaking over the years is the tremendous growth in the number of brick types and sizes that are now being manufactured.

There are, by some estimates, more than ten thousand different types and sizes of bricks currently available worldwide. Fortunately, this *is* a world figure and not applicable to the United States. As it is, there are a sufficient number of types and sizes available in this country to make selection a bit complicated.

BASIC CATEGORIES

All bricks manufactured fall into one of four categories: common, face, paving, and fire.

COMMON BRICK

This is the workhorse brick, the utilitarian brick. It is used for almost everything: building walls, walks, floors, interior walls, and so forth. Common brick is "brick red" in color. It is the least expensive type of brick manufactured, which is the major reason it is used most often.

Common brick is manufactured in three grades: SW, MW, and NW. The letters stand for severe weathering, moderate weathering, and no weathering, respectively. This is the order of brick hardness (on a descending scale, from hardest to softest), and the order of cost (again on a descending scale, from highest to lowest cost). The harder the brick, the less water permeable it is and the less vulnerable to damage done by frost. (It is the action of the cold on the absorbed water that actually destroys the brick, not the cold itself.)

SW brick can be used anywhere, in any climate. MW brick should not be exposed to the weather where anything more than a mild winter is expected. NW brick should not be used outdoors where any frost at all is expected. NW brick can be used indoors, or inside walls surfaced with MW or SW bricks.

USED BRICK

This is not a separate category. This is simply brick that has been salvaged from destroyed structures. Used brick can be any grade; there is no practical way of checking the brick's original specification and method of manufacture. Used brick's desirability stems not from its resistance to weathering but from its cost and appearance. Used bricks are the least expensive bricks of all. Coloring may vary from black through red to yellow, in a single brick. And time has twisted some of them badly (or perhaps they were made that poorly to begin with), so that, to some extent, they appear to have been handmade. Many people find used brick more attractive than common brick.

FACE BRICK

This is a type of brick designed and manufactured to be seen. (The full name is facing brick.) Face brick is harder than common brick and much more carefully made. Face brick dimensions are held close to uniform size P, whereas common bricks may vary as much as half an inch in one or more dimensions from brick to brick. And whereas common bricks may have a slight twist or bend, face bricks never do.

Face brick is made in a wide variety of colors, surfaces, and finishes. Some of the bricks have a smooth facing surface, others have striated, dimpled, grained, or grooved facing surfaces. And some are glazed, meaning they have faces that look like porcelain—in fact, they are, actually, a form of porcelain. And some are not simply one color; they may be multicolored, decorative works of art.

PAVING BRICK

This is brick especially formulated and fired to withstand vehicular traffic. Paving brick is used to pave public roads and commerical driveways. There is no need to use paving brick for a residential driveway. SW common brick will do.

FIRE BRICK

This is a pale yellow brick designed to withstand high temperatures. Fire brick is used to line furnaces and fireplaces. It must be laid up in fire clay or aluminum oxide mortar, both of which will withstand extremely

high temperatures. (Ordinary cement mortar will disintegrate in extreme heat.) Both are available at the masonry yard.

DIMENSIONS

Here is where we encounter the "sticky wicket." All bricks have two dimensions, nominal and actual. A brick's nominal dimension(s) is the space it will occupy when laid up in mortar. Since the mortar bed (joint) may be either ⅜ inch or ½ inch thick, there are really *two* nominal dimensions. A brick's actual dimension(s) is what its manufacturer says it is. This means you must ask your yardman what the brick's size is. *You cannot measure the brick* because common brick dimensions may vary as much as ½ an inch from brick to brick. To measure a brick's dimensions accurately you need to line up a dozen and *average* the resulting measurement. This is not really a problem in practice, because brick dimension errors will average themselves out as the wall or like structure is built.

Added to this confusion is nomenclature. Some brick sizes are called nonmodular. Others are classified as modular. Some yardmen call the nonmodular standard brick a building brick, others call the same brick a common brick.

SOLVING THE DIMENSION PROBLEM

There are three approaches. Ask the yardman either for the dimensions of the bricks he has to offer, or to supply bricks to your dimensions. Or just ask for common bricks and lay them out dry with the desired spacing and see what you get. This may be easier than deciding on wall dimensions first and then, in the end, having to cut bricks for every course (row) you lay.

CLEANING BRICKWORK

Excess mortar that discolors the face of less than day-old brickwork can be cleaned with hot water, a strong arm, and a scrub brush.

Older mortar that disfigures brickwork can be removed with a solution of muriatic acid and water or one of the commercial cleaners such as Brick Bath.

Use one part acid to ten parts water. *Always* add the acid to the water. *Always* wear rubber gloves when using the muriatic solution or one of the commercial cleaning solutions. Give the acid an hour or more to do its job, then, using plenty of water, wash the bricks clean of acid or cleaner.

MORTAR REQUIREMENTS

For standard modular bricks—2⅔ × 4 × 8 inches

Wall area in square feet	1-Brick wall Number of bricks	Cu. ft. mortar	2-Brick wall Number of bricks	Cu. ft. mortar	3-Brick wall Number of bricks	Cu. ft. mortar
10	61.7	.8	123.3	2.	184.9	3.2
25	154.25	2.	307.5	5.	462.25	8.
50	308.50	4.	615.	10.	920.5	16.
100	617.	8.	1,230.	20.	1,849.	32.

The above mortar figures assume ½-inch joints. If ⅜-inch joints are used, multiply mortar quantity by 80 percent. If ⅜-inch joints are used, multiply quantity by 120 percent. NOTE: Changing joint thickness will increase or reduce square footage of wall proportionally. Mortar quantity includes waste. See CEMENT and MORTAR for more data on same.

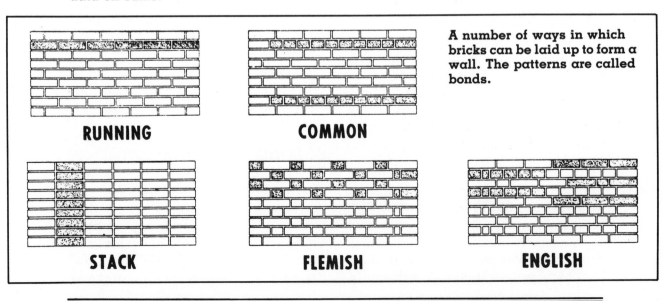

RUNNING   COMMON

A number of ways in which bricks can be laid up to form a wall. The patterns are called bonds.

STACK   FLEMISH   ENGLISH

	Nominal Dimensions, in.			Joint Thickness in.	Manufactured Dimensions in.			Modular Coursing in.
Unit Designation	T	H	L		T	H	L	
Standard Modular	4	2⅔	8	⅜	3⅝	2¼	7⅝	3C = 8
				½	3½	2¼	7½	
Engineer	4	3⅕	8	⅜	3⅝	2¹³⁄₁₆	7⅝	5C = 16
				½	3½	2¹¹⁄₁₆	7½	
Economy 8 or Jumbo Closure	4	4	8	⅜	3⅝	3⅝	7⅝	1C = 4
				½	3½	3½	7½	
Double	4	5⅓	8	⅜	3⅝	4¹⁵⁄₁₆	7⅝	3C = 16
				½	3½	4¹³⁄₁₆	7½	
Roman	4	2	12	⅜	3⅝	1⅝	11⅝	2C = 4
				½	3½	1½	11½	
Norman	4	2⅔	12	⅜	3⅝	2¼	11⅝	3C = 8
				½	3½	2¼	11½	
Norwegian	4	3⅕	12	⅜	3⅝	2¹³⁄₁₆	11⅝	5C = 16
				½	3½	2¹¹⁄₁₆	11½	
Economy 12 or Jumbo Utility	4	4	12	⅜	3⅝	3⅝	11⅝	1C = 4
				½	3½	3½	11½	
Triple	4	5⅓	12	⅜	3⅝	4¹⁵⁄₁₆	11⅝	3C = 16
				½	3½	4¹³⁄₁₆	11½	
SCR brick [2]	6	2⅔	12	⅜	5⅝	2¼	11⅝	3C = 8
				½	5½	2¼	11½	
6-in. Norwegian	6	3⅕	12	⅜	5⅝	2¹³⁄₁₆	11⅝	5C = 16
				½	5½	2¹¹⁄₁₆	11½	
6-in. Jumbo	6	4	12	⅜	5⅝	3⅝	11⅝	1C = 4
				½	5½	3½	11½	
8-in. Jumbo	8	4	12	⅜	7⅝	3⅝	11⅝	1C = 4
				½	7½	3½	11½	

Sizes of Modular Brick[1]

[1] Available as solid units conforming to ASTM C 216- or ASTM C 62-, or, in a number of cases, as hollow brick conforming to ASTM C 652-.

[2] Reg. U.S. Pat. Off., SCPI.

Sizes of popular modular brick. Note that a course (C) is one row of bricks. Courtesy Brick Institute of America

Steps in laying brick. A. The first brick is always an end brick, laid down on a bed of ½- to 1-inch-thick mortar. B. The second brick is always the brick at the other end of the wall. Note lines scratched in footing to indicate front edge of wall. Note nail marking desired corner of the wall. Mason is leveling a brick with the aid of a brick hammer and a spirit level. C. Buttering the end of a brick with mortar.

D. Here the wall is to make a turn. The second brick is slid into place on a bed of mortar. Joint between the two bricks is made with mortar already placed on brick end. E. A mason's line has been stretched between the two end bricks. Here a brick is slid into position against an in-place brick. Mason's line serves as guide to help mason lay bricks in a straight line. F. Installing the closure brick. Both ends of this brick must be mortared. If mortar slips off, trowel is used to hold or replace the mortar.

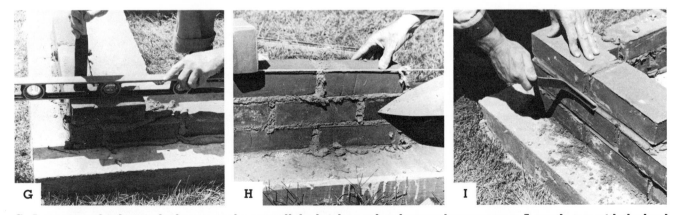

G. A constant check must be kept to make sure all the bricks are level as work progresses. A gentle tap with the heel of the hammer is all that should be needed. H. As work progresses the edge of the trowel is used to remove excess mortar. I. When the mortar has hardened a bit, the joints are compacted with a joint tool.

J. As the ends of the wall are erected they are checked for vertical evenness and correct alignment with the aid of a spirit level.

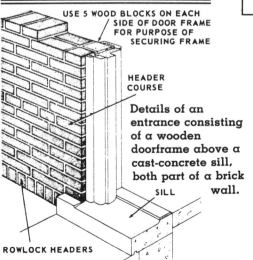

K. To cut a brick, place it on a firm surface such as a plank and strike with a mason's chisel.

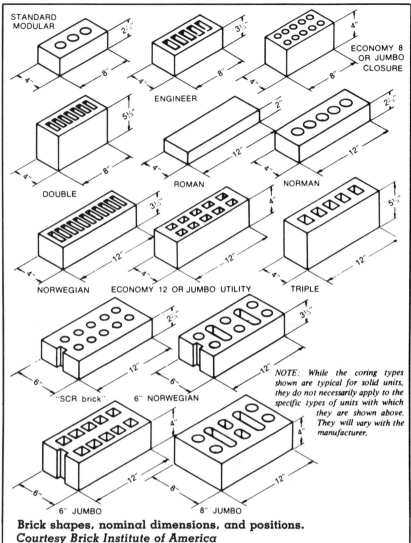

Brick shapes, nominal dimensions, and positions.
Courtesy Brick Institute of America

Details of an entrance consisting of a wooden doorframe above a cast-concrete sill, both part of a brick wall.

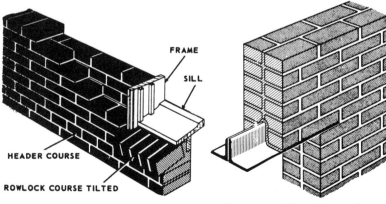

How a wooden window frame is positioned within a brick wall.

How a steel lintel may be positioned above an opening in a brick wall.

Height of Courses: 2 1/4-Inch Brick, 3/8-Inch Joint

Courses	Height	Courses	Height	Courses	Height	Courses	Height	Courses	Height
1	0' 2⅝''	21	4' 7⅛''	41	8' 11⅝''	61	13' 4⅛''	81	17' 8⅝''
2	0' 5¼''	22	4' 9¾''	42	9' 2¼''	62	13' 6¾''	82	17' 11¼''
3	0' 7⅞''	23	5' 0⅜''	43	9' 4⅞''	63	13' 9⅜''	83	18' 1⅞''
4	0' 10½''	24	5' 3''	44	9' 7½''	64	14' 0''	84	18' 4½''
5	1' 1⅛''	25	5' 5⅝''	45	9' 10⅛''	65	14' 2⅝''	85	18' 7⅛''
6	1' 3¾''	26	5' 8¼''	46	10' 0¾''	66	14' 5¼''	86	18' 9¾''
7	1' 6⅜''	27	5' 10⅞''	47	10' 3⅜''	67	14' 7⅞''	87	19' 0⅜''
8	1' 9''	28	6' 1½''	48	10' 6''	68	14' 10½''	88	19' 3''
9	1' 11⅝''	29	6' 4⅛''	49	10' 8⅝''	69	15' 1⅛''	89	19' 5⅝''
10	2' 2¼''	30	6' 6¾''	50	10' 11¼''	70	15' 3¾''	90	19' 8¼''
11	2' 4⅞''	31	6' 9⅜''	51	11' 1⅞''	71	15' 6⅜''	91	19' 10⅞''
12	2' 7½''	32	7' 0''	52	11' 4½''	72	15' 9''	92	20' 1½''
13	2' 10⅛''	33	7' 2⅝''	53	11' 7⅛''	73	15' 11⅝''	93	20' 4⅛''
14	3' 0¾''	34	7' 5¼''	54	11' 9¾''	74	16' 2¼''	94	20' 6¾''
15	3' 3⅜''	35	7' 7⅞''	55	12' 0⅜''	75	16' 4⅞''	95	20' 9⅜''
16	3' 6''	36	7' 10½''	56	12' 3''	76	16' 7½''	96	21' 0''
17	3' 8⅝''	37	8' 1⅛''	57	12' 5⅝''	77	16' 10⅛''	97	21' 2⅝''
18	3' 11¼''	38	8' 3¾''	58	12' 8¼''	78	17' 0¾''	98	21' 5¼''
19	4' 1⅞''	39	8' 6⅜''	59	12' 10⅞''	79	17' 3⅜''	99	21' 7⅞''
20	4' 4½''	40	8' 9''	60	13' 1½''	80	17' 6''	100	21' 10½''

Lintel Sizes

WALL THICKNESS	SPAN						
	3 FEET		4 FEET* STEEL ANGLES	5 FEET* STEEL ANGLES	6 FEET* STEEL ANGLES	7 FEET* STEEL ANGLES	8 FEET* STEEL ANGLES
	STEEL ANGLES	WOOD					
8"	2-3 x 3 x ¼	2 x 8 2-2 x 4	2-3 x 3 x ¼	2-3 x 3 x ¼	2-3½ x 3½ x ¼	2-3½ x 3½ x ¼	2-3½ x 3½ x ¼
12"	2-3 x 3 x ¼	2 x 12 2-2 x 6	2-3 x 3 x ¼	2-3½ x 3½ x ¼	2-3½ x 3½ x ¼	2-4 x 4 x ¼	2-4 x 4 x 4¼

* Wood lintels should not be used for spans over 3 feet since they burn out in case of fire and allow the brick to fall.

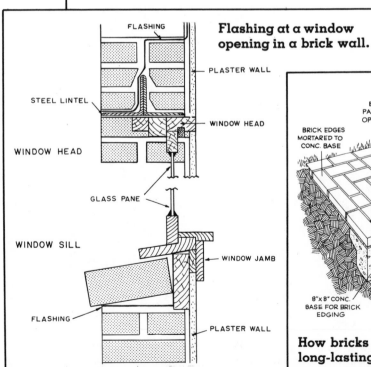

Flashing at a window opening in a brick wall.

FLASHING

PLASTER WALL

STEEL LINTEL

WINDOW HEAD

WINDOW HEAD

GLASS PANE

WINDOW SILL

WINDOW JAMB

FLASHING

PLASTER WALL

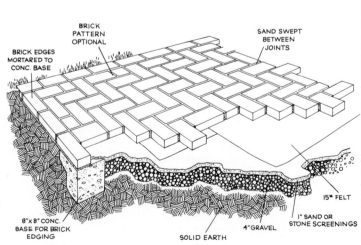

BRICK PATTERN OPTIONAL

SAND SWEPT BETWEEN JOINTS

BRICK EDGES MORTARED TO CONC. BASE

15# FELT

1" SAND OR STONE SCREENINGS

8"x 8" CONC. BASE FOR BRICK EDGING

4" GRAVEL

SOLID EARTH

How bricks may be laid up dry to form a solid long-lasting patio. *Courtesy Brick Institute of America*

5 CABINETS

Standard-sized cabinets in various woods, finishes, and designs are available from any number of local and national manufacturers and distributors. The cabinets are designed to be used in kitchens, baths, powder rooms, and wherever else you may care to use them. Cabinets are selected according to your taste, needs, and available space. Since no group of cabinets can possibly fit every room size, cabinets are made in varying widths with "filler" boards to bridge openings between cabinets and adjoining walls. Thus you select cabinet widths to fill your space and either neglect remaining openings or cover them with fillers.

Vanities, which are cabinets designed for bathrooms and powder and dressing rooms, generally come with their own tops. Kitchen cabinets usually consist of several units arranged in any number of ways, and manufacturers usually stock cabinet tops built to fit about a dozen fairly standard arrangements. If your cabinet arrangement differs from the standard set ups, you will have to get your cabinet tops made to order. Kitchen cabinet tops are, of course, counter tops. This is a financially important factor to bear in mind when you design your kitchen.

BASIC CONSIDERATIONS

CABINET MATERIAL AND FINISH
Most cabinets are made of plywood. Those with thicker walls and harder surface woods (maple instead of knotty pine, for example) stand up better to time and abuse. Stained and varnished wood does not stand up any better than painted wood, but scratches and dents in varnish are less visible than the same damage on a painted surface.

Metal cabinets are far less expensive and much stronger than wood cabinets. But unless you purchase metal cabinets that have been heavily porcelanized, the cabinets will look shoddy very quickly. The paint is easily scratched and chipped and then rust spots appear.

CABINET DIMENSIONS
You need at least a full half inch of clearance in order to slip a cabinet or group of cabinets between two walls. But since many walls are crooked, it's best to take measurements in several places to make certain you have full clearance all the way into the space.

If the end of a cabinet must project beyond a door opening, keep the side of that cabinet at least 15 inches shy of the door wall. You need that clearance to pass easily through the doorway.

CABINET CONSTRUCTION
There isn't sufficient space here to detail the many differences between well-constructed and poorly constructed cabinets. But there are some general guidelines you can easily follow.

Examine the products of a number of cabinet manufacturers. You will quickly appreciate the better-made ones. Look for heft—thickness and weight—in the materials used for sides, drawers, doors. Look for dovetailed, clean, tight joints. Check for smoothly opening and closing doors. Look for slides or runners guiding drawers.

Note that most cabinets are made without bottoms, which are not necessary. And most cabinets have only partial backs, which is satisfactory if the sides of the cabinet are properly braced by the partial back.

Cabinet sides that abut walls or other cabinet sides do not have to be stained and varnished, but they should be sealed. If they are not it is advisable to give them a coat of varnish (a spray can of varnish is all you need for the job).

TOPS

The best top consists of a single piece of Micarta or Formica that is continuous from the backboard (or splashboard) to over the front edge. Next is the top with Micarta or Formica edges (see that the joint lines are tight and clean). Least desirable and least expensive are the tops with metal edges (soil collects at and under the joint between the metal and the Micarta).

WATCH THE PIPES

When selecting cabinets make certain that no two cabinets meet in front of your sink or lavatory pipes. If they do you will have either to move the pipes, which is difficult, or to cut into the sides of the cabinets, which will greatly weaken them.

WATCH THE APPLIANCES

Make certain the cabinets you select can accommodate your disposal unit and/or dishwasher. The fact that the front of the cabinet is large enough doesn't always mean there is sufficient clearance on the inside.

TOP OPENINGS

Generally the company that supplies the cabinet top also cuts the opening(s) for the sink, range, faucets, etc. These holes not only must be correctly located but also be of the correct size. This takes careful planning. For example, rim-mounted and overlapping sinks, which may be identical in size, require different-sized openings. You can enlarge an opening with a fine-tooth keyhole saw, but you can never reduce it, so take care.

TIPS ON CABINET SELECTION

National Kitchen Cabinet Association makes the following suggestions:

• Open and shut the drawers and doors several times. Drawers should glide easily and quietly. Doors should have magnetized catches to stay shut. They should fit snugly against the cabinets at all edges when closed.

• Pull open a drawer and check how the sides are joined to the front and rear panels. Quality constructed drawers will have dovetailed joints at all four corners and be made of oak or another hardwood.

• Look underneath the drawer. Well-crafted drawers will have bottoms set into grooves in the sides and ends, not nailed to them. Bottoms should be sanded.

• Feel the cabinet's finish. It should

be smooth to the touch inside and out, with no bubbles or other imperfections. Variations in wood grain pattern, however, are part of the natural beauty of wood. Many wood species, such as oak and hickory, may also have small "distress" marks that give the cabinets a desirable, warm, antiqued appearance.

• Open the doors and examine the framing. Sturdy cabinets will have thick hardwood frames, ¾ inch to 1 inch thick, lock-jointed to the ends with mortise-tenon construction. This can be seen on display cabinets not covered by counter tops.

• Look inside the cabinet door for the round blue-and-white certification seal from the National Kitchen Cabinet Association. Cabinets that bear the NKCA seal must prove, through stringent laboratory tests, the ability to withstand hard daily use for years. Tests measure structural and finish resistance to common abuses such as heat, humidity, the overloading of shelves and drawers, splashes, and spills.

Kitchen cabinets of elm. *Courtesy Haas Cabinet Co.*

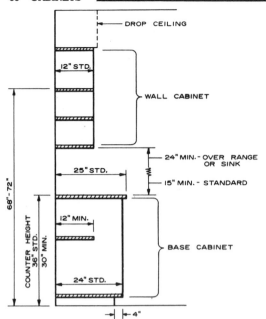

Standard kitchen cabinet dimensions.

A mortise and tenon joint—one hallmark of cabinet quality. *Courtesy Haas Cabinet Co.*

Well-made drawers always have their sides joined by dovetailed joints. *Courtesy Haas Cabinet Co.*

Single Formica-top bathroom vanity. Note lavatory bowl edge rests on top of the Formica. *Courtesy Haas Cabinet Co.*

WALL CABINETS

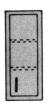 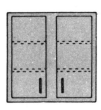   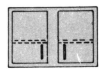

30" High   12" High   15" High   18" High   20" High

All wall cabinets are 12" deep. They come in a wide variety of sizes which can be combined to fit any area. The standard wall cabinet is 30" high. To take advantage of space over the refrigerator, cooking surface, or other areas, wall cabinets of less height are available. Angular and Lazy Susan cabinets fit into corners.

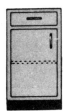 

BASE CABINETS

All base cabinets are 24" deep and 34½" high. The addition of the top provides a standard 36" counter height. Base cabinets also are offered in a variety of widths which combine to fit any area. Lazy Susan cabinets utilize corner space.

RANGE OR SINK BASES

Base cabinets in various widths are designed for a sink or cooking top. Where there are other cabinets on each side of the sink or cooking top area, it is possible to use a front only instead of a complete cabinet.

23⅛"

34½"

END PANELS

41⅞"

4½"

FILLERS AND MOULDINGS

To fill out an extra inch or two of wall space when cabinets do not quite fill the area, matching filler strips are available. Mouldings to match the cabinet finish add the finishing touch.

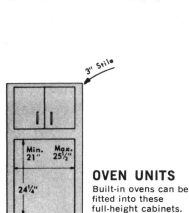

3" Stile

Min. 21"   Max. 25½"

24¼"

OVEN UNITS

Built-in ovens can be fitted into these full-height cabinets. They provide storage above the oven and drawers below.

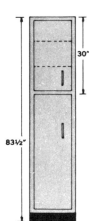

30"

83½"

UTILITY CABINETS

Full-height cabinets are useful in many areas. The upper area has two shelves. The lower area is perfect for brooms, mops, etc.

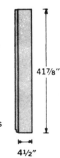

⅞"   ½"   1"   1"

(Top View) 30½" in height   1"

Typical cabinets and accessories.
Courtesy Haas Cabinet Co.

Four practical cabinet arrangements. *Courtesy Haas Cabinet Co.*

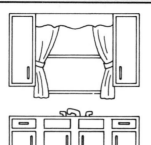

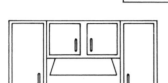

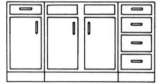

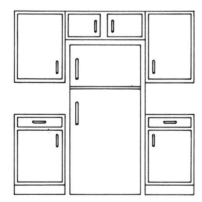

Four basic kitchen arrangements. The lines connecting the dots indicate work paths. *Courtesy Haas Cabinet Co.*

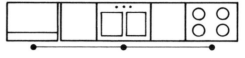

The "In-Line" Shape

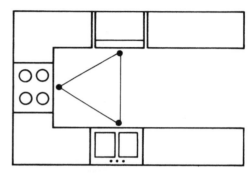

The "U" Shape

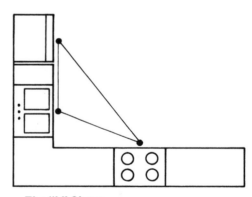

The "L" Shape

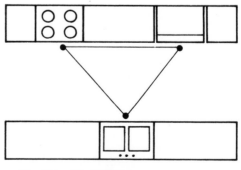

The "Corridor" Shape

1

Locate the position of all wall studs where cabinets are to hang by tapping with a hammer. Mark their position where the marks can easily be seen when the cabinets are in position.

2

Find the highest point on the floor with a level. This is important for both base and wall cabinet installation later.

Typical kitchen cabinet installation procedure. *Courtesy Haas Cabinet Co.*

3

Remove the baseboard from all walls where cabinets are to be installed. This will allow them to go flush against the walls.

4

Start the installation with a corner or end unit. Slide it into place then continue to slide the other base cabinets into the proper position.

5

When all base cabinets are in position, fasten the cabinets together. This is done by drilling a ¼" diameter hole through the face frames and using the 3" screws and T-nuts provided. To get maximum holding power from the screw, one hole should be close to the top of the end stile and one should be close to the bottom.

6

Check the position of each cabinet with a spirit level, going from the front of the cabinet to the back of the cabinet. Next shim between the cabinet and the wall for a perfect base cabinet installation.

7

Starting at the high point in the floor, level the leading edges of the cabinets. Continue to shim between the cabinets and the floor until all the base cabinets have been brought to level.

8

After the cabinets have been leveled, both front to back and across the front, fasten the cabinets to the wall at the stud locations. This is done by drilling a ³⁄₃₂" diameter hole 2¼" deep through both the hanging strips for the 2½" x 8 screws that are provided.

9

Fit the counter top into position and attach it to the base cabinets by predrilling and screwing through the front corner blocks into the top. Use caution not to drill through the top. Cover the counter top for protection while the wall cabinets are being installed.

10

Position the bottom of the 30" wall cabinets 19" from the top of the base cabinet, unless the cabinets are to be installed against a soffit. A brace can be made to help hold the wall cabinets in place while they are being fastened. Start the wall cabinets installation with a corner or end cabinet. Use care in getting this cabinet installed plumb and level, since this is the key for the entire installation.

11

Temporarily secure the adjoining wall cabinets so that leveling may be done without removing them. Drill through the end stiles of the cabinets and fasten them together as was done with the base cabinets.

12

Use a spirit level to check the horizontal surfaces. Shim between the cabinet and the wall until the cabinet is level. This is necessary if doors are to fit properly.

13

Check the perpendicular surface of each frame at the front. When the cabinets are level, both front to back and across the front, permanently attach the cabinets to the wall. This is done by predrilling a ³⁄₃₂" diameter hole 2¼" deep through the hanging strip inside the top and below the bottom of the cabinets at the stud location. Enough number 8 screws should be used to fasten the cabinets securely to the wall.

6 CAULK

When Noah built his ark he sealed the cracks between the timbers with pitch. He knew that no matter how tightly he joined the timbers they would come apart a little and water would enter his craft. Only a flexible, waterproof adhesive would keep those cracks sealed. In modern-day idiom, he caulked his boat. Wooden ships are still caulked as are modern homes. The reason is that the parts of a building move and shift in response to wind and temperature, but the movement of the various parts is different—and unequal. For example, a metal window frame set within a brick wall will not contract and expand at the same rate as the wall. Therefore, cracks will always form between the metal and the brick. Flexible caulking seals the cracks.

SELECTION

There are five basic formulations of caulking, each with its own characteristics. When selecting the type best for your purpose, remember to evaluate all the factors: materials to be sealed, presence or absence of paint, temperature, life of the caulk color, cost, environment, etc.

OIL BASE
Usually made from a combination of linseed oil, whiting; sometimes asbestine, kerosene, asbestos fiber, talc. This is the oldest, cheapest, and least desirable of them all (because it does not last as well as newer types). But it will adhere to wood,
masonry, metal, and clean-painted surfaces.

ACRYLIC LATEX
Good indoors and out, generally high on latex (rubber) content, resists temperatures ranging from −30° to 180°F. Takes all kinds of paints, including acrylics. Sets and is ready for painting in two hours; can be had in colors if you do not wish to paint. Good for all materials.

BUTYL RUBBER
Best for sealing metal to metal or metal to masonry; especially good with aluminum. Lasts five times longer than oil and latex caulks; comes in several colors; produces a rubberlike, watertight seal.

POLYVINYL
Available in several colors, adheres well to all surfaces, including paint and fiberglass. Some forms of polyvinyl come with fiberglass reinforcement and dry translucent. Like the other caulks, polyvinyl also bonds materials together but to a greater degree. In its liquid form polyvinyl caulk can be spread with a brush and applied like a paint. The wet brush or drips can be cleaned up with soap and water.

SILICON
This is probably the best all around. It will last longer than any of the others. It adheres well to everything except paint.

Variations of caulking abound. The DAP company, for example, has some seventeen caulking compounds, each with special properties. Other companies probably have as many of their own variations. All you can do is study their literature, compare their major ingredients to those listed here, and judge for yourself what is best for your needs.

APPLICATION

Caulk can be had in small, medium, and large squeeze tubes, cartridges, and cans. The cartridges fit into a caulking gun. Working its handle forces caulk out of the gun nozzle.

No matter what type of caulking you use or the method with which you apply it, the surfaces to be caulked must be perfectly dry, dust- and dirt-free.

When using a squeeze tube or gun, cut the nozzle directly across, as directed, and not at an angle. Doing this will produce a rounder bead of caulking. Holding the nozzle at an angle will produce proper adhesion. Once the bead is laid down there is usually no need to fuss with it. Just let it be.

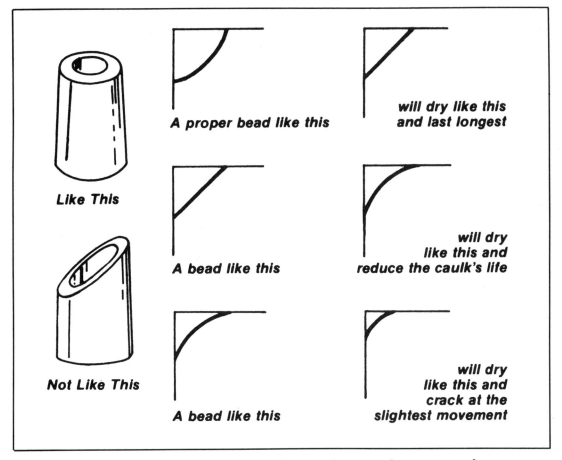

Like This

Not Like This

A proper bead like this

A bead like this

A bead like this

will dry like this
and last longest

will dry
like this and
reduce the caulk's life

will dry
like this and
crack at the
slightest movement

It is advisable to cut the nozzle of the caulking tube straight across and not at an angle. The straight-cut nozzle produces a rounder bead that fills the joint better. *Courtesy H. B. Fuller Co.*

7 CEMENT–MASONRY

Modern cement, the kind that is used to make concrete and mortar for joining bricks and stucco, is called portland cement because it looks like the stone that comes from the English island of Portland. Invented by one Josep Aspin, a brickmason from Leeds, England, in 1824, it differs from earlier cements in that it will harden underwater.

Modern cement is made by heating a mixture of clay and limestone in a giant rotary oven to some 2,800°F. The clay and stone melt and form clinkers, which are cooled and then ground into a very fine powder.

GENERAL CHARACTERISTICS

If you mix cement with water to form a mass with the consistency of, let us say, putty, a chemical action called hydration will take place. Depending on temperature, the cement-putty will turn into a kind of permanent stone within forty-eight hours. Once the water hits the cement there is no way the chemical reaction can be stopped or reversed. (Cold will slow it down.) If you were to place the still-soft mass of cement-putty underwater, the hardening would not be stopped; it would continue as before. If you mixed the cement-putty mass with the water, you still would not stop the hardening process. All that would happen would be that you would have a multitude of tiny bits of cement stone.

STRENGTH

Cement is, essentially, a kind of glue. Used by itself it has little strength. Maximum strength is secured when the dry cement is mixed with two parts clean sand and sufficient water to make an almost soupy mixture.

TYPES

There are five basic types of cement, and a number of variations, in common use today. They are all equal in strength and resistance to time and weather.

TYPE 1. General purpose.
TYPE 2. Same as Type 1 but has a lower hydration temperature, which means it doesn't get as hot after being poured. Used for thick, massive structures.
TYPE 3. High early. It hardens more quickly then the others.
TYPE 4. Low heat. Generates even less heat than Type 2. This is the cement used for giant dams.
TYPE 5. Alkali resistant. Used when contact with highly alkaline water and soil is expected.

AIR-ENTRAINING CEMENT

Certain chemicals are added to the cement that forms billions of microscopic air bubbles. The presence of the air bubbles affects the cement in a number of desirable ways. The water required for mixing is reduced by approximately one half gallon per bag of cement. The cement becomes more plastic and is more easily worked. The entrained air bubbles greatly increase the resistance of the cement to frost and the action of ice-melting chemicals such as calcium chloride and sodium chloride (table salt).

All types of cement can be made air entraining by the addition of the necessary chemicals. These chemicals can be purchased at the masonry yard. To secure the full advantage of air-entraining cement, however, the chemicals and the cement (plus whatever else is going to be added) must be mixed by machine. Hand mixing may not distribute the chemicals properly.

If you are going to hand mix, purchase air-entraining cement. These bags will be marked Type 1A, 2A, and 3A. They will have the characteristics of the type of cement, plus the air-entraining qualities.

MORTAR CEMENT

This is cement mixed with slaked lime. Generally the proportions are three parts cement to one part lime. Usually, the cement is Type 1. (See MORTAR.)

WHITE CEMENT

Standard cement is green while it is still soft. With time it turns to a pale gray. White cement hardens to a nearly white color. It is used when you want the end product to be white or when you want to add color. Naturally, brighter colors result when they are mixed with white rather than gray.

BROWN CEMENT

This cement handles like ordinary cement but hardens to a warm buff color, much like adobe.

OTHER ADDITIVES

Any number of different additives are currently manufactured and marketed under a variety of trade names. They are added to cement to alter its characteristics. Some act to slow the setting rate; some act to hasten setting. Some increase the wet cement's resistance to freezing; some make the hard cement more resistant to water penetration.

BUYING AND STORING CEMENT

STANDARD BAGS

Cement is sold in paper bags. Each bag contains exactly 1 cubic foot of cement and weighs about 94 pounds. Each bag is marked by type number and additive, if any. Bags containing cement and lime are marked mortar cement. They weigh about 76 pounds and contain a total of 1 cubic foot of both cement and mortar.

SELECTING A CEMENT

The quality of the cement produced by one company does not differ from the quality of the cement produced by any other company, so choose the cheapest you can find.

All types of cement will work equally well in the construction of ordinary buildings, walks, drives, and the like. There is no point in paying a premium for any special type of cement. Even the greater plasticity of air-entraining cement does not warrant its extra cost for ordinary cement (and concrete) work.

SMALL QUANTITIES

Cement can also be purchased in hardware shops and do-it-yourself shops in much less than 1-cubic-foot quantities. These packages contain standard cements (and cement mixtures). Their only drawback is their cost. Very often you can purchase a standard bag for the price of two or three small bags.

STORAGE

The paper bags in which cement is packed are neither waterproof nor water-resistant, and cement is hydrophilic—that is, it absorbs moisture. Outdoors, you cannot place a bag of cement on the earth for any length of time because it will soon absorb moisture. Outdoors, the bags must be raised above the ground and covered by a waterproof sheet of plastic or similar material. Cement may be stored for years indoors if the area is perfectly dry. In a damp cellar or basement, the cement will eventually absorb water and harden.

Lumpy cement should not be used. Still-powdery cement from the same bag can be used without problem, however.

Type 1 portland cement on the left. This bag weighs over 90 pounds. Type 1 masonry cement weighs only 69½ pounds. That's because it contains about 25 percent lime. Both bags contain exactly 1 cubic foot.

8 CONCRETE

Concrete is made by mixing cement, sand, small stones, and water together to form a thick soup or slurry. The concrete is then poured into a mold and permitted to harden. Any and all sorts of molds are used. Some produce artwork, some concrete blocks, some walls, walks, and drives. (The form used for a walk is an open pan with a dirt bottom. Once the concrete hardens it becomes a kind of rock that can withstand—and has withstood—the weather for thousands of years.)

BASIC CHARACTERISTICS

Wet concrete weighs about 150 pounds per cubic foot and roughly 2 tons per cubic yard. Wet concrete reaches initial set in about one hour; this takes less time in hot, dry weather, more time in cool weather. Wet concrete cannot withstand frost, though it can do so somewhat better than water. The chemical change that starts when water is added to cement is called hydration, and this action produces heat. This heat will delay freezing somewhat, but will not prevent it at very low temperatures. When wet concrete freezes the result is a kind of sand.

When concrete reaches initial set it is ready for finishing. Shine and surface water disappear and you should float and trowel the concrete at this time, since this is when it responds best.

During the following ten hours or so—again depending on temperature—you can, if you wish, break up the concrete, mix it with water, and handle it as you would fresh concrete. After ten hours the concrete reaches a condition known as final set. If you break up the concrete after final set, you will have pieces of stone that cannot be dissolved.

From initial set through final set and for days and possibly weeks following, the concrete looks green and is called green. Given time and sufficient water—which the concrete can draw from the air, when it is moist, or the soil when it, too, is moist, or which is sprayed on when the air is dry—the concrete slowly loses its green color and turns to a pale gray. This color change indicates a process called curing, which is accompanied by tremendous increase in the strength of the concrete.

Typically, three-day-old concrete may have a compressive strength of 1,500 psi. Seven-day-old concrete will have increased in strength to 2,000 psi. Twenty-eight-day-old concrete will have a rating of up to 4,000 psi. Year-old concrete will be able to withstand a compressive load of 5,500 psi. As time goes by, the concrete will grow increasingly stronger, though at a diminishing rate. Measurements have shown that this process goes on for at least thirty years.

As stated, concrete's compressive strength is very high. Its tensile strength (resistance to pull and bending), however, is comparatively low. The same concrete that can withstand 5,500 psi in compression is rated at no more than 650 psi in tension. This means that concrete cannot be used alone as a support beam. It must be reinforced. This is most often done by placing steel reinforcing bars within its length.

Although all concrete increases in strength as it is cured, maximum strength is dependent upon the ratio of the materials used to make it, specifically cement and water. Decreasing the cement content or increasing the quantity of water added to the mix decreases the strength of the concrete.

EFFECT OF WATER

The water content in a mix is measured as gallons of water per bag (1 cubic foot) of cement. Typically as you increase water content from 4½ gallons per bag to 10½ gallons per bag you reduce the twenty-eight-day compressive strength of the concrete from 4,000 psi to 1,000 psi. On the other hand, if you do not use sufficient water to thoroughly wet all the cement and provide the correct amount of water necessary for hydration, you will end up with concrete that will break in your hand.

At the same time, the less water used the more difficult it is to mix and place the concrete. In practice, the ratio used is about seven gallons of water per bag of concrete. This makes for easy mixing, easy placement, and a concrete with a twenty-eight-day, 3,000 psi rating. This is several times more strength than is needed for walls, walks, house footings, and foundations.

ADDITIVES

By using a Type A cement or adding air-entraining chemicals to the mix, you can secure an easier-to-work concrete that will have slightly greater resistance to wet freezing. The addition of calcium chloride at a rate not to exceed 2 pounds per bag of cement will also increase wet concrete's resistance to freezing. By using Type 3 cement, plus calcium chloride, time lapse to initial set can be cut in half. This makes for speedier placement and finishing while also reducing the danger of freezing. Note that calcium chloride makes the concrete a bit stiffer and more difficult to work.

Anti-Hydros is a trade name for another chemical additive used with concrete. It speeds setting time, increases frost resistance, and also increases concrete's resistance to water penetration.

MIX VOLUME

It might appear that if you were to mix 1 cubic foot of cement with 3 cubic feet of sand plus 5 cubic feet of stones and then add lots of water you would end up with at least 9 cubic feet of concrete. You won't. Instead you will have about 6.25 cubic feet of concrete.

The reason is the relative sizes of the materials involved. Cement, which is a very fine powder, will slip into the voids or spaces between the grains of sand. The sand will fit into the voids between the stones and the water will fit into whatever cracks and spaces remain.

To get a rough estimate of mix volumes, multiply the quantity of stone used in the 1:3:5 formula by 1.25. Multiply the stone in the 1:2¾:4 formula by 1.32, and the stone in the 1:2¼:3 formula by 1.5. This is something to bear in mind when you are considering the relative merits and costs of purchasing already mixed concrete to be delivered by truck versus purchasing the materials and mixing your own concrete.

CONCRETE MIX FORMULAS

Cement	Sand	Stone	
1	2¼	3	Strongest, most expensive, most wear-resistant, most weather-resistant, watertight. Use for swimming pools, walks, driveways, floors.
1	2¾	4	Moderately strong, moderately expensive, moderately weather- and wear-resistant. Used for foundations, walls, etc., structures not directly exposed to the elements.
1	3	5	Weakest, least expensive. Used for massive structures such as retaining walls, thick foundations, and the like.

FORMULAS FOR MAKING CONCRETE*

to make

1:2¼:3 mixture

	1 cubic yard	2 cubic yards	3 cubic yards
cement	6 bags	12 bags	18 bags
sand	16 cu. ft.	32 cu. ft.	48 cu. ft.
stone	18 cu. ft.	37 cu. ft.	54 cu. ft.
water	36 gallons	72 gallons	108 gallons

1:2¾:4 mixture

cement	5 bags	10 bags	15 bags
sand	16 cu. ft.	32 cu. ft.	48 cu. ft.
stone	20 cu. ft.	34 cu. ft.	60 cu. ft.
water	30 gallons	60 gallons	90 gallons

1:3:5 mixture

cement	4.5 bags	9 bags	13.5 bags
sand	16 cu. ft.	32 cu. ft.	48 cu. ft.
stone	22 cu. ft.	24 cu. ft.	65 cu. ft.
water	27 gallons	54 gallons	82 gallons

*Sand quantities have been increased 15 percent to account for bulking caused by the absorption of water.

Water is calculated on the basis of 6.15 gallons per bag of cement.

There are 27 cubic feet to 1 cubic yard.

WORKING WITH CONCRETE

FORMS

Concrete is ordinarily poured into a form where it goes through the chemical process that turns it to stone. The inner shape and surface of the form determines the finished shape and surface of the concrete. The top of the form is usually left open and the concrete permitted to find its own level, or screeded level, with the top of the form.

The outward pressure on the sides of the form depends on the depth of the form. Wet concrete behaves like water, and when the form is more than a foot or so deep, pressure can run to tons.

Once in the form and screeded, the concrete goes through a stage called initial set. This is when the free water comes to the surface. It is at this time that the concrete's surface is "finished." For a flat but frictive surface, such as a walk, the concrete is "floated," or rubbed flat with a float. For a smoother surface, floating is followed by a rub with a steel trowel. In the case of a walk the concrete will be "edged," which consists of running an edging tool down the border of the concrete.

Following, the concrete is kept moist for a few days until it is partially cured, which means it is hard enough to walk on.

COLORING CONCRETE

Concrete can be colored by dusting, integral coloring, and staining. A variety of colors are available. For best results, use white cement to make the concrete.

DUSTING

Dry color is dusted over freshly floated cement. Then the surface is troweled and allowed to cure the usual way. Dry colors or dry colors mixed with some white cement (for more even dispersal) can be purchased at the masonry yard. The latter are sold as "dust-on" colors and cost a little more.

INTEGRAL COLORING

Dry concrete pigment is mixed into the concrete at a rate of five to ten pounds of color per bag of cement. White cement is used for best results. The concrete is then positioned and treated as usual.

To save on the cost of color, the concrete walk or floor is poured in two layers. The first layer is not colored. The second layer, poured shortly after the first, is colored and is no more than ½ inch thick. This method reduces the amount of coloring needed by a considerable amount and still produces a deep shade of color.

STAINING

Three types of stains may be used: organic, solvent, or oxidizing.

The organic stains work by altering the concrete chemically, in this way producing a reasonably permanent color change. These stains produce brown, green, black, rust, and beige colors. They are simply brushed onto the finished concrete surface. See manufacturer's instructions for specifics. NOTE: When used on patched concrete the stains will accentuate the patches.

Solvent stains work by soaking into the pores of the concrete. Solvent stains for concrete are similar in a way to the stains used with wood, but for best results only stains specifically made for concrete should be used. Usually, these stains are simply brushed evenly over cured concrete.

Oxidizing stains are not currently available in ready-to-use form. You have to mix them yourself. To secure a reddish-brown or buff color, mix ferrous sulfate (sulfate or iron) with water. Use two full tablespoons to a pint of water. Stir until the chemical is completely dissolved. Then spread it over freshly finished concrete. The concrete should be so fresh you can still mar its surface with your hand. Be careful with the staining mixture because it will permanently stain your clothing and kill whatever grass it contacts. NOTE: This mixture will first turn the concrete green, so don't be surprised.

To secure a green color, use copper sulfate in place of ferrous sulfate.

PACKAGED CONCRETE

Dry concrete mixes are sold in hardware and similar stores. The packages are fine for small jobs and patching, but impossibly expensive when anything exceeding a cubic foot of concrete is required. Mix and use as you would ordinary concrete.

BONDING AGENTS

When patching concrete, when applying a layer of fresh concrete over old, or when butting fresh concrete up against old, it is advisable to use a bonding agent to help the new and the old concrete form a strong bond. Two of the better-known bonding agents are Permaweld-Z and Weld-Crete. Both are found only in liquid form and are applied with a brush.

REINFORCING CONCRETE

Concrete has very little tensile strength, meaning that it does not resist bending very well, so it must be reinforced when it is used in slabs meant to span an open area. Reinforcement is usually provided by steel bars placed within the concrete when it is poured. These rebars, special bars of steel, have been deformed so that their surfaces are very rough. The thickness of the bars used, their number and spacing depend on the distance the concrete slab is to span, the load it is to carry, the thickness of the concrete, and whether the concrete is to be supported at two sides or four sides. Concrete that is supported only at its ends (two sides)—for example, a bridge—must have more steel than a slab that is supported at four sides—for example, a porch floor.

NO-STEEL SPANS

Concrete that is 4 inches thick and supported on two sides only can span a distance up to 4 feet and carry a residential load, which is a maximum of 50 pounds per square foot. Increase the concrete's thickness to 6 inches and the span can be lengthened, safely, to 4½ feet.

Supported on four sides, a 4-inch slab can span 5 feet, and a 6-inch thick slab can safely span 5½ feet with the same residential load.

REBAR DATA (Reinforcing Bar)

Bar designation number	Bar diameter	Weight lbs./ft.	Cross section sq. in.
2	¼ in.	0.166	0.05
3	⅜ in.	0.376	0.1105
4	½ in.	0.668	0.1963
5	⅝ in.	1.043	0.3068
6	¾ in.	1.502	0.4418
7	⅞ in.	2.044	0.6013
8	1 in.	2.670	0.7854
9	1 sq. in.	3.400	1.000
10	1⅛ sq. in.	4.303	1.2656
11	1¼ sq. in.	5.313	1.5625

REQUIRED REINFORCEMENT FOR SLABS SUPPORTED ON FOUR SIDES*

Slab thickness	Bar diameter	Span	Spacing between bars
4 in.	⅜ in.	5 ft.	18 in.
4	⅜	6	14
4	⅜	8	10
4	½	10	10
6 in.	⅜ in.	5 ft.	20 in.
6	⅜	6	18
6	⅜	8	14
6	½	10	12

*It is assumed that the slab will be roughly square and that the bars will be of approximately equal lengths in both directions.

REQUIRED REINFORCEMENT FOR SLABS SUPPORTED ON TWO SIDES

Slab thickness	Span	Long bar diameter	Long bar spacing	Cross bar diameter	Cross bar spacing
4 in.	4 in.	⅜ in.	10 in.	⅜ in.	18 in.
4	5	⅜	8	⅜	18
4	6	⅜	6	⅜	18
4	8	½	7	⅜	12
4	10	½	4	⅜	6
6 in.	4 ft.	⅜ in.	12 in.	⅜ in.	18 in.
6	5	⅜	10	⅜	18
6	6	½	10	⅜	14
6	8	½	7	⅜	12
6	10	½	5	⅜	10

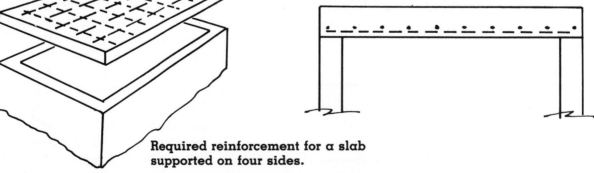

Required reinforcement for a slab supported on two sides.

Required reinforcement for a slab supported on four sides.

Mixing concrete in a mortar box.

The concrete has been placed in a form. Here it is being screeded. This action makes the top surface of the concrete level with the sides of the form. In this case, the form produces a walk.

Rough ridges left by the screed are removed by floating. The surface of the concrete is lightly rubbed down with a metal float.

For a smoother, harder surface the concrete is rubbed down with a steel trowel.

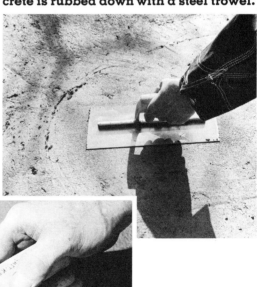

An edging tool is run along between the inside edge of the form and the concrete. The tool produces a rounded, finished edge.

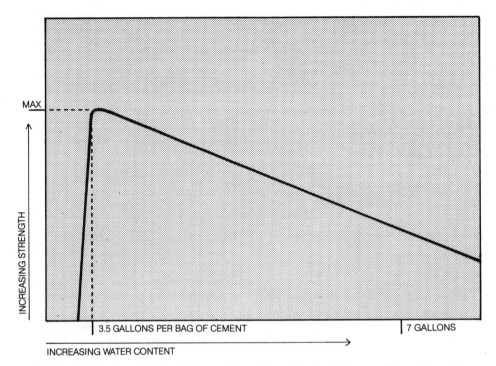

MAX

INCREASING STRENGTH

3.5 GALLONS PER BAG OF CEMENT   7 GALLONS

INCREASING WATER CONTENT

The effect of water content on the strength of concrete. Note that if you have too little water, the concrete will fall apart.

Form used to construct a concrete wall.

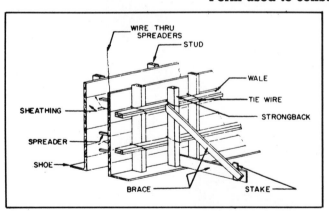

Erected form.

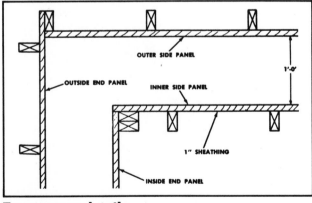

Form corner details.

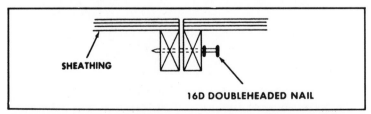

How form walls may be joined for easy disassembly.

DOORS

Doors for residential buildings, as distinct from commercial structures, doghouses, and barns, are divided into two basic categories. These catagories subdivide into a number of subgroups which further subdivide several times more.

The two primary groups are exterior and interior. Very simply, exterior doors must withstand the elements and intruders. Interior doors need not. From these two basic divisions we go on to a large variety of styles, materials, and ornamentations.

MAJOR PARTS

Residential doors are hung from hinges that are fastened to a doorframe, which in turn is fitted within the wall. The vertical sides of the frame are called side jambs. The top of the frame is called the head jamb. The bottom of the frame consists of a sill topped, in most instances, by a strip of wood, metal, and/or plastic called the threshold, which provides a flexible seal between the sill and the bottom of the door.

The strips of wood that prevent the door from swinging all the way through the frame are called doorstops. The trim around the doorframe, which hides the joint between the frame and the edges of the wall, is called the casing.

IDENTIFYING DIMENSIONS

When we speak of door widths, we speak of the door's actual width. The width of the opening in the frame for that door will always be a fraction of an inch larger. Generally, there is 1/16-inch clearance between the door and its frame on the hinge side and ⅛ inch of space to spare on the latch side. Generally, there is ⅛ inch clearance at the top of the door and ½ inch clearance between the sill and the bottom of the door. (This is the space sealed by the flexible threshold.)

ROUGH OPENINGS

The opening in the wall into which the doorframe fits is always larger than the frame by at least ¾ of an inch. This space is necessary in order to position the frame perfectly vertical despite bends and inaccuracies in the placement of the studs that frame the door opening. Top height clearance is the same ¾ to 1 inch.

Doorjamb width depends on the thickness of the wall. Jamb width is always such that the jamb will terminate flush with the finished inside wall and the house sheathing. If you don't know what this dimension is, or will be, purchase a two-piece, split-jamb doorframe. The width of the split jamb is adjustable.

EXTERIOR DOORS

DIMENSIONS

It is without a doubt, penny-wise, pound-foolish to install a front-of-the-house door that is less than 36 inches wide. You need this width to allow the movement of furniture in and out of the building. Rear doors can be smaller but should not be under 32 inches. The same goes for basement doors. Exterior door height is generally the standard 6 feet 8 inches. There are also 7-foot-high doors and frames to be had, but there is no particular need for them.

ENTRANCE SYSTEMS

This is the term most often used to describe anything more than a simple door and frame. Door systems vary, from frames with extra-wide and ornamented trim to frames that also include lights (windows) to one or both sides of the door. Entrance systems add cost, increase heat loss, but do provide some additional visual interest.

REDUCING ENTRANCE HEAT LOSS

Windowless entrance systems have considerably higher R values (insulating values) than do systems with windows. Ordinary windows conduct heat; glass is a very poor insulator. If you must have windows, you can secure doors and entrance systems with insulated windows. These consist of two panes of glass separated by a layer of air. On doors the two panes amount to a thickness of ½ inch with ¼ inch of air separating them. On sliding doors the total thickness is generally ⅝ of an inch with each piece of glass 3/16 inch thick.

The passage of air through the spaces between the door and its frame can account for a greater loss of heat than that lost through the door's glass. But this passage of air is easily

stopped by weather stripping. Years ago metal weather stripping was used. Today nylon is used, with the nylon kerfed (fitted into a slot) in place. Thresholds usually consist of an aluminum strip that encloses a flexible fold of nylon that seals the bottom of the door opening. In addition, it is customary today to further seal the front and rear doors of a home with a second, lighter door called a storm door. Generally, this is made of aluminum.

SECURITY

Single- and double-acting locks are only as strong as the door in which they are mounted, and the door and lock combination in the front of the house is no stronger than the rear door and its lock. But the strongest door and lock are of no avail when there is a window in the door or entrance system that can be broken and through which an intruder can reach to work the lock. All this is, of course, also true of a sliding door. It is just as easy to break through a large pane of glass as it is to penetrate a small pane of glass. If you install a sliding door of glass you give up all physical security and should install an electronic guard system or have a well-trained watchdog.

STYLES AND MATERIALS

To some extent the style of a door determines its material of construction. Panel doors are always made of solid wood. Two kinds of wood are used: pine, generally ponderosa, and fir. Doors made of number 1 pine are free of all knots. Doors made of number 2 pine have some small, tight knots. Both grades can be stained and varnished without problem. Number 1 can be painted without pretreating. Number 2 should have its knots coated with shellac prior to painting.

On the other hand, fir does not take stain and varnish well, but it is considerably stronger than pine.

All exterior doors, both the panel and the flush types to be discussed here, are made in thicknesses of 1⅜ and 1¾ inches. The thicker door is by far the stronger and more desirable door.

Flush, or flat, exterior doors should have interiors made of strips of wood glued together. There should not be any air spaces. The veneers, which are glued to the wood strips, are usually beautiful, so beautiful, in fact, that you can varnish them directly without staining, if you wish. Of course, they will also take paint.

Some of the flush doors are ornamented with wood moldings nailed into place. The moldings add to the cost, but not to the strength of the door. When you varnish or paint such doors be certain to thoroughly fill the joints between the molding and the veneer.

There are also all-metal doors available for residential use. They are considerably less expensive, and are stronger, fire-resistant, and rot-proof. They come completely pre-drilled. When painted they look exactly the same as flush doors of wood. It is only when you open them that you realize they are much heavier than wooden doors.

SLIDING (PATIO) DOORS

Sometimes called sliding doors, sometimes called patio or gliding doors, these doors fit into a prefabri-

cated frame that contains all the necessary hardware. Generally, the doors, which hang from rollers rather than ride on them are less troublesome; debris doesn't block the track as easily.

INSTALLATION

When the doorframe proper is pre-fastened within a wide, wood frame, the frame is positioned directly within the rough wall opening. Openings between the frame and the wall studs are filled with shims at several points. The frame is made perfectly vertical, then face-nailed through the shims to the studs. When there is no such frame, but the door is mounted within a narrow wood or metal frame, it is necessary to "case" the rough opening, which means frame it out. The doorframe is then positioned within the in-place frame. Obviously this is much more difficult, since you must make the fit between the two frames fairly close. Small openings between them can be caulked.

INTERIOR DOORS

DIMENSIONS

Interior doors leading from room to room should be 30 inches wide at a minimum, though some architects specify 28-inch doors for bathrooms. Closet doors can be 24 inches wide. Door height is almost always 6 feet 8 inches.

STYLES AND MATERIALS

Years ago, when wood and labor were both far less expensive, interior doors were made with panels. Today, cost has made most of us switch to flush doors. Flush doors consist of two parts: the veneer exterior and the core that supports the veneer. Cores may be made of solid strips of wood glued side by side to make a solid slab of wood, or the core may be fashioned from pieces of wood, leaving hollow areas. Both types of doors look alike. Both function equally well and last long. However, you can kick through a hollow-core door (should you want to or need to) and you have to take care when cutting this type of door down (shortening) that you don't cut through the frame and into the hollow area. There is still a third type of door made with a composition core. If you can examine the core (see it at the edge of the door) and it is firm chipboard, it will be satisfactory. If the core is of some type of paper composition, however, it won't stand up.

The price of a flush, interior door is based on its thickness—1⅜ or 1¾ inch—and on the type of wood used for veneer. The harder and more beautiful veneers fetch higher prices. But so far as ordinary service life is concerned, one veneer is no better than another.

LOUVERED DOORS

These may be fully or partially louvered. They may be of clear pine or slightly knotted pine. Unless there is a big fat knot visible somewhere, the only differences between one door and another are cost and appearance, and the knots are not visible beneath paint. Generally, louvered doors are available in thicknesses of 1¼ and 1⅜ inches only. Louvered doors are used for closets, to permit air to enter, between master bedrooms and children's rooms so that sounds can pass through, and in a few other spots.

DUTCH DOORS

These are horizontally split doors that open in one or two sections. When insects are no problem and you want the fresh air to waft in without the hinderance of a screen, these are the doors to choose. Be certain, however, to purchase solidly made 1¾-inch-thick doors, and bear in mind that you need twice the hardware—hinges, etc.—and that they are more than twice as difficult to hang (mount in their frame).

DOOR FRAMES AND TRIM

The purpose of the frame is to provide a "clean" passageway through the wall and a support for the door. The purpose of the trim is to hide the joints between the frame and the rough opening in the wall.

There isn't much to choose from among frames, except for the quality of the wood and the joint (or lack of joint) at the top of the frame. The better frames have head jambs that are dadoed into place (fitted into a groove). The others have head jambs that simply rest on top of the side jambs. The better frames are made of clear pine, the others of pine with small knots.

DIMENSIONS

The width of the jambs forming the frame must be exactly equal to the thickness of the wall. On interior walls, this would be the thickness from the surface of the wall on one side of the door to the surface of the other side of the same wall. As you can see, this dimension would depend on the thickness of the gypsum board you were using or whether or not you were working with a plastered wall. On an exterior wall, jamb width would be equal to the distance from the surface of the finished inner side of the wall through to the surface of the sheathing. When you are not certain what this dimension will be, purchase split-jamb doorframes. The width of these jambs can be varied.

INSTALLING FRAMES AND DOORS

ROUGH OPENINGS

The rough opening you leave in a wall when building it, or cut into an existing wall, is always approximately ¾ of an inch larger on the top and the sides than the outside dimensions of the doorframe. This clearance is necessary to permit you to correct for errors in the opening.

FRAME HEIGHT

Frame sides are made overly long. They almost always have to be shortened. When you cut an indoor frame, bear in mind necessary door clearances, rough and finished flooring, and whether or not there will be a threshold. You want the hung door to be ⅛ of an inch clear of the top jamb, and the bottom of the door to clear the finished flooring, threshold, or carpet by ½ inch.

External doorframes require the same careful planning, but here you have to consider the sill as well as the flooring and the threshold. The bottom of an exterior door should make contact with the threshold.

FASTENING THE FRAME

Pieces of wood shingles are used as shims to hold the doorframe perfectly vertical and to provide a support through which nails can be driven. Two shims are positioned above the head jamb and two more behind each side jamb. The portions of the shims that extend beyond the doorframe are then cut flush with the frame.

HANGING THE DOOR

Now comes the job that has driven many carpenters to distraction—hanging the door. There isn't room to detail the steps here, but suffice it to say that if the butt hinges are not mounted perfectly correctly, the door will neither hang correctly nor swing correctly. Two solutions are feasible. Hire an experienced carpenter or purchase a prehung door. The latter is a door that is supplied with mounted hinges that fit into hinges already mounted in the frame.

FIRE DOORS

These are fireproof or fire-resistant doors that are positioned at the entrance to a brick or block-enclosed furnace room. They are a safety measure and are required by many building codes. The standard fire door is made of metal and comes with prefastened hinges positioned and sized to fit hinges in a metal frame. (See BLOCK, CONCRETE, for installation details.)

Some building codes will accept a standard, flush wood door that has been covered on one side with a sheet of galvanized iron or ¼-inch Transite (a fireproof asbestos cement sheeting). Use a carbide-tipped bit to drill holes in the Transite.

OVERHEAD GARAGE DOORS

These doors are made of wood, metal, and fiberglass. The wood doors come in two thicknesses (frame thickness only) of 1⅜ and 1¾ inches. Without windows they have an R value of 2.0 to 2.9. When the metal doors are insulated they have an R factor of 7.7. The fiberglass doors have little insulating value. Their R factor is only approximately 1.05. They do pass considerable light, however. The green fiberglass will pass as much as 50 percent of the light that strikes it.

DOOR DIMENSIONS

In order to fit an overhead door into your garage you need approximately 18 inches of headroom. This is the distance from the top of the door opening to the ceiling. You also need 4 to 6 inches of side clearance for hardware.

The dimensions of the door itself depend upon the method you will use to mount it. The door may be the same size as the opening or it may be 2 inches wider and 1 inch higher than the opening depending on how it is to be hung.

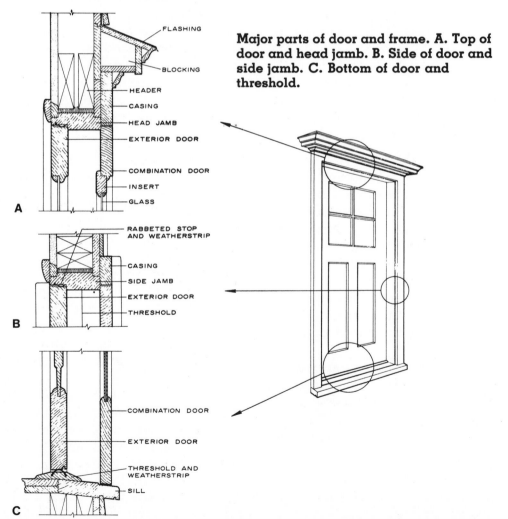

Major parts of door and frame. A. Top of door and head jamb. B. Side of door and side jamb. C. Bottom of door and threshold.

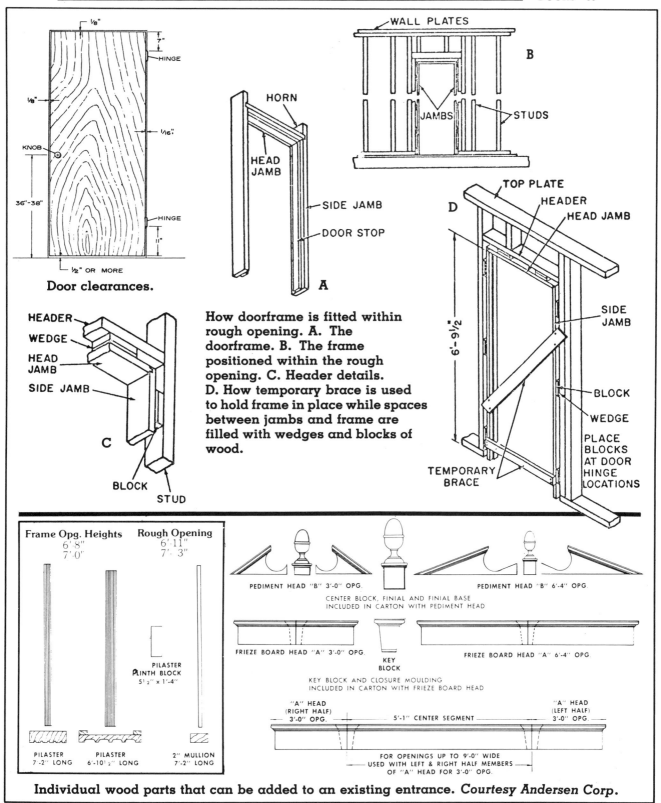

Door clearances.

HORN
HEAD JAMB
SIDE JAMB
DOOR STOP

A

WALL PLATES
JAMBS
STUDS

B

TOP PLATE
HEADER
HEAD JAMB
SIDE JAMB
BLOCK
WEDGE
PLACE BLOCKS AT DOOR HINGE LOCATIONS
TEMPORARY BRACE

D

HEADER
WEDGE
HEAD JAMB
SIDE JAMB
BLOCK
STUD

C

How doorframe is fitted within rough opening. A. The doorframe. B. The frame positioned within the rough opening. C. Header details. D. How temporary brace is used to hold frame in place while spaces between jambs and frame are filled with wedges and blocks of wood.

Frame Opg. Heights	Rough Opening
6'-8"	6'-11"
7'-0"	7'-3"

PILASTER PLINTH BLOCK
5½" x 1'-4"

PILASTER
7'-2" LONG

PILASTER
6'-10½" LONG

2" MULLION
7'-2" LONG

PEDIMENT HEAD "B" 3'-0" OPG.

PEDIMENT HEAD "B" 6'-4" OPG.

CENTER BLOCK, FINIAL AND FINIAL BASE
INCLUDED IN CARTON WITH PEDIMENT HEAD

FRIEZE BOARD HEAD "A" 3'-0" OPG.

KEY BLOCK

FRIEZE BOARD HEAD "A" 6'-4" OPG.

KEY BLOCK AND CLOSURE MOULDING
INCLUDED IN CARTON WITH FRIEZE BOARD HEAD

"A" HEAD
(RIGHT HALF)
3'-0" OPG.

5'-1" CENTER SEGMENT

"A" HEAD
(LEFT HALF)
3'-0" OPG.

FOR OPENINGS UP TO 9'-0" WIDE
USED WITH LEFT & RIGHT HALF MEMBERS
OF "A" HEAD FOR 3'-0" OPG.

Individual wood parts that can be added to an existing entrance. *Courtesy Andersen Corp.*

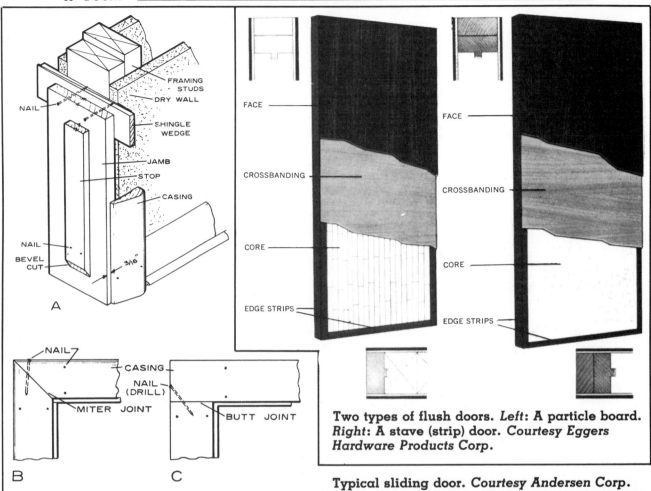

FRAMING STUDS
DRY WALL
SHINGLE WEDGE
NAIL
JAMB
STOP
CASING
NAIL
BEVEL CUT
3/16"
A

FACE
CROSSBANDING
CORE
EDGE STRIPS

FACE
CROSSBANDING
CORE
EDGE STRIPS

Two types of flush doors. *Left:* **A particle board.** *Right:* **A stave (strip) door.** *Courtesy Eggers Hardware Products Corp.*

NAIL
CASING
NAIL (DRILL)
MITER JOINT
BUTT JOINT
B
C

Typical sliding door. Courtesy Andersen Corp.

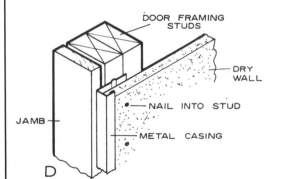

DOOR FRAMING STUDS
DRY WALL
JAMB
NAIL INTO STUD
METAL CASING
D

Doorframe and trim details. A. Relation of stop, jamb trim (sometimes called casing), and dry wall. B. How trim is fastened with a miter joint. C. How butt-joined trim is fastened. D. How metal casing is used to hold edge of dry wall.

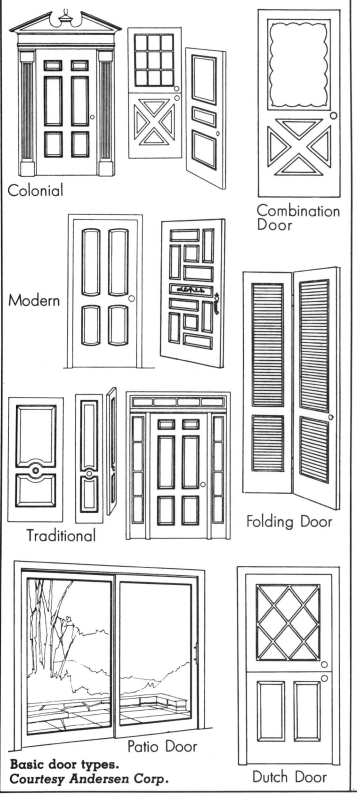

Colonial

Modern

Traditional

Combination Door

Folding Door

Patio Door

Dutch Door

Basic door types.
Courtesy Andersen Corp.

Method used to frame rough opening for a window or door. *Courtesy Andersen Corp.*

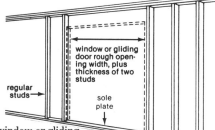

window or gliding door rough opening width, plus thickness of two studs

regular studs

sole plate

A. Lay out window or gliding door opening width between regular studs. It may be necessary to move an existing stud or add a new one. Make sure the distance between regular studs equals the suggested rough opening width of the window or gliding door unit, plus the thickness of two regular wall studs.

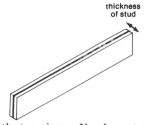

thickness of stud

B. Cut two pieces of header material (usually 2×8's, 2×10's, 2×12's, etc.) equal to the rough opening width of the window or gliding door unit, plus the thickness of two regular studs. (Same dimension as opening in Step A.)

Nail the two pieces of header material together using adequate spacer so header is as thick as a regular stud.

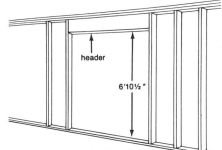

header

6'10½"

C. In most home construction, header should be 6'10½" from sub-floor. Position header at this height between regular studs. Nail through the regular studs into each end of header to hold in place until completing next step.

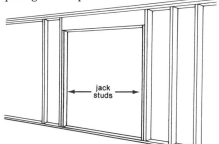

jack studs

D. Cut jack studs to fit snugly between sole plate and header. Nail jack studs to regular studs. Toe-nail jack studs to header.

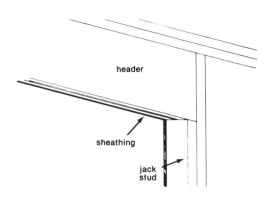

header

sheathing

jack stud

1. Run caulking compound across underside of sill to provide a tight seal between door sill and floor. If door frame is unassembled, follow the assembly instructions included. If sill is placed on concrete use sill filler insulation beneath.

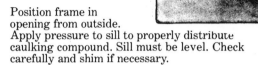

Position frame in opening from outside. Apply pressure to sill to properly distribute caulking compound. Sill must be level. Check carefully and shim if necessary.

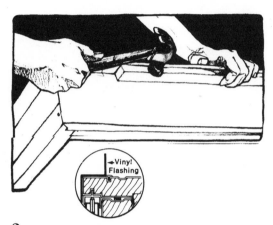

Vinyl Flashing

3. Temporarily secure frame in opening, using clamps to draw flanges tight against sheathing. Check jambs for plumb, and sill and head for level. Note that side jamb members have pre-drilled holes for installation screws.

Shim between jambs and rough opening members at these points, and complete frame installation.

2. Note that wide vinyl flanges are used at the head and side jambs which provide flashing. Place barbed leg in groove on side jambs and tap on a wood block to firmly seat flange. Apply white head flashing in similar manner.

4. Slide aluminum sill support into groove in outside edge of sill, and drive screws through holes into exterior wall.

Installing a sliding door in a prepared, rough opening. *Courtesy Andersen Corp.*

1. Insert pivot pins into pre-drilled holes.

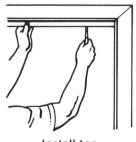

2. Install top and bottom tracks.

3. Install doors in pivots and slides.

Installing a bifold, louvered, sliding door that rides on top and bottom tracks. *Courtesy Southeaster-Kusan, Inc.*

1. Remove any trim from outside. Remove the sliding screen by lifting and pulling out at bottom.

2. Slide operating panel to center of frame, lift, and pull out of track.

3. To remove stationary panel, locate bracket(s) holding panel frame to side jamb or sill. Remove screw(s) and bracket(s). Screws may also be located at the sill and/or head of the panel. If so, remove these, too.

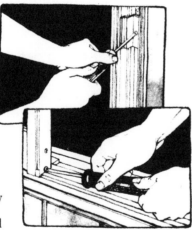

4. Slide stationary panel to center of frame, lift, and pull out of track.

5. Remove all screws holding frame to wall members. It may be necessary to use a cold chisel to cut inaccessible or tight screws.

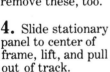
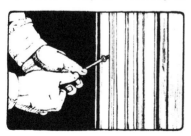

Replacing an old sliding door with a new, Perma-Shield door. _Courtesy Andersen Corp._

6. In some cases frame is attached to wall studs with a flange beneath exterior siding. Most metal frames will pull away easily. However, if necessary, use a sabre saw to cut flange between frame and wall stud.

7. Clean away any material from opening, including insulation. Remove any interior trim which may interfere with placement of Andersen® gliding door frame.

8. Check rough opening for plumb, level and square. Measure opening width at head, center, and sill. Measure height at both jambs and center.

9. If opening is too wide or high, fill with boards of the appropriate thickness. Caulk beneath boards before installation.

10. Assemble gliding door frame, following closely the instructions included in carton.

Continue with Step 1 of Perma-Shield® gliding door installation instructions, page 9. In many replacement installations, side jamb flashing cannot be used as indicated in step 2, page 10. In this case caulk well all around frame.

A. Installing the frame of a sliding door in a prepared opening. B. Installing the trim around a sliding-door frame. *Courtesy C. E. Morgan*

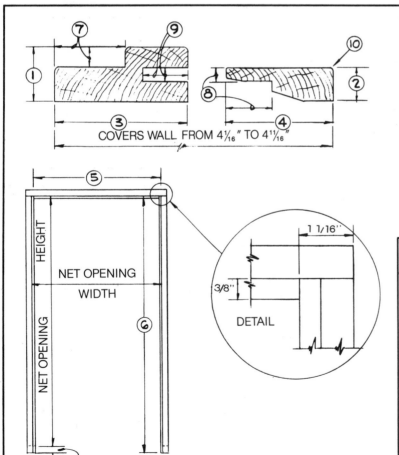

THICKNESS: Main member 1-1/16" (1)
             Extender member 11/16" (2)
WIDTHS: Main member 2-3/4" (3)
        Extender member 2-1/4" (4)
LENGTHS: Head — Dadoed for net opening size (5)
          Sides — 1" over net opening height (6)
RABBET: 3/8" x 1-7/16" (7)
TONGUE: 9/32" x 15/16" (8)
PLOW: 1/32" over tongue thickness x 15/16" depth (9)
FACE CORNERS: Slightly eased (10)
BUNDLING: Style A Standard (Main and extender
            members bundled separately)

Details of a two-piece split jamb.
Courtesy C. E. Morgan

COVERS WALL FROM 4 1/16" TO 4 11/16"

NET OPENING WIDTH

HEIGHT

NET OPENING

DETAIL

1 1/16"

3/8"

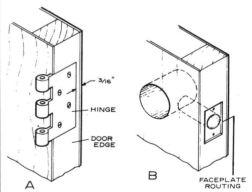

A. Door butt in position. B. Holes necessary for the insertion of a lock.

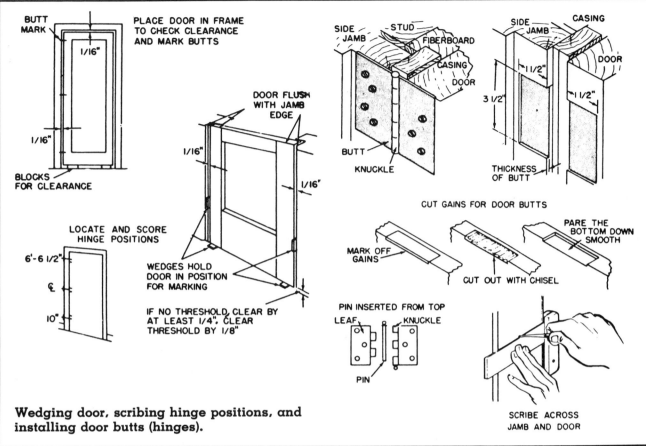

Wedging door, scribing hinge positions, and installing door butts (hinges).

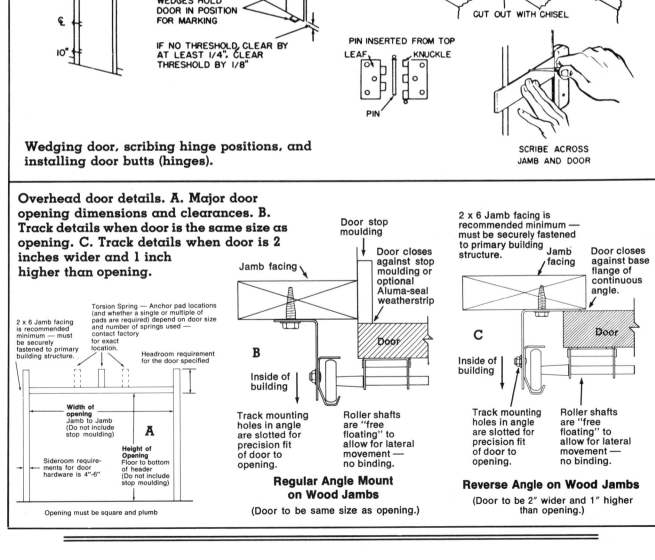

Overhead door details. A. Major door opening dimensions and clearances. B. Track details when door is the same size as opening. C. Track details when door is 2 inches wider and 1 inch higher than opening.

Regular Angle Mount on Wood Jambs

(Door to be same size as opening.)

Reverse Angle on Wood Jambs

(Door to be 2" wider and 1" higher than opening.)

10

ELECTRICAL WIRING

Sad experience has proven the need for caution and care in the installation of electrical wiring in residential and commercial structures. To ensure safety, a code has been developed over the years, which is now interpreted and administered by local building departments. Compliance with this code ensures that all known electrical dangers will be forestalled.

In some communities the building department will permit the homeowner to do his own wiring. In others, only licensed electricians are permitted to install wiring. In both cases proper procedure involves securing a permit for the work and written approval following its completion and inspection.

Many homeowners ignore their building department, which is a double risk. Without the experience of the building inspector, they have only their limited knowledge to guide them. If caught, they can be fined and even can be legally forced to remove all the wiring—quite a chore if the walls are already covered.

SIZE

Wire size is designated by an American Wire Gauge (AWG) number, which is based on the diameter of the core of a solid wire, or the total cross-sectional area of the wires, making up the core of a flexible wire. Choice of wire size depends on the current

expected to flow through the wire. This figure is easily found by dividing the wattage rating of the device(s) by the voltage. For example, a deep-fat fryer can draw 1,650 watts. This figure divided by 110 volts indicates a current draw of 15 amperes. On checking the current-carrying capacities for the flexible wire and the solid, within-the-wall wire, you will find you need a number 14 (rated at 18 amperes). If you have more than one appliance at the end of a line, you must, naturally, add up all the currents to find the total amount and use that to select wire size. NOTE: If you use an undersized wire it will get hot.

INSULATION

Whenever and wherever the wire will be subjected to great heat—for example, within a light fixture or leading to a toaster—special asbestos-insulated wire is used. In other areas the insulation normally provided is more than sufficient. Generally, the insulation is rated at better than 600 volts.

TYPE

High-voltage, permanent house wiring may be run with either of two types of wire or cable. One type, called BX, consists of one to any number of insulated conductors within a semiflexible metal shield. The other type is called by any number of trade names such as Romex. It consists of one of any number of insulated conductors within a woven cloth covering. BX is much more expensive than Romex and is somewhat more difficult to install. But BX has two distinct advantages: (1) the metal covering provides a continuous ground, and (2) the metal is protection against stray nails and small animals. Hidden within a wall, cloth-covered electrical cables can be pierced by a nail or chewed up by hungry little creatures.

JUNCTION BOXES

The code requires that all high-voltage connections be made within a metal box and that the box be accessible after the building is completed. Very simply, a junction box is literally a box with holes and a cover. The cables are brought into the box, and there, within the box, the wires are joined as required. The chance of a conductor breaking along the length of a cable is nil, but the chance of a joint coming apart is not unheard of. Since an open or partially open joint leads to sparks, heat, and fire, common sense dictates that the joint be protected by metal.

GEM BOXES

Sometimes called switch boxes, they are made of galvanized steel, are approximately 2 × 3 inches in size, and either 1½ or 2 inches deep. They are used as the termination point for cables, for which four openings are provided, plus two or four "knockouts." These are partially cut circles in the sides of the box that can be poked out with a screwdriver. The cables are slipped into any of the openings and

clamped in position. Boxes designed for Romex have clamps to accommodate cloth-covered cables. Boxes made for BX have clamps suitable for BX. Gem boxes are designed to be nailed to the side of a stud either by means of nails through the holes in the side of the box or by nails through a side bracket welded to the box. The box is positioned forward of the stud by a little less than the thickness of the gypsum board or plaster that is to follow. Thus, when the wall is installed the box projects through the wall.

Gem boxes are designed to encompass a switch or an outlet or a combination switch and outlet. When more than a single switch or outlet is desired, two boxes are ganged. This is done by taking the boxes apart. There is no limit to the number of boxes that can be ganged, except for the amount of space available. When the switch or receptacle (outlet) has been connected and positioned, a matching cover is fastened over it with machine screws.

ROUND BOXES

Actually octagonal in shape, they come in two sizes: 4 or 5 inches across and 2 inches deep. They are used as junction boxes, which means that wires are joined to other wires within them, and they are used to support lights. When they are used as a junction box, they are closed with a flat metal cover. One type, designed to support a light, comes with a side bracket, another comes with an adjustable bar. The bar is nailed to a pair of joists, suspending the round box between them. Depending on the type of light to be supported, the box may have a short stump of pipe fastened to its center. A hickey on the end of the chain holding the light fastens to the pipe. Smaller lights are usually supported by long bolts passing through the light and entering threaded holes in the side of the box. As with the gem box, when the round box is used to support a light, it is positioned so that its lower surface is almost flush with the finished ceiling.

UTILITY BOX

This is a narrow, rounded-corner version of the gem box. It is designed to be surface mounted. It accommodates a single switch or outlet and cover.

SQUARE BOX

This is a double-width version of the utility box. It is used as a junction box and as a support for a pair of switches or outlets. You will find these boxes on the walls of laundry rooms and the like where appearance is unimportant.

CONNECTIONS

Connections between wires are made in one of two ways. The bared wire end is slipped beneath a terminal bolt. Or the bare ends of two or more wires, skinned back for an inch or so, are lightly twisted together. Then the wires are cut off at an angle with a pair of cutting pliers, leaving about ½ inch of bare metal. A wire nut is then threaded down on the wires. Use a nut suited to the wire sizes and the number of wires joined.

Soldered and taped joints are no longer used.

STANDARD ANNEALED COPPER WIRE A.W.G. (B & S) — Theoretical Values

AWG	Diameter Inches Nom.	Area Circular Mils	Weight Pounds per M'	Length Feet per Lb.	Resistance at 68° F Ohms per M'	Ohms per Lb.
0000	.4600	211,600.	640.5	1.561	.04901	.00007652
000	.4096	167,800.	507.9	1.968	.06180	.0001217
00	.3648	133,100.	402.8	2.482	.07793	.0001935
0	.3249	105,500.	319.5	3.130	.09827	.0003076
1	.2893	83,690.	253.3	3.947	.1239	.0004891
2	.2576	66,370.	200.9	4.977	.1563	.0007778
3	.2294	52,640.	159.3	6.276	.1970	.001237
4	.2043	41,740.	126.4	7.914	.2485	.001966
5	.1819	33,100.	100.2	9.980	.3133	.003127
6	.1620	26,250.	79.46	12.58	.3951	.004972
7	.1443	20,820.	63.02	15.87	.4982	.007905
8	.1285	16,510.	49.98	20.01	.6282	.01257
9	.1144	13,090.	39.63	25.23	.7921	.01999
10	.1019	10,380.	31.43	31.82	.9989	.03178
11	.09074	8,234.	24.92	40.12	1.260	.05053
12	.08081	6,530.	19.77	50.59	1.588	.08035
13	.07196	5,178.	15.68	63.80	2.003	.1278
14	.06408	4,107.	12.43	80.44	2.525	.2032
15	.05707	3,257.	9.858	101.4	3.184	.3230
16	.05082	2,583.	7.818	127.9	4.016	.5136
17	.04526	2,048.	6.200	161.3	5.064	.8167
18	.04030	1,624.	4.917	203.4	6.385	1.299
19	.03589	1,288.	3.899	256.5	8.051	2.065
20	.03196	1,022.	3.092	323.4	10.15	3.283
21	.02846	810.1	2.452	407.8	12.80	5.221
22	.02535	642.4	1.945	514.2	16.14	8.301
23	.02257	509.5	1.542	648.4	20.36	13.20
24	.02010	404.0	1.223	817.7	25.67	20.99
25	.01790	320.4	.9699	1031.	32.37	33.37
26	.01594	254.1	.7692	1300.	40.81	53.06
27	.01420	201.5	.6100	1639.	51.47	84.37
28	.01264	159.8	.4837	2067.	64.90	134.2
29	.01126	126.7	.3836	2607.	81.83	213.3
30	.01003	100.5	.3042	3287.	103.2	339.2
31	.008928	79.7	.2413	4145.	130.1	539.3
32	.007950	63.21	.1913	5227.	164.1	857.6
33	.007080	50.13	.1517	6591.	206.9	1,364.
34	.006305	39.75	.1203	8310.	260.9	2,168.
35	.005615	31.52	.09542	10480.	329.0	3,448.
36	.005000	25.00	.07568	13210.	414.8	5,482.
37	.004453	19.83	.06001	16660.	523.1	8,717.
38	.003965	15.72	.04759	21010.	659.6	13,860.
39	.003531	12.47	.03774	26500.	831.8	22,040.
40	.003145	9.888	.02993	33410.	1049.	35,040.
41	.00280	7 8400	.02373	42140.	1323.	55,750.
42	.00249	6.2001	.01877	53270.	1673.	89,120.
43	.00222	4.9284	.01492	67020.	2104.	141,000.
44	.00197	3.8809	.01175	85100.	2672.	227,380.
45	.00176	3.0976	.00938	106600.	3348.	356,890.
46	.00157	2.4649	.00746	134040.	4207.	563,900.
47	.00140	1.951	.00590	169400.	5317.	900,500.
48	.00124	1.547	.00468	213600.	6705.	1,432,000.
49	.00111	1.227	.00371	269300.	8454.	2,277,000.
50	.00098	0.973	.00294	339600.	10660.	3,620,000.

Courtesy Daburn Electronics and Cable Corp.

Cord, Wire and Insulation

Designator	Type of Insulation	General Uses
WIRE		
R	Rubber	All purpose building wire. 600V. 60°C.
RH	Rubber & cotton braid	Same as R with heat resistance to 75°C.
RW	Rubber	Same as R with moisture resistance.
RHH	Rubber & cotton braid	Same as R with heat resistance to 90°C.
RHW	Rubber & cotton braid	Same as R with heat and moisture resistance to 75°C wet or dry.
RH/RW	Rubber & cotton braid	Same as R but 75°C dry and 60°C wet.
T	Thermoplastic vinyl	All purpose building wire. 60°C.
THW	Thermoplastic vinyl	Same capacity as RHW.
TW	Thermoplastic vinyl	Same as RW.
WP	Cotton braid	Weatherproof for suspended outdoor use.
NONMETALLIC CABLE		
NM	Paper overlaid with cotton braid or plastic	For dry use only, 60°C.
NMC	Plastic or neoprene coating.	Wet or dry use, 60°C. Only cable approved for barns.
USE	Rubber & neoprene	Underground service entrance. Fusing or additional covering not required.
UF	Thermoplastic	Underground feeder and branch cable. Can be buried but must be fused.
ARMORED CABLE		
ACT	Armored cable on plastic insulated wires	Branch circuits and feeders.
ACU	Armored cable on rubber insulated wires	Same as ACT.
CORDS		
C	Rubber and cotton braid	Lamps and portable appliances in dry areas. 300V. and 600V., 60°C.
HPD	Rubber and asbestos with overall braid	Heat resistant for toasters, heaters, irons, etc.
HPN	Neoprene	Same as HPD with moisture resistance.
SP-1	Rubber	Lightweight for lamps, clocks, etc. 300V.
SP-2	Rubber	Same as SP-1 with heavier construction for more general use. 300V.
SP-3	Rubber	Heavier construction than SP-2 for use with refrigerators, air conditioners, etc. 300V.
SPT-1, SPT-2, SPT-3	Thermoplastic	Correspond to SP-1, SP-2 and SP-3.
S	Rubber and jute twine	Heavy duty for power tools, battery chargers, etc. 600V.
SJ	Rubber and jute twine	Same as S but only 300V.
SJO	Rubber and jute twine	Same as SJ but oil resistant. 300V.

Guide to cord and wire insulation. *Courtesy Hardware Retailing*

A Checklist for Health, Safety to Conform to OSHA Standards

The Occupational Safety & Health Administration has set standards that affect the operation of all hardware/home center stores. Although OSHA's regulations directly affect the safety and health aspects of the stores themselves (and all places where people work) and how they are operated, you should relate the same standards to the items you sell. Have your electrical suppliers made sure their products comply with governmental safety standards? In the area of electrical equipment, some manufacturers say little change was needed—"the standards we have maintained meet the regulations." Some have redesigned entire lines of electrical specialties.

Here is a checklist of some important OSHA rules for both you and your customers. Be sure you comply, and be sure they are able to comply with the products you sell them and with the installation you recommend.

(See other checklists in other parts of the **Product Knowledge Handbook**. A full copy of OSHA electrical and other standards can be obtained from the Department of Labor, Occupational Safety & Health Administration, in your area.)

1. Be sure all electrical installations are in accord with the National Electrical Code. OSHA says they must be.

2. All live parts of electrical equipment operating at 50 volts or more must be guarded against accidental contact.

3. Protect all equipment against overcurrent.

4. Overcurrent devices in damp and wet locations must be of the type approved for this use.

5. Fuses and circuit breakers must be located and shielded to prevent burns or injuries.

6. All fixed electrical equipment must be grounded.

7. All electrical equipment—air conditioners, sump pumps, portable tools, others—must be effectively grounded.

8. All boxes and fittings in wet locations must be waterproof.

9. All electrical outlet boxes must be durably and legibly marked with the manufacturer's name and/or trademark. They must be rigidly and securely fastened to the surface to which they are mounted. All outlet boxes must have a cover.

10. Flexible cords must be in a continuous length when used—without splices. They cannot be worn, frayed or taped. They must be connected so that tension will not be transmitted to joints or terminal screws. Flexible cords cannot be used where fixed wiring is required.

Courtesy Hardware Retailing

Non-Metallic Sheath Cable

Armored Cable

Types S and SJ Cord

Type SPT Cord

Type HPD Cord

Cables and cords. *Courtesy Hardware Retailing*

GLOSSARY

Alternating Current—Abbreviated AC. A current of electricity which alternates at a rate of 60 hertz (cylces per second). This is, it flows first in one direction, then in the other. Only at very low frequencies is this charge visible to the eye through the flickering of lamps.

Ampacity—Current-carrying capacity of electrical conductors expressed in amperes.

Ampere—Abbreviated "amp." The amount of electricity delivered to an appliance or group of appliances, limited by the diameter of the wire it flows through.

Candle-Power—A measure of the intensity of light produced by a source. This standard of measurement is used in France, Britain and the U.S. One candle-power corresponds approximately to the light produced in the horizontal direction by an ordinary sperm candle.

Circuit—An electrical system using two or more wires where the current flows from the source to one or more electrical devices, and back again to the source of supply.

Circuit Breaker— A protective device to open a circuit (stop the flow of electricity) when that circuit is overloaded with damage to the circuit breaker. Must be re-set manually.

Conductors—Any wire or other component which carries electricity.

Conduit—Metal sleeve through which electrical wires pass.

Cycle—The period of a complete alternation of alternating current. Ordinary 60-cycle current thus has 60 cycles (120 alternations) each second.

Direct Current—Abbreviated DC. A flow of electric current continuous in one direction as long as the circuit is closed.

Direct Lighting—A system of lighting which delivers a majority of light in useful directions without being deflected from the ceiling or walls. Any lamp equipped with a glass or metal reflector, arranged to reflect the light toward the object to be illuminated is classified as direct lighting.

Electrical Service Entrance—A combination of intake wires and equipment —including the service entrance wires, electric meter, main switch or circuit breaker and main distribution or service panel—through which the supply of power enters the home.

Filament—A slender thread of material such as carbon or tungsten which emits light when raised to a high temperature by an electric current (as in an incandescent light bulb).

Foot Candle—The amount of illumination on a surface one sq. ft. in area on which one lumen of light is uniformly distributed.

Frequency—The number of complete cycles per second in an alternating current circuit. The frequency of a 60-cycle circuit, for instance, is 60.

Fuse—A replaceable safety device used to break the flow of current when a circuit becomes overloaded.

Grounding—Connects the electrical system with the earth to prevent shock. Ground wires are usually bare; grounding connections are normally black or green in color.

Indirect Lighting—A system of lighting where all the light is directed to the ceiling or walls which in turn reflect it to the objects to be illuminated.

Kilowatt—1,000 watts. From "watt" and Greek word "kilo" meaning 1,000.

Kilowatt Hours—Abbreviated K.W.H. A 1,000 watt lamp burning one hour will use one kilowatt hour of electricity. If the rate were 3 cents per K.W.H., the cost would be 3 cents per hour to operate.

Lumen—A unit of light emitted from a point light source of one candle through a unit solid angle. All lamps are rated in their output in lumens of light.

Main Service Panel—Includes the main electrical switch or circuit breaker and the circuit panel box which houses the circuit breakers or fuses for the branch circuit.

Ohm—A unit of electrical resistance. (Electrical resistance is the opposition by a body to the flow of electrical current.)

Outlet—A point on the wiring system which can be tapped to provide electrical current for appliances or lights.

Receptacle—A contact device installed at the outlet. Allows the connection of external electric cords from lamps or appliances.

Relay—Switching device to open or close circuits.

Switch—Completes or interrupts an electrical circuit.

Transformer—Steps up or steps down amount of alternating current available from circuit to that required by the appliance.

Volt—Amount of pressure needed to push electricity through a wire.

Watt—The unit of measurement of electrical power. Is calculated by multiplying volts times amperes. For instance, 746 watts equal one electrical horsepower; that is, a one horsepower electric motor uses 746 watts.

Two-wire BX cable. Bare wire is the ground wire.

Top: BX offset connectors. *Center:* Regular BC connectors. *Bottom:* Wire nuts (wire connectors).

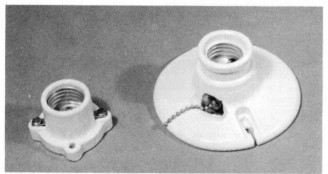

Left: Surface-mounted light socket. *Right:* Porcelain pull-chain fixture.

Left: Standard gem box (utility box). *Right:* Half-sized gem box with mounting strap.

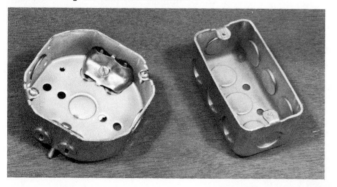

Left: 3-inch-round box. *Right:* Surface-mounted utility box.

Outlet and switch plates.

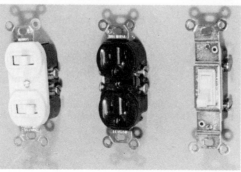

Left: Dual switch. *Center:* Dual receptacles. *Right:* Single pole switch.

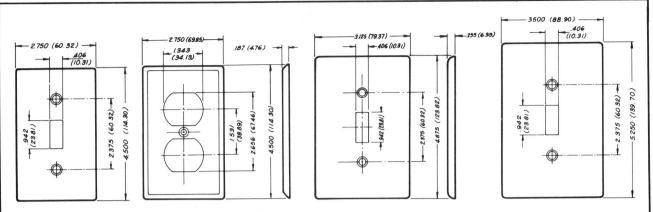

Wall plate dimensions. *Courtesy Leviton*

A few types of wall plates. *Courtesy Leviton*

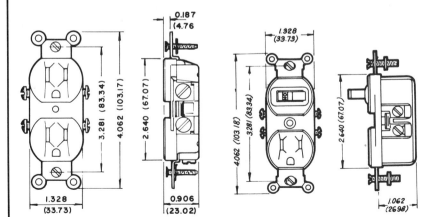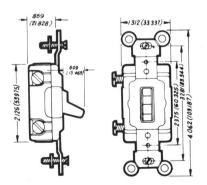

Left: A duplex receptacle. *Right*: A duplex receptacle and a switch. *Courtesy Leviton*

Dimensions of a toggle switch. *Courtesy Hardware Retailing*

11 FASTENERS

NAILS

Although adhesives are making strong headway in the joining of wood, nails have been, and still are, the most frequently used means of fastening anything to wood. Nails are easy to use, low in cost, available everywhere, and manufactured in some 1,500 different sizes and shapes.

Nails are not, by any means, new. The Romans forged them by hand as did everyone else up until about 1830 or so. Nails were not all made of metal. Some, called tree nails, were made of wood, usually locust because it resists rot and insects. Split into rough dowels, the tree nails were forced through undersized holes in the timbers they were to join. Their farther ends were then split and expanded with a wedge of wood. Tree nails were often used for early boat and house frame construction.

Some of the early colonial "pegged" homes and barns are still standing.

WHY NAILS HOLD

When you drive a nail through the grain in a piece of wood (and not with the grain), the nail cuts through the fibers that form the grain and pushes them aside. When pressure is applied to pull the nail out, the fibers tend to jam against the sides of the nail and lock it in place. This is why wood has no holding power when you drive a nail into the end of the grain. And this is why wood has no holding power when you drive home a nail so thick it splits the board. Different woods have different holding pow-

ers. Very hard woods do not hold nails well because the wood tends to split. When nailing woods such as oak and hickory it is best to drill pilot holes for the nails, or not to use nails at all, but screws instead.

SELECTING THE PROPER NAIL

Common practice calls for driving the nail through the thinner board into the thicker board. For maximum holding power, the length of the nail should be such that it passes almost, but not quite, through the thicker board. Thus, to fasten a ⅞-inch board to a 2⅝-inch board, a twelve penny (written 12d) nail, which is 3½ inches long, would be just right.

When there is no need to hide the nailhead, or when maximum holding power is required, common nails are used. They have flat, medium-diameter heads. When you may want to pull the nail out again, it's best to use double-headed or scaffold nails. When you want to "set" the nail (drive its head below the surface of the wood and then putty the opening), use finishing nails, which have small heads. When you must compromise between strength and appearance, you should use casing nails. They have heads sized between finishing nailheads and common nailheads.

When the material to be fastened is soft—for example roofing paper or shingles—roofing nails are used. They have large, flat heads.

When you are doing fine work, use nails designated by their lengths in inches and body diameter in wire gauge sizes. The larger the gauge number the smaller the nail's diameter. This group of slender wire nails are called brads. They have heads similar to finishing nails, like those of common nails.

For special work use special nails. These are generally described by their application. For example, floor nails are made for nailing wood floors to wood subflooring. The best have spiral bodies. For applying gypsum board, gypsum (Sheetrock) nails are used. The best are annular (they have ringed bodies). For finished plywood you can get nails with heads that match the color of the wood.

NAIL METALS AND FINISHES

Ordinary nails are made of steel. They rust. As a way to avoid rusting, many types of nails are made with zinc coatings. While zinc itself does not rust, zinc-coated nails sometimes do because the zinc often gets knocked off by the hammer, and the exposed iron usually rusts a bit. A better solution lies in using aluminum nails. They cost more, but they don't rust.

Some of the special nails—for example those made for furniture and fine brads—are made of brass.

WOOD SCREWS

When it comes to resisting in-line pull, screws have many times the holding power of nails. In addition, they can provide a clamping effect to pull parts together and they can be removed and replaced at will, something that cannot be done easily with nails. A nail driven into an old hole has no holding power. Wood screws not only cost more than nails, but also require pilot holes. Should you try to force a screw into anything but the softest wood without first drilling a pilot hole, you will either split the wood or break the screw.

DIMENSIONS

Wood screws start with a point called a gimlet, which expands to a fairly coarse spiral thread. The body of the screw is designated by a number that defines the diameter of the body. The overall length of the screw is given in inches. Thus a 1-inch No. 8 screw would be 1 inch long and have a body with the same thickness as that of a 2-inch No. 8 screw.

HEADS

The most common are flatheads, oval heads, and round heads with either a single slot for a standard screwdriver or a cross-slotted head for a Phillips screwdriver. The Phillips is easier to use, since the screwdriver doesn't jump out of the head as easily. Flatheads have the greatest holding power.

METALS, FINISHES

Most wood screws are made of mild steel and are given no further treatment. A small percentage are bright finished (polished). Some screws are blued, some are zinc, cadmium, or chrome-plated. A few are made of brass. Plain, blued, and bright-finished screws will rust. The others will not.

TAPPING SCREWS

These are case-hardened, steel screws designed to cut their own threads into wood, metal, and plastic. They are made in a number of different shapes and differ from wood screws mainly in that the tapping screw threads are thinner and wider spaced than the wood screw threads.

DIMENSIONS, TYPES
Tapping screws are designated in the same way as wood screws. A number indicates body thickness. Body length is given in inches.

METALS, FINISHES
Almost all tapping screws are made of hardened steel. A small percentage are made of brass. Some are untreated, some are cadmium-plated, a few are plated with nickel or zinc, and some are painted.

HEADS
In addition to the heads common to wood screws, tapping screws also come with panheads and hex washer heads. The latter is a hexagonal head incorporating a permanent washer.

STARTING AND DRIVING
When using gimlet-ended or pointed-end tapping screws to join thin sheets of soft metal or to penetrate a single thin sheet of metal, all you need do in many cases is to drive a small hole into the sheet metal. This can be done with a hammer and nail or center punch. Once the point of the screw is within the metal, you can generally drive the screw home.

This cannot be done when the metal involved is more than 1/32 inch thick. In such cases you must first drill a pilot hole equal in size to the shank diameter of the screw, less its threads. In other words, you need a hole a fraction of an inch smaller

than the overall diameter of the tapping screw. To insert the tapping screw into wood or plastic, you might try using the bit size suggested for the shank-clearance hole for a screw with the same number as the bit. For metal you had best experiment with a number of drill sizes in pieces of scrap until you find the hole diameter best suited to that metal and the tapping screw you plan to use.

LAG BOLTS (OR SCREWS)
These are a series of very large wood screws with square heads that require a wrench rather than a screwdriver. Made of mild steel, generally unfinished but sometimes zinc-plated, these screws are used for joining heavy timbers. They are also used with shields for bolting things to masonry.

MACHINE SCREWS
Machine screws are made to be driven into drilled and tapped holes including nuts. In order for the screw to enter the hole properly, not only must the screw diameter be correct, but the thread of the hole must also match that of the machine screw.

METALS, SHAPES, AND DIMENSIONS
Machine screws and nuts are routinely made of mild steel and brass and, lately, of aluminum. The steel may be bright finished, or plated in cadmium or chrome. Heads are usually flat, round, oval, and fillister, with any number of special shapes

made for limited applications. In addition to being designated by its head shape and metal, a screw is also identified by its body thickness, body length, and thread. The first two are easy. Screw length is computed from the surface of the metal that the screw will hold down. Thus the length of a flathead screw is measured up to the top of the head. The length of a round-head screw stops just beneath its head, as that head will be above the metal when the screw is in place and tightened.

Screw body thickness follows the numbers of the American Screw Gauge up to ¼ inch in diameter and in fractions of an inch from there on up.

THREAD
The general designations are coarse and fine. After a little experience, it is possible to pick up a bolt and determine its thread by feel. But most often it is not. Counting threads per inch is not much help either. The best method is by test. Try the nut on the bolt or vice versa. The nut should be "solid" on the screw and you should not need more than finger pressure to run it up.

BOLTS
A bolt is a special type of machine screw. The difference between a bolt and a regular machine screw lies in the length of the thread. Whereas a machine bolt has thread all the way up to its head, a bolt doesn't. A carriage bolt has a square head beneath a conical cap. The square head locks in the hole and prevents the bolt from turning. Stove bolts are simply machine bolts with coarse threads.

TOGGLE BOLTS
A toggle bolt consists of a standard machine screw and a more or less ordinary machine screw nut. Attached to the nut are a pair of spring-loaded arms that, in their normal position, are spread apart in a straight line on either side of the bolt.

To use the toggle bolt, drill a hole in the wall or ceiling large enough to permit the nut and its folded arms to pass through. After drilling the hole, remove the nut from its bolt, and then pass the bolt through the object to be fastened. Run the nut partway up on the bolt. Fold back the arms on the nut and then slide the nut and arms into the hole. Once inside the hole the arms spring apart. With one hand pull the object to be fastened away from the wall. With the other use a screwdriver to take up on the bolt. As you can see from illustration 00-00, toggle bolts can be used only where there is an open space behind the drilled hole.

MOLLY BOLTS
These consist of standard machine bolts with a long, sheet metal nut. Like toggle bolts, Mollies also need a space behind the drilled hole, but not very much. To use a Molly bolt, first drill a clearance hole through the wall. Then insert the Molly. With one hand hold the "nut" on the Molly to keep it from turning. With the other hand take up on the bolt. As you take up on the bolt, the nut is compressed and locks itself in place in the hole. Now you can remove the bolt and replace it as you wish. The Molly's nut remains in position. When you re-

move a toggle bolt its nut falls down behind the wall.

DRIVE MOLLY

This is a Molly with a point. It is driven into Sheetrock and similar walls, and then, as with the standard Molly, the internal bolt is tightened. The nut is compressed and locks itself in the hole. With the drive Molly you do not have to drill a hole for its entrance.

FASTENING TO MASONRY

NAILS

There are special steel nails that can be driven into concrete, cement joints, and very soft stone. Steel cut nails were the first to be made and used and are still used today. They have a blunt end and are the most difficult to use, as they often break and sometimes spring away at dangerous speeds. Modern concrete nails have points and are designed to be driven with the aid of a special holder and, preferably, a small sledgehammer.

SCREW DEVICES

These provide a more positive and permanent grip on masonry than do nails. To use, first drill into the masonry a hole that is the proper diameter and at least as deep as the length of the screw. In this case, masonry hardness is limited only by your ability to drill the hole. These devices can be used even with glass. The device, which can be in the form of a fiber tube or a split tube of plastic, is inserted into the hole. The screw is driven into the device, which then expands and grips the walls of the hole. The screw can be removed and replaced at will.

SHIELD DEVICES

A pre-drilled hole is again required. The shield, which consists of two metal halves, is inserted into the hole. Then the screw is driven home. Shields are generally made in sizes that can accommodate ¼-inch and larger diameter lag bolts.

EXPANSION PLUGS

One type consists of two pieces of lead on a machine bolt. The lead portion of the device is placed in the hole. Whatever is to be held against the wall is positioned beneath the bolt head. When the bolt is tightened, the two pieces of lead are brought together causing them to expand and lock themselves tightly against the walls of the hole.

Another type consists of a round plug of lead with a threaded section of steel in its center. The plug is placed in the bottom of the hole. A tool is then used to expand the plug and lock it into place. A bolt can now be threaded into the steel section of the plug.

EXPANSION BOLTS

These are steel bolts with split or otherwise shaped ends. A bolt is inserted into a tight-fitting hole in the masonry. The top of the bolt is then struck with a hammer causing its inserted end to expand and grip the walls of the hole. Once installed, expansion bolts cannot be removed by ordinary means.

ADHESIVE

The bolt or hook or whatever else is to be fastened to the masonry wall is first fastened to a small, pierced metal piece or plastic plate. Then the plate is cemented to the wall with epoxy cement.

Common and box nails: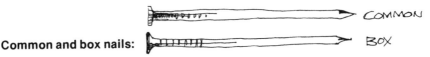

16d common and box, for general framing. 8d and 10d common and box nails, for toenailing. 6d and 8d common and box nails, for subfloor, wall and roof sheathing. Size depends on thickness of plywood sheathing.

Scaffold nails:

8d and 10d most common, for scaffolds, bracing and any temporary fastening that must be later removed.

Siding nails:

Nonstaining nails of size specified for siding thickness.

Casing and finish nails:

4d, 6d and 8d most common, for exterior and interior trim and installation of siding and paneling where large nailheads should not show.

Roofing nails:

A special type, commonly available. Size depends on thickness of roofing and deck material.

Drywall nails:

4d to 6d size depends on drywall thickness; for 1/2-inch drywall use 4d drywall nails.

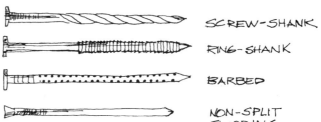

For underlayment and finish floor: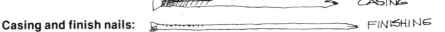

Special nail types are also available. For hardwood strip flooring, use either 8d hardwood nails or 2-1/2 inch hardened, spiral-threaded (screw-shanked) nails. For 3/8-inch Underlayment grade plywood (over subflooring), use 3d ring-shanks; for 5/8-inch Underlayment (over subflooring), use 4d ring-shanks. For 19/32 through 3/4-inch Sturd-I-Floor panels, use 6d deformed-shank nails.

Nails commonly used for residential construction.
Courtesy American Plywood Association

COMMON NAILS

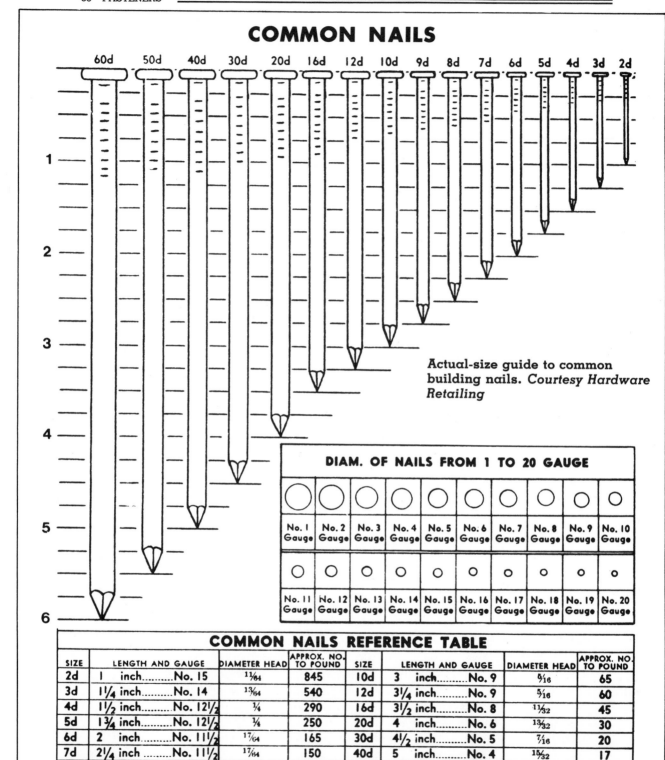

Actual-size guide to common building nails. *Courtesy Hardware Retailing*

DIAM. OF NAILS FROM 1 TO 20 GAUGE

No. 1 Gauge	No. 2 Gauge	No. 3 Gauge	No. 4 Gauge	No. 5 Gauge	No. 6 Gauge	No. 7 Gauge	No. 8 Gauge	No. 9 Gauge	No. 10 Gauge
○	○	○	○	○	○	○	○	○	○

No. 11 Gauge	No. 12 Gauge	No. 13 Gauge	No. 14 Gauge	No. 15 Gauge	No. 16 Gauge	No. 17 Gauge	No. 18 Gauge	No. 19 Gauge	No. 20 Gauge
○	○	○	○	○	○	○	○	○	○

COMMON NAILS REFERENCE TABLE

SIZE	LENGTH AND GAUGE	DIAMETER HEAD	APPROX. NO. TO POUND	SIZE	LENGTH AND GAUGE	DIAMETER HEAD	APPROX. NO. TO POUND
2d	1 inch..........No. 15	$\frac{11}{64}$	845	10d	3 inch..........No. 9	$\frac{5}{16}$	65
3d	1¼ inch..........No. 14	$\frac{13}{64}$	540	12d	3¼ inch..........No. 9	$\frac{5}{16}$	60
4d	1½ inch..........No. 12½	¼	290	16d	3½ inch..........No. 8	$\frac{11}{32}$	45
5d	1¾ inch..........No. 12½	¼	250	20d	4 inch..........No. 6	$\frac{13}{32}$	30
6d	2 inch..........No. 11½	$\frac{17}{64}$	165	30d	4½ inch..........No. 5	$\frac{7}{16}$	20
7d	2¼ inch..........No. 11½	$\frac{17}{64}$	150	40d	5 inch..........No. 4	$\frac{15}{32}$	17
8d	2½ inch..........No. 10¼	$\frac{9}{32}$	100	50d	5½ inch..........No. 3	½	13
9d	2¾ inch..........No. 10¼	$\frac{9}{32}$	90	60d	6 inch..........No. 2	$\frac{17}{32}$	10

Joining	Nailing method	Nails		
		Number	Size	Placement
Header to joist	End-nail	3	16d	
Joist to sill or girder	Toenail	2–3	10d or 8d	
Header and stringer joist to sill	Toenail		10d	16 inches on center.
Bridging to joist	Toenail each end	2	8d	
Ledger strip to beam, 2 inches thick		3	16d	At each joist.
Subfloor, boards:				
1 by 6 inches and smaller		2	8d	To each joist.
1 by 8 inches		3	8d	To each joist.
Subfloor, plywood:				
At edges			8d	6 inches on center.
At intermediate joists			8d	8 inches on center.
Subfloor (2 by 6 inches, T&G) to joist or girder	*blind-nail* (casing) and face-nail.	2	16d	
Soleplate to stud, horizontal assembly	End-nail	2	16d	At each stud.
Top plate to stud	End-nail	2	16d	
Stud to soleplate	Toenail	4	8d	
Soleplate to joist or blocking	*Face-nail*		16d	16 inches on center.
Doubled studs	Face-nail, stagger		10d	16 inches on center.
End stud of intersecting wall to exterior wall stud	Face-nail		16d	16 inches on center.
Upper top plate to lower top plate	Face-nail		16d	16 inches on center.
Upper top plate, laps and intersections	Face-nail	2	16d	
Continous header, 2 pieces, each edge			12d	12 inches on center.
Ceiling joist to top wall plates	Toenail	3	8d	
Ceiling joist laps at partition	Face-nail	4	16d	
Rafter to top plate	Toenail	2	8d	
Rafter to ceiling joist	Face-nail	5	10d	
Rafter to valley or hip rafter	Toenail	3	10d	
Ridge board to rafter	End-nail	3	10d	
Rafter to rafter through ridge board	{ Toenail	4	8d	
	{ Edge-nail	1	10d	
Collar beam to rafter:				
2-inch member	Face-nail	2	12d	
1-inch member	Face-nail	3	8d	
1-inch diagonal let-in brace to each stud and plate (4 nails at top).		2	8d	
Built-up corner studs:				
Studs to blocking	Face-nail	2	10d	Each side.
Intersecting stud to corner studs	Face-nail		16d	12 inches on center.
Built-up girders and beams, 3 or more members	Face-nail		20d	32 inches on center, each side.
Wall sheathing:				
1 by 8 inches or less, horizontal	Face-nail	2	8d	At each stud.
1 by 6 inches or greater, diagonal	Face-nail	3	8d	At each stud.
Wall sheathing, vertically applied plywood:				
⅜ inch and less thick	Face-nail		6d	} 6-inch edge.
½ inch and over thick	Face-nail		8d	} 12-inch intermediate.
Wall sheathing, vertically applied fiberboard:				
½ inch thick	Face-nail			1½-inch roofing nail.[1]
²⁵⁄₃₂ inch thick	Face-nail			1¾-inch roofing nail.[1]
Roof sheathing, boards, 4-, 6-, 8-inch width	Face-nail	2	8d	At each rafter.
Roof sheathing plywood:				
⅜ inch and less thick	Face-nail		6d	} 6-inch edge and 12-
½ inch and over thick	Face-nail		8d	} inch intermediate.

[1] 3-inch edge and 6-inch intermediate.

Recommended schedule for nailing the framing and sheathing of a well-constructed, wood-frame house.

Lag bolt (screw) and dimensions.

LAG SCREWS—LENGTHS AND DIAMETERS
(in inches)

Lengths	Diameters				
	¼	⅜, ⁷⁄₁₆, ½	⅝, ¾	⅞, 1	
1	x	x			
1½	x	x	x		
2, 2½, etc., to 10	x	x	x	x	
11 & 12		x	x	x	
13 to 16			x	x	

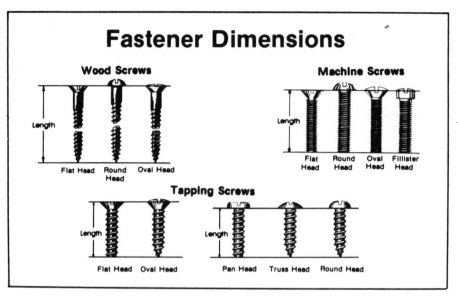

Courtesy Hardware Retailing

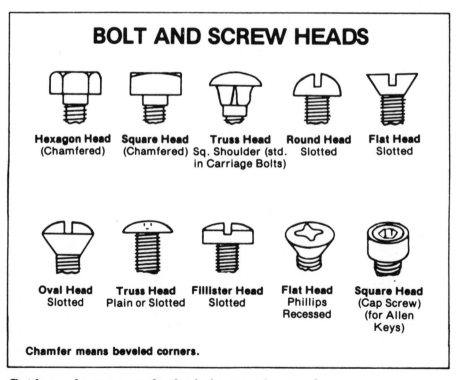

Guide to clearance and pilot hole sizes for wood screws.
Courtesy American Screw Co.

Size of Drivers to Use for Different Size Screws

SCREW NUMBER	0	1	2	3	4	5	6	7	8	9
REGULAR BLADE WIDTH	3/32''	1/8''	1/8''	1/8''	5/32''	3/16''	3/16''	7/32''	1/4''	1/4''
CROSS SLOT BLADE	No. 0		No. 1			No. 2				

SCREW NUMBER	10	12	14	16	18	20	24	7/16	1/2	9/16
REGULAR BLADE WIDTH	5/16''	3/8''	3/8''	3/8''	1/2''	1/2''	1/2''	1/2''	1/2''	1/2''
CROSS SLOT BLADE	No. 3				No. 4					

Standard Types of Screwdriver Tips and Screw Recesses

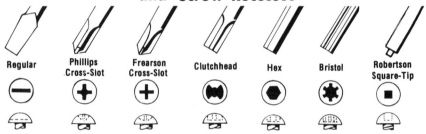

Regular   Phillips Cross-Slot   Frearson Cross-Slot   Clutchhead   Hex   Bristol   Robertson Square-Tip

Guide to screwdriver types and sizes to match various types and sizes of screws. *Courtesy Hardware Retailing*

Carriage Bolt Sizes

Lengths (inches)	Diameters (inches)			
	3/16, 1/4, 5/16, 3/8	7/16, 1/2	9/16, 5/8 3/4	
¾	X			
1	X	X		
1¼	X	X	X	
1½, 2, 2½, etc., 9½, 10 to 20.	X	X	X	X

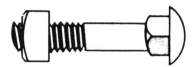

Square or common bolt.

Optimum Metric Fastener System

The following are the proposed diameter-pitch sizes of threaded fasteners under the OFMS program. Twenty-five new metric diameters are slated to replace 59 different size and thread combinations utilized under the current inch system. The coarse and fine thread distinction will be eliminated and a new single thread will fall somewhere in between the two.

Approximate diameter equivalents in inches appear in parenthesis as examples.

Nominal Diameter (mm)	Thread Pitch (mm)
1.6 (1/16'')	0.35
2	0.4
2.5	0.45
3	0.5
3.5 (1/8'')	0.6
4	0.7
5	0.8
6.3 (1/4'')	1.0
8	1.25
10	1.5
12	1.75
14	2
16	2
20	2.5
24	3
30	3.5
36	4
42	4.5
48	5
56	5.5
64	6
72	6
80	6
90	6
100 (4'')	6

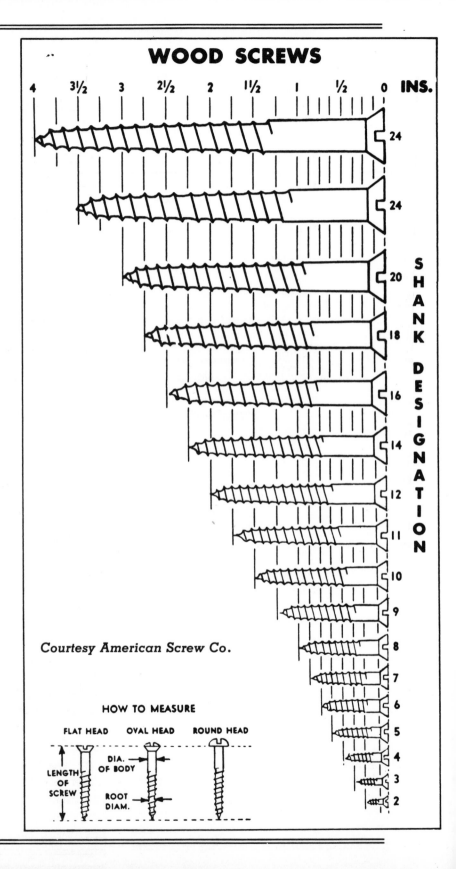

WOOD SCREWS

SHANK DESIGNATION

Courtesy American Screw Co.

HOW TO MEASURE

FLAT HEAD   OVAL HEAD   ROUND HEAD

LENGTH OF SCREW

DIA. OF BODY

ROOT DIAM.

STANDARD TAPPING SCREWS

TYPE A (ASA-A): A thread forming screw for use in thin metal .015 to .050 thick. Used with drilled, punched or nested holes in sheet metal, resin impregnated plywood, asbestos combinations, among others.

TYPE B (ASA-B): A thread forming screw for use in heavier metal .050 to .200 thick. Larger root diameter with finer thread pitch for light and heavy sheet metal non-ferrous castings, plastics, impregnated plywoods, asbestos combinations, and other materials.

TYPE BA (ASA-BA): A thread forming screw combining locating type point of Type A with thread size and pitch of Type B. Normal limitations of Type B apply.

TYPE BP (ASA-BP): Thread forming screw. Same as Type B but has a cone point for use where holes are slightly misaligned. Spaced thread.

TYPE C (ASA-C): A thread forming screw with either coarse or fine pitch machine screw thread and blunt tapered point. Eliminates chips and permits replacement with standard screw in the field. Higher driving torque required. Usable in heavy sheet metal and die castings.

TYPE 17 (ASA-17): A thread cutting screw for wood with a coarse tapping screw thread and a special long sharp point fluted to capture chips.

TYPE 1 (ASA-D): A thread cutting screw with single flute for general use. Produces a fine standard machine screw thread for field replacement.

TYPE F (ASA-F): A thread cutting screw with machine screw thread with blunt tapered point, having multi-cutting edges and chip cavities. For heavy gauge sheet metal, aluminum, zinc, and lead die castings, cast iron, brass and plastic.

TYPE G (ASA-G): Thread cutting. Blunt Die Point with a single through slot to form two cutting edges. Machine screw threads. For same general use as Type C but where less driving torque is required. For low strength metals and plastics.

TYPE 23 (ASA-T): A thread cutting screw in the fine thread series offering maximum thread cutting area and excellent chip clearing, with minimum tightening torques.

TYPE FZ (ASA-BF): A thread cutting screw with a tapping screw thread with blunt tapered point and multi-cutting edges and chip cavities. For plastics, die castings, metal clad and resin impregnated plywoods, and asbestos.

TYPE H (ASA-BG): Thread cutting. Spaced thread, blunt Die Point. Single slot has 2 cutting edges. Useful for brittle or friable material where threads too close together may cause material to crumble. Good in plastics and soft materials.

TYPE 25 (ASA-BT): A thread cutting screw similar to Type 23 point except with coarse Type B thread. For plastics and other soft materials with large chip clearing and cutting edges.

TYPE U (ASA-U): A thread forming screw with high Helix thread for driving or hammering into sheet metal, castings, fiber or plastics for permanent, quick assemblies.

Points and threads of standard tapping screws. *Courtesy American Screw Co.*

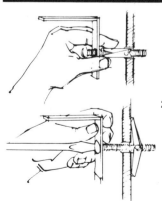

1. Insert bolt through item to be fastened, turn on wings, then fold wings completely back and insert through hole until wings spring open.

2. Pull back on assembly to hold wings against inside wall — this prevents the wings from spinning while tightening bolt. Turn bolt with screwdriver until firmly tightened.

NOTE: When installation is complete, the wings form a perfect 90° angle with the masonry. The entire length of the wings is supported by the masonry providing a full wall bearing distribution of the load.

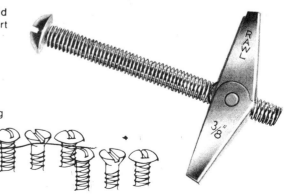

Toggle bolt and its application.

FASTENERS	WEDGE ANCHORS	PLASTIC ANCHORS	NYLON ANCHORS	SCREW ANCHOR	TOGGLE BOLTS	ZINC or ALUM DRIVE ANCHORS	MACHINE SCREW ANCHORS	LEAD ANCHORS	STEEL EXPANSION ANCHORS	ZINC LAG SHIELD	HOLLOW WALL ANCHOR
BRICK	M	M	L	H	M	H	H	M	H	M	H
CONCRETE	H	M	L	H	M	H	H	M	H	M	H
CONCRETE BLOCK	O	M	L	H	M	H	H	M	H	M	H
CINDER BLOCK	O	M	L	H	H	M	M	M	M	M	H
FIBERBOARD SIDING-DECKING	O	M	L	H	H	O	O	O	O	O	H
GLASS	O	O	O	H	H	O	O	O	O	O	H
GYPSUM	O	H	L	H	H	O	O	O	O	O	H
MARBLE	H	M	L	H	M	H	H	M	H	O	H
PLASTER	O	L	L	H	H	O	O	O	O	O	H
PLASTERBOARD	O	M	L	H	H	O	O	O	O	O	H
STONE	H	M	L	H	M	H	H	M	H	M	H
STUCCO	O	M	L	H	M	O	O	M	O	O	H
TERRAZZO	H	M	L	H	M	H	H	M	H	O	H
TERRA COTTA	H	M	L	H	M	O	O	M	O	O	H
TILE (Building)	O	M	L	H	M	O	O	M	O	O	H
TILE (Ceramic)	O	M	L	H	M	O	O	M	O	O	H
ACCESSORIES - BOLT or SCREW REQUIRED	None Anchor Complete	Sheet Metal or Wood Screw	None Anchor Complete	Sheet Metal or Wood Screw	None Anchor Complete	None Anchor Complete	Machine Screw	Sheet Metal or Wood Screw	None Anchor Complete	Lag Screw	None Anchor Complete
METHOD TOOLS	Drill Hammer Wrench	Drill Screw Driver Wrench	Drill Hammer	Drill Screw Driver	Drill Screw Driver	Drill Hammer	Drill, Hammer Screw Driver. Wrench Setting Tools	Drill Hammer Screw Driver	Drill Wrench Screw Driver	Drill Wrench	Drill Screw Driver
COMMENTS	Fastest growing anchor for heavy loads	Works in any material Excellent all purpose anchor	Works in all materials All purpose light duty—fast installation anchor with threaded or un-threaded nail	Works in any material Excellent all purpose anchor	Will work on all material backed by a hollow □ See legend	Will work on all hard materials	Will work on all hard materials	Will work on all hard materials	Will work on all hard materials	Will work on all hard materials	Will work on all material backed by a hollow □ See legend

LEGEND

H— Best or heaviest duty anchor for this material

M— Good anchor for this material

L— Light duty for this material

□— Anchor will work if material contains hollow

0— Not recommended

HARD MATERIALS
Brick-Concrete
Block-Stone, etc.

SOFT MATERIALS
Plaster
Plasterboard
Gypsum, etc.
Fiberboard, etc.

TAP SIZE		DRILL SIZE NO.	DRILL DIAMETER IN INCHES
DIAMETER	THREADS PER IN.		
2 — 56		51	.0670
3 — 48		5/64"	.0781
4 — 40		43	.0890
6 — 32		36	.1065
8 — 32		29	.1360
10 — 24		25	.1495
12 — 24		17	.1730
1/4" — 20		8	.1990
5/16" — 18		F	.2570
3/8" — 16		5/16"	.3125
1/2" — 13		27/64"	.4219

* American Screw Co.

Guide to tap size for various machine screws. Courtesy American Screw Co.

Lag-Shield and its method of installation. Courtesy Rawlplug Co.

A common use for Lag-Shields is in anchoring in the mortar joints between brick or building block, where it would be a disadvantage to permanently mar the masonry or to reduce the time required to drill the holes. For this application, the Lag-Shield should be installed so that its two halves will expand against the brick or building block.

←

Guide to selecting fasteners for stone and similar hard materials. Courtesy Hardware Retailing

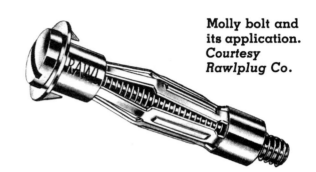

Molly bolt and its application. Courtesy Rawlplug Co.

INSTALLATION INSTRUCTIONS

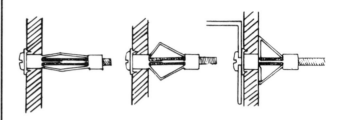

1. Drill proper size hole and insert Rawly. Tap head of Rawly until prongs are embedded in wall.

2. With a screwdriver, turn in screw until a definite resistance is felt. This indicates the Rawly is set.

3. Remove screw. Place object to be fastened in position and tighten screw.

Courtesy Hardware Retailing

Drive Molly, called Drive-Rawly by its manufacturer. Courtesy Rawlplug Co.

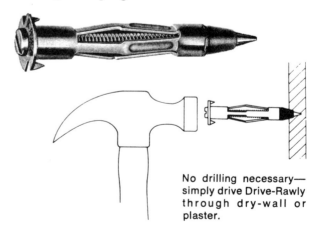

No drilling necessary— simply drive Drive-Rawly through dry-wall or plaster.

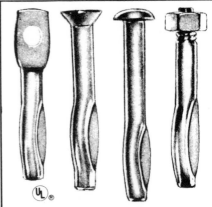

Rawlplug dimensions, associate screw dimensions, and plug installation. *Courtesy Rawlplug Co.*

Available in 40 sizes from #6 x 5/8" to 5/8" x 3 1/2"

GSA Specification FF-S-325 Group IV, Type 2

SHEET METAL AND WOOD SCREWS SIZES

Rawlplug Size	Rawl-drill Size & Diam.
6 x 5/8" 3/4" 1"	#6 (5/32")
8 x 5/8" 3/4" 1" 1 1/4" 1 1/2" 2"	#8 (11/64")
10 x 3/4" 1" 1 1/4" 1 1/2" 2"	#10 (3/16")
12 x 3/4" 1" 1 1/4" 1 1/2" 2"	#12 (1/4")
14 x 1" or 1/4" lag screw 1 1/4" 1 1/2" 2"	#14 (9/32")
16 x 1" 1 1/2" 2"	#16 (5/16")
20 x 1" or 5/16" lag screw 1 1/2" 2"	#20 (3/8")
22 x 2"	#20 (3/8")

LAG SCREW SIZES

3/8x1 1/2" 2" 2 1/2" 3"	7/16"
1/2x2" 2 1/2" 3"	5/8"
5/8x2 1/2" 3" 3 1/2"	3/4"

Installation

Installation of Rawlplugs is very simple — Rawldrill proper size hole through fixture, insert Rawlplug, and turn screw home.

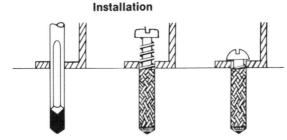

For maximum performance, use same size drill, Rawlplug and screw

The first, and most important rule in the installation of Rawlplugs is to us the *same size* Rawldrill, Rawlplug and screw. For instance, if using a #12 screw, drill the hole with a #12 Rawldrill and use a #12 Rawlplug.

The Rawlplug depends on tremendous compression for its holding power — the flexibility of the jute permits it to be forced and compressed into every irregularity in the walls of the hole, so it is absolutely necessary that Rawlplug, Rawldrill and screw sizes all be the same.

Measuring screws

The shoulders of wood or lag screws *should not* enter the Rawlplug. Forcing the screw shoulder into the Rawlplug adds nothing whatever to holding power, and may bind or "shear" the screw — that is, turn the head off.

1. With fixture in place drill hole to recommended depth.

2. Insert Rawl-Drive and drive with hammer until fixture is firmly anchored.

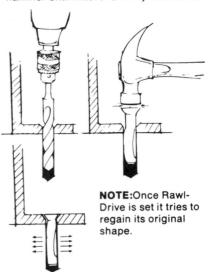

NOTE: Once Rawl-Drive is set it tries to regain its original shape.

INSTALLATION — STUD TYPE

Drill hole to total length of stud, with nut on, hammer flush and tighten. To move fixture, turn nut off, then hammer drive flush with surface.

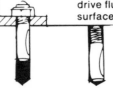

Types of Rawl-Drive bolts and how they may be installed. *Courtesy Rawlplug Co.*

12 FIBERBOARD

Fiberboard is made by separating the fibers of wood, sugar cane, or similar organic materials and then forming the individual fibers into sheets with the aid of heat and pressure. The process is somewhat akin to that used to make felt.

Fiberboard was probably the first "artificial" board or plank to be manufactured. While it has lost the popularity it once had, it is still the least expensive and most easily installed of all the man-made panels. It is light in weight and is easily cut with a razor knife or wood saw. If necessary, it can be bent in a gentle curve, something not possible with gypsum board and not easily done with plywood.

Fiberboard has an R factor or rating (see INSULATION) somewhat lower than that of rock wool and higher than that of softwood. Although fiberboard panels are not designed for sound absorption, rooms that have walls covered with fiberboard panels are considerably quieter than rooms made with gypsum board or plywood panels.

Fiberboard is normally light brown in color with a matte-textured surface that does not require painting. It reflects light well and is fairly easily cleaned with a damp sponge and a little mild soap. While it will burn, it is not highly combustible.

On the negative side, fiberboard is soft, and is easily dented and gouged. It must be supported on all four edges and should not be fastened to studs or furring strips more than 16 inches apart, center to

center. You cannot drive nails or screws into fiberboard and expect them to support any weight. You must first install a nailing base behind the fiberboard to carry these nails or screws.

Fiberboard is highly susceptible to moisture. It should never be used below ground or in a bathroom or kitchen. It swells and warps as it absorbs moisture. It is impractical to attempt to seal the fiberboard against moisture. But if you want to try, paint will do the job. Before you paint, even if it's just for decorative purposes, first you have to seal the board with shellac or it will soak up several coats of paint. This must be done on both sides and along the edges. The cost of the shellac, the paint, and the labor generally offsets fiberboard's other advantages.

Despite these limitations, fiberboard still has many practical applications. It is ideal for finishing an attic, or for covering the walls of a storage room or closet.

STYLES AND DIMENSIONS

Fiberboard is made in panels and planks. The panels may have square or beveled edges and may have V-grooves, which make the panels resemble a number of parallel planks. The panels generally come with tongue-and-groove edges.

Panels are made in thicknesses of ½ and 1 inch, widths of 4 feet, and lengths of 6, 7, 8, 9, 10, and 12 feet. Planks are made in the same thicknesses, in widths of 8, 12, and 16 inches, and in lengths of 8, 10, and 12 feet.

APPLICATION

Again, fiberboard is so soft it can be cut with a razor knife or an ordinary wood saw. But because it is so soft, the cut boards have very little strength and, therefore, no edge of any panel or board should be allowed to hang free. All fiberboard edges must be supported, including the joint edges where two planks meet. Lengthwise supports should not be more than 16 inches apart, center on center.

Let the fiberboard stabilize before nailing it in place. Do this by bringing the boards into the room they will occupy, several days before application. Separate the pieces so that the air can reach all sides. This will permit the moisture content of the boards to adjust until it matches that of the air in the room. Then you can nail them up.

Do not butt the edge of one plank or panel tightly against another; make sure to leave 1/16 of an inch of space between them. This will allow for a little expansion. Use 1¾-inch aluminum finishing nails when you are going to face-nail the boards; use the same size common nails where you are going to cover the joints with a molding of some sort. Use 1-inch cement-coated staples to fasten the tongue of a plank to its support. Position nails or staples at least ½ inch in from the edge of the panel. Space the fasteners about 3 inches apart. When you are fastening a long plank or panel, start nailing from the center and work outward. This will preclude buckling.

13 FLOORING— RESILIENT

Resilient flooring is made of many different materials, in many grades, patterns, colors, and in two basic forms: tiles and sheets. Resilient flooring is used as an alternative to wood and rigid flooring, as a replacement flooring atop badly worn existing flooring, and where it is impractical to use wood flooring—for example, below grade.

Resilient flooring resists water much better than wood floors, is more easily cleaned, and, depending on the type, may not need any waxing. It is made in many bright colors and intaglio patterns, neither of which is practical with wood. In addition, resilient flooring is far less expensive than wood flooring.

On the other hand, when the varnish wears off a wood floor it is a simple matter to revarnish it. Should the wood be stained or grooved it is not too difficult to power-sand it smooth and clean again. Generally, even when a floor is composed of individual resilient tiles it is impossible simply to replace only the worn tiles because of coloring differences, the difficulty of buying only a few tiles, and other similar reasons.

RESILIENT FLOOR TILE

The characteristics of resilient tiles depend on the materials from which the tiles are made. Therefore resilient tiles are always described by their material of composition.

ASPHALT TILES

These were the first of the resilient tiles to be manufactured and are still widely used today. They are the least expensive of all the tiles and in some ways the least desirable. They are brittle when cold. You have to bring them to room temperature before attempting to cut them, otherwise they will break. On the other hand, they flow (spread a bit) with time and temperature. In doing so they eventually fill all spaces and cracks between the individual tiles themselves and between the tiles and the walls, moldings, etc. Thus, you need not fit these tiles as closely as you must fit tiles of other materials. At the same time, the tendency of asphalt tiles to flow or give more than the other tiles makes it very important that they be laid on a perfectly smooth surface. Lay one of these tiles over a dime, for example, and in a few months the shape of the coin will appear through the tile.

Asphalt tiles are generally made in 9-×-9-inch squares, ⅛ inch thick. Their decorative pattern usually simulates marble. For best visual results, the "marble" veining of one tile should be positioned at right angles to that of an adjoining tile.

VINYL ASBESTOS

As the name indicates these tiles are basically a mixture of vinyl and asbestos. Note that the asbestos is fully combined with the vinyl. There is never any danger from asbestos particles. Generally made in 12-inch squares and in thickness of 1/16, 3/32, and 1/8 of an inch, they are far lighter and brighter in color than asphalt. They resist wear better, are more easily cleaned, do not require waxing—you can power-buff them to a dull gloss—but they cost more than asphalt tile.

SOLID VINYL

These tiles are all vinyl. This makes them brighter, tougher, longer lasting, and more easily cleaned than part-vinyl tiles. They also cost more. You can tell they are solid vinyl because whatever patterns appear run all the way through the tile. They are made in thicknesses of 4/5, 1/16, 3/32, and 1/8 of an inch and in square and rectangular shapes that are 12 × 12 and 12 × 18 inches in size.

PRINTED VINYL AND VINYL ASBESTOS

The difference between the solids and the printed is that the latter have their designs literally printed on one side. This makes a more detailed, more realistic design or pattern possible. But it also limits the life of the tile, since the printing is on the surface and wears off faster than the tile itself wears out. Printed vinyl tiles *look* worn out more quickly than do vinyl asbestos tiles.

EMBOSSED VINYL AND VINYL ASBESTOS

The process of embossing—shaping the surface—of resilient flooring can be—and is—employed with all types of tile except asphalt. The value of embossing is that it lends visual character to the flooring. The disadvantages are twofold: (1) The indentations tend to collect dust and grime far faster than a perfectly smooth suface; and (2) ridges and high spots tend to wear faster than low areas. Embossed resilient flooring is not the first choice for high-traffic areas.

CUSHIONED TILE

Vinyl tile is manufactured with a variety of backings that cushion the tile, which means walking on these tiles is a little easier on one's feet. A number of cushion backings are used. They include felt, felt and foam, asbestos, and foam. The latter two can be used below grade, the first two cannot; they will mildew and rot if they become wet and stay wet.

Cushion-backed resilient flooring has two drawbacks, in addition to costing more. One is that the presence of the cushioning layer makes application very difficult. The other is that the softness of the floor's surface makes it necessary to provide supports beneath the legs of furniture. If this is not done, the surface of the floor will become permanently indented.

NO-WAX RESILIENT FLOORING

Introduced in 1970, the no-wax feature is, actually, a special hard, shiny surface that is applied in a layer atop the flooring. Each manufacturer has his own formulation and brand name. But some also sell their formulations by the bottle so that you can re-cover worn spots by yourself.

RUBBER

Available in 12-inch squares, ⅛ and ¼ inch thick, rubber flooring provides a naturally soft footing. However, it does not come in as many colors as does vinyl and neither is it as bright. But it is probably longer lasting, since it is not as readily abraded as is the much harder vinyl.

CORK

This is the softest of the resilient floorings and it is, to some extent, noise-reducing. Its natural soft brown color is very pleasing, but it is neither highly wear-resistant nor easily cleaned. It can be waxed but will not take a shine. It is fairly easily patched, however. Cork tiles are available in 12-×-12 and 12-×-18-inch tiles, ⅛ and ¼ inch thick.

VINYL CORK

A combination of cork and vinyl that has many of the best features of each.

RESILIENT SHEET FLOORING

Sometimes called flat goods or roll goods, resilient sheet flooring was invented in 1860 by an Englishman named Frederic Walton when he noticed the film that formed in time over an open can of paint. He removed the "skin" that formed when the linseed oil oxidized, and from this he "worked" his way up to linoleum, the last of which was reportedly manufactured in 1974.

Modern sheet flooring is currently made from everything used to make modern resilient tile, with the exception of asphalt. Sheet flooring comes in the same materials, with the same finishes and backings as the tile. Or, quite simply, resilient tile is resilient sheet flooring that has been cut into squares and rectangles.

DIFFERENCES

Sheet flooring differs from tile flooring only in that the former is a continuous surface, which means there is less chance of water and soil creeping beneath the surface. This is a big plus. But sheet flooring is a lot more difficult to install. Whereas tile can be had in sizes as small as 9 inches square, sheet flooring comes in rolls from 6 to 15 feet wide. The need for greater care and accuracy when cutting and installing sheet flooring is obvious.

Linoleum floor at the left was the height of style back in the 1930s. Today, linoleum is no longer manufactured in this country. The gleaming, no-wax flooring on the right has replaced it. *Courtesy Armstrong Cork Co.*

Installing adhesive-backed resilient floor tile.
A. The room is squared off with chalk lines. The protective paper is peeled from the back of a tile.

B. With chalk lines as a guide the tiles are maneuvered into position and pressed into place.

Installing resilient sheet flooring. A. Read the instructions provided. You will need a carpenter's square, chalk line, sheet flooring adhesive, notched trowel, and a hook knife or scissors. B. Measure the room very accurately. Make a scale drawing of the floor. The square is used to make certain your measurements are at right angles to each other. C. Permit sheeting to warm up, if cold. Lay it out perfectly flat. Transfer measurements to sheeting. Cut along your lines. A piece of heavy cardboard beneath the lines will prevent your knife from damaging the floor.

C

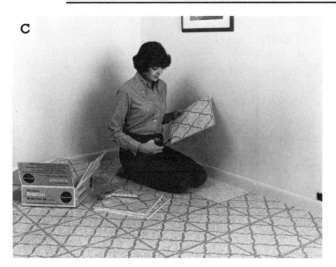

C. Where necessary, tiles are easily cut with ordinary scissors.

D

D. The job can be completed in a few hours. The tile used here is a no-wax tile called Rafina. *Courtesy Armstrong Cork Co.*

C

D

D. Carefully position the sheeting on the floor it will occupy. Check to make certain it is not too large in areas and does not curl or fold back. Then roll back half of the sheet. Spread the adhesive evenly over the entire area, making certain the edge of the trowel touches the floor. In this way the adhesive is spread evenly. Unroll the sheeting. Press it firmly onto the adhesive. Then

E

repeat with the other half.

E. Once the entire sheet of flooring has been secured with adhesive, you can replace the furniture and go about your business. Nothing more need be done. *Courtesy Armstrong Cork Co.*

FLOORING— SEAMLESS

Seamless flooring is truly seamless because it is applied like a thick paint. When it hardens it forms a resilient flooring. The thickness of the flooring depends on how many layers you apply and how thick you make each layer.

Seamless flooring can be applied to any surface that can be painted. Unless you pour on sufficient liquid to fill any and all indentations and valleys, however, the finished flooring will show most of the original surface variations. Thus before applying the liquid flooring you should either fill the holes with a special cement made for this purpose or power-sand the floor perfectly smooth.

Seamless flooring can be poured over concrete, but if the concrete has been stained, you should cover it with a coat of sealer. Otherwise the stain may bleed through and discolor the flooring.

Seamless flooring should not be poured over an old linoleum floor or a plastic tile floor. If the supporting surface is not solid and substantial, the seamless flooring will not lay down properly, and it could peel in a short time.

If you wish, a layer of colored flakes can be spread over the seamless flooring and sealed in place with a transparent, plastic liquid that dries to a hard, durable finish. Should wear marks appear because of concentrated traffic, additional coats of acrylic plastic glaze can be applied to refinish the surface. No waxing is necessary.

APPLICATION TIPS

Make sure the surface is perfectly clean, dust- and dirt-free. Make sure the solution is at room temperature. Provide plenty of ventilation. Work rapidly in order to keep the liquid as fluid as possible while you are applying it. Do not apply a thicker coat than suggested by the manufacturer. Let each coat dry thoroughly to a hard finish before applying the following coat.

15 FLOORING-WOOD

In the good old days when there wasn't much choice, flooring was cut in wide, square-edge hardwood planks and either pegged down or face-nailed to the floor joists. This type of flooring is still available if you are willing to pay the price and wait for your special order to be delivered. Today we make do with narrower, smaller pieces of hardwood and get better results, because modern flooring is machine cut.

Two types of wood flooring are common. One is called strips, because it consists of long, comparatively narrow boards. The other is called block, because it consists of squares of wood that in turn are composed of smaller pieces of wood.

STRIP FLOORING

HARDWOOD

Five different kinds of wood are commonly used to make hardwood flooring. They are hard maple, oak, beech, birch, and pecan. Their hardness or toughness are more or less equal. Maple is most often used for sport surfaces such as basketball courts. Oak is most often selected for residential use. Oak is sawn two ways: plain and quarter. Plain cutting tends to show the flat side of the grain. Quarter sawing tends to show the edge of the grain. The latter type is available on special order only.

GRADES, WIDTHS, WASTE

Once the wood has been cut into flooring it is graded and packed into bundles. Each bundle will contain a specific number of *nominal* square feet of flooring. No bundle will contain any pieces less than 9 inches long. The better and more expensive grades of flooring contain fewer knots and discolorations; the average length of the pieces will also be longer.

Width designations for hardwood flooring are confusing. There is the actual dimension and the counted dimension. The counted dimension is simply a convenient designation. For example, ¾-×-3¼-inch flooring is counted as—or called—1 × 4.

Further, the actual size of the flooring cannot be used to compute needed quantity because the actual size includes the tongue, which enters the groove and does not contribute to the floor area. This means that you must calculate quantities needed by multiplying the floor area to be covered by the loss factor. For example, when laying 1½-inch strip flooring, only 45 percent of the width of the strip goes to cover the floor. Thus, to cover 100 square feet of floor, you will need 220 square feet of the 1½-inch flooring plus another 5 percent for normal cutting waste.

As the width of the board increases, waste decreases, with the lowest waste figure being 29 percent for the 3¼-inch stock. As board width increases, however, cost goes up. Your assignment therefore is to find where the upward-moving cost line crosses the downward-moving waste line. At the same time, keep in mind that it takes more than twice as much labor to lay down 1½-inch flooring than it does to lay down 3¼-inch flooring.

TONGUED AND GROOVE (T&G) VS. SQUARE EDGE

Tongue-and-groove hardwood flooring is tongued and grooved along both sides and both ends. This locks the boards solidly together and helps keep the floor smooth and flat. But, as mentioned, a lot of wood gets wasted in making the tongues. Square-edge flooring is less costly because there isn't this tremendous waste. However, you still have to compute coverage by the actual size of the lumber and not its nominal size, which may or may not be the same. Individual lumber yards often have their own designations.

Square-edge flooring is face-nailed. T&G is blind-nailed (you do not see the nails).

Square-edge boards will never lie as perfectly flat over as long a time as T&G. And in addition, there is always the possibility that the boards will shrink a little, causing cracks to form between them.

THICKNESS

Hardwood strip flooring thicknesses range from 5/16 to 33/32 of an inch, with the most common thickness being ¾ inch. The thinner boards are cheaper, but the thicker lay down more easily, tend to correct floor errors, and generally are much easier to work with. The best compromise is probably the ¾-inch thickness.

SOFTWOOD

Fir and yellow pine are two fairly hard "softwoods" that are used for flooring. They are sawn plain, which shows the sides of the grain, and rift, which shows the narrow edges of the grain. Rift-sawn fir approaches the hardwoods in appearance and wear resistance. Plain sawn does not, and in high-traffic areas will soon wear down unevenly.

These woods are often used in 1¼- to 1½-inch thicknesses for single-layer flooring in attic playrooms and porches. In the latter location they must be given a "fat" pitch to ensure rapid water runoff.

PREFINISHED

Hardwood flooring is also made with slightly beveled edges to simulate antique flooring, and is sealed and varnished at the factory. The cost of this type of flooring is obviously higher than that of unfinished flooring.

BLOCK FLOORING

Block flooring may be considered to be a poor man's parquetry. Parquetry is a wood floor made of many small pieces of wood fitted together to form squares, diamonds, and other patterns. It is very beautiful, very expensive, and very difficult to lay. Although the pieces of wood are precut at the factory, the cutting is not precise; corrections have to be made; joint quality approaches that of cabinetmaking.

Block flooring differs from parquetry in that the pieces of wood are prejoined into 9-×-9- and 12-×-12-inch squares. Each square may be made of small, solid pieces of wood, or each square may actually be a square cut from multilayer plywood. Block flooring is sold in various woods, colors, patterns, and thicknesses. It comes either bare or prefinished, and either square edge or tongue and groove. Thicknesses range from as little as ¼ inch up to 25/32 inch. The T&G can be blind-nailed. The square-edge blocks must be face-nailed. An alternative is to lay them down in mastic.

While it may appear that block flooring is easier to lay than strip, because there is no nailing when you work with a mastic, good results are more difficult with block than strip flooring. Strips align themselves; blocks do not. You must keep them in perfect alignment. If each succeeding block is off a fraction, the last block in the row will be visibly off and then all the adjoining blocks will not fit properly. When you work with resilient tile that can be cut with shears, it is no problem to correct for errors; no one notices an undersized tile. But when you work with tongue-and-groove blocks, reducing the size of a block means cutting a new tongue or groove.

Strip flooring tends to level a floor. The long pieces of wood tend to hide floor imperfections. Even T&G blocks will tend to go up and down with every subfloor variation.

SUBFLOORING

MATERIALS USED
When a subfloor is to be covered by a finished wood floor, either plywood or square-edge boards may be used. When the subfloor is to be covered by carpeting or resilient flooring—neither of which has much stiffness or strength—plywood must be used. Whatever softwood is least expen-sive at the time is used, preferably in 6-inch widths, because there is less waste, and always in a nominal 1-inch thickness. When a nominal 1-inch finished floor is to be laid down, interior grade plywood as lit-tle as ⅜ inch thick may be used with floor joists 16 inches on center. When nothing but a single layer of plywood is to be used, its thickness will range from 1 inch to 1¼ inches minimum, depending on whether or not the wood's edges are joined by clips, or tongues and grooves, or are simply butted. NOTE: Local building codes specify these dimensions.

APPLYING STRIP SUBFLOORING
The strips should, preferably, be run at a 45-degree angle to the joists. Two 6d common nails should be used where each strip crosses a joist. Strips should be spaced ¼ inch apart, and all strip ends should terminate at a joist.

APPLYING PLYWOOD SUBFLOORING
There is much less work involved in applying plywood than strip sub-flooring. Joists must be positioned accurately, however, as the sides of the plywood must center on the joists. The sheets can be nailed down, with one 6d common nail every 8 inches, or the sheets may be glued down with a construction adhesive. Generally the use of an adhesive is limited to 1-inch plywood, edge-joined by tongues and grooves or clips.

LAYING STRIP FLOORING

PRELIMINARY PRECAUTIONS
Finished flooring should never even

be brought into a house before the building is completely enclosed, the plaster has been given a week to fully dry, or the taping job has been given two days to dry out completely. If the floor is to be laid in a basement, give the concrete two weeks to dry out. Then bring the bundles of flooring inside, open them up, and wait two days for the flooring to stabilize.

APPLICATION

Cover the floor with a layer of red or white building paper or polyethylene film. Start parallel to the longest wall, and groove to the wall with ½- to ⅝-inch clearance. NOTE: The base and shoe molding are not in place at this time. Face-nail the edge of the flooring strip that is nearest the wall. Blind-nail its other edge. If you are nailing by hand use a heavy flooring hammer and a nail set. If you are nailing by machine, make sure the machine is properly positioned before you strike it. Use 7d floor nails, or 2-inch machine fasteners 8 to 10 inches apart.

After the first strip is nailed down, position the second strip alongside. Use a piece of scrap flooring and a hammer to drive the second strip tightly against the first. Continue on across the room, taking care to stagger the joints in a random pattern.

LAYING BLOCK FLOORING

Before you lay block flooring, let the building dry out and let the moisture content of the flooring reach equilibrium with the moisture content of the building. Cover the supporting surface with building paper or plastic. Snap a chalk line four or five blocks distant from one wall and exactly parallel to that wall. Snap a second line at right angles to the first. Position the second line an even number of blocks from either wall. Your first block is positioned within one of the angles formed by the two lines. Succeeding blocks are placed around the first block. If you are nailing, follow the manufacturer's nailing instructions. If you are working with a mastic, spread the mastic where the first few blocks are to go. Resnap the lines atop the mastic as best you can. It is very important to get the first few blocks positioned exactly right.

Of course, you do not use building paper or plastic sheeting beneath the flooring when you are going to bond it in place with a mastic.

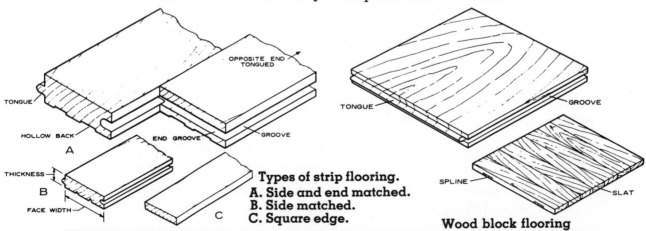

Types of strip flooring.
A. Side and end matched.
B. Side matched.
C. Square edge.

Wood block flooring

Guide to Hardwood Flooring Grades

A brief grade description, for comparison only. NOFMA flooring is bundled by averaging the lengths. A bundle may include pieces from 6 inches under to 6 inches over the nominal length of the bundle. No piece shorter than 9 inches admitted. The percentages under 4 ft. referred to apply on total footage in any one shipment of the item. ¾ inch added to face length when measuring length of each piece.

UNFINISHED OAK FLOORING (Red & White Separated)		BEECH, BIRCH & HARD MAPLE		PECAN FLOORING	PREFINISHED OAK FLOORING (Red & White Separated—graded after finishing)	
CLEAR (Plain or Quarter Sawn)** Best Appearance Best grade, most uniform color, limited small character marks. Bundles 1¼ ft. and up. Average length 3¾ ft.	*SELECT AND BETTER*	**FIRST GRADE WHITE HARD MAPLE** (Spec. Order) Same as FIRST GRADE except face all bright sapwood. **FIRST GRADE RED BEECH & BIRCH** (Spec. Order) Same as FIRST GRADE except face all red heartwood **FIRST GRADE** Best Appearance. Natural color variation, limited character marks, unlimited sap. Bdles. 2 ft. & up. 2 & 3 ft. bdles. up to 33% footage.	*SECOND AND BETTER*	***FIRST GRADE RED** (Spec. Order) Same as FIRST GRADE except face all heartwood. ***FIRST GRADE WHITE** (Spec. Order) Same as FIRST GRADE except face all bright sapwood. **FIRST GRADE** Excellent Appearance. Natural color variation, limited character marks, unlimited sap Bdles. 2 ft. & up. 2 & 3 ft. Bdles. up to 25% footage.	***PRIME** (Special Order Only) Excellent Appearance Natural color variation, limited character marks, unlimited sap. Bundles 1¼ ft. and up. Average length 3½ ft.	*STANDARD AND BETTER*
SELECT & BETTER (Special Order) A Combination of Clear and Select grades **SELECT (Plain or Quarter Sawn)**** Excellent Appearance Limited character marks, unlimited sound sap. Bundles 1¼ ft. and up. Average length 3¼ ft.		**SECOND & BETTER GRADE** Excellent Appearance. A combination of FIRST and SECOND GRADES. Bdles. 2 ft. & up. 2 & 3 ft. Bdles. up to 40% footage. (NOTE: 5% 1¼ ft. bdles. allowed in SECOND & BETTER jointed flg. only.) **SECOND GRADE** Variegated Appearance. Varying sound wood characteristics of species. Bdles. 2 ft. & up. 2 & 3 ft. Bdles. up to 45% footage.	*THIRD AND BETTER*	***SECOND GRADE RED** (Special Order Only) Same as SECOND GRADE except face all heartwood. **SECOND GRADE** Variegated Appearance Varying sound wood characteristics of species. Bundles 1¼ ft. and up. 1¼ ft. to 3 ft. bundles as produced up to 40% footage.	**STANDARD & BETTER GRADE** Combination of STANDARD and PRIME. Bundles 1¼ ft. and up. Average length 3 ft. **STANDARD GRADE** Variegated Appearance Varying sound wood characteristics of species. A sound floor. Bundles 1¼ ft. and up. Average length 2¾ ft.	*TAVERN AND BETTER*
NO. 1 COMMON Variegated Appearance *Light and dark colors; knots, flags, worm holes and other character marks allowed to provide a variegated appearance, after imperfections are filled and finished. Bundles 1¼ ft. and up. Average length 2¾ ft.		**THIRD & BETTER GRADE** A combination of FIRST, SECOND and THIRD GRADES. Bundles 1¼ ft. and up. 1¼ ft. to 3 ft. bundles as produced up to 50% footage. **THIRD GRADE** Rustic Appearance All wood characteristics of species. Serviceable, economical floor after filling. Bundles 1¼ ft. and up. 1¼ ft. to 3 ft. bundles as produced up to 65% footage.		**THIRD GRADE** Rustic Appearance All wood characteristics of species. A serviceable, economical floor after filling. Bundles 1¼ ft. and up. 1¼ ft. to 3 ft. bundles as produced up to 60% footage.	***TAVERN & BETTER GRADE** (Special Order Only) Combination of PRIME, STANDARD and TAVERN. All wood characteristics of species. Bundles 1¼ ft. and up. Average length 3 ft. **TAVERN GRADE** Rustic Appearance All wood characteristics of species. A serviceable, economical floor. Bundles 1¼ ft. and up. Average length 2¼ ft.	
NO. 2 COMMON (Red & White may be mixed) Rustic Appearance All wood characteristics of species. A serviceable, economical floor after knot holes, worm holes, checks and other imperfections are filled and finished. Bundles 1¼ ft. and up. Average length 2¼ ft.						

*1¼ FT. SHORTS (Red & White may be mixed)
Unique Variegated Appearance. Lengths 9 inches to 18 inches. Bundles average nominal 1¼ ft. Production limited.

*NO. 1 COMMON & BETTER SHORTS
A combination grade, CLEAR, SELECT, & NO. 1 COMMON 9 inches to 18 inches.

*NO. 2 COMMON SHORTS
Same as No. 2 COMMON, except length 9 inches to 18 inches.

** Quarter Sawn — Special Order Only
*Check with supplier for grade and species available.
†NESTED FLOORING: Random length tongued and grooved, end-matched flooring is bundled end to end continuously to form 8 ft. long (nominal) bundles. Regular grade requirements apply.
‡NESTED FLOORING: If put up in 8 ft. nested bundles, 9 to 18 inch pieces will be admitted in ¾" x 2¼" as follows in the species of Beech, Birch & Hard Maple: FIRST GRADE, 4 pcs. per bundle; SECOND GRADE, 8 pcs.; THIRD GRADE, as develops. Average lengths: FIRST GRADE, 42 inches; SECOND GRADE, 33 inches; THIRD GRADE, 30 inches.

PREFINISHED BEECH & PECAN FLOORING
*TAVERN & BETTER GRADE (Special Order Only)
Combination of PRIME, STANDARD and TAVERN. All wood characteristics of species. Bundles 1¼ ft. and up. Average length 3 ft.

Courtesy National Oak Flooring Manufacturing Association

HOW TO ARRIVE AT THE AMOUNT OF HARDWOOD FLOORING REQUIRED

To determine the board feet of flooring needed to cover a given space, first find the area in square feet then add to it the percentage of that figure which applies to the size flooring to be used, as indicated below. The additions provide an allowance for side-matching plus an additional 5% for end-matching and normal waste.

Courtesy National Oak Flooring Manufacturing Association

55% for	¾"x1½"
42½% for	¾"x2"
38⅓% for	¾"x2¼"
29% for	¾"x3¼"
38⅓% for	⅜"x1½"
30% for	⅜"x2"
38⅓% for	½"x1½"
30% for	½"x2"

The above figures are based on laying flooring straight across the room. Where there are bay windows or other projections, allowance should be made for additional flooring.

Nail Schedule

Tongue and Groove Flooring Must Be Blind Nailed

¾x1½, 2¼ & 3¼ in.	2 in. machine driven fasteners, 7d or 8d screw or cut nail.	10-12 in. apart*
¾x3 in. to 8 in.** Plank	2 in. machine driven fasteners, 7d or 8d screw or cut nail.	8" apart into and between joists.

*If subfloor is ½ inch plywood, fasten into each joist, with additional fastening between.
**Plank Flooring over 4" wide must be installed over a subfloor.

Following flooring must be laid on a subfloor.

½x1½ & 2 in.	1½ in. machine driven fastener, 5d screw, cut steel or wire casing nail.	10 in. apart
⅜x1½ & 2 in.	1¼ in. machine driven fastener, or 4d bright wire casing nail.	8 in. apart
Square-edge flooring as follows, face-nailed — through top face		
5/16x1½ & 2 in.	1 inch 15 gauge fully barbed flooring brad. 2 nails every 7 inches.	
5/16x1⅓ in.	1 inch 15 gauge fully barbed flooring brad. 1 nail every 5 inches on alternate sides of strip.	

Standard Sizes, Counts & Weights

Nominal	Actual	Counted	Weights M Ft.
TONGUE AND GROOVE-END MATCHED			
** ¾x3¼ in.	¾x3¼ in.	1x4 in.	2210 lbs.
¾x2¼ in.	¾x2¼ in.	1x3 in.	2020 lbs.
¾x2 in.	¾x2 in.	1x2¾ in.	1920 lbs.
¾x1½ in.	¾x1½ in.	1x2¼ in.	1820 lbs.
** ⅜x2 in.	11/32x2 in.	1x2½ in.	1000 lbs.
** ⅜x1½ in.	11/32x1½ in.	1x2 in.	1000 lbs.
** ½x2 in.	15/32x2 in.	1x2½ in.	1350 lbs.
** ½x1½ in.	15/32x1½ in.	1x2 in.	1300 lbs.
SQUARE EDGE			
** 5/16x2 in.	5/16x2 in.	face count	1200 lbs.
** 5/16x1½ in.	5/16x1½ in.	face count	1200 lbs.
Nominal	**Actual**	**Counted**	**Weights M Ft.**
SPECIAL THICKNESSES (T and G, End Matched)			
** 33/32x3¼ in.	33/32x3¼ in.	5/4x4 in.	2400 lbs.
** 33/32x2¼ in.	33/32x2¼ in.	5/4x3 in.	2250 lbs.
** 33/32x2 in.	33/32x2 in.	5/4x2¾ in.	2250 lbs.
JOINTED FLOORING — i.e., SQUARE EDGE			
** ¾x2½ in.	¾x2½ in.	1x3¼ in.	2160 lbs.
** ¾x3¼ in.	¾x3¼ in.	1x4 in.	2300 lbs.
** ¾x3½ in.	¾x3½ in.	1x4¼ in.	2400 lbs.
** 33/32x2½ in.	33/32x2½ in.	5/4x3¼ in.	2500 lbs.
** 33/32x3½ in.	33/32x3½ in.	5/4x4¼ in.	2600 lbs.

**Special Order Only

Courtesy National Oak Flooring Manufacturing Association

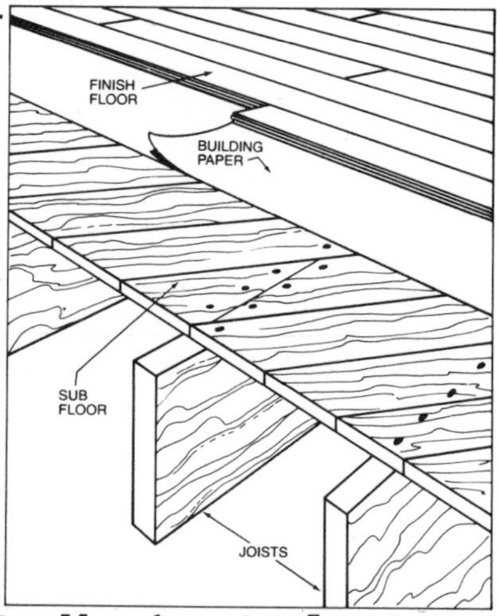

How square-edge boards are laid at an angle to provide a subfloor for finished flooring. *Courtesy National Oak Flooring Manufacturing Association*

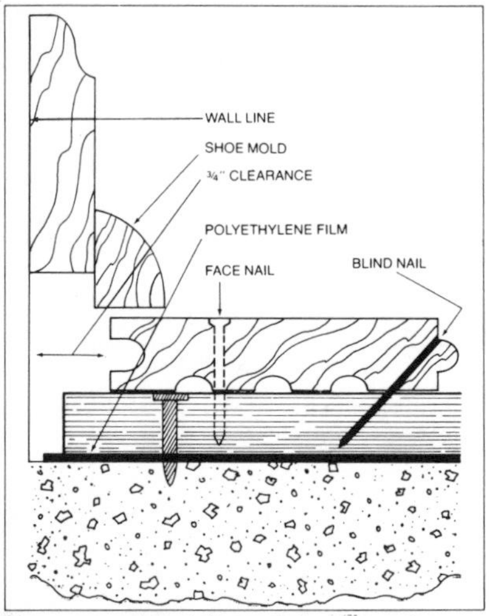

How a plywood subfloor may be used atop concrete to provide a nailing support for strip flooring.

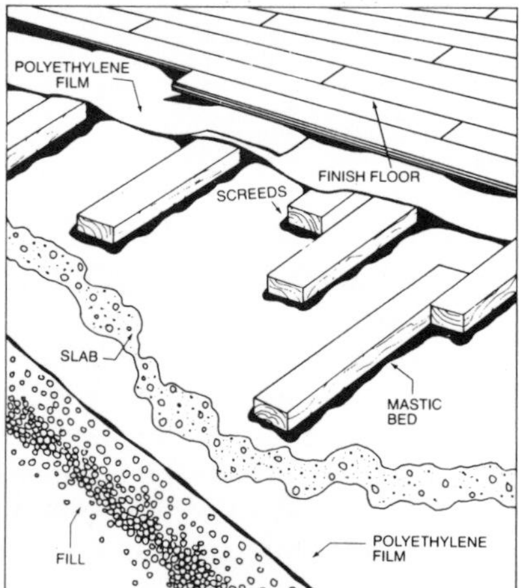

How strip flooring may be laid atop screeds (sleepers), in turn laid atop a concrete slab. *Courtesy National Oak Flooring Manufacturing Association*

How the first flooring strip is positioned and nailed. Note that the groove is toward the wall. Note the face nails and the blind nails.

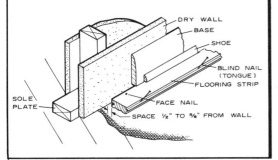

DRY WALL
BASE
SHOE
BLIND NAIL (TONGUE)
FLOORING STRIP
FACE NAIL
SPACE ½" TO ⅝" FROM WALL
SOLE PLATE

Subfloor adhesive bonding instructions.

1. Chalk line the joist at 4' intervals. Apply PL-400 for one sheet at a time. Apply a 1/4" high bead to each joist where sheet will fall. (Two beads will be used on butt joint.)

2. Start at corner and lay a full course of subfloor to the next corner. Position sheet with a minimum of sideways slippage. Nail each sheet as you go.

3. Apply a 3/16" bead in groove of plywood.

4. Lay 2X4 on tongue side and use sledge to secure T&G fit. Be sure to stagger end joints.

5. Nail sheet 12" O.C. with 6d annular ring or spiral nails.

6. Use putty knife or wood scrap to remove any adhesive squeeze-out.

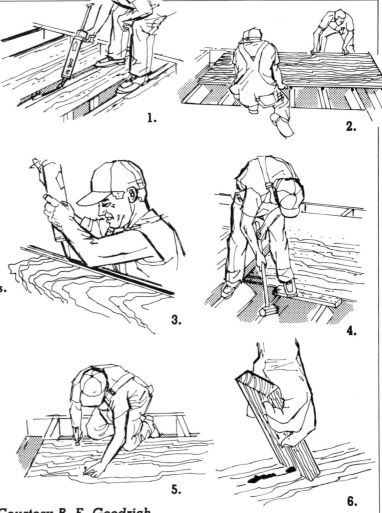

Courtesy B. F. Goodrich

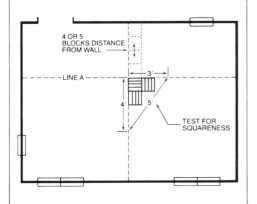

Courtesy National Oak Flooring Manufacturing Association

4 OR 5 BLOCKS DISTANCE FROM WALL — LINE A — 3' — 4' — 5' — TEST FOR SQUARENESS

Working lines for laying block in a square pattern.

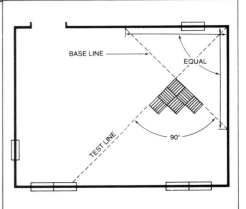

BASE LINE — EQUAL — TEST LINE — 90°

Working lines for laying block in a diagonal pattern.

16 FRAMING HARDWARE

The faster and stronger alternative to nailing frame timbers to one another is to join them with framing hardware. These are pressed or stamped pieces of heavy gauge sheet metal. They are shaped to join a joist to a girder, a purlin to a joist, a sheet of subflooring plywood to floor joists, steps to a stringer, porch posts to a stoop, studs to a sill plate, and more.

Some types of framing hardware have sharp metal projections that eliminate the need for nails. This type of framing hardware is positioned then pounded home with a hammer. The other types require standard nails.

Common framing practices and a few examples of framing hardware are illustrated on the accompanying pages.

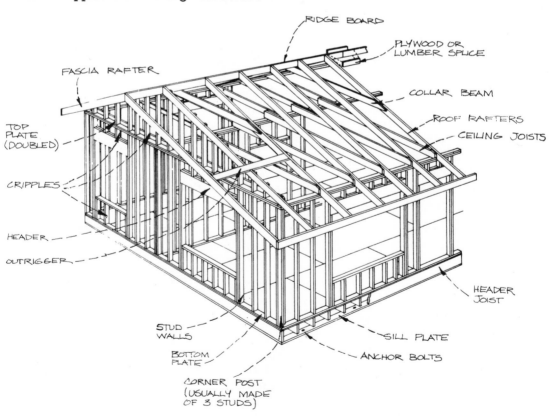

RIDGE BOARD
PLYWOOD OR LUMBER SPLICE
FASCIA RAFTER
COLLAR BEAM
ROOF RAFTERS
CEILING JOISTS
TOP PLATE (DOUBLED)
CRIPPLES
HEADER
OUTRIGGER
HEADER JOIST
STUD WALLS
BOTTOM PLATE
SILL PLATE
ANCHOR BOLTS
CORNER POST (USUALLY MADE OF 3 STUDS)

Typical single-story frame house showing wall and roof details. *Courtesy American Plywood Association*

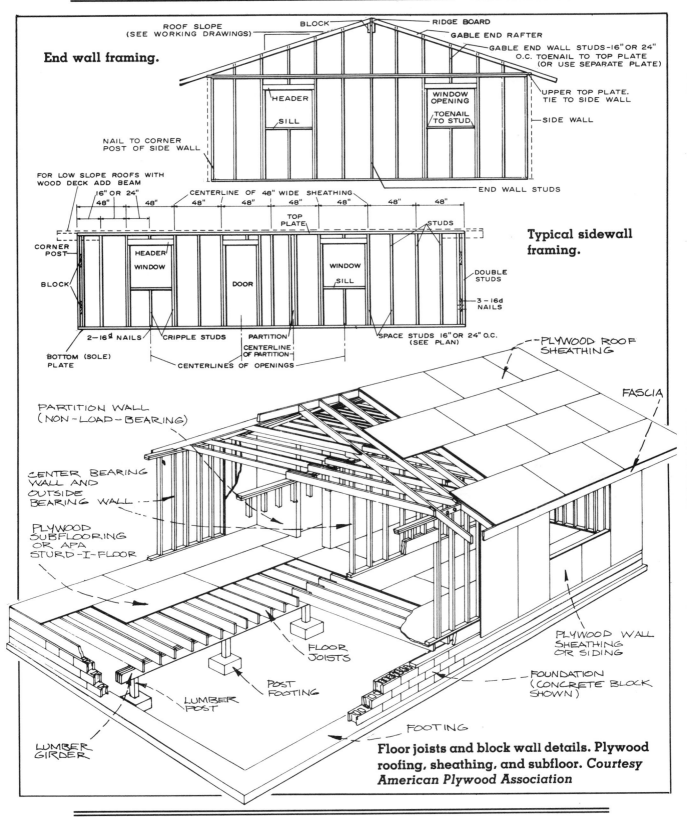

End wall framing.

ROOF SLOPE (SEE WORKING DRAWINGS)
BLOCK
RIDGE BOARD
GABLE END RAFTER
GABLE END WALL STUDS-16" OR 24" O.C. TOENAIL TO TOP PLATE (OR USE SEPARATE PLATE)
HEADER
SILL
WINDOW OPENING
TOENAIL TO STUD
UPPER TOP PLATE. TIE TO SIDE WALL
SIDE WALL
NAIL TO CORNER POST OF SIDE WALL
END WALL STUDS

FOR LOW SLOPE ROOFS WITH WOOD DECK ADD BEAM
16" OR 24"
48"
48"
CENTERLINE OF 48" WIDE SHEATHING
48"
48"
48"
48"
48"
48"
TOP PLATE
STUDS

Typical sidewall framing.

CORNER POST
BLOCK
HEADER WINDOW
DOOR
WINDOW SILL
DOUBLE STUDS
3 – 16d NAILS
2 – 16d NAILS
CRIPPLE STUDS
PARTITION
CENTERLINE OF PARTITION
SPACE STUDS 16" OR 24" O.C. (SEE PLAN)
BOTTOM (SOLE) PLATE
CENTERLINES OF OPENINGS

PARTITION WALL (NON-LOAD-BEARING)
CENTER BEARING WALL AND OUTSIDE BEARING WALL
PLYWOOD SUBFLOORING OR APA STURD-I-FLOOR
PLYWOOD ROOF SHEATHING
FASCIA
FLOOR JOISTS
POST FOOTING
LUMBER POST
LUMBER GIRDER
PLYWOOD WALL SHEATHING OR SIDING
FOUNDATION (CONCRETE BLOCK SHOWN)
FOOTING

Floor joists and block wall details. Plywood roofing, sheathing, and subfloor. *Courtesy American Plywood Association*

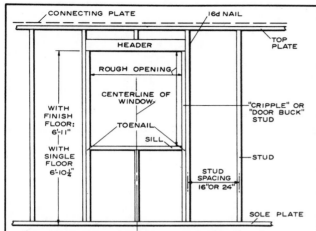

Framing details and rough opening dimensions for double-hung wood windows.

Window glass size (each sash)		Rough frame opening size	
Width *Inches*	Height *Inches*	Width *Inches*	Height *Inches*
24	16	30	42
28	20	34	50
32	24	38	58
36	24	42	58

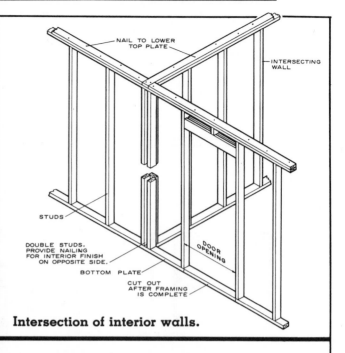

Intersection of interior walls.

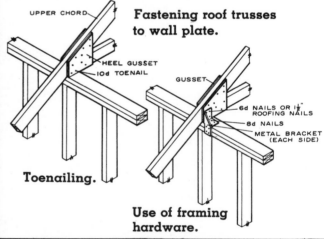

Fastening roof trusses to wall plate.

Toenailing.

Use of framing hardware.

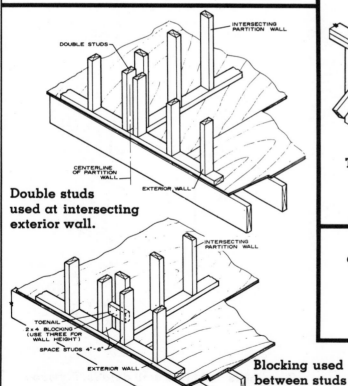

Double studs used at intersecting exterior wall.

Blocking used between studs intersecting exterior wall.

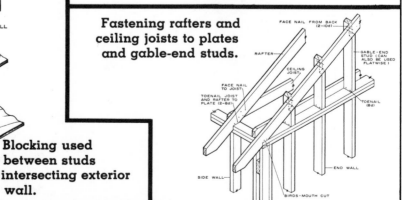

Fastening rafters and ceiling joists to plates and gable-end studs.

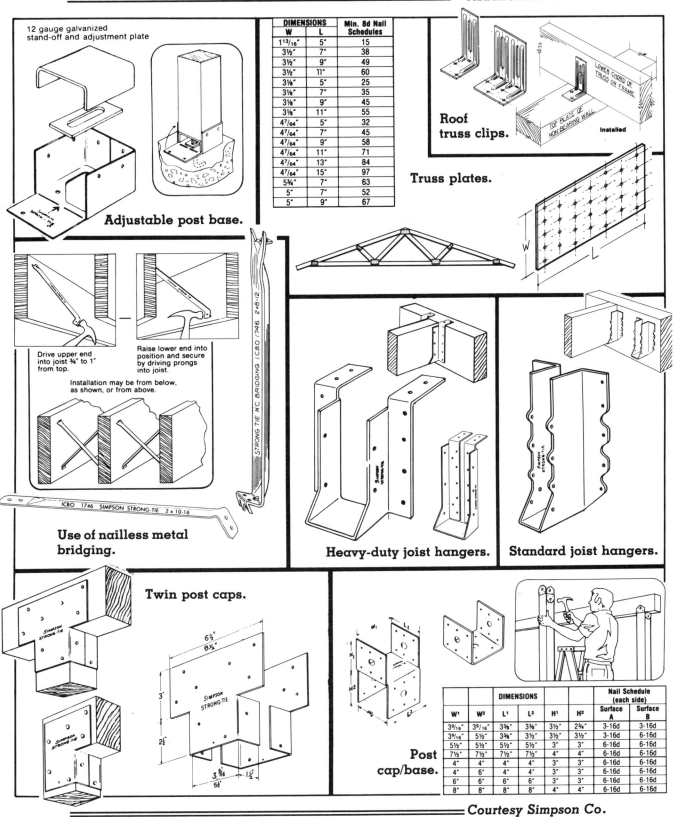

12 gauge galvanized
stand-off and adjustment plate

Adjustable post base.

| DIMENSIONS | | Min. 8d Nail |
W	L	Schedules
1¹³/₁₆″	5″	15
3½″	7″	38
3½″	9″	49
3½″	11″	60
3⅛″	5″	25
3⅛″	7″	35
3⅛″	9″	45
3⅛″	11″	55
4⁷/₆₄″	5″	32
4⁷/₆₄″	7″	45
4⁷/₆₄″	9″	58
4⁷/₆₄″	11″	71
4⁷/₆₄″	13″	84
4⁷/₆₄″	15″	97
5¾″	7″	63
5″	7″	52
5″	9″	67

Roof truss clips.

LOWER CHORD OF TRUSS OR FRAME

TOP PLATE OF NON-BEARING WALL

Installed

Truss plates.

Drive upper end into joist ¾″ to 1″ from top.

Raise lower end into position and secure by driving prongs into joist.

Installation may be from below, as shown, or from above.

STRONG-TIE NC BRIDGING ICBO 1746 2×8-12

ICBO 1746 SIMPSON STRONG-TIE 2×10-16

Use of nailless metal bridging.

Heavy-duty joist hangers.

Standard joist hangers.

Twin post caps.

SIMPSON STRONG-TIE

6⅛″
8⅛″

3″

2½″

3⁹/₁₆″   1½″
5¼″

Post cap/base.

| | | DIMENSIONS | | | | Nail Schedule (each side) | |
W¹	W²	L¹	L²	H¹	H²	Surface A	Surface B
3⁹/₁₆″	3⁹/₁₆″	3⅜″	3⅜″	3½″	2¾″	3-16d	3-16d
3⁹/₁₆″	5½″	3⅜″	3½″	3½″	3½″	3-16d	6-16d
5½″	5½″	5½″	5½″	3″	3″	6-16d	6-16d
7½″	7½″	7½″	7½″	4″	4″	6-16d	6-16d
4″	4″	4″	4″	3″	3″	6-16d	6-16d
4″	6″	4″	4″	3″	3″	6-16d	6-16d
6″	6″	6″	6″	3″	4″	6-16d	6-16d
8″	8″	8″	8″	4″	4″	6-16d	6-16d

Courtesy Simpson Co.

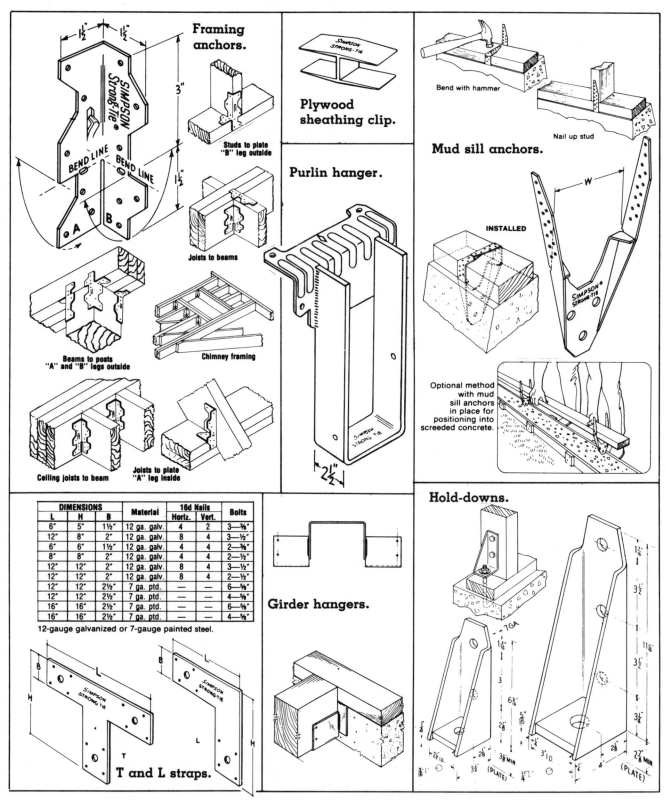

Framing anchors.

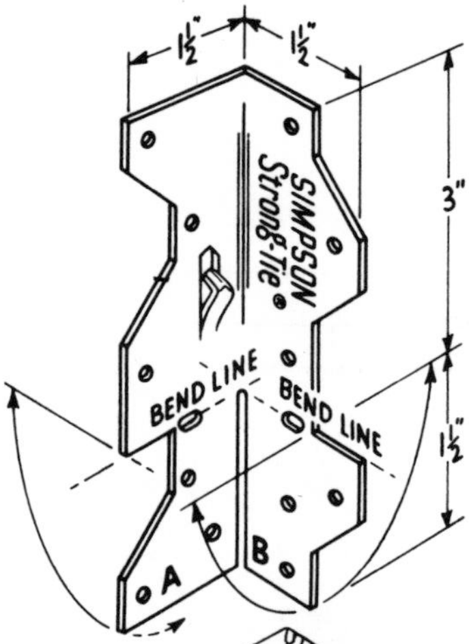
1½"
1½"
SIMPSON
Strong-Tie®
3"
BEND LINE
BEND LINE
1½"
A
B

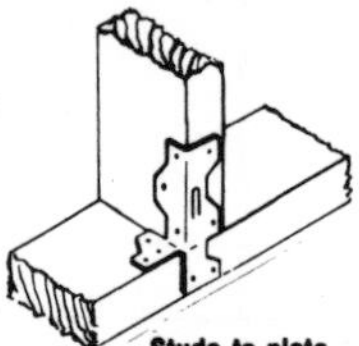

Studs to plate "B" leg outside

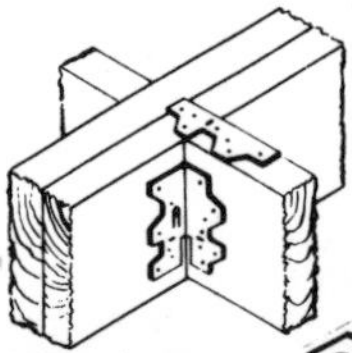

Joists to beams

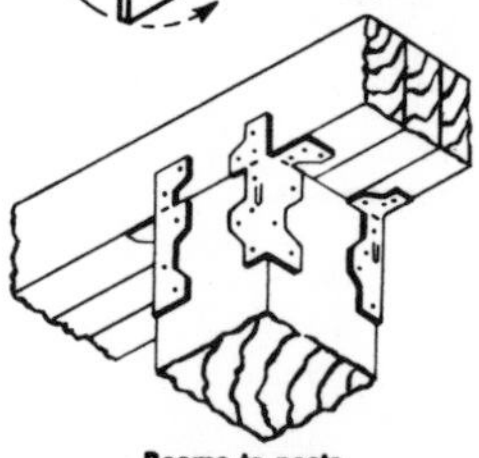

Beams to posts "A" and "B" legs outside

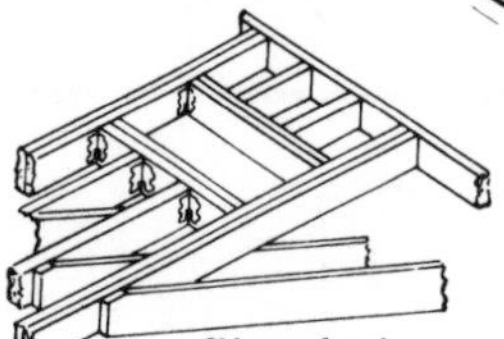

Chimney framing

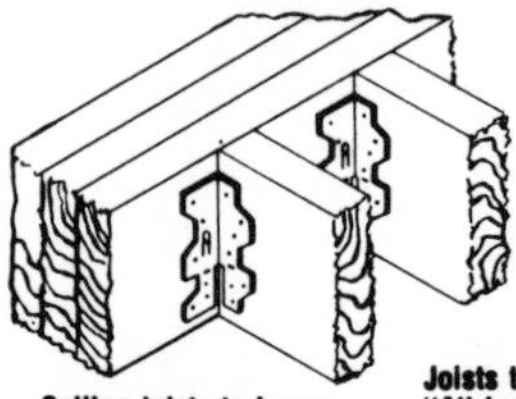

Ceiling joists to beam

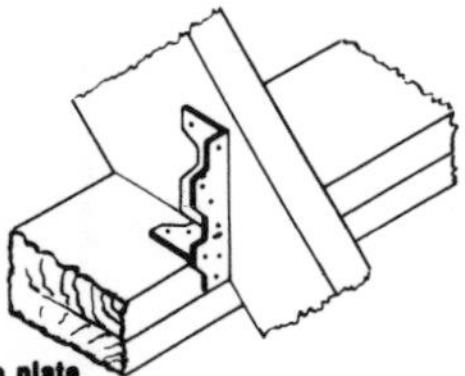

Joists to plate "A" leg inside

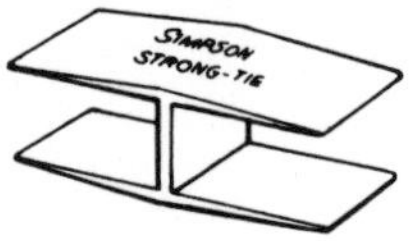
SIMPSON
STRONG-TIE

Plywood sheathing clip.

Purlin hanger.

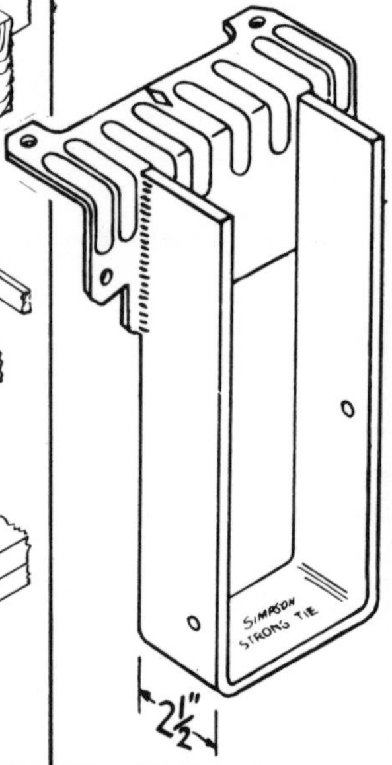
SIMPSON
STRONG-TIE
2½"

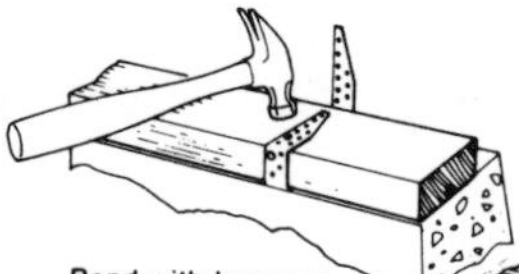

Bend with hammer

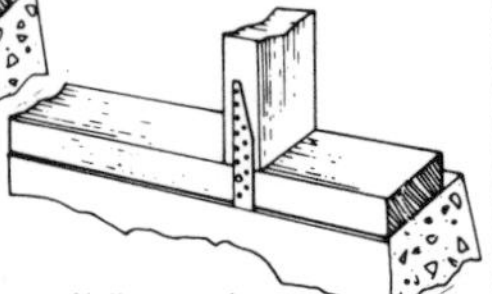

Nail up stud

Mud sill anchors.

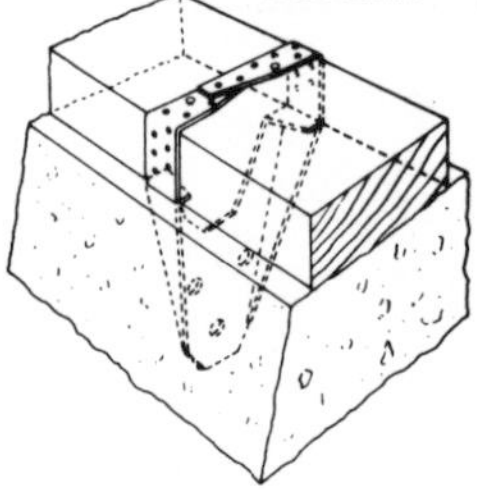
INSTALLED

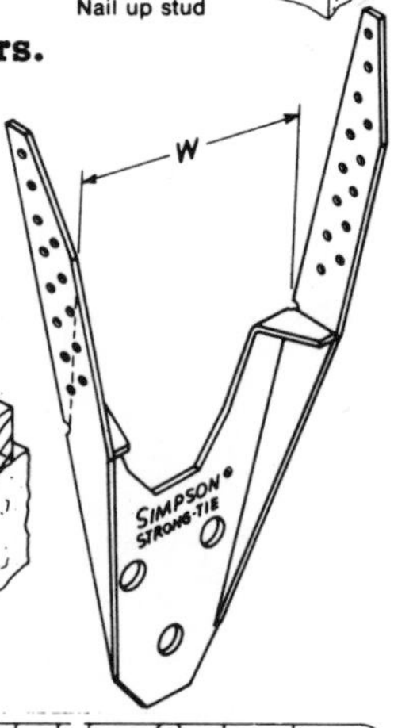
W
SIMPSON®
STRONG-TIE

Optional method with mud sill anchors in place for positioning into screeded concrete.

DIMENSIONS			Material	16d Nails		Bolts
L	H	B		Horiz.	Vert.	
6"	5"	1½"	12 ga. galv.	4	2	3—⅜"
12"	8"	2"	12 ga. galv.	8	4	3—½"
6"	6"	1½"	12 ga. galv.	4	4	2—⅜"
8"	8"	2"	12 ga. galv.	4	4	2—½"
12"	12"	2"	12 ga. galv.	8	4	3—½"
12"	12"	2"	12 ga. galv.	8	4	2—½"
12"	12"	2½"	7 ga. ptd.	—	—	6—⅝"
12"	12"	2½"	7 ga. ptd.	—	—	4—⅝"
16"	16"	2½"	7 ga. ptd.	—	—	6—⅝"
16"	16"	2½"	7 ga. ptd.	—	—	4—⅝"

12-gauge galvanized or 7-gauge painted steel.

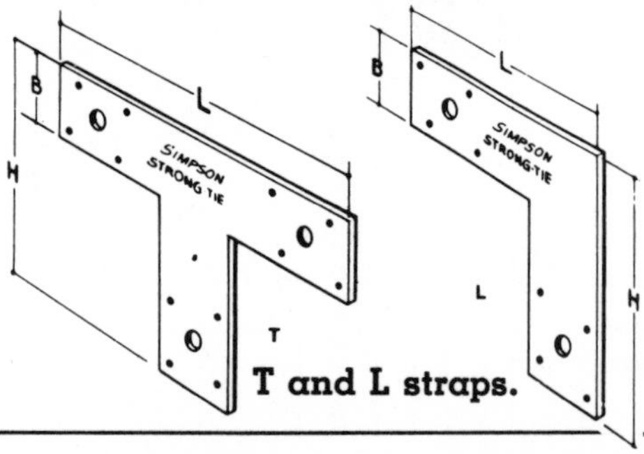
B
L
H
SIMPSON
STRONG TIE
T
B
L
SIMPSON
STRONG-TIE
L
H

T and L straps.

Girder hangers.

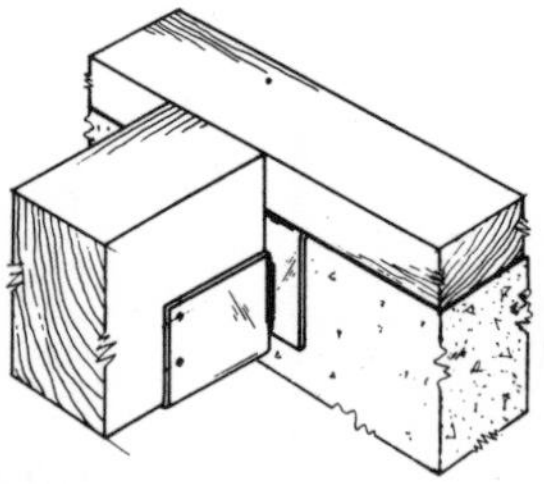

Hold-downs.

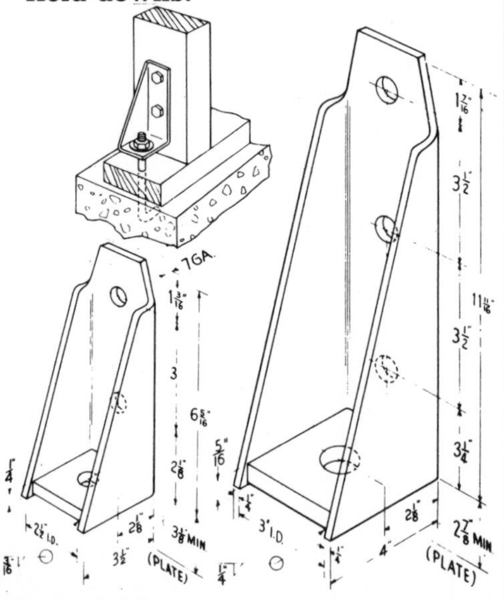
7GA.
(PLATE)
(PLATE)

Courtesy Simpson Co.

GLASS

(ALSO SEE INSULATION, PLASTIC, WINDOWS)

The invention of glass is attributed to the Egyptians. At least four thousand years ago, they used glass for the making of jewelry, and for several centuries glass jewels were more highly prized than nature's own gems. Glass was not used for windows until some time in the thirteenth century. The first glass used for windows were roundels, more or less flat, circular plates of glass made by rapidly spinning a molten glob of glass on a glassblower's pipe. Roundels are still available for use in stained-glass construction.

WINDOW GLASS

Window glass is rated two ways: by quality and by type, which is simply another term for thickness.

QUALITIES

The best is rated AA. This is glass with almost no flaws. People don't "run" and "wave" when you look at them through this glass. Naturally, it costs much more than the lower-quality types, and not too many shops stock this glass, but it can be secured on order.

Second best rates a single A. It is almost free of imperfections. If you sight through it carefully and move your head, you may notice that some lines bend a little, but not much. This is the grade that is chosen for the better-built house.

Third on the list is rated B. This grade always has some minor defects. Hold it above a newpaper and you will see that some of the print is out of line. This is the glass you might select for attic or basement windows.

TYPES

The thinnest type is called picture glass. It is used for picture framing, where there is no special need for strength. Picture glass is approximately 1/16 inch thick.

The next type is called single-strength window glass. It is 3/32 inch thick and is used for most small windows.

Double-strength window glass is approximately twice as thick as single-strength glass; that is to say, it is usually close to ⅛ inch thick. This is the glass to use in doors, in large windows that run 3 × 4 feet, in storm windows and storm doors.

Heavy sheet glass is still thicker and comes in two thicknesses: 3/16 and 7/32 of an inch. This is the glass you might use for any of the aforementioned heavy-duty areas and for things such as coffee-table tops and the like. This is the glass that is used for picture windows when and where you don't want to go to the expense of plate glass.

QUALITIY VS. TYPE

With the exception of the two types of heavy sheet glass, which are available only in A and B qualities, all the other types of glass can be had in AA, A, and B quality.

This means that if you want to glaze a large picture of Aunt Sue, and you want a flawless cover for the picture, you don't need to go to the expense of double-weight glass. You can use the thinnest, lightest weight glass of AA quality.

PURCHASING WINDOW GLASS

Most hardware shops carry a supply of standard glass sizes. If they don't have glass to match your needs, they will cut it for a small fee, but you have to pay for the whole sheet from which it is cut.

MEASURING FOR WINDOW GLASS

First remove the old glass. To avoid cutting yourself it is best to wear gloves. Carefully remove the old putty and glazier's points. The points can be reused. Now measure the empty space, allowing 1/16 inch clearance all around. If the glass does not have to fit into a rabbet (or slot), you don't have to worry about its thickness. If one edge has to slip into a slot, you must use glass thin enough to fit that slot. Now check to make certain the frame is square. If it is not, and many old frames are not, you will have to get glass cut to match, or it won't fit.

INSTALLING THE GLASS

When working with a wood frame, you slip the glass into the frame. Use a few triangular points to hold it fast. Then putty the glass in place. When working with a metal frame, you first lay down a thin layer of putty all around. The glass is then rested within the putty and more putty is added to lock it in place.

PLATE GLASS

Plate glass is polished glass. Whereas window glass is simply cast, plate glass is ground flat. While the surface of plate glass is not as near optical perfection as optical glass (which is true to a fraction of a wavelength), plate glass is more than perfect enough for any of our needs.

Plate glass is also thicker and heavier than window glass. Plate starts at ¼ inch and goes on up through 1 inch and more. Plate glass 1¼ inches thick weighs 16.45 pounds per square foot. Picture glass weighs only 14 ounces per square foot.

Plate glass is the first choice for picture windows, tabletops, and, when tempered, bulletproof automobile windows.

SPECIAL GLASS

The types of glass described in this section are classified as special only because they were originally used in comparatively small quantities. Today, some of these "special" types of glass are used in far larger quantities than common glass. You will find special glass in many glass shops, but rarely in hardware or similar stores. Hardware stores limit their stock to the common glasses in standard sizes.

BENT GLASS

This is double-strength or plate glass that is bent at the factory. Very little bent glass is stocked even by the glass manufacturers; almost all of it is bent to order. Since this is a one-of-a-kind operation involving the building of a form, the cost is considerable. Bear in mind that you need a curved molding to support the bent sheet of glass.

SURFACE-ALTERED GLASS

Glass is routinely chipped, ground, etched, and otherwise altered to make it more attractive and to provide special effects. Surface-altered glass is several times more costly than standard glass when purchased in sizes cut to your specifications. Generally, it is difficult to cut some surface-altered types of glass without a good chance of breakage. Therefore, if you cannot tailor your needs to already available sizes, your costs can go up very rapidly.

COLORED GLASS

This type of glass is made in two forms. One is ordinary flat-surface glass that has been tinted. The most common colors are blue and a kind of pink, both available in a thickness of 13/64 of an inch. The second form is that used by stained-glass artisans. This form or type subdivides into literally hundreds of different colors and surface textures. There are greens, purples, blues, yellows, variegated colors; sandy, wavy, and indented surfaces. It is here that you find the use of roundels and the handmade French and Belgium glass that goes for five and ten dollars a square foot. Look for these glasses in art-supply and craft shops. NOTE: The red colors cost the most.

HEAT-ABSORBING GLASS

This is not an insulating glass but is, rather, glass with the unique optical property of transmitting some 75 percent of the visible light while retarding some 55 percent of the lower frequency, infrared light, or heat. Generally available only in a thickness of ¼ of an inch, this glass has a relatively high coefficient of expansion, which ordinary glass does not. Thus you must provide for some expansion and contraction when installing heat-absorbing glass.

INSULATING GLASS

At the present time there is no such thing as a true insulating glass. The term *insulating glass* refers to a double pane of glass separated by an air space. There are also insulating glass windows made of three panes of glass containing two air spaces. It is the enclosed air that provides the insulation. The air spaces vary from ¼ to ½ an inch. Obviously, the wider the space the greater the insulation. (See INSULATION for data on the R values of insulating glass.)

Insulating glass can be used in place of a standard pane plus a storm window. When considering the change, however, you must not only provide a 1-inch or more rabbet in the window sash, but also make sure that when the new glass is installed there is sufficient clearance for the sash to move.

STRUCTURAL GLASS

You will see more and more of this glass being used to cover the exterior walls of office buildings and even walls and halls in private homes. Structural glass is made in colors, but, unlike ordinary colored glass, structural glass is opaque.

This glass is made in a number of thicknesses; 11/32, 7/16, ¾, ⅞, and 1¼ inches. Some of the glass is cut into "tile" dimensions of 8 × 16 and 16

× 16 inches. It also comes in sheets up to 72 × 130 inches.

Structural glass can be cut, drilled, and its edges polished for use as tabletops, counter tops, and half-walls. Using special plastic cement formulated for the purpose, architectural glass can be installed over any hard, flat, firm surface, except wood. A space of 1/64 of an inch is left between sheets and is later pointed with joint cement. Recommended circumferential clearance is ⅜ of an inch. This space, too, can be pointed.

GLASS BLOCK

Each glass block is made of two halves, cast independently and later fused together, leaving a sealed, dry, dead-air space within the block. One half of the block is designed for ex-terior exposure; the other goes on the inside of the structure.

A glass block wall is strong, rot-, rust-, and weather-resistant, but, un-like stone, in which place it is often used, glass block passes light. As for the passage of heat, ordinary glass block has the insulating value of single-air space insulating glass. Glass block made to exclude heat—for example solar-reflective glass block—rejects 72 percent of the sun's heat that strikes it.

Glass blocks are made in many colors, surfaces, and even in a solid (no interior air space) form called Vis-tabrik. As single units they may be installed within a wood or metal frame. As blocks they are laid up just like bricks using mortar with a little lime. (See BRICKS and MORTAR.)

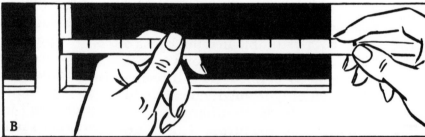

A. The old glass is removed. B. The opening is measured. The new glass is cut 1/16 to 3/16 of an inch smaller to allow for irregularity and expansion. C. The glass is positioned and held in place with a number of glazier's points. D. Putty is applied. E. Use the putty knife to make a smooth, triangular bevel, the mark of a true craftsman. *Courtesy Libbey-Owens-Ford Co.*

Basic steps in replacing a windowpane.

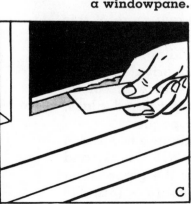
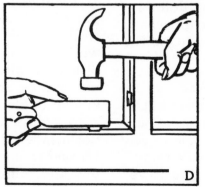
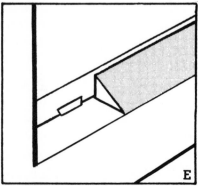

MAXIMUM HEAT GAIN BY TYPE OF GLASS

Glass	Glass Thickness	*Relative Heat Gain BTU/H Square Foot
CLEAR GLASS		
Single-Pane	3/32″ or 1/8″	218
Single-Pane	3/16″	208
Double-Pane Insulating	3/16″	176
Double-Pane Xi Insulating	3/32″ or 1/8″	186
TINTED GLASS		
Grey, Single-Pane	3/16″	165
Bronze, Single-Pane	3/16″	168
Grey, Double-Pane Insulating	3/16″	130
Bronze, Double-Pane Insulating	3/16″	134
MEDIUM PERFORMANCE REFLECTIVE GLASS		
Bronze, Single-Pane	3/16″	106
Bronze, Single-Pane	1/4″	105
Bronze, Double-Pane Insulating	1/8″	92
Bronze, Double-Pane Insulating	3/16″	78
TRIPLE GLAZING Double-pane insulating glass with medium performance bronze reflective triple glazing panel.	3/32″ or 1/8″	81
TRIPLE GLAZING Double-pane insulating glass with clear triple glazing panel	3/32″ or 1/8″	165

HEAT GAIN DATA

In those southern areas of the U.S. where cooling is the major energy cost, glazing may be the most important cost factor in energy-saving considerations. That's because cooling costs are based almost solely on heat gains transmitted through the glass.

A glance at the table shows how your choice of single glass, double-pane insulating glass, environmental glass, triple glazing (double insulating glass with an environmental panel) can greatly influence the amount of window and gliding door heat gain.

*When ASHRAE solar heat gain factor is 200 BTU/HR-Sq. Ft. and the outdoor air temperature is 14° warmer than the indoor temperature.

Courtesy Libbey-Owens-Ford Co.

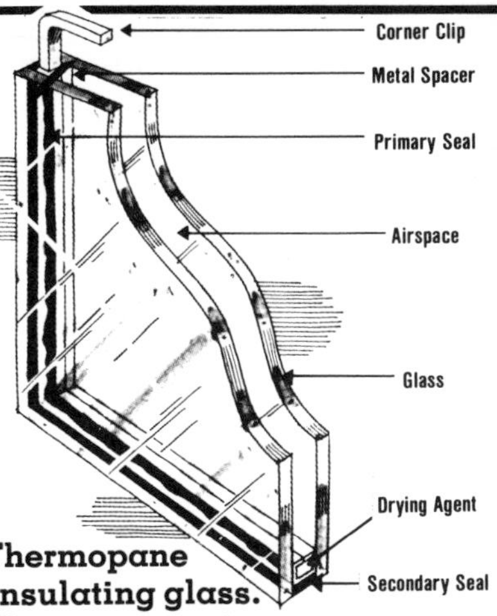

Corner Clip
Metal Spacer
Primary Seal
Airspace
Glass
Drying Agent
Secondary Seal

Thermopane insulating glass. The air space is permanently sealed. *Courtesy Libbey-Owens-Ford Co.*

Maximum sizes in which various types of glass are normally manufactured.

Type of glass	Use or quality	Thickness (in.)	Max. size (in.)
Window glass	Photo	1/16	36 x 50
	Picture	5/64	36 x 50
	Single strength	3/32	40 x 50
	Double strength	1/8	60 x 80
	Sheet	3/16	120 x 84
		7/32	120 x 84
		1/4	120 x 84
		3/8	60 x 84
		7/16	60 x 84
	Greenhouse	1/8	20 x 24
Clear polished plate	Glazing	1/8	76 x 128
		1/4	127 x 226
	Mirrors	1/4	127 x 226
	Commercial	5/16	127 x 226
		3/8	125 x 281
		1/2	125 x 281
		3/4	120 x 280
		1	74 x 148
		1 1/4	74 x 148
Float glass	Glazing, mirrors	1/4	122 x 200

INSULATING GLASS—STANDARD SIZES

METAL EDGE

2 Pieces ¼″ Polished Plate Glass—½″ Air Space

UNIT SIZE		UNIT SIZE		UNIT SIZE	
33″	x 76¾″	46⅛″	x 56½″	56½″	x 58⅛″
35½″	x 36″	47⅞″	x 50⅜″	56½″	x 66″
35½″	x 48⅛″	47⅞″	x 66⅝″	56½″	x 70⅛″
35½″	x 60⅜″	48″	x 48″	57″	x 76¾″
36″	x 44½″	48″	x 60″	58″	x 64½″
36″	x 55¼″	48″	x 72″	58″	x 72½″
36″	x 68¾″	48⅛″	x 55¼″	58″	x 80½″
36″	x 75″	48⅛″	x 68¾″	58″	x 96½″
36″	x 93″	48⅛″	x 75″	58″	x 116½″
42″	x 48½″	48⅛″	x 93″	60″	x 72″
42″	x 56½″	48½″	x 50″	60¼″	x 66⅝″
42″	x 66″	48½″	x 58″	60⅜″	x 68¾″
42″	x 72″	50″	x 56½″	60⅜″	x 75″
44½″	x 48⅛″	50″	x 64½″	60⅜″	x 93″
44½″	x 60⅜″	50″	x 72½″	64½″	x 66″
45″	x 76¾″	50″	x 80½″	66″	x 72½″
45⅛″	x 52″	50″	x 96½″	66″	x 84″
46″	x 48½″	50⅜″	x 60¼″	66″	x 96″
46″	x 64½″	52½″	x 58⅛″	72″	x 84″
46″	x 72½″	52½″	x 70⅛″	72″	x 96″
46⅛″	x 52½″	55¼″	x 60⅜″		

2 Pieces 3/16″ Window Glass—½″ Air Space

35½″	x 36″	48½″	x 42″	64½″	x 46″
35½″	x 48⅛″	48½″	x 46″	64½″	x 50″
35½″	x 60⅜″	48½″	x 50″	64½″	x 58″
42″	x 66″	55¼″	x 36″	68¾″	x 36″
42″	x 72″	55¼″	x 48⅛″	68¾″	x 48⅛″
44½″	x 36″	55¼″	x 60⅜″	72″	x 48″
44½″	x 48⅛″	56½″	x 42″	72½″	x 46″
44½″	x 60⅜″	56½″	x 46⅛″	72½″	x 50″
45⅜″	x 52″	56½″	x 50″	75″	x 36″
48″	x 48″	56½″	x 58⅛″	75″	x 48⅛″
48″	x 60″				

Insulating glass, standard sizes. *Courtesy Pittsburgh Plate Glass Co.*

GLASS EDGE (DS premium)

2 Pieces ⅛″ Window Glass—3/16″ Air Space

Picture window sizes

DOUBLE HUNG WINDOWS W	H	AWNING WINDOWS W	H	CASEMENT WINDOWS W	H
49 3/16″	x 46″	36⅝″	x 49¼″	35 7/16″	x 36 1/16″
49 3/16″	x 50″	39⅝″	x 49¼″	35 7/16″	x 48¼″
49 3/16″	x 58″	44⅝″	x 49¼″	35 7/16″	x 60 7/16″
57 3/16″	x 46″			44 7/16″	x 36 1/16″
57 3/16″	x 50″			44 7/16″	x 48¼″
65 3/16″	x 46″			44 7/16″	x 60 7/16″
65 3/16″	x 50″			55 3/16″	x 36 1/16″
				55 3/16″	x 48¼″
				68 11/16″	x 36 1/16″
				68 11/16″	x 48¼″

GLASS EDGE (SSA)

2 Pieces 3/32″ Window Glass—3/16″ Air Space

W	H	W	H	W	H
16″	x 24″	21 1/16″	x 49″	36″	x 16″
16″	x 32″	21 1/16″	x 61 3/16″	36″	x 20″
16″	x 36″	22″	x 18″	36″	x 24″
16″	x 48″	22″	x 55 9/16″	36⅝″	x 14¼″
16″	x 60″	24″	x 16″	36⅝″	x 18¼″
16 9/16″	x 24⅝″	24″	x 20″	36⅝″	x 22¼″
16 9/16″	x 30 13/16″	24″	x 24″	36⅝″	x 30¼″
16 9/16″	x 36 13/16″	24″	x 32″	39⅝″	x 14¼″
16 9/16″	x 49″	24″	x 36″	39⅝″	x 18¼″
16 9/16″	x 61 3/16″	24″	x 48″	39⅝″	x 22¼″
19″	x 15″	24″	x 60″	39⅝″	x 30¼″
19½″	x 53″	24¼″	x 15¼″	40″	x 16″
20″	x 16″	27¼″	x 14¼″	40″	x 20″
20″	x 20″	27¼″	x 18¼″	40″	x 24″
20″	x 24″	27¼″	x 22¼″	42½″	x 22½″
20″	x 32″	27¼″	x 30¼″	44″	x 16″
20″	x 36″	28″	x 16″	44⅝″	x 14¼″
20″	x 48″	28″	x 20″	44⅝″	x 18¼″
20″	x 60″	28″	x 24″	44⅝″	x 22¼″
21 1/16″	x 24⅝″	32″	x 16″	44⅝″	x 30¼″
21 1/16″	x 30 13/16″	32″	x 20″	45½″	x 25½″
21 1/16″	x 36 13/16″	32″	x 24″		

Glass Thickness	Air Space	Max. Area Sq. Ft.	Dimensional Tolerances	Unit Thickness	Approx. Avg. Net Weights Per Sq. Ft.
⅛″	3/16″	24	± 1/16″	7/16″ ± 1/32″	3¼ lbs.
3/32″	3/16″	10	± 1/16″	⅜″ ± 1/32″	2½ lbs.

18 GYPSUM BOARD

Also known as Sheetrock, plaster-board, and wallboard, gypsum board is made from gypsum, a kind of rock. It is the only material known that can be reduced to powder and returned to its rocklike condition by adding water and letting it dry. Gypsum is the basis of plaster of Paris.

Gypsum board is manufactured by mixing powered gypsum with various chemicals and water to form a paste, which is then sandwiched between two sheets of heavy paper, passed between rollers to form a panel, and then oven-dried.

Gypsum board is rot- and fireproof with a rating of forty-five minutes to three hours, depending on panel thickness and the materials to which it is fastened. As a thermal insulator it is rated at approximately 1.0 R per inch of thickness. It is not normally waterproof. Unless protected, ordinary grades of gypsum board soften as they absorb water.

ADVANTAGES

A single layer of gypsum boards over wood studs (called dry-wall construction) is by far the most widely used residential inner wall. It is the cheapest and most easily applied material available for this purpose. When properly installed it is hardly distinguishable from plaster. In some ways it is more resistant to cracking than plaster, since the paper cover provides the gypsum with a small degree of flexibility; plaster has none

at all. Many architects believe that a double layer of gypsum board is superior to plaster in many ways.

TYPES AND DIMENSIONS

Gypsum board is manufactured with several different kinds of cores, surfaces, sizes, and edge shapes.

TYPES OF CORES

The standard or basic core is rot-proof, vermin-proof, and fireproof gypsum. It will withstand an occasional wetting, but constant exposure to moisture will cause it to disintegrate.

A variation of the basic gypsum core designed for greater fire resistance is mixed with glass fibers, which helps it resist heat.

Sound-deadening cores do just that. But they are not as sound deadening as a layer of cork or similar material. They just transmit far less sound than standard gypsum board.

Waterproof cores contain the usual gypsum plus asphalt waxes. One side is covered with light blue paper designed to accept the adhesive used with tile. Some companies call these boards tile backers.

Black-top or sheathing-core gypsum board contains an asphalt emulsion that makes it resistant to water. Some manufacturers call these boards exterior Sheetrock panels.

SURFACES
Standard gypsum board comes with a

light brown paper covering on one side and a gray covering on the other. The brown (or face) side is designed to accept all types of paint and wallpaper.

There are also boards that come with a layer of aluminum foil attached to one surface (the foil side is always fastened against the studs). The foil acts as a vapor barrier and also provides some degree of reflective insulation.

Still another type is made with a laminated vinyl surface, in any of a dozen colors and surface textures. These boards can withstand scrubbing, and eliminate the need for painting. They have square edges that are butted tightly against one another.

To support either a skim or a full thickness of plaster, gypsum boards are made with either a highly absorptive paper surface or a perforated surface.

DIMENSIONS

Gypsum boards are made in a range of thicknesses that begin at ¼ of an inch and continue up to 1 inch. The most commonly used thickness, ½ inch, weighs 2 pounds per square foot. Thus the common two-sheet package of 4-×-8-foot panels weighs 128 pounds—something to consider when you are thinking about carrying panels in your car.

Panels are made in widths of 2 and 4 feet and in lengths of 6 and 12 feet. The ends of all sheets are cut square across, exposing the core. The sides are shaped.

SIDE SHAPES

The most widely used sheets have tapered edges. The taper permits two adjoining sheets to be joined most readily and invisibly by taping (see below).

Other sheets have beveled edges. These sheets are used to produce a paneled appearance.

Some sheets have tongue-and-groove edges, which makes it possible to lock exterior gypsum panel sheets together.

Still other sheets have square edges. The face material is wrapped around the edge, so when two are butted together, nothing but a line is visible.

AVAILABILITY

NOTE: Not all gypsum boards are manufactured in all sizes with all types of edges and surfaces. What is more important, few yards carry more than ⅜-, ½-, and ⅝-inch panels 4 × 8 feet in size.

APPLICATION

If you are installing gypsum board as a fire barrier, check with the local building department. Most require ⅝-inch panels. If you are covering an interior wall, opt for the ½-inch panels. They go up more easily, tend to correct minor wall variations, and are more easily taped because of the more deeply tapered sides.

PANEL PLACEMENT

If at all possible, run the gypsum board panels across the ceiling joists, using as many uncut panels as possible. Every cut means a tape joint. If wall height permits you to run the panels horizontally without ending up with a narrow strip and three horizontal joints, run them this way. Remember the ceiling goes up first, and there is no need for Sheetrock behind the floor trim.

CUTTING

Use a steel straightedge as a guide and cut with a razor knife. Cut through the face paper and bend the panel away from the cut. It will snap apart. Cut the gray back paper. To make a hole, cut through the paper on both sides of the panel and gently tap out the circumscribed area.

APPLYING THE PANELS

Do the ceiling first (almost impossible to install without help). Measure and cut the panel as necessary and lift into position. Nail one end, then the middle, and then the other end. Use annular ring nails only. Place them about 1 inch in from the panel edge, one nail every 9 inches. Drive the nails so as to dimple the paper. *Do not mash the board.*

Do the walls next. Let the top sheet touch the underside of the ceiling sheets. One nail every foot is sufficient.

TAPING

Taping is something of an art. If you have never done it before practice on an out-of-sight area, or set up some practice joints before you attempt to tape the visible areas.

TOOLS, EQUIPMENT, AND MATERIALS

You will need a 3-inch-wide scraper and a 7-inch scraper, plus an aluminum hawk. If you are over six feet six, you are all set. If not, rent a pair of stilts (no kidding), or set up a couple of planks on low sawhorses. You cannot do a ceiling from a ladder without a lot of pain.

Use either premixed taping compound or mix your own. In the latter case you must mix very thoroughly. To keep the compound from drying out overnight, cover it with a thin layer of water. Do not reuse any compound that falls to the floor. Pick up all droppings—the compound will bleach or stain whatever it rests on. Use tapered-edge tape with the crease mark down its middle. Do not use perforated tape.

Keep your tools clean by constantly running the scraper across the hawk's edge. Discard the semihardened compound you remove.

JOIN THE BEVELED EDGES FIRST

With the narrow scraper, apply a layer of compound ⅛ inch thick and 3 inches wide in the center of the valley formed by the adjoining beveled edges. Spread the compound the full length of the valley joint. Place the end of the tape on the compound, starting 1 inch short of the end of the valley. Unroll the tape and cut it off 1 inch short of the other end of the valley. With your scraper, gently center the tape down the length of the valley and press it firmly and smoothly into the compound. Do not press so hard that the tape curls up.

INSIDE CORNERS NEXT

These include the joints between the walls and the ceiling. Unroll 8 feet of tape and cut it off. Carefully fold it down the center line. Go to an inside corner. Beginning at the top, apply a thin, wedge-shaped band of compound down the length of one side of the joint. Now gently press the folded tape into the corner, and press one half of the tape against the compound. Run the scraper down the surface of the tape, feathering the edge, and removing the excess compound. Do the same at the ceiling, but start 1 inch short of the corners. Now go back and do the other half of the joint.

END JOINTS NEXT

Lay down a very thin, 2- to 3-inch-wide band of compound over the length of the joint. Press a strip of tape gently into the compound. Next, run your scraper gently down the length of the tape. You want to force the tape to lie flat and smooth atop end joints and to leave no excess compound on top of the tape. Make certain the tape's ends are short of all other joints by an inch or so. Now give the compound in the joints sufficient time to dry completely.

REPEAT PERFORMANCE

Twelve or more hours have passed and all the joints are perfectly dry. Go to the valley joints and spread a 4-inch-wide band of compound down the length of the joint. Run the 4-inch or wider scraper down the length of the joint, using the valley sides as your guide. Do not make the compound more than ⅛ inch thick at any point. Later, when this joint has hardened, you will go over it a third time, laying down a very thin layer of compound and finishing it off with an 8-inch-wide scraper.

Return to the corners. Cover one side of the corner with a 2-inch-wide band of compound; go over the band with your 4-inch scraper, feathering the joint edge that is away from the corner. Let this compound dry before you do the other side of the joint the same way.

Return to the end joint. Apply a 2-inch-wide band of compound to one half of the tape. Let the compound go as much as 1/64 of an inch over the center of the tape. Feather the other edge of the compound. When this strip or band has dried, repeat the operation on the other side of the tape. In a sense you are constructing a very gentle hill over the tape. Again, let the compound dry hard. Repeat the same operation, one side of the tape (which is now hidden) at a time. But this time feather the compound as far out as you can, using the 8-inch scraper.

OUTSIDE CORNERS

Cut a length of aluminum corner molding. Using a few nails, fasten it over the corner with its bottom edge ½ inch above the top of the floor trim to be installed and the same distance clear of the ceiling. Using the bead on the molding as a guide, apply a thin band of compound down both sides. Let it dry hard, then follow with a second band down both sides.

NAILHEADS

Apply a daub of compound to each indented nailhead. Run the scraper over the surface of the panel making the daub flush with the surface of the panel. Since compound shrinks when it dries, you will have to go over each nailhead at least three times to hide it completely.

INTERSECTIONS

These are formed where one tape joint meets another, usually at a right angle. They are the hardest to tape. You have to bring your scraper around in successive curves so as to meld one surface into another. If there are any lumps and bumps when you have finished and the compound is bone hard, you can sandpaper them down.

Types of edges available.

TAPERED EDGE:

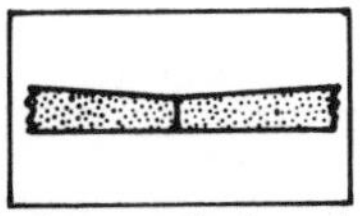

The tapered edge was originally called the "recessed edge." This taper allows space for tape and joint treatment to be applied and the completed job will be flat, smooth, and monolithic. Width of taper is about 2″.

SQUARE EDGE:

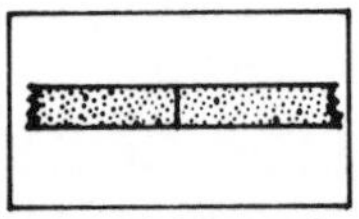

The gypsum board square edge was the original wallboard edge. Initially designed to be a base with a final covering such as wallpaper, paneling, or tile, square edge can be finished with joint compounds to form a clean monolithic wall suitable for paint. Also can be used where an exposed joint is desired for a panelled effect.

TAPERED w/ROUND EDGE:

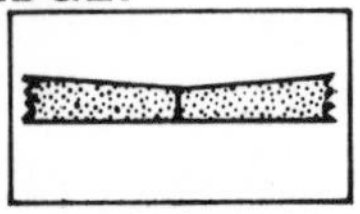

G-P round edge (RE) gypsum board can be used for wall and ceilings in both new construction and remodeling. It is designed to reduce the beading and ridging problems commonly associated with standard type gypsum board. The edge formation provides a stronger, more rigid joint and reduces joint beading or ridging.

BEVELED EDGE:

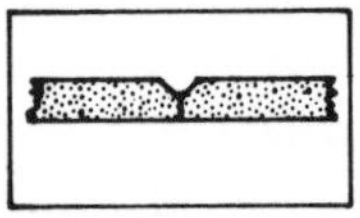

The beveled edge is a suitable edge to give a paneled effect. After fasteners are covered with joint compound the board is ready for paint with grooves exposed.

"T & G" EDGE:

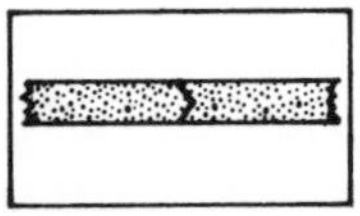

G-P's "tongue and groove" edge is used on 2″wide sheathing and backer boards. (available only in certain areas)

MODIFIED BEVELED EDGE:

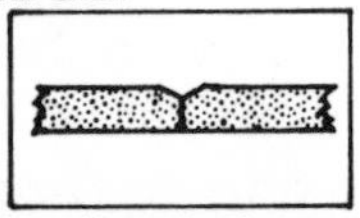

The modified beveled edge is available only on Eternawall™ panels. This particular edge more readily accommodates the vinyl surface decoration, which is delivered completely edge wrapped. The vinyl surface material is available in 15 standard patterns and colors and 15 new colors and textures.

GYPSUM BOARD NAILS & SCREWS SELECTOR GUIDE

	Description	Applications
	1¼″ GWB-54 Annular Ring Nail 12½ ga.; with a slight taper to a small fillet at shank. Bright finish; med. diamond point.	½″, ⅜″ and ¼″ Gypsum board, ½″ and ⅜″ Gypsum Backer Board to wood frame
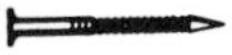	1⅜″ Annular Ring Nail (Same as GWB-54 except for length)	⅝″ Gypsum board to wood frame
	2½″ 7d nail 13 ga., ¼″ diamond head	⅝″ Firestop® Gypsum board face layers over ½″ Sound Deadening Board or 2 layers ⅝″ Firestop to Wood Studs
	1⅞″ 6d Nail 13 ga., ¼″ diamond head	⅜″ and ¼″ Gypsum board over existing surface, wood frame
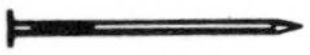	1⅞″ 6d Nail 13 ga., ¼″ diamond head	⅝″ Firestop Gypsum board to wood frame
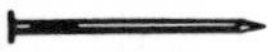	1⅝″ 5d Nail 13½″ ga., 15/64″ diamond head	½″ Firestop Gypsum board to wood frame
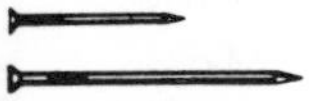	1⅛″ Matching Color Head Nail (Steel) 1⅞″ Matching Color Head Nail (Steel)	Predecorated Gypsum board to wood frame over existing surface, wood frame
	1⅜″ Matching Color Head Nail (Brass)	Predecorated Gypsum board (colors) to wood frame
Gypsum board to Metal Framing 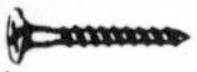	1″ Gypsum board Screw Type S	Single Layer Gypsum board to 25 Gauge Steel Studs. Gypsum board to Resilient Channel. Gypsum board to Metal Furring.
	1¼″ Gypsum board Screw Type S 1⅜″ Gypsum board Screw Type S	1″ core units to L Runner in 2″ Solid and Semi-Solid Partition Systems
	1⅝″ Gypsum board Screw Type S	Double-Layer Gypsum board to 25 gauge Steel Studs. Double-Layer Gypsum board to Metal Furring.
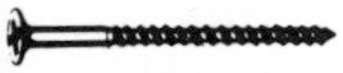	1⅞″ Gypsum board Screw Type S	Double-Layer Gypsum board
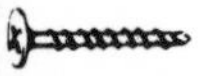	1″ Gypsum board Screw Type S-12 Also available in ¾″, 1⅛″ and 1 5/16″ lengths	For single or multi-layer application of Gypsum board to heavy gauge steel (up to 12 gauge).
Gypsum board to Wood Framing 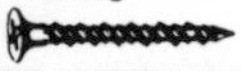	1¼″ Gypsum board Screw Type W	Single Layer Gypsum board to Wood Framing.
Gypsum board to Gypsum Ribs 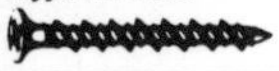	1½″ Gypsum board Screw Type G 1⅝″ Gypsum board Screw Type G	Gypsum board to Gypsum Ribs in Semi-Solid Partition Systems.
Wood Trim to Metal Framing 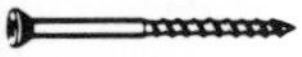	1⅝″ Gypsum board Screw Type S Trim Head 2¼″ Gypsum board Screw Type S Trim Head	Wood trim over single layer of Gypsum board on 25 gauge Steel Studs. Wood trim over double layer Gypsum board on 25 gauge Steel Studs.
Metal Studs to Door Frames and Runners 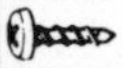	⅜″ Gypsum board Screw S-12 Pan-Head	Metal Door frame to 12 gauge (max.) Steel Studs. Metal Studs to Metal Runners.
Metal Trim & Door Hinges to Metal Framing 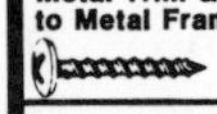	⅞″ Type S-18 Oval Head Also avalable in ¾″, 1⅛″ & 1 5/16″ lengths	Door hinges to door frame and aluminum components to metal.
Gypsum Sheathing 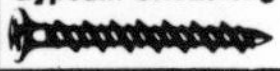	11 gauge, ⅜″ head, 1½″ long	

Horizontal and Vertical Application: TYPE S—Metal studs or furring spaced 24″ on center. Screws should be spaced 12″ on center unless otherwise noted in the detailed assemblies shown in Georgia-Pacific literature.

TYPE G—Laminated systems and other gypsum to gypsum applications.

TYPE W—Wood studs 16″ or 24″ on center. Screws should be spaced 12″ on center unless otherwise noted in the detailed assemblies shown in G-P literature.

Selection of the proper nail for each application is extremely important, particularly for fire-rated construction. The nails recommended comply with performance standards adopted by the Gypsum Association.

Courtesy Georgia-Pacific Corp.

Product	Thickness	Width	Length	ASTM & CSA Standards	USDA Federal Specification
G-P REGULAR GYPSUM BOARD Tapered Edge	¼″	4′	6′ to 12′	C 36 ■ CSA A82.27	SS-L-30d Type III—Grade R
Square, Tapered or Round Edge	⅜″	4′	6′ to 16′		
	½″	4′	6′ to 16′		
	⅝″	4′	6′ to 16′		
G-P FOIL BACK GYPSUM BOARD Square, Tapered Edge or Round Edge	⅜″	4′	6′ to 16′	C 36 ■ CSA A82.27	SS-L-30d Type III—Grade R
	½″	4′	6′ to 16′		
	⅝″	4′	6′ to 16′		
***ETERNAWALL*™ GYPSUM BOARD** Modified Beveled Edge	½″	4′	8′ Std.†	C 36 ■ CSA A82.27	SS-L-30d Type III—Grade R or Grade X Class III
	⅝″	4′	8′ Std.†		
***FIRESTOP*® GYPSUM BOARD** Square, Tapered Edge or Round Edge	½″	4′	6′ to 16′	C 36 ■ CSA A82.27	SS-L-30d Type III—Grade X
	⅝″	4′	6′ to 16′		
***FIRESTOP*® FOIL BACK GYPSUM BOARD** Square, Tapered Edge or Round Edge	½″	4′	6′ to 16′	C 36 ■ CSA A82.27	SS-L-30d Type III—Grade X
	⅝″	4′	6′ to 16′		
G-P TILE BACKER BOARD Tapered Edge	½″ ⅝″	4′ 4′	8′, 11′ and 12′	C 630 ■ CSA A82.27	SS-L-30d Type VII Grade R, X, W
G-P GYPSUM SOUND DEADENING BOARD Square Edge	¼″	4′	8′ Std.†	C 442 ■ CSA A82.35	SS-L-30d Type IV—Grade R
G-P BACKER BOARD Square or T & G Edge	⅜″	4′	8′ Std.†	C 442 ■ CSA A82.35	SS-L-30d Type IV Grade R Grade X
	½″	2′	8′ Std.†		
	⅝″	2′	8′ Std.†		
GYPSUM SHEATHING Long-Edges—Square Edge Core-treated or non core-treated	½″ (or ⅝″ Firestop gypsum board)	4′	8′ & 9′	C 79 ■ CSA A82.27	SS-L-30d Type II Grade R&W (½″) or Grade X&W (⅝″)
Square or Tongue and Groove Core-treated or non core-treated (available in certain areas only)	½″ (or ⅝″ Firestop gypsum board)	2′	8′ Std.†	C 79 ■ CSA A82.27	
***DENS-COTE*® PLASTER BASE**	½″ ⅝″	4′	6′ to 12′	C 588 ■ CSA A82.27	SS-L-30d Type VI Grade R
***FIRESTOP*® *DENS-COTE*® PLASTER BASE**	⅝″	4′	6′ to 12′	C 588 ■ CSA A82.27	SS-L-30d Type VI Grade X
***DENS-COTE*® PLASTER**				C 587	SS-P-00402b Type VI

Brand	Product	ASTM* Standards	Federal Spec.
G-P	JOINT SYSTEM MATERIALS	C 475	SS-J-570a 10/24/66
G-P	*METRO-MIX*™	C 317	—

†Standard Length—Other Lengths on Order.
*All ASTM Standards—Per Latest Revision.
■All Canadian Standards in Blue

Popular types of gypsum boards and their dimensions. *Courtesy Georgia-Pacific Corp.*

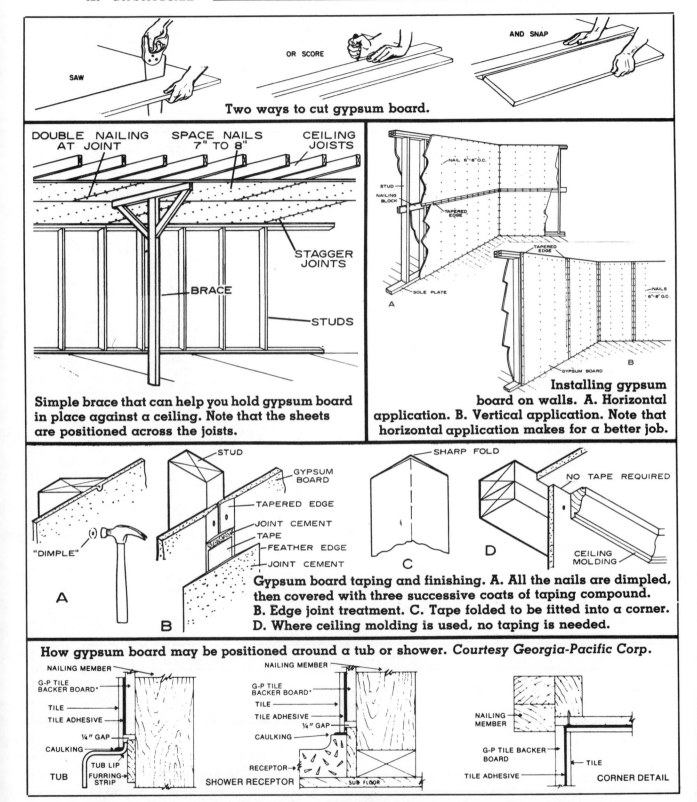

Two ways to cut gypsum board.

DOUBLE NAILING AT JOINT   SPACE NAILS 7" TO 8"   CEILING JOISTS

STAGGER JOINTS

BRACE

STUDS

Simple brace that can help you hold gypsum board in place against a ceiling. Note that the sheets are positioned across the joists.

NAIL 6"-8" O.C.

STUD NAILING BLOCK

TAPERED EDGE

TAPERED EDGE

SOLE PLATE

NAILS 6"-8" O.C.

A

B

GYPSUM BOARD

Installing gypsum board on walls. A. Horizontal application. B. Vertical application. Note that horizontal application makes for a better job.

STUD

GYPSUM BOARD

TAPERED EDGE

JOINT CEMENT

TAPE

FEATHER EDGE

JOINT CEMENT

"DIMPLE"

A

B

SHARP FOLD

C

D

NO TAPE REQUIRED

CEILING MOLDING

Gypsum board taping and finishing. A. All the nails are dimpled, then covered with three successive coats of taping compound. B. Edge joint treatment. C. Tape folded to be fitted into a corner. D. Where ceiling molding is used, no taping is needed.

How gypsum board may be positioned around a tub or shower. *Courtesy Georgia-Pacific Corp.*

NAILING MEMBER

G-P TILE BACKER BOARD*

TILE

TILE ADHESIVE

¼" GAP

CAULKING

TUB LIP

FURRING STRIP

TUB

NAILING MEMBER

G-P TILE BACKER BOARD*

TILE

TILE ADHESIVE

¼" GAP

CAULKING

RECEPTOR

SHOWER RECEPTOR

SUB FLOOR

NAILING MEMBER

G-P TILE BACKER BOARD

TILE

TILE ADHESIVE

CORNER DETAIL

19 HARDBOARD

Hardboard is made from wood. The wood is separated into tiny fibers that are then formed into a board and permanently bonded together in a hot-press, which forces the lignin—the original wood-cell material—to act as a glue. Some hardboard is made with the addition of a chemical binder that acts to make the hardboard harder and more water-resistant.

GRADES

Hardboard is made in a number of grades that denote the hardness of the board and its resistance to water. The major grade or class divisions are, in ascending order of hardness, service, service-tempered, standard, and tempered. All manufacturers do not grade their products in exactly the same way, however, and most lumberyards stock no more than two grades, which they classify as standard and tempered. Visually, the only difference between the two is color. The standard is a light brown, the tempered a darker brown. One surface of all grades or classes of hardboard is always smooth. The other is almost always matted. Hardboard with two sides smooth is also available.

BASIC CHARACTERISTICS

Hardboard can be cut with a saw just like wood. It can be fastened in place with nails, screws, or adhesives. In many ways it is easier to work with

than wood because it has no grain. It will not split. But hardboard will not take nails the way wood will. You can drive a nail into hardboard without problem, but unless the nail penetrates the hardboard and enters wood, the nail will not hold—you can pull it out with your hand. Screws also do not hold well in hardboard. If you must use screws, use sheet metal screws—they hold best.

Since it has no grain, you can cut hardboard in various patterns without breaking off any pieces. Hardboard bends more easily and evenly than wood. To make a really sharp bend in hardboard, first soak it in water overnight.

Standard or soft hardboard should never be used outdoors. Preferably it should never be used indoors where there is or might be moisture—for example, on a basement wall. Hardboard does not absorb water as readily as does fiberboard, but it does absorb it readily enough. Placed near a cellar wall, the hardboard will buckle as it grows moist on one side. However, you can use tempered hardboard in damp areas and outdoors. Should you do so, provide a moisture barrier, which can be either a polyethylene sheet between the hardboard and the concrete or several layers of paint on the rear of the hardboard. The edges of the hardboard—all types—should be sealed with paint or varnish when the board is to be exposed to moisture.

Hardboard offers somewhat less thermal insulation than an equal thickness of wood. To some degree it burns like wood and it takes all kinds of paints and varnishes just as well as wood. But hardboard is not as strong as wood. Whereas a ¼-inch-thick strip of wood will remain flat when suspended at its ends, a hardboard panel will sag. Hardboard is considerably less expensive, however, than ordinary wood or even plywood.

TYPES AND DIMENSIONS

COMMON PANELS

The panels most often stocked by local yards are 4 × 8 feet, ⅛ and ¼ inch thick, one side smooth and one side matted. If only one grade is stocked it will usually be standard. A second grade will usually be tempered. Other thicknesses manufactured include 1/10, 3/16, and 5/16 of an inch. Generally, these are available only on special order.

PEGBOARD

This is a hardboard panel with a pattern of evenly spaced holes. It may be used as an ordinary panel on a wall or ceiling. The holes provide a visual change from the solid smooth surface offered by a standard wall panel. Sometimes pegboard is installed because the holes reduce the percentage of sound that would normally be reflected; to a small degree pegboard is a sound-absorbent surface.

Pegboard panels come in thicknesses of ⅛ and ¼ of an inch and in standard and tempered grades. If you are going to use the pegboard to hang hooks (or fixtures) bear in mind that you need 3/16-inch clearance behind the board to insert and re-move the hooks, and that you must use ⅛-inch hooks with ⅛-inch pegboard and ¼-inch hooks with ¼-inch pegboard.

PLANKS

Hardboard planks are 16 inches wide and 8 feet long. They are tongued and grooved and may be positioned horizontally or vertically. The planks come in standard and tempered grades and in thicknesses of ¼ and 5/16 of an inch.

UNDERLAY

This is hardboard made to be used as a base. It may be nailed or glued to an existing wood floor or a subfloor. Its purpose is to provide a smooth support for linoleum, tile, or carpeting. It is made in 4- × -4-foot squares and 4- × -3-foot rectangles, ¾-inch thick.

TILE PANELS

These are panels with V-shaped grooves that divide the panels into 4-inch squares and give the appearance of ceramic tiles. Tile panels have an exceptionally hard and moisture-resistant finish. These panels are designed to be used as an alternative to ceramic tile in kitchens and bathrooms. They are made in 4-foot widths and in lengths ranging from 3 to 16 feet. It comes in one thickness only—⅛ of an inch.

SIDING

Hardboard siding is available in a wide range of colors, finishes, and in two thicknesses—¼ and 5/16 of an inch. It is more easily and quickly applied than is conventional wood siding. This is due to the size of the hardboard siding. Widths range from 12 to 24 inches and lengths range from 8 to 12 feet. The siding is designed for either horizontal or vertical application.

PREFINISHED PANELS

These are mostly 4- × -8-feet- × -¼-inch panels that are harder than standard grade panels and possibly as hard as tempered panels. The choice of colors, surface textures, and finishes is almost endless. Almost all the natural woods have been duplicated, along with various wood widths. In addition, panels are made with surfaces that duplicate brick, stone, and stucco. Finishes are so durable that some of the manufacturers guarantee their product for the lifetime of the building (with certain limitations).

APPLICATION

As stated, like wood, hardboard can be drilled and sawn as well as glued or nailed in place. The hardboard itself, however, will not hold nails. Should you want to install a shelf or affix something to a hardboard panel, first you must provide a wood support behind the panel at the point where you wish to drive the nails. Hardboard will, to some extent, hold sheet metal screws, at least firmly enough to hang a picture.

STABILIZATION

Take the hardboard panels into the room they will enhance several days prior to application. Separate them and let them rest on their long edges. This will allow them to adjust to the moisture and temperature conditions of the room and will reduce the chance of buckling later.

MOISTURE PROTECTION

Always install a continuous vapor barrier of polyethylene or similar material between the panels and any wall (such as a basement wall) that may become moist at some time. If a single sheet of plastic will not cover it, let the edges of a second sheet overlap the first by a foot or more.

Panels made for bathrooms, kitchens, and the like must have their edges sealed. This is best done with waterproof caulking and metal moldings made for that purpose. The companies that make bathroom hardboard also make or supply the moldings and caulking.

NAILING

Use matching-color nails, also furnished by the maker of the panels, 1 inch long for boards up to ¼-inch thick and 1¼-inch-long nails for thicker hardboards. Keep your nails at least ⅜ of an inch in from the edges of the panels. Space them 4 inches apart around the perimeter and 8 inches apart elsewhere. If, for some reason, you have to drive nails very close to one another, drill clearance holes for those nails. Keep the nails out of whatever grooves may be present in the panels.

CLEARANCES

The tops and bottoms of the panels should clear both the ceiling and the floor by ¼ of an inch. The edge of one panel should not touch the edge of an adjoining panel. They should be clear of each other by a hairbreadth.

SUPPORT

The panels can be fastened directly to wall studs spaced 16 inches apart on centers or to furring strips spaced an equal distance apart. Nailing supports must be provided for the tops and bottoms of the panels and for any mid-panel joints that may be necessary.

GLUING

Lay down a ⅛-inch-thick layer of neoprene adhesive in the center of every support surface. Use shims to lift your panel the required ¼ inch, hold it vertically against the wall, and then, with a few nails, fasten its top edge in position. Press the panel against the adhesive. Pull it free and re-press it into position after two minutes. Reapply pressure after another twenty minutes. Remove the nails.

Hardwood panel application procedure using an adhesive. A. Measure the length, width, and height of the wall areas to be paneled, then draw an outline plan showing overall dimensions. Include measurements and locations of windows, doors, stairways, pipes, ducts, and beams. Then take the plan to your local home center or lumber dealer.

He'll help you determine the number of panels and other materials you'll need. Most paneling comes in 4 × 8 sheets. B. Paneling can be installed over masonry, plaster, or dry wall. Where paneling is to be installed over masonry or concrete, as in the typical basement, first apply a vapor barrier of foil or plastic over the walls. Then, using concrete nails, install 1 × 2 furring

strips horizontally at top and bottom of wall and vertically along the wall on 16-inch centers. (For additional stability, you may want to add horizontal furring strips between the vertical strips.) Place extra furring on each side and under all window openings. (If you have to build a wall to section off a portion of your room, use 2 × 4 construction. If you're paneling over an existing smooth plas-

ter or dry-wall surface, mount the panels directly to the wall.) C. After the first nail is driven into a furring strip, use a level to check plumb. Shim if necessary with a strip of wood or piece of cedar shingle. Then complete nailing the furring strips into place. D. Unwrap panels after delivery and stand them on the long edge, in the area to be paneled. Let them

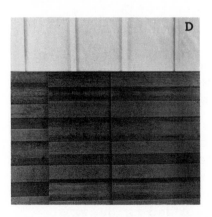

stand for at least forty-eight hours before installation so that the panels can adjust to room temperature and humidity. E. Match grain and color before installation by standing the panels around the walls. This will show the most pleasing pattern for the room.

F. When cutting panels with a circular saw, cut from the *back side* of the panel. If using a handsaw, mark and saw on the

surface side. This will ensure that the rough edge of the cut is on the back side of the panel. When cutting for height, *deduct ½ inch* from your wall height measurement. The installed panel should be ¼ of an inch above the floor and a ¼ of an inch below the ceiling. G. To cut openings for electrical outlets, use as a pattern a junction box that

matches the one in the wall. Drill holes in each corner of the pattern, keeping the holes *inside* your drawn pattern to avoid overcutting. Then cut out the opening with a vertical saw or keyhole saw. H. Panels can be mounted with nails or panel adhesive. For nail installation, set the panel in place ¼ of an inch below the ceiling and tack with one nail

to hold in place while checking plumb. I. Place level on the edge of the panel to check true plumb. *This is important* because the first panel establishes vertical alignment for all panels to follow. J. Using color-coordinated nails, tack

the panel at the top corner to hold in place, then place nails *4 inches apart* along the panel edges. K. Nails on intermediate studs should be *8 inches apart*.

L. For adhesive installation,

first clean all studs with a wire brush to assure a good adhesive bond. Trim the applicator end of your adhesive cartridge to lay a ⅛-of-an-inch bead. Apply a *continuous* strip of adhesive at panel joints and to top and bottom panel edges.

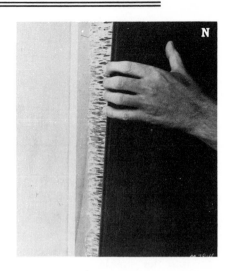

Place 3-inch beads of adhesive 6 inches apart on the studs. Do not skimp — beads must be *at least* 3 inches long. M. Set panel into place (¼ of an inch from ceiling) and tack at the top with one nail to hold the panel in place. Check the plumb and adjust as necessary. Then press the panel into

place with a firm, uniform pressure. This will spread the adhesive bead evenly between studs and panel. N. Grasp the bottom of the panel at the edges and slowly pull the panel out and away from the studs. *After two minutes, repress the panel at all stud points. After 20 minutes, re-*

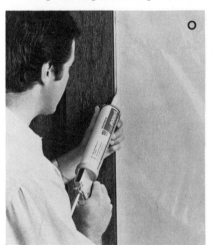

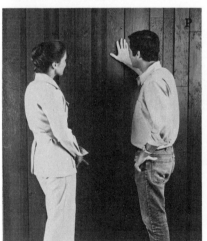

HOOKS

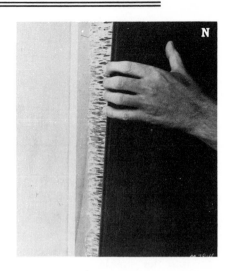

BRACKETS

A
8"
10"
12"
16"

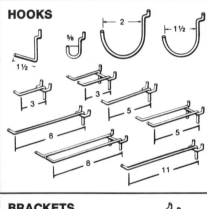

TOOL HOLDERS

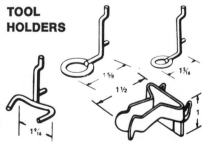

check the panel and apply pressure at all edges and intermediate stud points to assure firm adhesion and an even panel surface. O. Install successive panels, applying ⅛-of-an-inch continuous bead of adhesive at panel joints and at top and bottom edges, and 3-inch beads 6 inches apart on

studs as before. P. When paneling job is complete, you're ready to finish the room with ceiling and floor materials. If desired, add matching moldings and furnish to taste. *Courtesy Masonite Corp.*

Hardware used to hang tools, etc., from pegboard. *Courtesy Masonite Corp.*

Basic requirements for the interior installation of hardboard paneling. A. Panels applied to furring strips over a continuous vapor barrier over masonry wall. B. Panels applied to furring strips fastened to irregular walls. C. Panels applied over Sheetrock or plaster walls. D. Panels applied directly to studs with glue or nails.

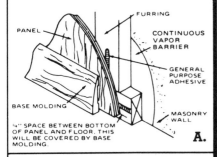

PANEL
FURRING
CONTINUOUS VAPOR BARRIER
GENERAL PURPOSE ADHESIVE
BASE MOLDING
MASONRY WALL

¼" SPACE BETWEEN BOTTOM OF PANEL AND FLOOR. THIS WILL BE COVERED BY BASE MOLDING.

A.

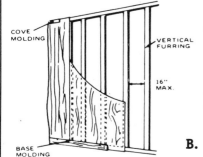

COVE MOLDING
VERTICAL FURRING
16" MAX.
BASE MOLDING

B.

1 5/8" NAILS 8" O.C. AT INTERMEDIATE SOLID BACKING SUPPORTS
8"
STUDS 16" O.C.
NAILS 4" O.C. AT JOINT AND ALONG ALL EDGES

NOTE: FOLLOW SAME PROCEDURE FOR NAILING OVER OPEN FRAMING BUT USE SPECIAL 1" NAILS.

C.

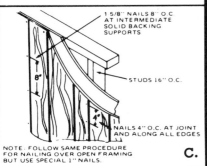

INTERMITTENT 3" ADHESIVE BEAD · 6" SPACE ON INTERMEDIATE STUDS
CONTINUOUS ADHESIVE BEAD ½" FROM ALL EDGES OF PANEL
16" O.C. MAX.
BASE MOLDING

D.

MARLITE BRAND MONOPLANK

FEATURE	BENEFIT	PROOF
6" x 96" x ¼" MODULE	DESIGN FLEXIBILITY	MONOPLANK APPLICATION DIRECTIONS
SHIPLAP JOINERY SYSTEM	APPLICATION EASE NOT REQUIRING NAILING OR DIVISIONAL MOLDINGS	INSTALLATION DETAILS & BUTT EDGE FABRICATION DETAILS
BALANCED MATERIAL	RESISTS WARPAGE	3-5% MOISTURE ADDED TO THE FINISHED MONO-PLANK
OIL TEMPERED WOOD FIBERS	IMPACT RESISTANCE & SURFACE QUALITY	A. IZOD IMPACT 30 in/lbs. B. MINIMUM SURFACE CHIPPING AT SAW CUTS
DESIGN TREND AESTHETICS	MEETS THE INTERIOR DESIGN COLOR, TEXTURE, PATTERN REQUIREMENTS	SAMPLES, PHOTOGRAPHS, ILLUSTRATIONS
HIGH BAKE COATING SYSTEM	EXCEPTIONAL SURFACE DURABILITY	CLASS I FINISH AS PER U.S. DEPT. OF COMMERCE SPEC (PS-59). TEST RESULTS: A. SAND DROP ABRASION -8 LITERS B. BELL MAR SCRAPE 6 kg. C. UNAFFECTED BY COMMON STAINS

BUTT EDGE FABRICATION DETAILS

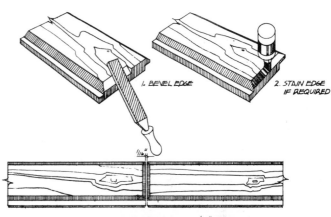

1. BEVEL EDGE
2. STAIN EDGE IF REQUIRED
3. BUTT EDGES, ALLOW 1/16" SPACE FOR MONOPLANK EXPANSION

(cont. on next page)

Applying "plank" hardboard, shiplap edge. Courtesy Masonite Corp.

5 3/4"   ¼"

96"

¼"

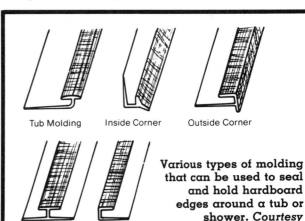

Tub Molding   Inside Corner   Outside Corner

Division   Edging

Various types of molding that can be used to seal and hold hardboard edges around a tub or shower. *Courtesy Masonite Corp.*

(cont. from previous page)

MONOPLANK APPLICATION DIRECTIONS
SCALE 1/4"=1'-0"

VERTICAL STACK   HORIZONTAL STACK

VERTICAL STRIP   HORIZONTAL STRIP

45° DIAGONAL   60° DIAGONAL

CHEVRON   BOOKMATCH

GEOMETRIC

INSTALLATION DETAILS

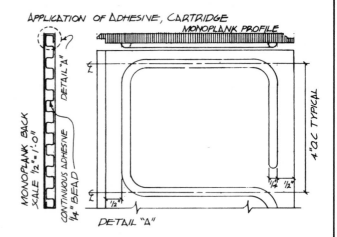

APPLICATION OF ADHESIVE, CARTRIDGE
MONOPLANK PROFILE
MONOPLANK BACK
SCALE 1/2"=1'-0"
CONTINUOUS ADHESIVE 1/4" BEAD
DETAIL "A"
4"O.C. TYPICAL
DETAIL "A"

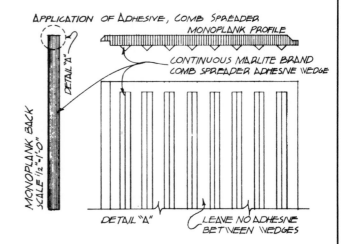

APPLICATION OF ADHESIVE, COMB SPREADER
MONOPLANK PROFILE
MONOPLANK BACK
SCALE 1/2"=1'-0"
DETAIL "A"
CONTINUOUS MARLITE BRAND COMB SPREADER ADHESIVE WEDGE
DETAIL "A"
LEAVE NO ADHESIVE BETWEEN WEDGES

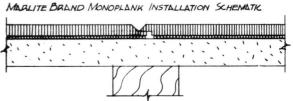

MARLITE BRAND MONOPLANK INSTALLATION SCHEMATIC

MARLITE BRAND MONOPLANK
MARLITE BRAND ADHESIVE
GYPSUM SHEET
STUD OR FURRING

APPLICATION PROCEDURE
1. APPLY ADHESIVE
2. PRESS IN PLACE
3. BREATH APPLICATION BY REMOVING MONOPLANK FROM GYPSUM SHEET
4. REPRESS MONOPLANK IN PLACE

FEATURE	BENEFIT	PROOF
16"x96"x1/4" MODULE	APPLICATION EASE AND FLEXIBILITY	APPLICATION & INSTALLATION DIRECTIONS & DETAILS
TONGUE & GROOVE JOINERY APPLICATION SYSTEM	MONOLITHIC WALL AESTHETICS WITH AN EXPANSION & CONTRACTION INTERLOCK	TONGUE & GROOVE INSTALLATION SCHEMATIC AND THE MARLITE BRAND PLANK CLIP FUNCTION
HIGH BAKE COATING SYSTEM	EXCEPTIONAL SURFACE DURABILITY & AESTHETICS	CLASS I FINISH AS PER U.S. DEPT. OF COMMERCE SPEC. (PS-59). TEST RESULTS: A. SAND DROP ABRASION - 8 LITERS B. BELL MAR SCRAPE 6-kg. C. UNAFFECTED BY COMMON STAINS D. SCRUBABILITY---NO MORE THAN 5° GLOSS CHANGE AFTER 3000 CYCLES ON G.E. SCRUB TESTER
OIL TEMPERED WOOD FIBERS	IMPACT RESISTANCE AND SURFACE QUALITY	A. IZOD IMPACT 30 IN/lbs. B. MINIMUM FINISH CHIPPING AT SAW CUTS. C. UNIFORM SURFACE
BALANCED MATERIAL	RESISTS WARPAGE	3-5% MOISTURE ADDED TO THE FINISHED PLANK
DESIGN TREND AESTHETICS	MEETS THE INTERIOR DESIGN COLOR, TEXTURE, PATTERN REQUIREMENTS	SAMPLES, PHOTOGRAPHS, ILLUSTRATIONS

MARLITE BRAND PLANK — TONGUE EDGE, WOOD FIBER SUBSTRATE, GROOVE EDGE, SURFACE AESTHETICS

Applying "plank" hardboard, tongue-and-groove edged. Courtesy Masonite Corp.

Tongue & Groove Plank Installation Schematic
1/16" SPACE — TYPICAL WALL SKINNING SECTION

- PREFINISHED MARLITE BRAND PLANK
- MARLITE BRAND C-375 ADHESIVE
- MARLITE BRAND PLANK CLIP
- STANDARD GYPSUM SHEET
- MARLITE BRAND PLANK CLIP NAIL
- WOOD STUD OR FURRING STRIP

Marlite Brand Plank Clip Function

THE FUNCTION OF THE PLANK CLIP IS TO PROPERLY SPACE THE MARLITE BRAND PLANK AT THE TONGUE & GROOVE JOINT DURING INSTALLATION. THE CLIP, ALSO, SUPPORTS THE PLANKS TO THE WALL SYSTEM WHILE THE PLANK ADHESIVE TAKES HOLD.

1/16" SPACING BETWEEN PLANKS IS REQUIRED TO ACCOMMODATE POTENTIAL EXPANSION OF THE WOOD FIBER PLANK DURING A CHANGE OF INTERIOR ROOM HUMIDITY. THE CLIP IS NAILED TO THE WALL SYSTEM TO MAINTAIN THE CLIP SPACING PLUS HOLD THE PLANK WHILE THE ADHESIVE SETS UP.

CLIP FACE

(cont. on next page)

(cont. from previous page)

16" PLANK APPLICATION DIRECTIONS & DETAILS
SCALE 1/4"=1'-0"

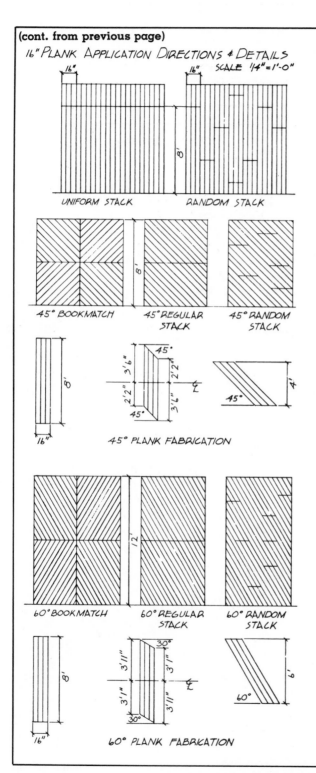

UNIFORM STACK   RANDOM STACK

45° BOOKMATCH   45° REGULAR   45° RANDOM
                     STACK   STACK

45° PLANK FABRICATION

60° BOOKMATCH   60° REGULAR   60° RANDOM
                     STACK   STACK

60° PLANK FABRICATION

INSTALLATION DETAILS

ADHESIVE APPLICATION, CARTRIDGE

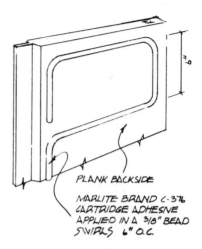

PLANK BACKSIDE

MARLITE BRAND C-376
CARTRIDGE ADHESIVE
APPLIED IN A 3/8" BEAD
SWIRLS 6" O.C.

ADHESIVE APPLICATION, COMB SPREADER

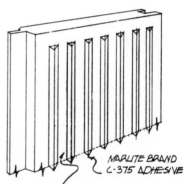

MARLITE BRAND
C-375 ADHESIVE

LEAVE NO ADHESIVE
BETWEEN WEDGES
USE MARLITE BRAND NOTCHED
STEEL COMB SPREADER.

PLANK APPLICATION PROCEDURE

1. APPLY ADHESIVE TO BACKSIDE OF
THE PLANK USING EITHER MARLITE
BRAND C-375 OR C-376 ADHESIVE
2. PRESS PLANK IN PLACE
3. BREATH PLANK APPLICATION BY
REMOVING PLANK FROM GYPSUM
SHEET. THIS PERMITS A QUICK CO-ADHESION
BOND & ALLOWS ADHESIVE GASSES TO VENT.
4. RE-PRESS PLANK IN PLACE

20 HARDWARE

(ALSO SEE FASTENERS, FRAMING, HARDWARE, LOCKS, METAL, PLUMBING, AND VENTILATION)

It used to be that hardware was something made of iron that the mighty smith forged beneath his giant chestnut tree. Today the term *hardware* has become an umbrella that includes almost everything used in construction and repair work, from metal to plastics and other synthetics. Modern hardware shops carry more items than modern drugstores. Therefore, to alleviate the congestion, the hardware covered in this chapter is limited to those items not covered in the chapters on fasteners, framing, locks, metal, plumbing, and ventilation.

CABINET HARDWARE

HINGES

Any of five different types of hinges may be used for cabinetwork. They are full mortise, half mortise, full surface, half surface, and invisible.

A full-mortise hinge is one that is mortised (countersunk) into both the doorframe and the door. Generally the hinge is mortised into the edge of the door and the inner edge of the frame. The door itself fits flush in the frame. Only the hinge pin portion of the hinge is visible from outside the cabinet. This is the type of hinge used by master craftsmen. It makes for a very neat job, but is very difficult to install correctly. A slight error in placement or angle and the door will not close properly.

Half-surface hinges are mortised into the frame or jamb, but not into the door itself. Generally the nonmortised half of the hinge is fastened to the inner surface of the door. Half-surface hinges are a little easier to install than full-mortise hinges.

Half-mortise hinges are mortised to the door and fastened atop the doorframe. They are the reverse of the half-surface hinges and no easier to install.

Full-surface hinges are easiest to install. One type fastens to the surface of the door and the face of the cabinet. The door fits into the frame. Another has an offset bent into one portion of the hinge; this is used with doors that cover the opening. Both of the above hinges are completely visible. Still another type is positioned behind the door and on the surface of the cabinet. This hinge is invisible when the cabinet door is closed, but its use results in a clearance space between the door and the face of the cabinet.

Invisible hinges fit into recesses cut into the edge of the door and the doorframe or doorjamb. These hinges are expensive and difficult to install properly, since both portions of the hinge fit into mortises, and it is the mortise that locks the hinge in position. Without the mortise surrounding the hinge, there is nothing but the screws to hold the hinge, and they are not enough on a cabinet where you cannot use large screws.

PIVOTS

These consist of two pieces of metal joined by a single pin on which the pieces of metal can rotate. By fastening the pivots atop and beneath the edges of a cabinet door and also fastening the other halves of the pivots to the cabinet, you secure a door that can swing open and shut just as if it were on hinges. The advantage is that very little of the pivot shows, and it is a lot easier to install than any of the other door supports.

HANDS

In speaking of hinges we must consider hands—whether the hinge is right-hand or left-hand. If we don't the hinge cannot be properly applied. Differentiation is easy. You are standing outside the building or cabinet. If the door swings away from you—that is to say if the door swings inward—you need a left-hand hinge if the hinge is to go on your left side; a right-hand hinge if it is to go on your right. If the door is to swing outward, the reverse is true: Outward-swinging doors take left-hand hinges on the right side, and right-hand hinges when the door is to swing on your left side.

PULLS

These are simply handles affixed to drawers and doors that are used to open and close them. Some are knobs held by a central screw. Some are ornamented handles held by two machine screws. Some types are recessed. Whatever the type, they are always centered on their horizontal line and usually also centered on their vertical line. In some instances they may be positioned a bit above the center of the door or drawer.

LATCHES

Some latches are surface mounted and some are mortised. They are made in plated steel and solid brass. There are also spring-loaded catches, which hold the door fairly firmly closed until you pull it open. There are magnetic catches that do the same. And there are "touch" latches. These are double-spring loaded. Like an ordinary spring or magnetic latch, you operate it by pushing the door closed. The latch holds the door in position. To open you push the door lightly. That releases the second spring, which then swings the door open.

SLIDES

Slides are used to facilitate the opening and closing of a drawer that is expected to be heavily weighted down: a drawer that would be difficult to move on ordinary wood rails or a drawer that you want to remove entirely from the cabinet and yet not hold its weight in your hands.

There are many types of slides, made of steel, aluminum, and brass. Some are two-section units that have limited extensions; others have three sections that extend one third farther. When selecting a pair of slides, in addition to securing slides that permit the extension you wish, you must make certain the slides will safely support the weight at full extension and that slide mounting holes and or brackets are such that they can be accommodated by your drawer and cabinet.

BUILDING DOOR HINGES

BUTT HINGES

These are full-mortise hinges. To some extent they are shaped much like full-mortise cabinet hinges, with the major difference being size and metal thickness. Butt hinges are made of steel and brass. Brass is the best for exterior door use. NOTE: For safety, hinge pins are always positioned inside the building.

But hinges are designed for high-, medium-, and low-frequencey use and light- and heavyweight doors. It is assumed that the average front door is generally subjected to medium use—that is, opened and closed some 16,000 times a year.

While there is a standard table for selecting hinge size, there is little in the way of savings to be gained by using butt hinges less than 4 inches long on standard doors, and 5-inch butts on heavy oak doors up to 36 inches wide. Wider doors should be carried by three hinges. As for hinge width, select a hinge that will leave a ¼-inch-wide strip of wood along one side when you mortise the hinge.

STRAP HINGES

These are full-surface hinges. One type consists of two long V-shaped hinges. The second has one V portion and one rectangular portion. Strap hinges are used for barn doors and the like.

SPRING HINGES

This is a surface hinge with an enclosed spring. When the hinge is in place and the spring has been adjusted, the spring tends to keep the door closed and the flies out.

SCREW HOOK AND STRAP HINGE

This is an old-fashioned hinge used primarily on gates. The hook portion can be lifted out of the strap. This makes it possible to lift the entire gate up and remove it.

SLIDING DOOR HARDWARE

Essentially, this hardware consists of a metal track fastened to the top of the doorframe or doorjamb. The door or doors are fastened to a set of rollers that ride on the track. As the track is either T-shaped or an angle, the door hangs from its rollers. The best rollers are made of nylon. They are friction-free and need no lubrication. The lower edges of the door or doors are simply held in place by guides screwed fast to the floor.

When selecting sliding door hardware, select "hangers" that are adjustable, and do not depend solely on mounting screw position. Also make sure that track and hangers are of a size to fit the thickness of the door or doors you are going to hang. NOTE: Sliding doors are never used when you want a tight fit between the doors and the door opening.

SHELF BRACKETS

In addition to the old-fashioned shelf brackets of years ago, which are still being made in sizes to accommodate shelving from widths of 3 to 14 inches, shelf brackets are now available in a variety of multiple-shelf supports.

MULTIPLE-SHELF SUPPORTS

Two basic designs are offered. One type fits in the facing sides of two shelf supports. For example, this type would be used in a bookcase to support the shelves. The support consists of a pair of pierced metal channels, spaced a distance apart and mounted vertically, one pair on each side of the bookcase. Small clips are fitted into the holes in the supports. The clips, four to each shelf, support the shelf. The advantage of this system of support is that you can quickly and easily vary the height and spacing of the shelves should you wish to do so.

The other type of multiple-shelf support is positioned alongside the shelves rather than at their ends. Generally the second type of support, also consisting of a pair of pierced metal channels, is positioned on a wall. In place of clips there are arms that may range up to 16 inches in length. The arms fit into the holes or slots in the vertical supports.

When selecting arm-type, multiple-shelf support hardware you must select arms that are not only long enough to hold the shelves, but also strong enough to carry the load you anticipate. Anodized aluminum is probably your best bet so far as cost, strength, and corrosion resistance is concerned. Aluminum is anodized in many colors and tones.

FLATIRON HARDWARE

Flatiron hardware includes corner irons, braces, and mending plates that are, literally, made from strips of flat iron.

Corner irons are right angles made by bending a strip of flat iron. They are sized by width and the length of one side (leg) of the angle. Standard sizes run from $1 \times \frac{1}{2}$ inch to $10 \times 1\frac{1}{4}$ inches, with a corresponding number of screw holes countersunk for flathead wood screws.

Corner braces are similar to corner irons, but the metal used is thinner and not as wide. Sizes run from 1 to 10 inches.

Flat corner irons are also made from iron, but whereas the braces are made by bending the metal, the flat corners are stamped out of heavy gauge sheet metal. Leg lengths and widths run from $1\frac{1}{2} \times \frac{3}{8}$ inch to $3\frac{1}{2} \times \frac{3}{4}$ inch.

Mending plates are straight lengths of strap iron, with two to six holes in each plate. Sizes run from $2 \times \frac{1}{2}$ inches to $10 \times 1\frac{1}{4}$ inches.

CASTERS

Casters are wheels mounted on swivel supports that are used to support chairs, hand trucks, and the like. There are, basically, two types. One is called snap fit; the other plate mounted or supported.

The snap-fit type consists of two parts. One is tubular and fits into a hole drilled vertically into the leg of the table or whatever. The tube portion is driven into the hole. The wheel portion terminates in a vertical rod with a knob on its end. This end is simply inserted into the tube. It snaps into place and needs force to be removed. In addition to selecting a snap-fit caster large enough to support its load easily, you also need a unit that does not require so large a diameter hole that the leg is weakened.

The plate-mounted caster is generally larger, running to wheels 5 and more inches in diameter. It is fastened to the underside of the object by four screws driven through mounting holes.

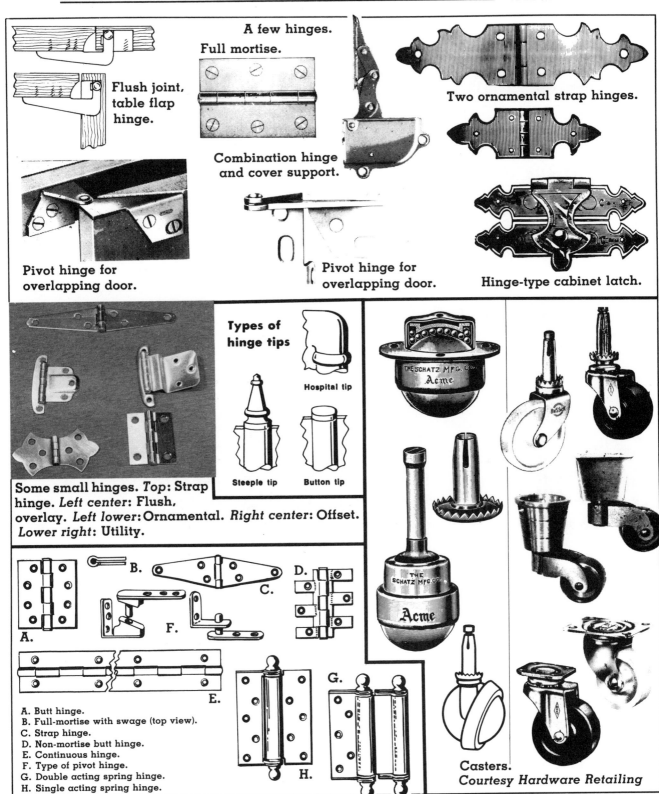

A few hinges.

Full mortise.

Flush joint, table flap hinge.

Combination hinge and cover support.

Two ornamental strap hinges.

Pivot hinge for overlapping door.

Pivot hinge for overlapping door.

Hinge-type cabinet latch.

Types of hinge tips

Hospital tip

Steeple tip

Button tip

Some small hinges. *Top:* Strap hinge. *Left center:* Flush, overlay. *Left lower:* Ornamental. *Right center:* Offset. *Lower right:* Utility.

A. Butt hinge.
B. Full-mortise with swage (top view).
C. Strap hinge.
D. Non-mortise butt hinge.
E. Continuous hinge.
F. Type of pivot hinge.
G. Double acting spring hinge.
H. Single acting spring hinge.

Casters.
Courtesy Hardware Retailing

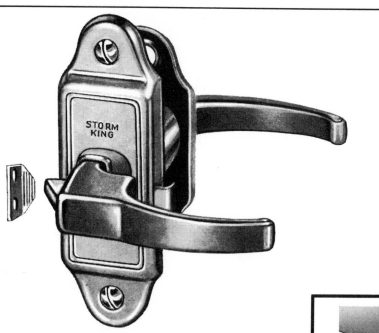

Spring-roller catch.
Courtesy Albert Constantine and Co.

Cabinet touch latch.

Latches.

Screen door latch.
Courtesy Storm King Manufacturing Co.

Two magnetic latches.
Courtesy McKinney Corp.

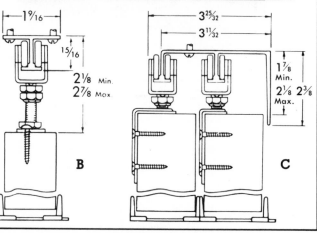

Sliding-door hardware.
A. Hardware fastened to door. Note adjustable fitting.
B. End view of single track arrangement.
C. End view of twin track arrangement.
Courtesy Grant Pulley and Hardware Co.

INSULATION

In the winter heat tends to leave our homes and so increase our discomfort or force us to increase our fuel costs. In the summer the reverse process takes place, and either we accept discomfort or we expend energy and money to power an air conditioner. The ways heat enters and leaves a building are manifold, and each structure loses and gains heat in somewhat different ways, but roughly, the movement of unwanted heat breaks down this way:

	Two stories (%)	One story (%)
Walls	38	23
Ceilings, roof	25	39
Windows	21	11
Air leaks	14	15
Floors	2	12

To reduce the flow of unwanted heat into and out of our homes it is necessary to know and understand not only the uses and application of insulation but also the basic nature of heat and heat flow.

PRINCIPLES OF HEAT

HEAT IS ENERGY

If you apply heat to water, convert the water to steam, and use the steam to drive a steam engine or a turbine, the power produced by the turbine will be exactly equal to the energy of the heat applied to the water, less the losses occurring in the process. Unfortunately, the losses are considerable.

The best turbine doesn't extract much more than 30 percent of the heat's energy. The best of the old-time steam engines didn't get much more than 6 percent.

HEAT IS UNSTABLE

Whereas a closed tank of gasoline will retain its energy indefinitely, there is no known method of storing heat. Heat will escape the best containers we can make. It will escape even from triple-walled glass vacuum bottles with fully mirrored surfaces. It will take time, but eventually the liquid, solid, or gas in the bottle will reach the same temperature as the air outside the bottle.

HEAT TRAVELS IN ONLY ONE DIRECTION

So far as we know, heat will travel only toward a colder point. If you heat the end of a cold length of iron, heat will travel up the iron to warm the cold end. The cold will not travel down the iron to chill the hot end.

SPEED OF MOVEMENT

Movement is not an accurate description of how heat moves, but the term is useful for our purpose here. In any case the movement of heat is directly related to the temperature differential. (Again, this is a general statement, not a precise one.) The greater the differential, the more rapidly the heat travels. For example, place an almost-boiling hot cup of coffee in a cool room and the coffee quickly becomes lukewarm. Once the coffee becomes lukewarm it will remain that way for a long time. In other words, the lower the temperature differential, the slower the temperature change—in this example—of the coffee. Eventually, the coffee in the cup will reach equilibrium with the air in the room. Until that condition is reached, heat will continue to move from the coffee to the air in the room.

Heat will stop its continuous movement only when everything in the universe reaches the same temperature, a condition called entropy. (Let's hope this state will not shortly be reached.)

METHOD OF TRAVEL

Heat moves or travels from one point or place to another by one or all of three methods. They are radiation, conduction, and convection.

The sun, for example, radiates heat. Heat travels 90 million miles from the sun to our planet in about eight seconds. But even much colder objects radiate heat, which travels at the same speed, 186,000 miles per second (the speed of light). For example, a wood fire that may not be hotter than 1,000°F radiates heat. Even a hot-water radiator at only 140°F radiates heat. Hold your palm next to the radiator and you will feel radiant heat strike and warm your hand. But an 80°F radiator in a 90°F room will not radiate heat. Instead the room will radiate heat to the radiator, and, in a sense, the cooler radiator will extract heat from the warmer room.

As noted above, heat will travel from the hot end of a piece of metal to its cold end. The metal conducts heat. Consequently, that method of heat travel is called conduction.

The movement of heat produced by the movement of air or liquids is called convection. When you heat the floor of a room you are also heating its ceiling. This is due to the movement of hot air from near the floor to the ceiling; the air carries or convects heat as it goes. When water heated in a boiler is driven by a pump through a distant radiator, the water heats the radiator which then radiates heat. The system is called forced convection heating because the water is forced to move by a pump.

MEASURING HEAT

Heat is measured several ways. The one most familiar to most of us is the use of a thermometer, a thin tube of glass filled with mercury or colored alcohol. The expansion of the mercury or the alcohol is a measure of temperature. To phrase it as non-technically as possible, temperature can be viewed as the strength of heat's activity. The higher the temperature the more active the heat (and the shorter its electromagnetic wavelength).

While temperature is useful in measuring the effect of the weather on our bodies and informing us of when the roast is ready and the sugar has turned to caramel, temperature is not particularly useful in determining the insulating properties of materials.

For this we use a method based on the cumulative effect of heat upon a specific quantity of water. This effect is measured in British Thermal Units (BTUs). A BTU is the amount of heat required to raise the temperature of one pound of water exactly 1 degree

Fahrenheit. It is a universally accepted unit of heat measurement and very handy. For example, BTUs are used to calibrate and specify the output of both a furnace and an air conditioner. An oil burner/furnace rated at 85,000 BTUs can raise 85,000 pounds of water 1 degree, or 850 pounds of water 100 degrees, in an hour. Since 850 pounds of water amounts to roughly 100 gallons, this boiler could heat 100 gallons of 60-degree water to 160 degrees every hour. Translated into horsepower (without any regard for the power loss that would occur in actual practice), 85,000 BTUs is roughly equal to 35 horsepower or 25 kilowatts per hour.

An 85,000-BTU air conditioner can, in one hour, cool 100 gallons of 160-degree water to 60 degrees.

HEAT STORAGE

It is only recently that any attention has been paid to heat storage, but it is a very important factor in moderating the temperature of a building and reducing its peak heating and cooling requirements.

Very simply, the heavier and more massive the substance from which a building is constructed, the more heat the building can absorb and later release. This is why an insulated concrete block building requires less heating and cooling energy than does an equally well insulated building made of wood. A study was done comparing the energy needs of the two types of building. Both buildings were the same size and had an identical amount of window area, and both thermostats were set to 70°F. The

wood-frame building required a 94,000-BTU furnace, whereas the block building needed no more than 70,000 BTUs. The frame building weighed less than 5 pounds per cubic foot, the block building weighed 70 pounds per cubic foot. Roughly the same power ratio was obtained when the buildings were cooled in the summer.

Heat storage by means of crushed stone, poured concrete, and concrete block is the basis of many passive solar heating/cooling systems. During a winter day, sun entering the windows strikes and warms the concrete floor and other massive heat sinks. At night curtains insulate the windows, and the heat stored in the stone provides a portion of the total heat necessary to warm the house. In the summer the stone is cooled during the night, and in the day it draws heat from the building.

REDUCING THE FLOW OF HEAT

Any material used to slow the flow of heat is known as an insulator, although, to repeat, nothing known can stop the flow of heat completely. Many different materials are used as insulators. They have been selected or fabricated for their insulating properties, fire- and rot-resistance, ease of installation, and cost.

EVALUATION

A number of formulas have been devised and used to rate in numbers the effectiveness of specific insulation. The results of these tests have been assigned the letters K, C, and U. The lower the K, C, or U number is, the better the insulator is.

APPROXIMATE R VALUES OF COMMON BUILDING MATERIALS

	R
Solid concrete	.08/inch
Stone	.08/inch
Standard concrete block	.105/inch
Light concrete block	.156/inch
Common brick	.205/inch
Face brick	.113/inch
Stucco	.20/inch
Plastic vapor barrier	.00/inch
Building paper	.06/single layer
Gypsum board	.879/inch
Sand plaster	.30/inch
Insulating plaster	1.50/inch
Ceiling tile	2.40/inch
Fiberboard sheathing	2.90/inch
Plywood	1.30/inch
Softwood sheathing	1.13/inch
Roll roofing	.15/single layer
Asphalt shingles	.16/layer
Wood shingles	.86/layer
Tile or slate shingles	.08/layer
Glass fiber batt	2.75/inch
Rock wool batt	3.6/inch
Glass fiber loose fill	2.2/inch
Rock wool loose fill	2.75/inch
Cellulose fiber loose	3.6/inch
Enclosed air	.25/inch
Foamglass	2.63/inch
Styrofoam batt	5.0/inch
Polystyrene batt	5.0/inch
Isocyanurate batt	5.0/inch
Single-weight glass	.13
Double-glazed ½-inch air space	1.72
Metal-edged insulating glass	1.85

NOTE: In some materials R factors vary with thickness. Generally (but not in all instances), doubling the thickness doubles the R value.

This has led to the introduction of R numbers, which stand for thermal resistance. These can be added directly. Today, most insulations are rated in R numbers. Should you encounter a U number, be advised that it is a reciprocal of R. This means you divide 1 by the U number to find R. NOTE: Some of the older insulations and older textbooks use the letter C in place of R. If the letter is followed by a figure greater than 1.0, it is probably and R figure and can be used as such.

COMPUTING TOTAL INSULATION

To do this simply add all the R numbers of the materials comprising the wall, roof, or floor. For example:

Exterior plywood siding	0.43
½-inch sheathing	1.32
R-11 insulation	11.00
½-inch gypsum wallboard	0.45
Total R =	13.20

Note that this figure applies to only those sections or areas of the wall that are so constructed and insulated. If there is a window or door in the wall, the window area and the door area R values must be calculated individually.

Note also that many architects and engineers assign an R value to the air films that exist on the outside and the inside surfaces of the wall. The R figures they use are 0.17 and 0.68, respectively. Naturally, including these figures increases the total R value of the wall. These numbers may be useful for presenting a better picture to the Energy Commission, but they are unreliable—any wind will blow the exterior air film away.

TYPES OF INSULATION

We can divide insulation into three categories: reflective, nonconductive, and vacuum.

REFLECTIVE

As its name indicates, this type works by reflecting radiant heat. In the summer it reflects heat outward. In the winter it reflects heat inward. Reflective insulation does not have to face the source of heat directly. For example, a layer of reflective insulation placed on the underside of a roof will reflect radiant energy that passes through the roof proper.

Aluminum foil is the material most often used for reflective insulating. It is sometimes cemented in thin layers to heavy kraft paper in order to save on metal. Sometimes it's used in single layers and sometimes in multiple layers, with each layer separated from the other by an air space. Reflective insulation is made with "nailing" flanges and is fastened between rafters and studs 16 and 24 inches on centers. Nails are not used. Instead just a few staples are driven through the flanges and into the wood to hold the insulation in place.

Metal does not permit the passage of moisture, so metal foil reflective insulation also serves as a vapor barrier.

To reduce the movement of radiant energy through nonconductive insulation, some nonconductive insulation is made with aluminum foil on one or both sides.

NONCONDUCTIVE

Each of the many types of nonconductive insulation currently made has its advantages and disadvantages. In terms of effectiveness, they are roughly equal. The thicker the insulation the better it insulates.

Loose fill. This type comes in bags or bales and is easily either poured into place as you would pour sand or blown into place. On the other hand, because it is loose, it tends to settle, thus compacting and reducing its insulating properties proportionately.

Loose-fill insulation made from expanded and treated wood fibers is not a good choice because the wood is combustible and susceptible to microbial and insect attack.

Loose fill made from expanded asbestos fibers is a very poor choice because there is always the danger of inhaling the fibers, which are a known carcinogen. On the other hand, asbestos is a stone, so it won't burn, rot, or deteriorate, and if it is used within a tightly and permanently enclosed space, its fibers can do no harm.

Mica that has been exploded and, therefore, expanded is also used for fill insulation. It too is stone and won't rot, burn, or deteriorate. It doesn't compact very much with time and is easy to handle.

Glass fibers, which are made from molten glass that is spun into a kind of wool, are also used for loose-fill insulation. Glass is inert and microbe-resistant. It is easy to handle, but when you work with it be sure to roll your sleeves down and wear gloves because the tiny glass fibers can pierce and irritate your skin.

Expanding chemical foam is also used as a kind of loose fill. Most often it is blown into the walls of an existing house. It is combustible, but since it is behind plaster or Sheetrock, it is considered acceptable by most building codes.

Blow-in. The first step in this procedure is to remove a section of siding from the exterior of the building. Then a few large holes are drilled through the sheathing and commercial applicators are used to blow the insulation or foam into the spaces between the studs. In newer homes there is generally no problem. But many older homes have fire stops. These are short horizontal sections of 2 × 4s placed between studs to keep flames from reaching up through the full height of the wall. On such homes you have to blow the insulation into the walls *below and above* the fire stops to do a complete job.

Glass wool batts and blankets are made of spun-glass fibers similar to those used for loose glass-fiber insulation. The difference is that the batts and blankets are somewhat self-supporting.

The batts are usually 48 inches long and just wide enough to fit between rafters and studs 16 and 24 inches on center. Batt thicknesses vary from 1 to 8 inches. Some batts are bare, some are enclosed in heavy, fire-resistant kraft paper that forms nailing flanges on both sides of the batts, and some have reflective foil on one or two sides. The blankets are made of similar material in various widths and thicknesses. Except for the insulation backed by foil, which adds its R factor to the insulation, all the glass wool insulation is alike in that its R factor is directly proportional to its thickness. A 4-inch batt has an R factor twice that of a 2-inch batt. If you position one 2-inch batt atop another the result is an insulator with an R factor equal to the total of the two batts.

Glass wool batts and blankets must be handled with gloves. They can be cut with a razor knife. Fasten the batts in place with staples every 18 inches or so, with the aluminum or heavy kraft paper facing the interior of the building.

Rigid insulation is made by combining air with polyurethane or isocyanurate (called R-guard by Georgia-Pacific and Styrofoam by Dow Chemical Corporation). Rigid foam insulation is manufactured in strips and sheets having tongue-and-groove edges and in a number of thicknesses with and without reflective foil.

Rigid foam insulation has an average R rating of between 4 and 5 R per inch of thickness. Glass wool batts and blankets have a rating of 3.5 R per inch of thickness.

Rigid foam insulation is rot- and vermin-proof and, to a high degree, moisture-proof. However, it is not fireproof. When it is installed in a wood-frame building the interior surface of that side or ceiling must be covered by ½-inch plasterboard (check local building code). Rigid plastic foam insulation can be cut with a razor knife and used as sheathing in place of wood or exterior Sheetrock. When so used, diagonal braces must be installed between or across the studs.

Rigid foam insulation has moderate compression resistance, but it is sufficiently strong to install atop a roof-deck and cover with built-up roofing. Then you can lay down 4 inches of concrete and use it to support automobiles. The foam is often used this way to insulate garage floors from the earth below.

Foamglass is a trade name for a new type of rigid insulation. Made by Pittsburgh Corning, it is composed of microscopic cells of glass. Since the cells are closed, this insulation is a perfect moisture barrier and never absorbs water, so it never loses its insulation value. Its R rating is approximately 4.0 per inch. It is much stronger than plastic foam. Foamglass has a compressive strength of 100 pounds per square inch, or more than 7 tons per square foot. The glass bead material is made in boards ranging in thickness from 1½ inches through 4 inches, and in sheets cemented between two layers of kraft paper. In addition, the cellular glass insulation is made in flat blocks 12 × 18 × 1¼ inches and 18-×-24-inch blocks in thicknesses of 2 to 5 inches. The company also makes tapered blocks that can be used when you want to provide a pitch on a flat surface.

SHAPED INSULATION

In addition to the blocks and sheets already listed, insulation is manufactured in specific shapes and sizes for specific applications. For large diameter pipes you can purchase split tubes of asbestos, which are held in place by metal bands. For small diameter tubes you will find a rubberlike split tube that adheres by itself. There are also "blankets" available with which you can cover a hot-water boiler or tank.

ASBESTOS CEMENT
Odd shapes, such as pipe joints and the like, can be covered and insulated with asbestos cement. This is sold in the form of a paste that is mixed with water into a putty and hand-molded into shape. When the paste hardens it forms a permanent insulator, smooth and pale gray in color. There is no need to worry about asbestos particles. The hardened paste will not deteriorate and disperse. If necessary, you can remove the hardened asbestos cement, soak the pieces in water, and reshape it as you wish.

VACUUM INSULATION
Removing the air from between two sheets of glass eliminates the transference of heat from one pane of glass to the other by conduction and/or convection. The only way heat can cross the vacuum barrier is by radiation. Glass insulated this way is ideal for homes, greenhouses, and similar structures. Sun enters the building, warms it, and remains inside. At night, heat is trapped within the building. It cannot escape through the evacuated space in any measurable quantity.

Unfortunately, such glass is not presently manufactured. Instead the space between the two panes is filled with dehydrated air. The results are not as good, but this setup is much better than a single pane of glass, which has an R rating of little better than 0. With a ¼-inch air space the R rating is about .07. In northern areas double-glazed windows are used, which results in a figure of .14. A tight storm window, with a 2-inch air space between it and the glass, would have an R of approximately .50.

HOW MUCH INSULATION DO YOU NEED?

Most homes constructed before World War II have no inner wall and ceiling insulation. Their external walls have an approximate R value of 4 to 5. Their ceilings, attic, and roof R values probably range from 6 through 8. Such buildings will benefit immeasurably from insulation. If you simply double the wall and ceiling R values you will reduce heat loss (and gain) through the walls and ceiling by half.

Homes built after World War II are generally insulated. Usually, 2-inch batts were installed in the walls and 4-inch batts in the ceilings. Doubling the insulation in these walls and ceilings will also reduce heat loss. But now you have to go to 4-inch batts (total) in the wall and 8-inch batts (total) in the ceiling. Because these houses had a lower heating bill to begin with, the savings gained from doubling the insulation will be proportionately lower.

Now, let's assume you have a modern home with 4-inch batts in the walls and 8-inch batts in the ceiling. You now have to go to 8 and 16 to cut your heat loss in half. As you can see, your heat loss was less to begin with, your savings in heat are less, but your cost of insulation has increased tremendously.

We are assuming in this discussion that it is a simple and inexpensive matter to open the walls and ceilings and add insulation. In most instances it is not. And when you try to get 8 inches of insulation into a wall that is less than 4 inches thick, you will have problems, to say the least.

On the other hand, it is not easy to add a lot of insulation to the exterior of a building either. There just isn't the space for it within the thickness of the siding. However, you can get an R as high as 2.50, which would be a considerable heat saving if added to an uninsulated wall having an R of only 4 or so.

VAPOR BARRIERS

Humans excrete an average of 2 pints of water per day and more in warm weather. This moisture, plus the moisture generated by cooking, collects in the interior of your home and, like heat, travels toward the cold. In this case the moisture will pass slowly, but continuously, through the plaster or Sheetrock of your home, through whatever insulation may be present in the wall, and will condense on the inner side of the exterior wall. It condenses there because that is the coldest surface. Water means trouble, and the least trouble it will cause you is to force the paint to peel off the exterior walls in large blisters. The most trouble it will cause—and this is plenty—will be to rot the water-soaked timbers in the walls.

Two steps must be taken to prevent this. A moisture-proof barrier must be positioned on the inner side of all house-frame insulation. If a wall is insulated, the barrier is positioned on the inner side of the insulation. Ceiling insulation calls for a barrier below the insulation. Floor insulation requires the barrier above the insulation. Loose insulation has no barrier, so one must be installed. This can be a sheet of plastic or metal foil, plain or on a kraft paper backer. Batt and blanket insulation comes with a vapor barrier. All you need do with this is install it properly. Rigid foam is, in itself, a moisture barrier. Nothing more need be done with it.

That is step one. The second step consists of ventilating the area(s) behind the insulation in the walls, and above and below the insulation in the attic and the cellar. An occupied cellar needs no special ventilation; opening and closing doors is enough. A crawl space needs openings in the foundation wall. Attics may be ventilated by attic louvers positioned *above* the insulation. Walls are ventilated by louvers in the eaves and small louvers in the walls themselves. If you are using rigid foam boards as sheathing, or an underlay for metal or plastic siding, leave small spaces between the foam boards or punch a few small holes here and there through the foam board itself.

Applying Styrofoam insulation. The lightweight, foam insulation is easily cut and positioned. *Courtesy Dow Chemical Co.*

Definitions of insulating terms. *Courtesy Pittsburgh Corning Corporation*

Btu, British Thermal Unit—The amount of heat required to raise the temperature of one pound of water 1°F.

k, thermal conductivity—The amount of heat that passes through 1 square foot of homogeneous material 1 inch thick in 1 hour's time, with a temperature difference of 1°F between the surfaces of the material.

C, thermal conductance—The amount of heat that passes through 1 square foot of material of any thickness in 1 hour's time with a temperature difference of 1°F between the surfaces of the material. C is determined by dividing k by the material thickness $\left(C = \dfrac{k}{\text{thickness}} \right)$.

R, thermal resistance—A measure of a material's ability to retard heat flow. R is the numerical reciprocal of C $\left(R = \dfrac{1}{C} \right)$.

U, overall coefficient of heat transmission — The total heat flow through a building wall or roof system. U is the reciprocal of the sum of the resistances of all the components of a system, including air space and air films $\left(U = \dfrac{1}{R_{\text{total}}} \right)$.

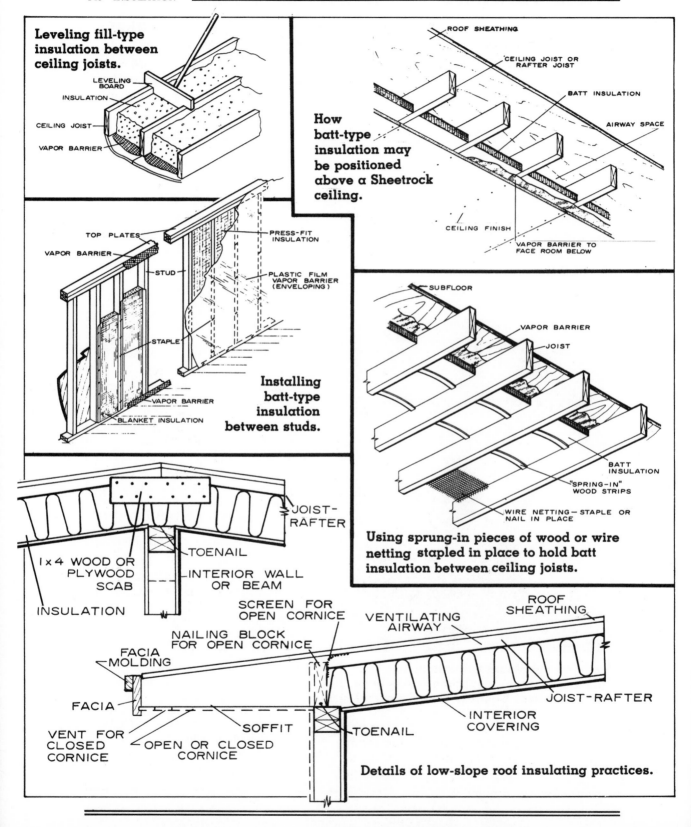

Leveling fill-type insulation between ceiling joists.

LEVELING BOARD
INSULATION
CEILING JOIST
VAPOR BARRIER

How batt-type insulation may be positioned above a Sheetrock ceiling.

ROOF SHEATHING
CEILING JOIST OR RAFTER JOIST
BATT INSULATION
AIRWAY SPACE
CEILING FINISH
VAPOR BARRIER TO FACE ROOM BELOW

Installing batt-type insulation between studs.

TOP PLATES
VAPOR BARRIER
STUD
STAPLE
VAPOR BARRIER
BLANKET INSULATION
PRESS-FIT INSULATION
PLASTIC FILM VAPOR BARRIER (ENVELOPING)

Using sprung-in pieces of wood or wire netting stapled in place to hold batt insulation between ceiling joists.

SUBFLOOR
VAPOR BARRIER
JOIST
BATT INSULATION
"SPRING-IN" WOOD STRIPS
WIRE NETTING—STAPLE OR NAIL IN PLACE

JOIST-RAFTER
1 x 4 WOOD OR PLYWOOD SCAB
TOENAIL
INTERIOR WALL OR BEAM
INSULATION

FACIA MOLDING
FACIA
VENT FOR CLOSED CORNICE
OPEN OR CLOSED CORNICE
SOFFIT
NAILING BLOCK FOR OPEN CORNICE
SCREEN FOR OPEN CORNICE
TOENAIL
VENTILATING AIRWAY
INTERIOR COVERING
ROOF SHEATHING
JOIST-RAFTER

Details of low-slope roof insulating practices.

HEATING DEGREE DAYS

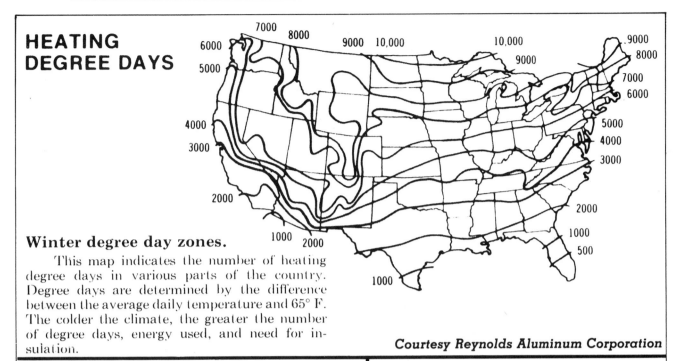

Winter degree day zones.

This map indicates the number of heating degree days in various parts of the country. Degree days are determined by the difference between the average daily temperature and 65° F. The colder the climate, the greater the number of degree days, energy used, and need for insulation.

Courtesy Reynolds Aluminum Corporation

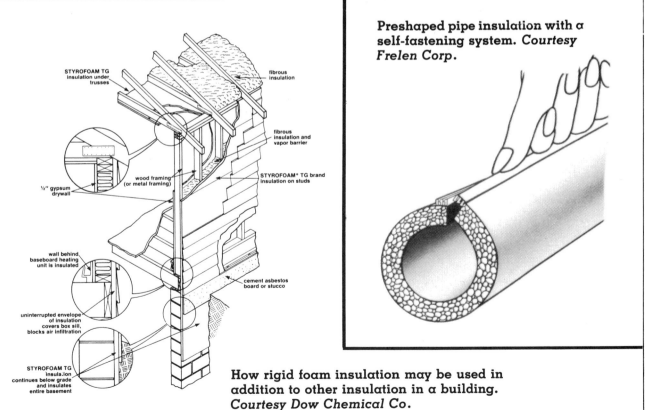

How rigid foam insulation may be used in addition to other insulation in a building. *Courtesy Dow Chemical Co.*

Preshaped pipe insulation with a self-fastening system. *Courtesy Frelen Corp.*

Laminates are a group of plastic and wood/plastic veneers designed to be applied to the surface of wood. The purpose of the laminate may be to make the wood surface more attractive or simply to present a surface different from the wood it covers, or to create a tougher, more wear- and heat-resistant surface that can be obtained by a mere coating of shellac and varnish.

MICARTA AND FORMICA

These are two copyrighted names for phenolic melanins—which are plastic veneers—produced under high pressures and temperatures. Generally available in sheets approximately 1/16 inch thick and 4 × 8 feet in size, they are very hard, tough, and heat-resistant. With some care they can retain their shine and bright colors, when used as counter tops and the like, for up to twenty years. But in time, the top surface wears through and the brown undersurface appears. They can withstand temperatures of up to boiling (212°F; 100°C), but will char and discolor under the touch of a soldering iron or a too-close tabletop stove.

The range of colors, patterns, and surfaces available is considerable and includes colors from off-white through dark brown; patterns with squares, circles, birds, and bees, wood grain and simulated marquetry; and surfaces from smooth and shiny to a texture that has the feel of wood under hand. You will find the latter style of laminate on low-priced office furniture in place of more expensive woods.

Lumberyards, which may not stock more than a dozen styles or so of the sheets of laminates, usually will order a sheet for you. Most yards insist that you purchase an entire sheet, but some will sell a portion of a sheet at a higher-than-full-sheet price.

PREMOUNTED LAMINATES

Lumberyards usually stock or will order premounted laminates for their customers. Generally, the laminate is contact-cemented to a panel of ¾-inch plywood. It is your assignment to cut the panel to fit your needs or have the panel cut for you. When ordering premounted panels, make sure the supporting lumber is suitable for your intended application; if the panel is to carry a sink, it's wise to purchase moisture-resistant or exterior grade plywood.

CURVED LAMINATES

Better counter tops and the like do not have right-angle splashboards but have curved front edges and splashboards. This is accomplished by bending the laminate in two tight curves; the process requires high pressure, heat, and a mold. It cannot be done at home. The cost of this type of counter top is high, but it is beautiful and has no corners for the collection of soil.

CUTTING AND APPLYING

High-pressure laminates such as Formica and Micarta are best cut with a high-speed power saw fitted with a fine-tooth blade. If you are going to cut the sheet by hand, use a trim saw, which is a crosscut saw with fine teeth. For minor cutting you can get by with a hacksaw. Make sure that you support the sheet firmly, as these laminates are hard and brittle.

Laminates are applied or fastened by means of contact cement. Some of the cements can be sprayed on, some require a brush, but the net results are the same. These cements are called contact because they work on contact. Once the laminate has touched the cemented surface of the plywood or whatever, the bond is made; there is no easy way to break it.

Therefore, the usual method of applying a laminate (or anything else) with the aid of contact cement is to cut the laminate to size, or slightly larger. Cover the supporting surface with cement. Cover the cement with a heavy sheet of brown paper. Position the laminate atop the paper. Then slide the paper out.

Laminate edges projecting beyond their support are best cut back with a Surform plane, or sandpaper on a block of wood.

HEAT-BONDED LAMINATES

These are high-pressure laminates backed by a layer of heat-sensitive cement. They are manufactured by Westvaco in a number of colors and patterns. The laminate is cut to size and placed on the surface it is to cover; then heat is applied via an ordinary household pressing iron. The heat penetrates the 1/64 inch plastic and converts the underlayer to a form of cement. Next, the surface is rolled with a cook's rolling pin, and except for trimming, the job is done.

REAL WOOD VENEER

It is now possible to purchase wood veneer backed by heat-sensitive cement in a number of wood types and grain patterns. Manufactured by Westvaco and a few other companies, the iron-on wood laminate is applied to any clean surface in the manner described immediately above.

Kitchen cabinets covered with heat-bonded laminates. *Courtesy Westvaco*

Steps in applying heat-bonded laminate. The laminate is cut to size.

The laminate is positioned and trimmed.

A pressing iron is used to provide the heat and pressure needed to effect the bond.

A rolling pin is used to make certain the laminate is in full contact with the supporting surface. *Courtesy Westvaco*

23 LEADERS & GUTTERS

Originally, buildings did not have leaders and gutters, which are, today, sometimes called downspouts. Originally, rain just ran down the roof to the earth and that was it. Some homeowners still utilize this method of rain disposal; to keep the rain from washing away the soil where it strikes the earth, they simply lay down a line of flagstones.

The first gutters were simply narrow boards fastened on edge atop the roof and near its edges. These directed the flow of rainwater off to one side. You can still see these gutters on some old homes, and they still work well.

Then came true (metal) gutters. These were originally (and often still are) made of copper, with soldered joints. They are very good, last a long time, and add an air of refinement to a building, especially as they age and develop a green patina. But copper has always been expensive and soldering takes a lot of time. In the main, copper has been replaced by galvanized iron with screw-fastened joints. Now aluminum is replacing the galvanized iron and, to some small extent, plastic gutters and leaders are replacing aluminum.

COMPARING THE MATERIALS

There is no doubt that copper leaders and gutters when made of sufficiently thick gauge, with carefully soldered joints and copper nails, will last fifty years or more. If the joints are not properly soldered, however, or if iron or galvanized nails are used, or if these metals are permitted in any way to touch the copper (for example, if a roofing nail falls into the gutter) holes will soon develop. Where cost is of no importance and the building's exterior is brick, stone, or natural wood, copper is the most attractive material you can use for gutters and leaders.

The major problem with galvanized iron is not just that it is harder to cut and join, and more difficult to lift up in place, but that it always rusts. The reason is simply that while the face of the metal is protected by zinc, the cut edges are not. Rust from these exposed edges can stain the sides of a building. And, as mentioned before, should a copper nail or a penny fall into the galvanized gutter, corrosion will proceed at an extremely rapid rate at that point.

Aluminum will last as long as copper, when it is of equal thickness. But, like copper, it is a relatively soft metal and, therefore, the parts of an aluminum rain system must be properly joined and supported. Bare aluminum will oxidize to a pale gray; once this happens, the gray oxide layer will prevent further oxidation.

151

In industrial areas the gray oxide will be very dark. Aluminum gutters and leaders can be had in a number of bonded colors, which are usually warranted for twenty years or more.

When choosing between rain systems offered by different manufacturers, go for the system with the thickest metal: 0.027 inch is good; thicker is even better.

Polyvinyl chloride (PVC), the same synthetic material that is now being used for water pipes, is also being formed into leaders and gutters. Rain systems made of polyvinyl chloride have the same advantages and disadvantages of other home construction materials made from the same compound. The color goes all the way through, but with time the color tends to fade a little and the shine on the surface will disappear. High temperature causes the material to sag a bit. How high a temperature? How much sag? These questions are difficult to answer because there is also a time element—length of exposure to heat, plus a pressure element. A gutter supported every half-dozen feet will not sag as badly or as quickly as the same gutter supported every dozen feet. In addition, PVC becomes brittle at low temperatures. You are not likely to place your ladder against a vinyl gutter when the temperature is below zero, but a tree limb striking a vinyl gutter at this temperature will break it, whereas the same blow to a metal gutter would only bend it.

INSTALLING LEADERS AND GUTTERS

HOW MANY LEADERS?
Figure an average of one leader every 20 linear feet of gutter, and/or one leader for every 500 square feet of roof surface. Figure, too, that you don't really want a gutter to round a corner because water (plus debris) doesn't round corners very well. It is better to "break" the gutter at the corner and lead the water away to two different leaders in two opposite directions.

PITCH THE GUTTER CORRECTLY
Make certain the fascia is in good condition, clean, and well painted. Then stretch a chalk line from one end of the fascia to the other. Start one end near the top of the fascia and lower the other end to produce a pitch of 1 inch in 20 feet. A little more won't hurt. Less will. Snap the line to give you the location of the top edge of the gutter.

MOUNTING THE SUPPORTS
Giant nail supports are the least desirable. The strongest but the most visible are the types that fasten beneath the roof shingles and reach down to and around the gutter. The types that are nailed to the fascia are the best compromise. In any event, use aluminum nails and try to place them where they will enter the rafters. (Nailheads in the fascia will locate them for you.)

ASSEMBLING THE GUTTER
Aluminum gutters come in lengths of 10, 16, 20, 25, and 30 feet. Plastic gutters come in lengths of 10 and 20 feet. It's best, whenever possible, to use a single length. Since this rarely is possible, you will have to join pieces to meet your needs. In any case, both the aluminum and the plastic gutters can be cut with a hacksaw.

To hold the sections in a perfectly

straight line it is best to assemble them on the ground, preferably on a perfectly level surface. Join the aluminum sections with the aid of slip-joint connectors. Seal the joints with gutter mastic and lock them by drilling holes through the gutter and joint and putting blind rivets through the holes. Five rivets at each joint (that would be a total of ten through the slip joint) is plenty. If you don't want to use rivets, use stainless steel, self-tapping screws. Do not use steel.

Fittings are joined to aluminum gutters the same way. The contacting surfaces are coated with gutter mastic; the joint is made, then drilled and locked with either rivets or screws.

The vinyl gutters are another story. If you play it safe and use mastic and rivets or screws, there's no problem. If you wish a tighter, possibly more permanent joint, you can cement it. The area to be covered with cement is lightly sanded, and cement is applied. The two pieces are brought together and held there for a minute or two. Then the holes are drilled and the rivets or screws installed. It is simple enough. The catch is that the cement—and you must use PVC cement—hardens very quickly. You have about twenty seconds in which to complete the joint. Once (properly) made, it will never come apart.

Aluminum rain system installed.
Courtesy Lifeguard Industries

Gutter Hangers

There are a great variety of gutter-hanger styles and arrangements. Some fasten to the fascia board; some wrap around the gutter and secure by straps nailed under the roof shingles. The free-floating gutter systems generally use the fascia board mounting method with a concealed bar bracket. Variations include fascia aprons and roof aprons. Generally fascia brackets are spaced approximately 32 inches so nail penetrates rafter ends, using 1-1/4-inch aluminum screw shank nails. The roof hanger types should be nailed through sheathing and into rafters. Nail at every other rafter (32 inches maximum).

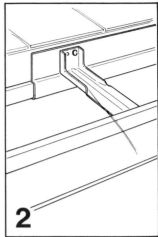

Mounting Methods

A combination hanger used with a free-floating system is shown in Fig. 1. This is a concealed hanger, fascia-mounted, and hooks into front and rear gutter beads.

A variation shown in Fig. 2 features a combination bar hanger and fascia apron for more flashing at the back.

A wrap-around hanger with roofing strap is shown in Figure 3. This traditional style is often used with open rafter ends and should be nailed under roof shingles at rafter location.

Figure 4 shows the spike-and-ferrule mounting. Insert a ferrule between gutter sides and in line with rafter end. Drive gutter spike through gutter, ferrule and into rafter end. Locate at every other rafter.

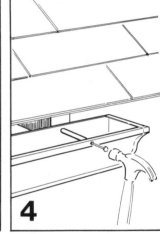

Downspouts

Downspout is installed after gutter is hung, and should be flush with wall for maximum support. Downspouts, elbows and outlet tubes should be riveted together. Locate drop outlets in gutter immediately above down-spout locations. Score and remove a piece of gutter bottom the same size as downspout. Insert drop tube through this hole and apply pop rivet and gutter sealer, (from the inside). Elbow and downspout sections should always slide inside the section immediately below to prevent leakage. Use enough outlets and downspouts to handle water from the roof. A 2x3 downspout can normally handle 600 sq. ft. of roof area, and a 3x4 section can accommodate 1200 sq. ft. Secure downspouts to house with pipe straps, using two per 10 foot length.

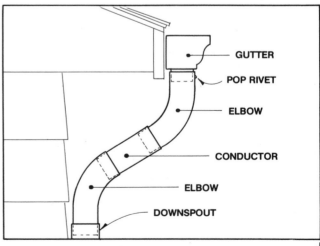

Steps in the installation of gutters and leaders.
Courtesy The Aluminum Association

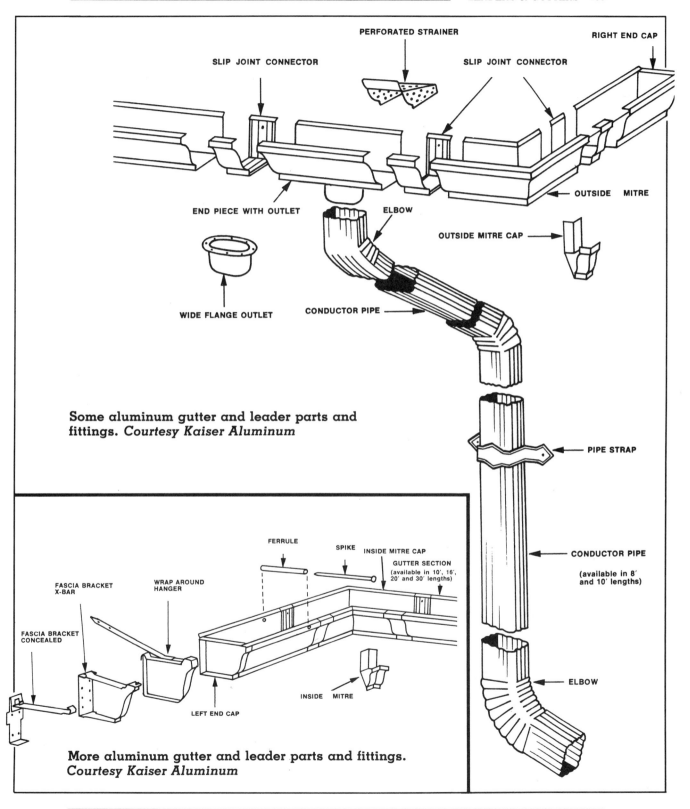

PERFORATED STRAINER

RIGHT END CAP

SLIP JOINT CONNECTOR

SLIP JOINT CONNECTOR

OUTSIDE   MITRE

END PIECE WITH OUTLET

ELBOW

OUTSIDE MITRE CAP

WIDE FLANGE OUTLET

CONDUCTOR PIPE

PIPE STRAP

Some aluminum gutter and leader parts and fittings. *Courtesy Kaiser Aluminum*

CONDUCTOR PIPE

(available in 8′ and 10′ lengths)

FERRULE

SPIKE

INSIDE MITRE CAP

GUTTER SECTION
(available in 10′, 16′, 20′ and 30′ lengths)

FASCIA BRACKET
X-BAR

WRAP AROUND
HANGER

FASCIA BRACKET
CONCEALED

INSIDE   MITRE

LEFT END CAP

ELBOW

More aluminum gutter and leader parts and fittings. *Courtesy Kaiser Aluminum*

The oldest lock ever found was made sometime between 722 and 705 B.C. by the artisans of the Emperor Sargon II, who occupied a 25-acre area in the mile-square city of Khorsabad, an ancient capital of Persia. The key, cut from a heavy, hardwood log, weighs perhaps 20 pounds. It fits into a keyhole large enough to accept a grown man's arm. Pegs on the key had to be matched to holes cut in a large, square bolt of wood. When the mating was accomplished, the key could be turned and the bolt slid free of the doorframe.

The Egyptians had locks and keys even earlier, but nothing but their keys remain, along with paintings of locks and keys. The ancient Egyptian keys were about 14 inches long and used pins of wood or iron. According to our records, the Egyptian locks and keys predated the Persian by some fifteen hundred years.

Greek locks followed chronologically, but not scientifically. They were far simpler than the Egyptian locks. In place of an arrangement of pins that had to fit predrilled holes, the Greeks made keys that were no more than long, curved pieces of metal. But they used a small keyhole so that you could not reach in with a hand and work the lock.

The Romans discarded the 3-foot-long keys the Greeks used and replaced them with iron keys similar to those we now call skeleton keys and use in our warded locks.

From Roman times on locks didn't see much improvement until the first really modern lock was invented in 1778. This was the work of Joseph Bramah, who invented a series of new and improved locks. In 1851, at the International Industrial Exhibition in London, an American locksmith named Alfred C. Hobbs picked two of the best locks England had to offer and won a prize of £200 that had gone uncollected for forty-five years. After this the struggle to invent pickproof locks developed in earnest.

TYPES OF LOCKS

WARDED LOCKS

This lock may be surface mounted or mortised into the thickness of the door. Almost always it consists of a rectangle of cast iron, with mounting holes and a keyhole. A few companies still manufacture these locks, but part interchangeability is almost nil. If yours is broken, carry it with you as you try to find parts in junk shops and the like. If it is important that you repair it, have the broken cast iron brazed. Nothing else will hold it.

These locks are easily surface mounted. All you need do is make the front of the lock flush with the door's edge and at right angles to the same edge. Long screws hold the lock to the door. A single hole through the door takes care of the key. But note that warded locks being made of cast iron are easily broken and more easily picked.

DISK-TUMBLER LOCKS

These are moderate-security, low-priced locks found in office desks, filing cabinets, and automobiles in all price ranges. Most disk-tumbler locks can be installed in a single hole drilled through the door or the doorframe. In some designs portions of the lock are positioned on the inside of the door, either surface mounted or partially mortised. In any case, the installation of this lock is relatively simple, but its hole diameter and location must be exact.

PIN-TUMBLER LOCKS

This is a very popular type of lock that depends on four to eight pins for its security. Only when all of its pins are moved a specific distance can the key be turned, and, along with the key, the bolt withdrawn. Pin position is determined by the cuts on the edge of the key. Pin-tumbler-lock mechanisms are made in a number of designs.

RIM LOCKS

This is a type of pin-tumbler lock that has the cylinder that holds the pins and accepts the key separate from the casing, which mounts the dead bolt and/or the angle-ended latch bolt. The cylinder passes through a hole in the door and is bolted in place. The lock case mounts on the side of the door over the cylinder. A flexible "tail" from the cylinder enters the lock case. When the proper key is introduced into the cylinder, the cylinder can be turned. When the cylinder turns, its tail turns and moves the bolts.

Rim locks have somewhat the same installation requirements that

drawer locks have. You must make sure to drill a hole of the proper size to accept the cylinder and make sure it's the right distance from the edge of the door to meet the lock case. But since the tail is flexible, you have a little leeway in placing the case on the backside of the door over the cylinder opening.

Rim locks can be repaired. Remove the screws holding the case to the door. Then remove the bolts holding the cylinder in place. Take the cylinder and its keys to the locksmith. The smith can not only repair the lock, but also change its keying which means he can make all existing keys inoperative and provide you with a new set of keys. But in many cases, you can do this yourself more economically by simply purchasing a new cylinder and set of keys.

MORTISED RIM LOCKS

The operation of these locks is similar to the aforementioned rim locks. They have the same type of key mechanism. But the cylinders differ in that they are threaded into the case. The case is mortised into the edge of the door. Then the cylinder is slipped through a predrilled hole and screwed into the case. Setscrews prevent the cylinder from being unscrewed and backed out from the front of the door.

Mortised rim locks are much more difficult to install. You must not only drill the correct size hole and locate it accurately, but also mortise the full depth of the lock case. Contrary to general opinion, mortised locks are no stronger than rim locks. Mortising actually weakens the door. Some mortised locks, however, have both a latch bolt and a dead bolt, which together provide the door with a more substantial grip on its frame.

Cylinder replacement is simple enough. The door is opened and the setscrews holding the cylinder are backed off. Then the cylinder may be unscrewed and removed.

TUBULAR LOCKS

These are pin-tumbler locks in which the lock-and-key mechanism is positioned within one knob. They are much easier to install than mortised locks, far less expensive, but not as secure. It is easier to force a tubular lock than it is to force a rim or a mortised lock. Still the tubular lock is more attractive than the rim lock, since the tubular has no case on the inner side of the door.

Tubular locks require two holes, a fairly large one through the door and a second, at right angles to the first,

that passes through the edge of the door. In most instances, new tubular locks are accompanied by a printed paper drilling guide that will accurately locate both holes for you. The lock is taken apart and portions of it are inserted in the holes. A pair of bolts through the inner spindle rose holds all the parts together. Tubular locks are rarely repaired. Generally the entire lock, knob, spindle, and key cylinder are replaced as a unit.

MAINTENANCE

The bolts and latches on a warded lock may be given a spot of grease now and again. The other types of locks are never greased or oiled. Instead they are lubricated annually with a spray of graphite. Powdered graphite can be purchased in flexible squeeze bottles made especially for this purpose.

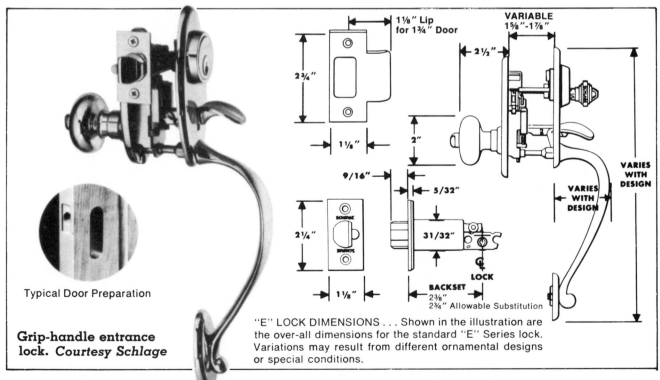

Typical Door Preparation

Grip-handle entrance lock. *Courtesy Schlage*

"E" LOCK DIMENSIONS . . . Shown in the illustration are the over-all dimensions for the standard "E" Series lock. Variations may result from different ornamental designs or special conditions.

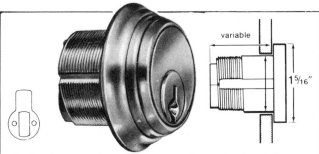

Cylinder used with mortised rim locks. This differs in that it is screwed into the mortised lock. Note threads and tailpiece, which fits on lock mechanism and actuates lock bolt. *Courtesy Schlage*

Two examples of disk-tumbler locks. These are mounted through a single hole. *Courtesy Schlage*

Cylinder used with a surface-mounted rim lock. Rectangular metal plate goes on inside of door. Bolts hold cylinder in place. To get at these bolts the lock must be removed, which means you must be on the inside of the door.

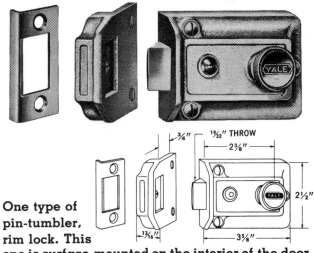

Left: Door preparation. *Right:* Lock installed. *Courtesy Schlage*

One type of pin-tumbler, rim lock. This one is surface-mounted on the interior of the door. The cylinder fits in a hole in the door. Its tail operates the lock's bolt. *Courtesy Yale Lock Co.*

Hand of Door Follow the illustration to correctly determine the hand of the door.

Courtesy Schlage

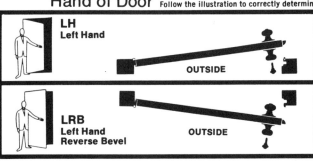

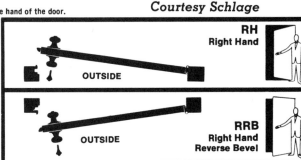

LH Left Hand OUTSIDE

RH Right Hand OUTSIDE

LRB Left Hand Reverse Bevel OUTSIDE

RRB Right Hand Reverse Bevel OUTSIDE

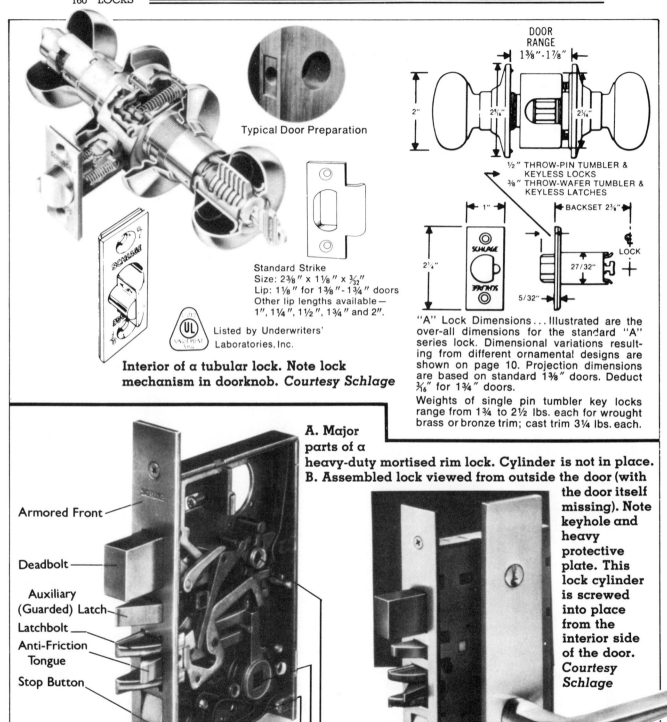

Typical Door Preparation

Standard Strike
Size: 2⅜″ x 1⅛″ x ³⁄₃₂″
Lip: 1⅛″ for 1⅜″ - 1¾″ doors
Other lip lengths available—
1″, 1¼″, 1½″, 1¾″ and 2″.

Listed by Underwriters'
Laboratories, Inc.

Interior of a tubular lock. Note lock mechanism in doorknob. *Courtesy Schlage*

DOOR RANGE 1⅜″ - 1⅞″

2″

2³⁄₁₆″   2¼″

½″ THROW-PIN TUMBLER &
KEYLESS LOCKS
⅜″ THROW-WAFER TUMBLER &
KEYLESS LATCHES

1″   BACKSET 2¾″

2¼″   27/32″   LOCK

5/32″

"A" Lock Dimensions . . . Illustrated are the over-all dimensions for the standard "A" series lock. Dimensional variations resulting from different ornamental designs are shown on page 10. Projection dimensions are based on standard 1⅜″ doors. Deduct ³⁄₁₆″ for 1¾″ doors.

Weights of single pin tumbler key locks range from 1¾ to 2½ lbs. each for wrought brass or bronze trim; cast trim 3¼ lbs. each.

A. Major parts of a heavy-duty mortised rim lock. Cylinder is not in place. B. Assembled lock viewed from outside the door (with the door itself missing). Note keyhole and heavy protective plate. This lock cylinder is screwed into place from the interior side of the door. *Courtesy Schlage*

Armored Front

Deadbolt

Auxiliary (Guarded) Latch

Latchbolt

Anti-Friction Tongue

Stop Button

Turn Unit Hub

Lever Hubs

Gun type springs

A

B

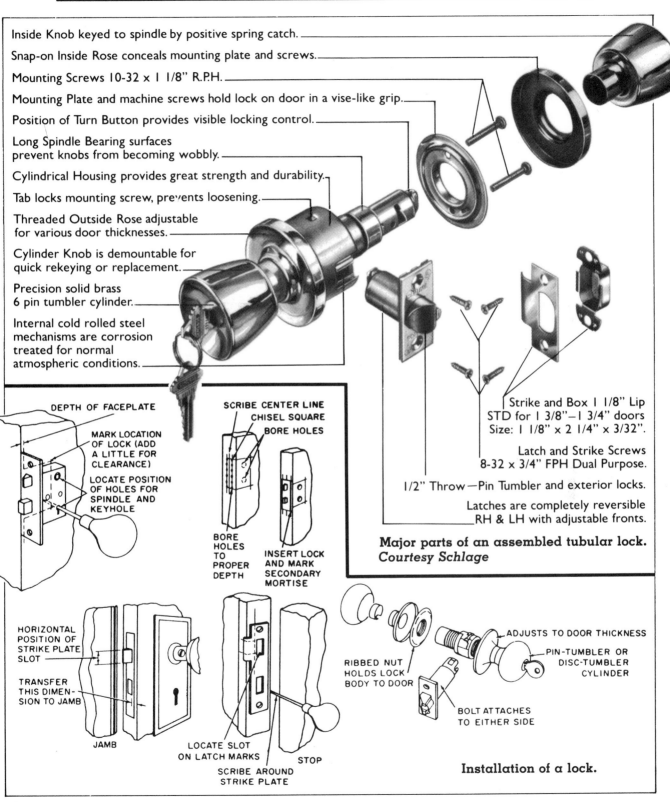

Inside Knob keyed to spindle by positive spring catch.

Snap-on Inside Rose conceals mounting plate and screws.

Mounting Screws 10-32 x 1 1/8" R.P.H.

Mounting Plate and machine screws hold lock on door in a vise-like grip.

Position of Turn Button provides visible locking control.

Long Spindle Bearing surfaces prevent knobs from becoming wobbly.

Cylindrical Housing provides great strength and durability.

Tab locks mounting screw, prevents loosening.

Threaded Outside Rose adjustable for various door thicknesses.

Cylinder Knob is demountable for quick rekeying or replacement.

Precision solid brass 6 pin tumbler cylinder.

Internal cold rolled steel mechanisms are corrosion treated for normal atmospheric conditions.

Strike and Box 1 1/8" Lip STD for 1 3/8"–1 3/4" doors Size: 1 1/8" x 2 1/4" x 3/32".

Latch and Strike Screws 8-32 x 3/4" FPH Dual Purpose.

1/2" Throw—Pin Tumbler and exterior locks.

Latches are completely reversible RH & LH with adjustable fronts.

Major parts of an assembled tubular lock.
Courtesy Schlage

DEPTH OF FACEPLATE

MARK LOCATION OF LOCK (ADD A LITTLE FOR CLEARANCE)

LOCATE POSITION OF HOLES FOR SPINDLE AND KEYHOLE

SCRIBE CENTER LINE
CHISEL SQUARE
BORE HOLES

BORE HOLES TO PROPER DEPTH

INSERT LOCK AND MARK SECONDARY MORTISE

HORIZONTAL POSITION OF STRIKE PLATE SLOT

TRANSFER THIS DIMENSION TO JAMB

JAMB

LOCATE SLOT ON LATCH MARKS

SCRIBE AROUND STRIKE PLATE

STOP

RIBBED NUT HOLDS LOCK BODY TO DOOR

ADJUSTS TO DOOR THICKNESS

PIN-TUMBLER OR DISC-TUMBLER CYLINDER

BOLT ATTACHES TO EITHER SIDE

Installation of a lock.

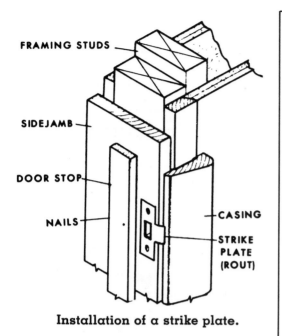

FRAMING STUDS

SIDEJAMB

DOOR STOP

NAILS

CASING

STRIKE PLATE (ROUT)

Installation of a strike plate.

Double-safety lock. The in-knob lock mechanism is used to lock the latch bolt. This bolt slips into place by itself when the door is closed. The dead bolt (the upper bolt) has its own keying mechanism. This bolt cannot be forced back with a sheet of plastic as can the in-knob lock. Thus you can lock the door with one bolt and one key or two bolts and two keys.

Housing and Linkage

Mounting Screws

Inside Rose and Turn

Inside Knob

One-Inch Throw Steel deadbolt with concealed Hardened Roller

Adjustable Front Flat or Beveled

7/8" Trim Ring and Hardened Steel Insert

1/8" Trim Ring and Hardened Steel Insert for 1 3/8" Doors

Precision Solid Brass Pin Tumbler Cylinder

Outside Knob and Lock Mechanism

1/2" Throw Deadlatch

Strike and Box

Deadbolt Strike, Box and Wood Frame Reinforcer with 3" screws

Latch and Strike Screws

25 METAL

Most of all the known elements are metal. Most of these metals we never see or handle *as* metals. Sodium, for example, a part of everyday salt, is a metal so volatile that when combined with oxygen will burst into flame immediately. It must be stored under kerosene to keep it inactive. Combined with chloride, it behaves itself.

Metal weights and strengths vary greatly. Iridium, used for the tips of better pens, weighs 1,400 pounds per cubic foot. Gold weighs less: 1,205 pounds; iron weighs only 490 pounds, aluminum weighs 166.7 pounds, and sodium weighs only 60.6 pounds per cubic foot.

Iron is, of course, stronger than aluminum. But some aluminum alloys are as strong as some of the steels, and aluminum weighs only a third as much as steel.

OXIDATION

All metals oxidize, which means they combine with oxygen. Some metals—iron for example—rust very quickly. Aluminum rusts even more quickly. Its rust, however, is aluminum oxide, which is a very stable compound. Aluminum turns a light gray almost the instant it is exposed to air. The oxide then protects the underlying metal almost indefinitely.

All metals are crystalline, which means their atoms are aligned in regular patterns. When a piece of metal is bent back and forth until it breaks, the broken ends appear to be crystalline. The metal has not actually crystallized, it has simply broken along its grain lines.

CORROSION

Corrosion differs from oxidation (rusting) in that it is not merely oxygen combining with the metal. True corrosion occurs when two dissimilar metals form part of an electrolytic cell (which is the wet form of the common dry cell battery used in flashlights). Thus corrosion requires two metals plus an electrolyte, which can be water. Since there is no such thing as absolutely pure water, even rainwater can serve as an electrolyte. Obviously, salt water or even rainwater that has passed through smog is a powerful electrolyte. As soon as the "cell" is set up, the movement of metal atoms takes place. The stronger the electrolyte and the more dissimilar the two metals, the faster atoms move from one metal to the other. In simpler terms, a hole is eaten into one metal.

The point of all this is that you should be very careful about mixing dissimilar metals in construction and repair work. Should you find a sagging copper tube in your basement, *don't* pull it up in to place with a piece of galvanized wire. If you have gone to the expense of installing copper gutters and leaders, *don't* fasten them in place with galvanized (zinc-covered) nails. By the same measure, don't use iron nails on aluminum or with aluminum. Use copper on copper, galvanized nails on galvanized iron, and aluminum nails on or with aluminum. If you are installing roof shingles and let a galvanized nail fall and remain in a copper or aluminum gutter, you are going to have a hole there in a few weeks.

Any time you place two dissimilar metals in contact where there is or may be moisture you accelerate corrosion a hundredfold. Where a sweaty copper tube held in place with copper clips may last several hundred years, if the same tube is held in place with a galvanized iron strap, it will open up in less than a year.

SOURCES OF SUPPLY

When all you require is a few small pieces of metal, the local hardware shop or lumberyard is probably the most convenient source. These places usually stock a variety of bars, rods, straps, and angles of aluminum and mild steel. Some also carry threaded rods. Generally, piece length is 36 or 48 inches.

In addition these shops and yards stock metal trim: 8-foot pieces of rounded flats and inside and outside corners of aluminum. A few of the yards stock 4-×-8-foot pierced sheets of mild steel and aluminum. These sheets are cut to size and used for radiator covers and the like.

A few of these shops will stock 3-×-4-foot sheets of metal, generally in 20-gauge (the larger the gauge number the thinner the sheet). The sheets are moderately soft and made of some rust-free alloy of iron. They, too, are expensive.

IRONWORKS

For an occasional piece of metal the aforementioned supply sources are fine. But when you need heavier and longer lengths, try the local ironworks. You will find them listed in the Yellow Pages as ironworks, iron-railing manufacturers, ornamental ironworks, and so on.

The ironworks is the metal equivalent of a lumberyard. Here they stock, cut, drill, and sometimes bend steel plate, strips, bars, rods, angles, I beams, and more. They will cut to order for a nominal fee and you pay for the metal by the pound.

Iron railing and ornamental ironworks are secondary sources. They buy from the ironworks or directly from the steel mill. They have a limited range of sizes and they charge more for the metal and for cutting.

METAL SUPPLY COMPANIES

These differ from the previously listed sources in that they carry a range of different metals. It is here that you can find aluminum, brass, bronze, copper, and more. They generally have a minimum charge. They too will cut and drill to your specifications. Their charge for cutting depends on the accuracy of your requirements. For a square edge the metal must be sawn. For a perfectly square edge the metal must be ground after sawing. On the other hand, power cutting takes but an instant. However, the edge produced by the giant snips is rough and the metal's end is somewhat distorted.

TINSMITHS

For sheets of galvanized iron, copper, and aluminum try the local tinsmith.

If there is none in your area, try the wholesale roofing supply companies.

They often stock sheet metal and sheet metal piping.

CORROSION CONTROL GUIDE

Magnesium (Mg)
Magnesium alloys
Aluminum (Al)
Zinc (Zn)
Iron (Fe)
Cadmium (Cd)
Steel and iron
Cast iron
Nickel (Ni)
Lead-tin
Lead (Pb)

Tin (Sn)
Hydrogen (H)
Brass
Copper (Cu)
Bronze
Copper-nickel
Silver (Ag)
Mercury (Hg)
Platinum (Pt)
Gold (Au)

When any two of the above metals are placed in contact with each other in the presence of an electrolyte—water plus any salt—or even some of the metals themselves in dissolved form, corrosion occurs. The metal physically higher on the list becomes the anode and corrodes with little damage to the metal or alloy lower on the list, which becomes the cathode. The closer the two metals are on the list, the less their galvanic difference and the less corrosion. The farther apart the two metals are on the list, the greater the rate of corrosion.

MILLWORK

(ALSO SEE CABINETS, DOORS, STAIRS, WINDOWS)

First there were carpenters. (Noah, for example, was a carpenter of the shipwright fraternity.) All work—cutting and shaping—was done by hand. To smooth a board carpenters used a plane with a straight cutting edge. To make a half-round shape they used a plane with a half-round indentation on its cutting blade. There was a time not too far back when carpenters carried dozens of different planes, each with differently shaped blades, to the job with them. Finishing out or trimming out the interior of a home in those golden days could take a single carpenter all winter.

Then along came the mill and changed most of it. With the advent of waterpower, and later steam power, the shaping of strips of wood to make ornamental moldings was accomplished in the mill. The carpenter now had merely to cut and position the preshaped wood. The wood and the house parts assembled from such mill-shaped pieces of wood came to be known as millwork.

MOLDING

SHAPES

The accompanying illustrations show the major molding shapes currently manufactured and their dimensions. These shapes and dimensions were classified by the wood molding industry some twenty-five years ago. They are the most popular and can be bought at or through any lumberyard. Other shapes or profiles can be made, but they require special order.

MANUFACTURE

Ponderosa pine is the major wood used for moldings. Sugar pine is also used, and some prefer it to ponderosa. In addition, Douglas fir, larch, white fir, cedar, and hemlock are used. The fir has a grain that tends to rise when painted and with the passage of time. It is probably the last choice for exposed molding.

The best molding is made from a single strip of wood. The least desirable molding is made from two or more short pieces joined by finger joints. Unfortunately, the glue used is not waterproof, so if you are going to use finger-jointed molding, use it indoors.

GRADES

Wood moldings are manufactured in two grades: N and P. N is clean enough to take light staining and varnish. It may have a few small knots and defects showing. P has many more knots and defects and it may contain finger joints. P is suitable only for opaque painting.

DIMENSIONS

Thickness and width are kept to plus or minus 1/32 of an inch.

OTHER MILLWORK

In addition to moldings mills also make wood railings, porch parts, fireplace mantels, various wood ornamentation, and special projects.

Most larger lumberyards have millwork facilities for making out of wood almost anything you may want. These items are individually priced based on the material requirements and labor that go into each one.

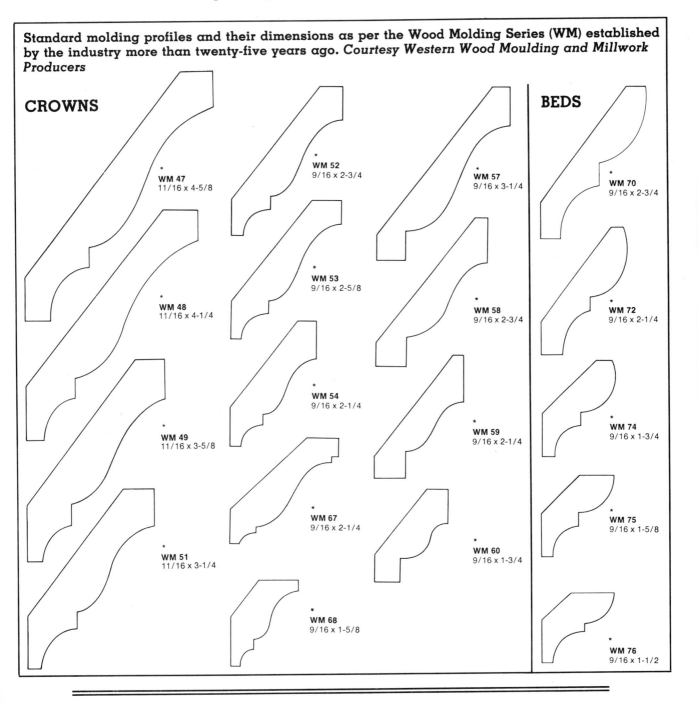

Standard molding profiles and their dimensions as per the Wood Molding Series (WM) established by the industry more than twenty-five years ago. *Courtesy Western Wood Moulding and Millwork Producers*

CROWNS

WM 47
11/16 x 4-5/8

WM 48
11/16 x 4-1/4

WM 49
11/16 x 3-5/8

WM 51
11/16 x 3-1/4

WM 52
9/16 x 2-3/4

WM 53
9/16 x 2-5/8

WM 54
9/16 x 2-1/4

WM 67
9/16 x 2-1/4

WM 68
9/16 x 1-5/8

WM 57
9/16 x 3-1/4

WM 58
9/16 x 2-3/4

WM 59
9/16 x 2-1/4

WM 60
9/16 x 1-3/4

BEDS

WM 70
9/16 x 2-3/4

WM 72
9/16 x 2-1/4

WM 74
9/16 x 1-3/4

WM 75
9/16 x 1-5/8

WM 76
9/16 x 1-1/2

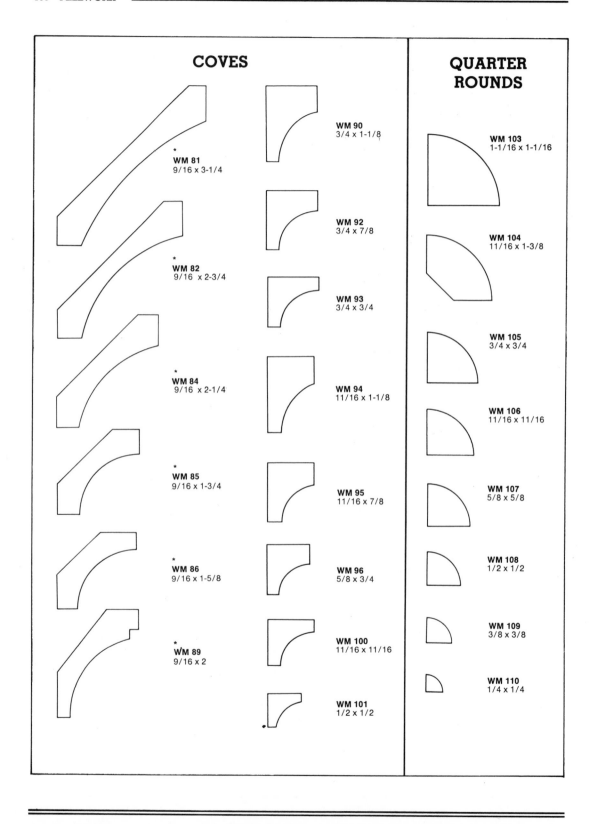

COVES

WM 81
9/16 x 3-1/4

WM 82
9/16 x 2-3/4

WM 84
9/16 x 2-1/4

WM 85
9/16 x 1-3/4

WM 86
9/16 x 1-5/8

WM 89
9/16 x 2

WM 90
3/4 x 1-1/8

WM 92
3/4 x 7/8

WM 93
3/4 x 3/4

WM 94
11/16 x 1-1/8

WM 95
11/16 x 7/8

WM 96
5/8 x 3/4

WM 100
11/16 x 11/16

WM 101
1/2 x 1/2

QUARTER ROUNDS

WM 103
1-1/16 x 1-1/16

WM 104
11/16 x 1-3/8

WM 105
3/4 x 3/4

WM 106
11/16 x 11/16

WM 107
5/8 x 5/8

WM 108
1/2 x 1/2

WM 109
3/8 x 3/8

WM 110
1/4 x 1/4

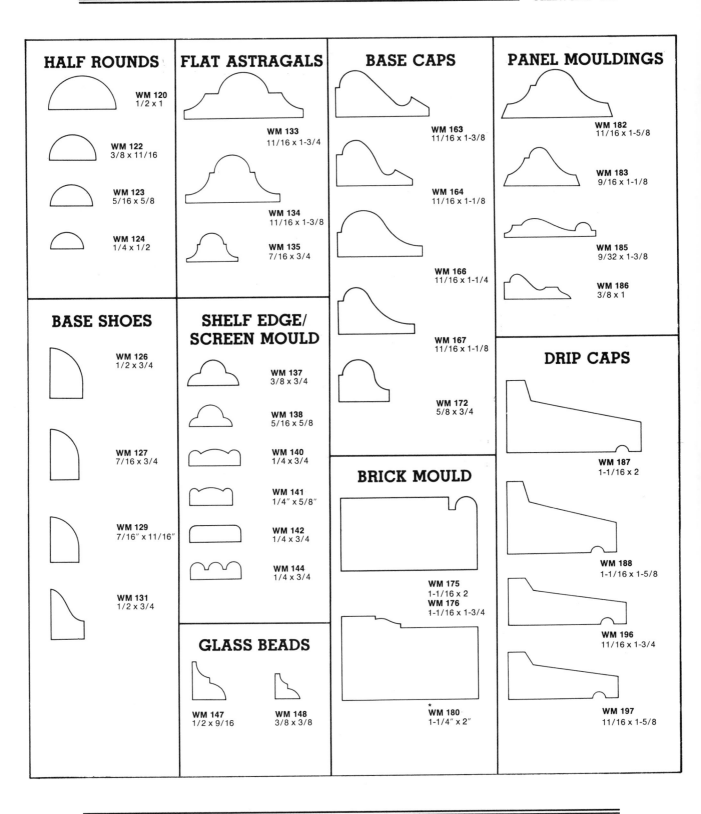

HALF ROUNDS

WM 120
1/2 x 1

WM 122
3/8 x 11/16

WM 123
5/16 x 5/8

WM 124
1/4 x 1/2

FLAT ASTRAGALS

WM 133
11/16 x 1-3/4

WM 134
11/16 x 1-3/8

WM 135
7/16 x 3/4

BASE CAPS

WM 163
11/16 x 1-3/8

WM 164
11/16 x 1-1/8

WM 166
11/16 x 1-1/4

WM 167
11/16 x 1-1/8

WM 172
5/8 x 3/4

PANEL MOULDINGS

WM 182
11/16 x 1-5/8

WM 183
9/16 x 1-1/8

WM 185
9/32 x 1-3/8

WM 186
3/8 x 1

BASE SHOES

WM 126
1/2 x 3/4

WM 127
7/16 x 3/4

WM 129
7/16" x 11/16"

WM 131
1/2 x 3/4

SHELF EDGE/ SCREEN MOULD

WM 137
3/8 x 3/4

WM 138
5/16 x 5/8

WM 140
1/4 x 3/4

WM 141
1/4" x 5/8"

WM 142
1/4 x 3/4

WM 144
1/4 x 3/4

GLASS BEADS

WM 147
1/2 x 9/16

WM 148
3/8 x 3/8

BRICK MOULD

WM 175
1-1/16 x 2
WM 176
1-1/16 x 1-3/4

*
WM 180
1-1/4" x 2"

DRIP CAPS

WM 187
1-1/16 x 2

WM 188
1-1/16 x 1-5/8

WM 196
11/16 x 1-3/4

WM 197
11/16 x 1-5/8

CASING

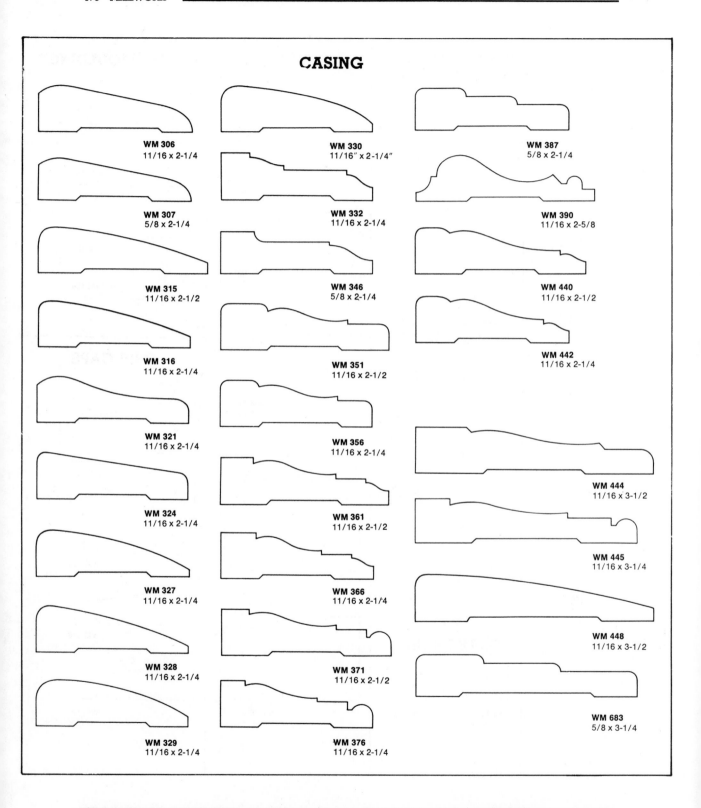

WM 306
11/16 x 2-1/4

WM 307
5/8 x 2-1/4

WM 315
11/16 x 2-1/2

WM 316
11/16 x 2-1/4

WM 321
11/16 x 2-1/4

WM 324
11/16 x 2-1/4

WM 327
11/16 x 2-1/4

WM 328
11/16 x 2-1/4

WM 329
11/16 x 2-1/4

WM 330
11/16" x 2-1/4"

WM 332
11/16 x 2-1/4

WM 346
5/8 x 2-1/4

WM 351
11/16 x 2-1/2

WM 356
11/16 x 2-1/4

WM 361
11/16 x 2-1/2

WM 366
11/16 x 2-1/4

WM 371
11/16 x 2-1/2

WM 376
11/16 x 2-1/4

WM 387
5/8 x 2-1/4

WM 390
11/16 x 2-5/8

WM 440
11/16 x 2-1/2

WM 442
11/16 x 2-1/4

WM 444
11/16 x 3-1/2

WM 445
11/16 x 3-1/4

WM 448
11/16 x 3-1/2

WM 683
5/8 x 3-1/4

CASING

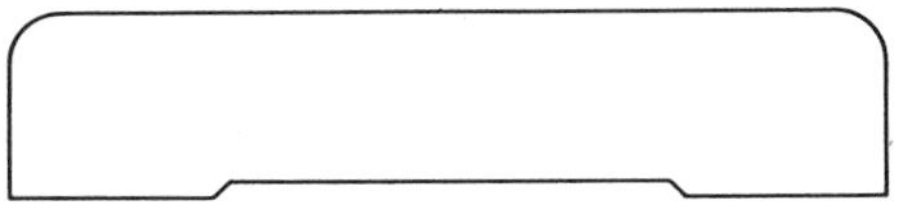

WM 410 11/16 x 4-1/4
WM 412 11/16 x 3-1/2
WM 413 11/16 x 3-1/4 (Illus).

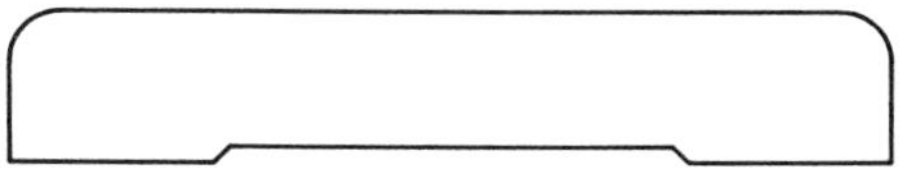

WM 430 9/16 x 4-1/4
WM 432 9/16 x 3-1/2
WM 433 9/16 x 3-1/4 (Illus.)

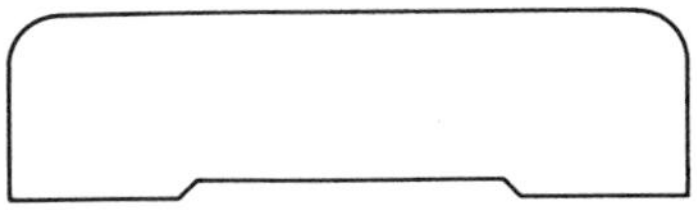

WM 452 11/16 x 2-1/2 (Illus.)
WM 453 11/16 x 2-1/4

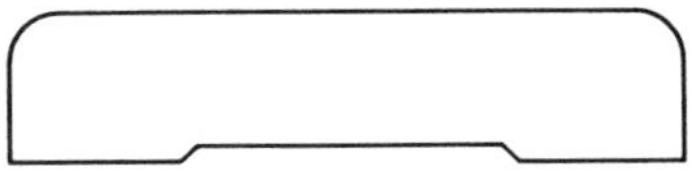

WM 492 7/16 x 2-1/2 (Illus.)
WM 493 7/16 x 2-1/4

WM 472 9/16 x 2-1/2 (Illus.)
WM 473 9/16 x 2-1/4

LATTICE

WM 265 9/32 x 1-3/4
WM 266 9/32 x 1-5/8
WM 267 9/32 x 1-3/8
WM 268 9/32 x 1-1/8

Lattice also available in 1/4 thickness.

PICTURE MOULDINGS

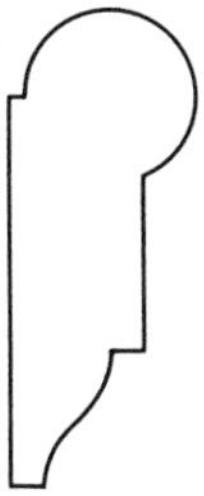

WM 273 11/16 x 1-3/4
WM 276 11/16 x 1-3/4 

BACK BANDS

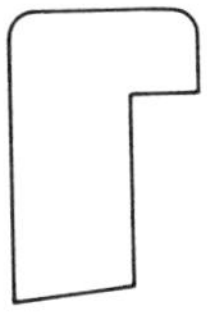

WM 280 11/16 x 1-1/16
WM 281 11/16 x 1-1/8 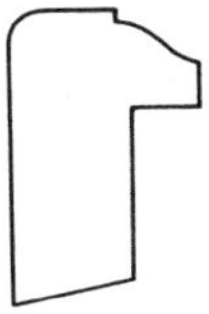

WAINSCOT/PLY CAP MOULDINGS

WM 290 11/16 x 1-3/8

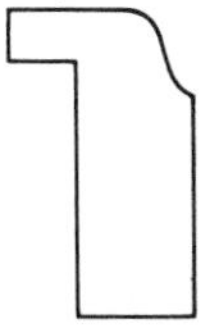

WM 294 11/16 x 1-1/8

WM 296 3/4 x 3/4

WM 292 9/16 x 1-1/8

WM 295 1/2 x 1-1/4

CHAIR RAILS

WM 298 11/16 x 2-1/2

WM 297 11/16 x 3

WM 303 9/16 x 2-1/2

WM 300 1-1/16 x 3

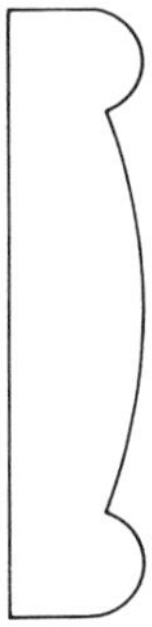

WM 304 1/2 x 2-1/4
WM 390 11/16 x 2-5/8

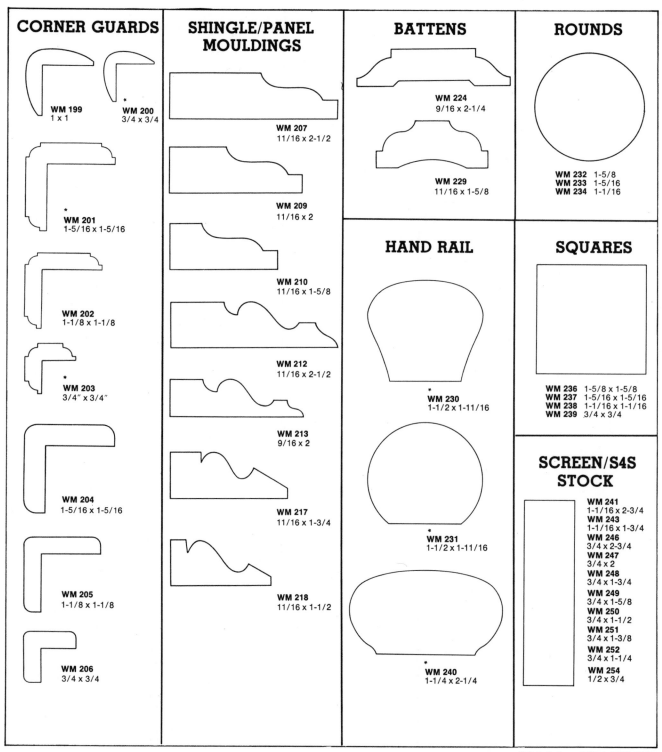

CORNER GUARDS

WM 199
1 x 1

* WM 200
3/4 x 3/4

* WM 201
1-5/16 x 1-5/16

WM 202
1-1/8 x 1-1/8

* WM 203
3/4" x 3/4"

WM 204
1-5/16 x 1-5/16

WM 205
1-1/8 x 1-1/8

WM 206
3/4 x 3/4

SHINGLE/PANEL MOULDINGS

WM 207
11/16 x 2-1/2

WM 209
11/16 x 2

WM 210
11/16 x 1-5/8

WM 212
11/16 x 2-1/2

WM 213
9/16 x 2

WM 217
11/16 x 1-3/4

WM 218
11/16 x 1-1/2

BATTENS

WM 224
9/16 x 2-1/4

WM 229
11/16 x 1-5/8

HAND RAIL

* WM 230
1-1/2 x 1-11/16

* WM 231
1-1/2 x 1-11/16

* WM 240
1-1/4 x 2-1/4

ROUNDS

WM 232   1-5/8
WM 233   1-5/16
WM 234   1-1/16

SQUARES

WM 236   1-5/8 x 1-5/8
WM 237   1-5/16 x 1-5/16
WM 238   1-1/16 x 1-1/16
WM 239   3/4 x 3/4

SCREEN/S4S STOCK

WM 241
1-1/16 x 2-3/4
WM 243
1-1/16 x 1-3/4
WM 246
3/4 x 2-3/4
WM 247
3/4 x 2
WM 248
3/4 x 1-3/4
WM 249
3/4 x 1-5/8
WM 250
3/4 x 1-1/2
WM 251
3/4 x 1-3/8
WM 252
3/4 x 1-1/4
WM 254
1/2 x 3/4

S4S stock also available in 7/16", 1/2", 9/16", 5/8" and 11/16" standard thickness.

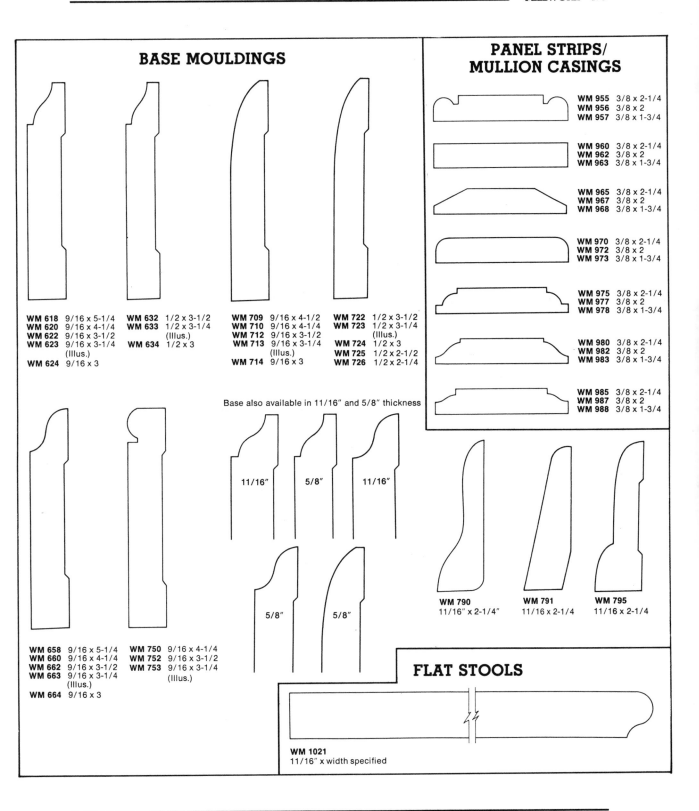

BASE MOULDINGS

WM 618	9/16 x 5-1/4
WM 620	9/16 x 4-1/4
WM 622	9/16 x 3-1/2
WM 623	9/16 x 3-1/4
	(Illus.)
WM 624	9/16 x 3

WM 632	1/2 x 3-1/2
WM 633	1/2 x 3-1/4
	(Illus.)
WM 634	1/2 x 3

WM 709	9/16 x 4-1/2
WM 710	9/16 x 4-1/4
WM 712	9/16 x 3-1/2
WM 713	9/16 x 3-1/4
	(Illus.)
WM 714	9/16 x 3

WM 722	1/2 x 3-1/2
WM 723	1/2 x 3-1/4
	(Illus.)
WM 724	1/2 x 3
WM 725	1/2 x 2-1/2
WM 726	1/2 x 2-1/4

Base also available in 11/16″ and 5/8″ thickness

11/16″ 5/8″ 11/16″

5/8″ 5/8″

WM 658	9/16 x 5-1/4
WM 660	9/16 x 4-1/4
WM 662	9/16 x 3-1/2
WM 663	9/16 x 3-1/4
	(Illus.)
WM 664	9/16 x 3

WM 750	9/16 x 4-1/4
WM 752	9/16 x 3-1/2
WM 753	9/16 x 3-1/4
	(Illus.)

PANEL STRIPS/ MULLION CASINGS

WM 955	3/8 x 2-1/4
WM 956	3/8 x 2
WM 957	3/8 x 1-3/4

WM 960	3/8 x 2-1/4
WM 962	3/8 x 2
WM 963	3/8 x 1-3/4

WM 965	3/8 x 2-1/4
WM 967	3/8 x 2
WM 968	3/8 x 1-3/4

WM 970	3/8 x 2-1/4
WM 972	3/8 x 2
WM 973	3/8 x 1-3/4

WM 975	3/8 x 2-1/4
WM 977	3/8 x 2
WM 978	3/8 x 1-3/4

WM 980	3/8 x 2-1/4
WM 982	3/8 x 2
WM 983	3/8 x 1-3/4

WM 985	3/8 x 2-1/4
WM 987	3/8 x 2
WM 988	3/8 x 1-3/4

WM 790	11/16″ x 2-1/4″
WM 791	11/16 x 2-1/4
WM 795	11/16 x 2-1/4

FLAT STOOLS

WM 1021
11/16″ x width specified

STOPS

WM 813	7/16 x 2-1/4
WM 814	7/16 x 1-3/4
WM 815	7/16 x 1-5/8
WM 816	7/16 x 1-3/8 (Illus.)
WM 817	7/16 x 1-1/4
WM 818	7/16 x 1-1/8
WM 820	7/16 x 7/8

WM 823	3/8 x 2-1/4
WM 824	3/8 x 1-3/4
WM 825	3/8 x 1-5/8
WM 826	3/8 x 1-3/8 (Illus.)
WM 827	3/8 x 1-1/4
WM 828	3/8 x 1-1/8
WM 830	3/8 x 7/8
WM 831	3/8 x 3/4

WM 843	7/16 x 2-1/4
WM 844	7/16 x 1-3/4
WM 845	7/16 x 1-5/8
WM 846	7/16 x 1-3/8 (Illus.)
WM 847	7/16 x 1-1/4
WM 848	7/16 x 1-1/8
WM 850	7/16 x 7/8
WM 851	7/16 x 3/4

WM 853	3/8 x 2-1/4
WM 854	3/8 x 1-3/4
WM 855	3/8 x 1-5/8
WM 856	3/8 x 1-3/8 (Illus.)
WM 857	3/8 x 1-1/4
WM 858	3/8 x 1-1/8
WM 860	3/8 x 7/8
WM 861	3/8 x 3/4

WM 873	7/16 x 2-1/4
WM 874	7/16 x 1-3/4
WM 875	7/16 x 1-5/8
WM 876	7/16 x 1-3/8 (Illus.)
WM 877	7/16 x 1-1/4
WM 878	7/16 x 1-1/8
WM 880	7/16 x 7/8
WM 881	7/16 x 3/4

WM 883	3/8 x 2-1/4
WM 884	3/8 x 1-3/4
WM 885	3/8 x 1-5/8
WM 886	3/8 x 1-3/8 (Illus.)
WM 887	3/8 x 1-1/4
WM 888	3/8 x 1-1/8
WM 890	3/8 x 7/8
WM 891	3/8 x 3/4

WM 903	7/16 x 2-1/4
WM 904	7/16 x 1-3/4
WM 905	7/16 x 1-5/8
WM 906	7/16 x 1-3/8 (Illus.)
WM 907	7/16 x 1-1/4
WM 908	7/16 x 1-1/8
WM 910	7/16 x 7/8
WM 911	7/16 x 3/4

WM 913	3/8 x 2-1/4
WM 914	3/8 x 1-3/4
WM 915	3/8 x 1-5/8
WM 916	3/8 x 1-3/8 (Illus.)
WM 917	3/8 x 1-1/4
WM 918	3/8 x 1-1/8
WM 920	3/8 x 7/8
WM 921	3/8 x 3/4

WM 933	7/16 x 2-1/4
WM 934	7/16 x 1-3/4
WM 935	7/16 x 1-5/8
WM 936	7/16 x 1-3/8 (Illus.)
WM 937	7/16 x 1-1/4
WM 938	7/16 x 1-1/8
WM 940	7/16 x 7/8
WM 941	7/16 x 3/4

WM 943	3/8 x 2-1/4
WM 944	3/8 x 1-3/4
WM 945	3/8 x 1-5/8
WM 946	3/8 x 1-3/8 (Illus.)
WM 947	3/8 x 1-1/4
WM 948	3/8 x 1-1/8
WM 950	3/8 x 7/8
WM 951	3/8 x 3/4

WM 953	7/16 x Width Specified

WM 954	3/8 x Width Specified

SHELF CLEAT

WM 990
11/16 x 1-1/2

CHAMFER STRIP

WM 995
3/4 x 3/4

INSIDE CORNER

WM 999
5/16 x 1

MOULDINGS

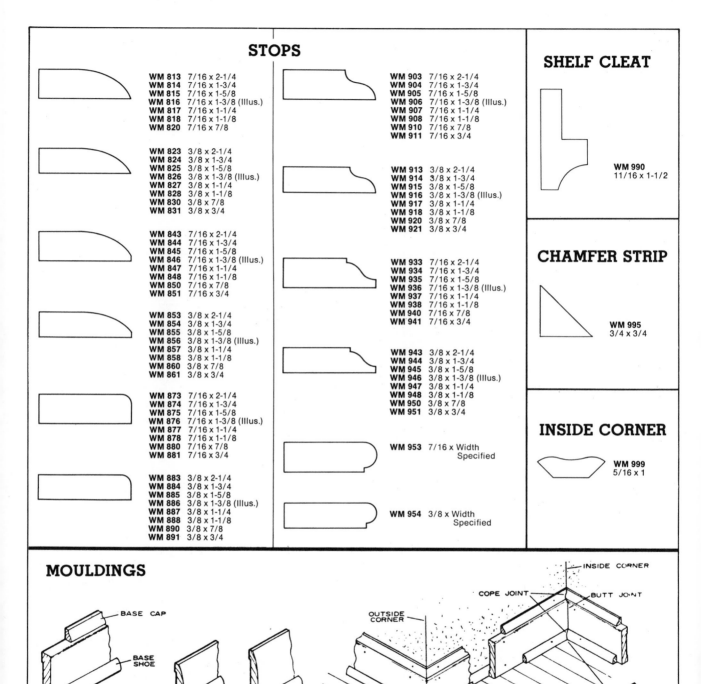

How various moldings may be used to "finish" a wall-to-floor joint.

RABBETED STOOLS

**SPECIFY WIDTH OF RABBET
AND DEGREE OF BEVEL**

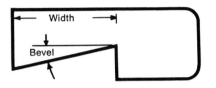

Width

Bevel

10°   14°

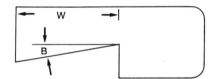

WM 1131	1-1/16 x 3-5/8
WM 1133	1-1/16 x 3-1/4
WM 1134	1-1/16 x 2-3/4

W

B

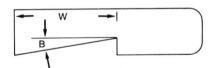

WM 1153	11/16 x 3-1/4
WM 1154	11/16 x 2-3/4
WM 1155	11/16 x 2-1/2
WM 1156	11/16 x 2-1/4

W

B

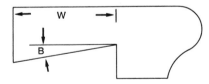

WM 1161	1-1/16 x 3-5/8
WM 1163	1-1/16 x 3-1/4
WM 1164	1-1/16 x 2-3/4

W

B

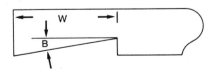

WM 1193	11/16 x 3-1/4
WM 1194	11/16 x 2-3/4
WM 1195	11/16 x 2-1/2
WM 1196	11/16 x 2-1/4

W

B

T-ASTRAGALS

WM 1300
1-1/4 x 2-1/4

WM 1305
1-1/4 x 2

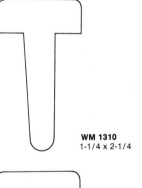

WM 1310
1-1/4 x 2-1/4

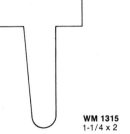

WM 1315
1-1/4 x 2

ROUND COLUMNS

Recommended Maximum Load Capability	Column Diameter	Column Length Ft.	Outside Diameter at Top of Column In.	Inside Diameter at Top of Column In.	Outside Diameter at Bottom of Column In.	Inside Diameter at Bottom of Column In.	Length of Column Shaft Ft.	Lbs. Weight
Lb.			A	B	C	D	E	
8,600	6"	8-0	4-1/4	2-1/4	5-5/8	3	7-7	31
16,600	8"	8-0	6-1/4	3-3/4	7-5/8	5-1/4	7-7	42
		10-0	6-1/4	3-3/4	7-5/8	5	9-7	47
20,000	10"	8-0	8-1/4	5-3/4	9-5/8	7-1/8	7-7	53
		10-0	8-1/4	5-3/4	9-5/8	7-1/4	9-7	62
		12-0	8-1/4	5-3/4	9-5/8	7-1/4	11-7	69
20,000	12"	8-0	10-1/4	7-3/4	11-5/8	9-1/4	7-7	61
		10-0	10-1/4	7-3/4	11-5/8	9	9-7	75
		12-0	10-1/4	7-3/4	11-5/8	9	11-7	87
		16-0	10-1/4	7-3/4	11-5/8	9	15-7	120
20,000	16"	16-0	13	10-1/4	15-5/8	13	15-5	222
		18-0	13	10-1/4	15-5/8	13	17-5	245
		20-0	13	10-1/4	15-5/8	13	19-5	266
20,000	18"	16-0	15	12-1/8	17-5/8	14-3/4	15-5	218
		18-0	15	12-1/8	17-5/8	14-3/4	17-5	274
		20-0	15	12-1/8	17-5/8	14-3/4	19-5	300
20,000	20"	16-0	17	14-1/4	19-5/8	16-7/8	15-5	280
		18-0	17	14-1/4	19-5/8	16-7/8	17-5	310
		20-0	17	14-1/4	19-5/8	16-7/8	19-5	339

STRESS DATA

Columns constructed with ponderosa/sugar pine, with allowable stresses per the National Design Specification for Stress-Grade Lumber and Its Fastenings.

Load to be applied concentrically at top of column. Design loads valid only if column caps and bases are stressed parallel to the grain, and only if uniform contact is made between the full area of the column ends and the cap and base units.

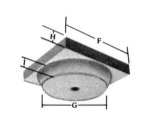

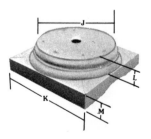

BASES				CAPITALS			
ROUND		SQUARE		ROUND		SQUARE	
Dia.	Thickness	Size	Thickness	Dia.	Thickness	Size	Thickness
J	L	K	M	G	I	F	H
6-1/8"	1-1/2"	8-1/8"	1-1/2"	5-1/8"	1-1/4"	6-3/4"	1-1/4"
8	1-1/2	10	1-1/2	6-3/4	1-1/4	8-3/8	1-1/4
10	1-1/2	12	1-1/2	10-3/8	1-1/2	10-3/8	1-1/2
12	1-1/2	14	1-1/2	10-3/8	1-1/2	12	1-1/2
16-3/8	2-1/4	18-3/4	2-1/4	13-3/4	2-1/4	16	2-1/4
18-1/2	3-1/8	22	3-1/8	15-3/4	3	18-3/4	3-1/8
20-1/2	3-1/8	24	3	17-5/8	3	20-3/4	3-1/8

capitals and bases

Caps and Bases (for 16", 18" and 20" diameter columns).* Manufactured of high density polyurethane, caps and bases are packed one set to a carton. Available exclusive of columns. Paint primed, ready to install and finish.

*Caps and Bases for smaller diameter columns are manufactured from ponderosa and/or sugar pine.

square box columns

6" x 6" x 8' - 0"
8" x 8" x 8' - 0"
8" x 8" x 10' - 0"

Typical wooden columns and bases. *Courtesy C. E. Morgan*

Mortar is used to join brick to brick, stone to stone, glass block to glass block, concrete block to concrete block, or any combination thereof.

Mortar is made by mixing cement, sand, and water to make a thick paste, or by mixing cement, lime, sand, and water together. In either case sufficient water must be added to wet the mixture thoroughly, and the ingredients must be mixed so thoroughly that the mortar has one even color throughout.

Normally, mortar should not set up—stiffen—for at least thirty minutes, even on a hot, dry day. If it stiffens more quickly than this, an insufficient quantity of water was used. Mortar that sets up after thirty minutes or so can be retempered by adding a little water and mixing again. Mortar that has not been used for two hours should be discarded.

MIXTURES

Within reason, the quantity of water used in any mix has little effect upon its strength and other characteristics. Water content just affects consistency. It is the ratio of the other ingredients that dictates a mortar's qualities.

NO-LIME MORTAR

Mortar made with cement, sand, and water is used for joining nonporous materials such as stone and glass brick. For average work, use a mixture of one part cement to three parts sand.

CEMENT-PLUS-LIME MORTAR

The addition of hydrated (slaked) lime to the mix increases its plasticity and adherence. This increases the mixture's workability, which means the mortar is easier to smooth and that it will stick more readily to the trowel and the masonry. For most work, use a mixture of one part cement, one quarter part lime, and three parts sand. The resulting mortar has, when fully hardened (cured), a compressive load rating of 400 psi. This figure has been established by the ASTM (American Society of Technical Materials), which is the recognized authority in these matters.

Cement-lime mortar is used with porous masonry materials such as brick and concrete block.

QUANTITIES

When cement is mixed with sand, the cement, which is an ultra-fine powder, fills the voids between the grains of sand. When water is added, the water pretty nearly fits into the spaces left between the cement and the sand. Therefore, you will not end up with much more mortar than the volume of the sand with which you began. For example, if you mix one part cement with three parts sand and add the necessary water, you will end up with just about three parts mortar. Thus, to estimate the results of mixing cement, lime, and sand, figure that the resulting mortar will not exceed the volume of sand used.

CEMENT-PLUS-LIME MORTAR MIXES BY VOLUME

ASTM classification	Cement	Hydrated lime	Sand	Maximum recommended compressive loading	Characteristics
M	1	¼	3	400 psi	High strength Good workability Used for exposed service
S	1	½	4½	350 psi	Excellent workability Moderate strength
N	1	1	6	300 psi	Used for unexposed service
O	1	2	9	250 psi	Excellent workability Low strength Used for unexposed service
					Excellent workability Highly adhesive and smooth
					Very low strength Used for unexposed service

MORTAR PER BLOCK/BRICK

As a rule of thumb you can figure you will need 1 cubic foot of mortar for every thirty to forty 8-×-16-inch blocks you lay. The exact quantity will depend on joint thickness and waste.

For brick, you need much less mortar. One cubic foot of mortar is all you need for approximately 200 to 300 common bricks. Exact numbers of bricks that can be laid with this quantity of mortar will depend on joint thickness and waste.

MIXING

First mix the cement with or without the lime added to the sand. Then add a little water at a time until the desired consistency is reached. For most applications you will need a consistency similar to ice cream. If you have added too much water, add a mixture of dry sand and cement (in the desired proportions) to the mixture. Be sure to mix until the mortar is of a single color and consistency throughout. No need to mix beyond that point.

When you mix, use a container several times larger than the quantity you are attempting to mix and the task will be easier and faster. For any quantity larger than half a shovelful use a mortar pan or a mortar box, which can be rented. Or, form your dry material into a circle on a concrete floor or drive. Add water to the center and mix inward. When finished, hose the mixing surface clean.

To save yourself the trouble of mixing lime into the cement, use mortar cement in place of regular cement. Mortar cement is about 25 percent lime, which means that when you add one part mortar cement to three parts sand, the resulting mix is rated M. M is a rating for high strength.

SPECIAL MORTARS

When laying down brick, flagstones, or slate atop a concrete base, use a no-lime mixture with very little water. Mix the cement and sand dry and then add just enough water to enable you to mold some of the mortar into a ball. When squeezed, the ball of mortar should not exude any water. If it does, it is too wet. Add more cement and mix again.

As stated previously, glass brick is generally laid up in lime-free mortar; at least this is the mortar used by old-timers. The manufacturers of glass bricks, however, recommend a standard mixture containing the usual 25 percent lime. You might try both and see which performs best for you.

28

PAINT & SHELLAC & VARNISH

(ALSO SEE STAIN)

Paint consists of pigment and a "vehicle." The pigment provides the color and hiding power, the vehicle makes the pigment fluid, and dries to form a bond between the particles of pigment and the surface over which the paint has been spread.

Early paints consisted of colored earth, oils, and greases. With time it was learned that oil pressed from flaxseeds would dry to a firm, hard layer. Later still, solvents were added to control the consistency of the paint, and then driers were added to speed drying.

So-called artists' colors as they were made and used by the masters of centuries past consisted of nothing more than ground color mixed with linseed oil. Modern artists' colors are made no differently, though the desire for lower-cost materials has brought acrylic colors into use. The colors used by the great masters have withstood the passage of centuries, just as modern linseed-oil colors will if, like the old paint, they are kept out of direct sunlight.

Up to around World War II, oil-based paint, with linseed oil as the major vehicle, was used for just about all residential painting. After the war new paints were introduced, not because the old, linseed-oil paint wasn't doing its job, but because

prices were going up, linseed oil included. So were labor costs and the cost of having to wash brushes in a solvent (though wise, old painters cleaned their brushes in cheap, highly effective kerosene, then removed the kerosene with a little solvent).

Another change in paint makeup, but one that did not take place until more recent years, was the legally mandated removal of white lead (oxide of lead). Since lead is poisonous when ingested, present law forbids any paint for home use to contain more than 0.06 percent lead. (Efforts by the Environmental Protection Agency may even reduce this figure.) In any case, lead has been replaced by zinc oxide and titanium dioxide.

CHOOSING A PAINT

Paint choice should be made on the basis of compatibility between the paint and the surface it will cover; the type of service to which the paint will be exposed; the length of service desired; and lastly, cost.

Bear in mind that a good exterior paint job should last four years or more. An interior paint job should last at least six. Preparation and painting require considerable work, so, in the long run, it's wasteful to save money on paint that won't stand up to the years.

PAINT QUALITY
While it is true that there are an infinite number of grades of paint manufactured, there are some things you can do to protect yourself against inferior paint.

Read the label. Every can of good-quality paint has a description of its makeup or formula on the label. Most important are the metals, or solids. The more solids the better the paint, with the exception of whiting, which is a kind of chalk. Then check the vehicle. The more oil or resin and the less solvent, motor oil, and water, the better the paint. One of the best paints, Dutch Boy, carries a label that reads something like this: "Pigment 40 percent zinc oxide, 5 percent titanium dioxide, 5 percent calcuim carbonate (whiting). Vehicle 40 percent linseed oil; 5 percent thinner, 5 percent drier." Compare this to Home Owner's Special: "Pigment 10 percent zinc, 5 percent titanium dioxide, 35 percent calcium carbonate. Vehicle 15 percent linseed oil, 20 percent mineral spirits (motor oil), 10 percent Tung oil, 5 percent drier."

The better paints always cover better, spread out better and further, are easier to apply, and last much longer.

CUTTING COSTS
Use as few colors as possible. Every partly used can is a dead waste. The chance that you will ever need the balance of the paint before it hardens is slim.

MIX YOUR OWN COLORS
Start with five gallon cans of white, which will save you some money. Then remove as much as you believe you will need and add one color a little at a time until you secure the color or tint you wish. Should your first batch be insufficient, it is always easy to mix up a little more IF YOU USE ONLY ONE COLOR. Use two or more and the job calls for a Rembrandt. In this way you can have several shades and still waste very little.

OIL-BASED PAINTS

Oil-based paints still consist of pigment and vehicle plus thinners and driers. When the thinners evaporate and the vehicle hardens the result is a hard coating. Flat, medium, high gloss, and enamel are similar in composition but differ in the relative ratios of pigment to vehicle. Flat paint has the least pigment, enamel has the most. It is for this reason that enamel is difficult to work with; its covering power is lower than the others.

Major advantages
    Better surface penetration
    Better adhesion
    Natural gloss
    Excellent hiding ability
    Good flow and spread
    Resists weathering very well
Major disadvantages
    Has a strong odor
    Slow to dry
    Cleanup is tedious and troublesome

LATEX PAINT

These paints are made by mixing or emulsifying acrylic or vinyl in water plus various other chemicals. Latex paints are made for both interior and exterior application. Generally they produce a flat, no-shine surface, but a few companies also manufacture semigloss, gloss, and enamel.

Major advantages
    Quick drying—one hour in warm weather
    Almost odorless
    Easy application
    Can be applied over damp surfaces
    Not as likely to blister and peel as oil-based paint
    Wash up with water
    Not damaged by alkalies in new masonry
    Nonflammable
    Touch-up no problem

Major disadvantages
    Doesn't flow as well as oil-based paint
    Doesn't adhere as well as oil-based paint
    Won't adhere well to chalky surfaces
    Doesn't hide as well as oil-based paint
    Bare wood requires special latex primer
    Damaged if touched by water in less than a week or two after application

ALKYD PAINTS

These are interior and exterior paints formulated with a man-made resin called alkyd. The paints are made in flat, semigloss, gloss, and enamel. They can be used as a base or primer for oil-based paints.

Major advantages
    Dries more rapidly than oil-based paint

    Is washed more easily than latex paints
    Forms a tough, nonporous surface

Major disadvantages
    Comparatively difficult to apply
    Requires constant mixing to maintain consistency
    Touch-up must be done almost immediately
    Requires thinners or turpentine for washup
    Has little odor, but its fumes are toxic

ONE-COAT PAINTS

These are paints that, their manufacturers say, can cover a surface beautifully with only a single coat. The promise is very attractive, but it is only a promise. These paints are thicker than standard paints. They have more pigment and less vehicle. They are more difficult to apply only in the sense that it is hard to cover a wall with a brush or even a roller evenly enough in one coat so that none of the under-color peeks through. If you are painting a clean, unpainted surface, or if you will be satisfied with less-than-excellent results, one-coat paint will do. If you are trying to cover a "difficult" color such as green, for example, or if you want a near-perfect job, you had best opt for two or more coats with a standard paint. This does not mean, however, that you'll be doubling either your labor or the cost of the paint because standard paints spread out much more quickly and easily than the one-coat formulations.

MASONRY PAINTS

When the surface of the masonry (which includes stucco, asbestos shingles, and brick, as well as cement and concrete) is clean and chalk-free, your best bet is a latex paint formulated for exterior or masonry application. The paint will adhere best when the masonry is a bit damp.

When the masonry surface is dusty with chalk (cement and stone powder), you need a special bonding agent; apply with a brush or roller before applying the latex masonry paint.

Powdered cement paints that contain a quantity of portland cement are mixed with water before they are applied. This paint can be used only over porous masonry, which excludes materials such as asbestos shingles. The masonry should be thoroughly wetted down before the paint is applied. The powdered cement paint should not be used atop any other paint.

SHELLAC

Actually made by dissolving the shells of lac bugs in alcohol, shellac is the traditional indoor wood floor "paint," and the wood sealer applied on furniture before the final coats of varnish are applied.

Shellac is made in two colors: white and orange. The white dries to a very pale yellow, which is clear when applied in a thin coat. The orange has a slight orange tint.

PURCHASING TIPS

Shellac is sold in "cuts." A gallon of 4-pound cut shellac has twice as much shellac as a gallon of 2-pound cut shellac. Since the lac is the expensive portion of the mix, price should correspond to cut. You can always reduce the quantity of lac in a mix by adding alcohol. You can use grain alcohol, but wood alcohol (which is poisonous when ingested) is commonly used.

Stored shellac deteriorates with time. The rate of deterioration is probably temperature related. In any case, "old" shellac will not dry and harden properly, but will remain tacky forever. Your only guide to the age of a can of shellac beyond the seller's word is its color. Aging turns shellac red. If the can is marked white shellac and it looks like orange shellac, that's due not to an error in labeling but to age. Old orange shellac will appear a deeper orange.

APPLICATION

Shellac can be thinned only with alcohol. The brush used with shellac will solidify into a lump unless you wash it perfectly clean with alcohol. Most painters use a large, cheap shellac brush for floors, which they discard after use.

To make a primer for varnish (a step to which some craftsmen object; they recommend varnish as a primer for varnish), the shellac is cut with an equal or larger quantity of alcohol. As a primer for floors the same cut, or thinned mixture, is used. Following coats should not be made with more than 4-pound shellac. When the shellac is thin you can literally slop it on and it will level itself. On a warm day, with all the windows wide open, you can start the second coat in thirty minutes.

Shellac is used for floors because it is somewhat flexible and not as easily scratched as varnish. Shellac is not used as a final coat on furniture because it softens with heat. Sit on a shellacked chair in the summer and you will stick to your seat.

VARNISH

Varnish is simply the vehicle used in paint, minus the pigment. It provides a hard, clear surface that is easily washed and cleaned. However, varnish does not stand up to weathering very well; even spar varnish, which is a type of top-quality oil-based varnish, has to be renewed frequently (sanded and revarnished) if it is to keep its appearance.

OIL-BASED VARNISHES
These are the traditional varnishes that are thinned with turpentine. They have many advantages. They do adhere well to a shellac primer and they do adhere well to themselves, if not too many months have

passed between coats. If time has passed, a thorough wash with alcohol followed by a light sanding will provide the "tooth" necessary for good adhesion. This means you can build up as thick a coat of varnish (almost) as you wish.

Oil-based varnishes are made in high-gloss, semigloss, and satin formulations. Many craftsmen prefer to work with the high-gloss type and change it to satin with a light touch of steel wool.

POLYURETHANE
This is probably the best varnish made today. It forms a hard, tough, clear finish that has excellent resistance to chipping, soaps, and detergents. But this is the varnish nonprofessionals had best stay clear of. It is difficult to apply. It will not adhere to some forms of stained wood no matter what you try—sanding the surface, even steel-wooling the surface with a pad soaked in the polyurethane. Worst of all, it will not adhere readily to itself. If you do not apply a second coat in short order of the first, the second coat will peel off.

The Light Reflectance of Various Colors

Do you wish to make the most of the natural and artificial light within a room? Or—do you wish to soften the skyglare that sometimes enters through large glass areas? Remember, dark colors absorb light while light ones reflect it. This chart will help you determine the colors that will best serve your purpose.

White 80%	Light Buff 56%	Light Green 41%
Ivory (Light) 71%	Peach 53%	Pale Blue 41%
Apricot-beige 66%	Salmon 53%	Deep Rose 12%
Lemon Yellow 65%	Pale Apple Green 51%	Dark Green 9%
Ivory 59%	Medium Gray 43%	

HOW TO ESTIMATE FOR HOUSE AND INTERIOR PAINTS

Distance Around House in Ft.	Average Height 12′	Average Height 15′	Average Height 18′	Average Height 21′	Average Height 24′
60 feet	1½ gal.	2 gal.	2¼ gal.	2½ gal.	3 gal.
92	2¼	2¾	3½	4	4½
124	3	3¾	4½	5¼	6
140	3½	4¼	5	6	7
172	4¼	5¼	6	7¼	8½

Distance in feet Around Room	Ceiling 8′	Ceiling 8½′	Ceiling 9′	Ceiling 9½′	Paint for Ceiling	Finish for Floors
30 feet	⅝ gal.	⅝ gal.	¾ gal.	¾ gal.	1 pt.	1 pt.
40	⅞	⅞	⅞	1	1 qt.	1 qt.
50	1	1⅛	1⅛	1¼	3 pts.	1 qt.
60	1¼	1¼	1⅜	1⅜	2 qts.	3 pts.
70	1⅜	1½	1½	1⅝	3 qts.	2 qts.
80	1½	1⅝	1¾	1⅞	1 gal.	5 pts.

Chart courtesy of Hyde Tools and Dutch Boy Paints.

SANDPAPER

GRIT	DESCRIPTION	USES
40 (1½)	Very Coarse	Removing paint, other rough jobs.
50 (1)	Coarse	Preliminary smoothing of rough surfaces.
80 (1/0)	Medium	General sanding. Smooth enough for most surfaces to be painted.
120 (3/0)	Fine	Finish sanding before varnishing or painting.
220 (6/0)	Very Fine	Good for "killing the gloss," i.e. light sanding of painted surfaces before painting over them.

Source: **Skil Makes It Easy,** published for Skil Corp., by Special Interest Publications, Magazine Div. of Meredith Corp., Des Moines.

DO'S AND DON'TS OF INTERIOR PAINTING

DO	DON'T
Wash all grease and dirt off walls and woodwork.	Don't expect good results on dirty surfaces.
Patch cracks in walls and ceilings before painting.	Don't paint over a damp surface with oil base paints.
Seal all new surfaces with a primer.	Don't apply the second coat of paint until the first coat has dried properly.
Scrape clean all loose paint and sand smooth.	Don't sand woodwork across the grain.
Stir paint thoroughly before any applications.	Don't change cans of paint in the middle of a wall area.
Allow new plaster to dry before painting.	Don't add thinner to the product unless the directions call for it.

What to use . . . and where

	FLAT PAINT	SEMI-GLOSS PAINT	ENAMEL	RUBBER BASE PAINT (NOT LATEX)	EMULSION PAINT (INCLUDING LATEX)	CASEIN PAINT	INTERIOR VARNISH	SHELLAC	WAX (LIQUID OR PASTE)	WAX (EMULSION)	STAIN	WOOD SEALER	FLOOR VARNISH	FLOOR PAINT OR ENAMEL	CEMENT BASE PAINT	ALUMINUM PAINT	SEALER OR UNDERCOATER	METAL PRIMER
PLASTER WALLS & CEILING	✔•	✔•		✔	✔	✔											✔	
WALL BOARD	✔•	✔•		✔	✔	✔											✔	
WOOD PANELING	✔•	✔•		✔	✔•		✔	✔	✔		✔	✔						
KITCHEN & BATHROOM WALLS		✔•	✔•	✔	✔												✔	
WOOD FLOORS							✔	✔	✔•	✔•	✔	✔	✔•					
CONCRETE FLOORS									✔•	✔•	✔			✔				
VINYL & RUBBER TILE FLOORS									✔	✔								
ASPHALT TILE FLOORS										✔								
LINOLEUM									✔	✔	✔		✔	✔				
STAIR TREADS									✔		✔	✔	✔	✔				
STAIR RISERS	✔•	✔•	✔•	✔			✔	✔			✔	✔						
WOOD TRIM	✔•	✔•	✔•	✔	✔•		✔	✔	✔			✔					✔	
STEEL WINDOWS	✔•	✔•	✔•	✔												✔		✔
ALUMINUM WINDOWS	✔•	✔•	✔•	✔												✔		✔
WINDOW SILLS		✔•					✔											
STEEL CABINETS	✔•	✔•	✔•	✔														✔
HEATING DUCTS	✔•	✔•	✔•	✔												✔		✔
RADIATORS & HEATING PIPES	✔•	✔•	✔•	✔												✔		✔
OLD MASONRY	✔	✔	✔	✔	✔	✔									✔	✔	✔	
NEW MASONRY	✔•	✔•	✔•	✔	✔										✔		✔	

 Black dot indicates that a primer or sealer may be necessary before the finishing coat (unless surface has been previously finished.)

Courtesy National Paint, Varnish, and Lacquer Association

Here are some suggested color schemes for your home:

If your house has shutters, paint the trim the same color as body of house—or white. If not, use these suggested colors for trim.

If the roof of your house is	You can paint the body	...and the trim or shutters and doors															
		Pink	Bright red	Red-orange	Tile red	Cream	Bright yellow	Light green	Dark green	Gray-green	Blue-green	Light blue	Dark blue	Blue-gray	Violet	Brown	White
GRAY	White	✗	✗	✗	✗	✗	✗	✗	✗	✗	✗	✗	✗	✗	✗	✗	
	Gray	✗	✗	✗	✗		✗	✗	✗	✗	✗	✗	✗	✗	✗		✗
	Cream-yellow		✗		✗		✗		✗	✗							✗
	Pale green				✗		✗		✗	✗							✗
	Dark green	✗				✗	✗	✗									✗
	Putty			✗	✗				✗	✗			✗	✗		✗	
	Dull red	✗			✗		✗							✗			✗
GREEN	White	✗	✗	✗	✗	✗	✗	✗	✗	✗	✗	✗	✗	✗	✗		
	Gray			✗		✗	✗	✗									✗
	Cream-yellow		✗		✗				✗	✗	✗					✗	✗
	Pale green			✗	✗	✗		✗									✗
	Dark green	✗		✗		✗	✗	✗									✗
	Beige				✗				✗	✗	✗			✗	✗		
	Brown	✗				✗	✗	✗									✗
	Dull red					✗		✗		✗							✗
RED	White		✗		✗				✗		✗			✗			
	Light gray		✗		✗				✗								✗
	Cream-yellow		✗		✗						✗	✗	✗				
	Pale green		✗		✗												✗
	Dull red					✗		✗		✗	✗						✗
BROWN	White			✗	✗		✗	✗	✗	✗	✗		✗	✗	✗	✗	
	Buff				✗				✗	✗	✗					✗	
	Pink-beige				✗				✗	✗						✗	✗
	Cream-yellow				✗				✗	✗	✗					✗	
	Pale green				✗				✗	✗						✗	
	Brown			✗		✗	✗										✗
BLUE	White			✗	✗	✗						✗	✗				
	Gray			✗	✗							✗	✗				✗
	Cream-yellow			✗	✗								✗	✗			
	Blue			✗		✗	✗					✗					✗

Courtesy National Paint, Varnish, and Lacquer Association

29

PARTICLE BOARD

Particle board, sometimes called wood-flake board because it does consist of tiny flakes of wood glued together, is a practical replacement for solid wood. It's practical because it's less expensive and in some ways it's better.

BASIC CHARACTERISTICS

Particle board is, for all practical purposes, solid wood. It can be drilled, chiseled, and sawn just like wood. But, unlike wood, it has no knots or grain; therefore it is just as strong in one direction as it is in another. It doesn't hold nails nearly as well as wood, however, and screws driven into its edge must be preceded by a pilot hole, otherwise the screw will burst the particle board. Even with the correct size pilot hole, standard wood screws do not hold too well in particle board; sheet metal screws hold better.

Particle boards are light to dark brown in color depending on the cement that was used to form them. The weight of the board, which is several times that of softwood, also depends on the glue and wood, and on the pressure employed in making the board. The denser boards weigh more.

Particle boards are not as stiff as ordinary boards. Whereas you might support a shelf of 1-inch pine every 3 feet, you would have to provide support every 2 feet for an equally thick particle board shelf.

Particle board is also sensitive to moisture. If you place particle board atop a subfloor in a house that has no basement, you must first lay down a continuous vapor barrier, otherwise the particle board may absorb moisture on one side and buckle.

Particle boards are ideal in some ways as an underlay for carpets and seamless flooring. One reason is that there are particle board compounds with which you can fill cracks and depressions in the underlay. Then you can sand these areas to produce an almost perfectly smooth surface.

Since these boards have no knots and no grain, they take paint evenly and smoothly. Properly painted, it is difficult to distinguish such boards from standard lumber. Because of this many manufacturers and craftsmen are now using particle board to build furniture, especially for out-of-view sections.

APPLICATION

Particle board may be handled exactly as ordinary lumber with a few limitations. One, already mentioned, is the need for pilot holes for screws. Another is nailing limitations. When you're driving nails through a particle board panel, you must make sure to keep them at least ½ inch in from the panel edges. When nailing panels up to ⅜ inch thick, use 4d nails. For panels ⅜ to ⅝ inch thick, use 6d nails. When nailing thicker panels with larger nails, keep the nails farther in from the board's edges. If you don't, you'll either have to drill clearance holes for the nails or take a chance that the board will break near the nail hole.

Always leave a small space, about 1/16 of an inch, between particle boards to allow for expansion.

DIMENSIONS

Most lumberyards stock particle boards in 4- × -8-foot panels ⅝ inch thick. For other thicknesses—for example ¼, ¾, and 1 inch—you will probably have to place a special order.

SPECIAL TYPES

In addition to the more or less standard particle board, sometimes called corestock, there are any number of special application variations. Some of the major types are listed in the following table.

	Particleboard Types	Uses
Corestock	Products of flakes or particles bonded with urea-formaldehyde or phenolic resins with various densities and related properties.	For furniture, casework, architectural paneling, doors and laminated components.
Wood Veneered Particleboard	Corestock overlaid at the mill with various wood veneers.	For furniture, panels, wainscots, dividers, cabinets, etc.
Overlaid Particleboard	Particleboard faced with impregnated fiber sheets, hardboard or decorative plastic sheets.	For applications such as furniture, doors, wall paneling, sink tops, cabinetry and store fixtures.
Embossed Particleboard	Surfaces are heavily textured in various decorative patterns by branding with heated roller.	For doors, architectural paneling, wainscots, display units and cabinet panels.
Filled Particleboard	Particleboard surface-filled and sanded ready for painting.	For painted end-products requiring firm, flat, true surfaces.
Primed or Undercoated	Factory painted base coat on either filled or regular board —exterior or interior.	For any painted products.
Floor Underlayment	Panels specifically engineered for floor underlayment.	Underlay for carpets or resilient floor coverings.

Courtesy Georgia-Pacific Corp.

30 PLASTICS

(ALSO SEE LAMINATES, LEADERS & GUTTERS, PLUMBING)

Although plastic is used in many ways in construction, it still is not used as a major structural component, except to make fiberglass-reinforced plastic panels.

FIBERGLASS PANELS

Made of fine filaments of glass embedded in plastic, the panels are translucent, shatterproof, frost-, rot- and waterproof. They are excellent for skylights, greenhouses, carport roofs, awnings, patio shelters, even windows and storm doors. A single sheet of corrugated fiberglass requires little support. It can be the roof and the shingles and the window all in one.

Fiberglass is made in many colors, sizes, and shapes. It is exceptionally strong for its weight. A standard 26-inch-×-10-foot panel weighs no more than 11 pounds.

LIGHT AND HEAT TRANSMISSION

Fiberglass panels are made in a range of colors and opacities. Different colors and opacities pass different amounts of heat and light. For specific figures refer to the manufacturer's literature. For general guidance you can use the following:

Red and reddish colors: passes more heat less light

Green: passes roughly equal quantities of heat and light

Blue and bluish colors: passes more light and less heat

White: passes the most heat and light

If you are seeking a panel that will provide shade, select one that transmits 30 percent or less of the solar energy that falls on it.

WEIGHTS

Panels are not classified by thickness or gauge. Instead they are classified by weight per square foot. Obviously, the thicker, heavier panels are the best and, obviously, they cost more.

The generally available weights are 4, 5, 6, and 8 ounces per square foot. The heavier panels are recommended for roofing where there may be a snow load.

SHAPES AND DIMENSIONS

These panels are most commonly stocked:

2½ inches corrugated, 26 inches wide, 8, 10, and 12 feet long
4-inch-×-⅝-inch ribbed, 26 inches wide, 8, 10, and 12 feet long
Flat sheets, 24, 30, 36, and 48 inches wide, 8, 10, and 12 feet long
50-foot rolls, 36 and 48 inches wide

CUTTING AND INSTALLATION

Fiberglass panels may be cut with a

fine-tooth hand or power saw. It is best to predrill holes through the panels for nails, screws, and other fasteners. Use a ⅝-inch bit and place a neoprene washer under the nail or screw. The oversized holes permit the panel to expand and contract with temperature changes without buckling. The washer allows the panel to move, yet holds it snugly.

Normally, the 26-inch panels are overlapped on joists spaced 20 inches on centers. The purlins—the supports that are placed at right angles to the joists—are spaced:

30 to 32 inches apart for 4 oz. panels
36 to 38 inches apart for 5 oz. panels

48 to 50 inches apart for 6 and 8 oz. panels

When the panels are mounted in a vertical position, these dimensions may be increased by 20 percent.

To seal the spaces between panel corrugations and a supporting purlin, you can purchase corrugated and rib-shaped wood fillers. To join overlapping panels use a clear sealant.

When installing a flat sheet of fiberglass in a wood or metal sash, provide at least ⅛ inch clearance all around the fiberglass to allow for expansion. Then seal with putty or a flexible glazing compound.

31

PLUMBING

In the main, plumbing systems consist of pipes, fittings, valves, and fixtures. Pipes are, of course, the conduits through which water and gas flow. Fittings are short conduits that connect pipes to pipes, and pipes to valves and/or fixtures. Valves control the flow of water and gas. Fixtures are the terminals, the end points to which the water is brought. The terminal for a run of gas pipe would be, of course, a furnace, hot-water tank, or cooking stove.

No single book, no matter what its size, could possibly include all the materials—pipes, fittings, valves, and fixtures—used in plumbing. The following pages simply cover the most commonly used materials. And, as you can see, even these are considerable.

PIPES AND TUBING

COPPER TUBING

Copper tubing is manufactured for plumbing applications in four different wall thicknesses. They are designated types K, L, M, and DWV (which stands for drain, waste, and vent). For any given size the external diameters of all the four types of tubing are alike. Their internal diameters differ, however, because the wall thicknesses of the four types differ in descending order. Type K has the thickest walls; type DWV has the thinnest. Cost corresponds to wall thickness; the heavier the tubing the higher its price.

Application. Most building codes will permit the use of type M for all pressure pipe that is not buried in the earth. Type DWV can be used for drain, waste, and venting. When the tubing is to be covered or in contact with the earth, it is best to use type K.

Size. Types K and L are made in ¼-inch diameters, starting at ¼ of an inch and going up. Type M is not made in anything smaller than ⅜ of an inch. Type DWV is not to be had in any size smaller than 1¼ inches. All these figures are nominal. The actual outside diameter of the tubing is somewhat larger for all sizes. For example, the actual outside diameter of 1-inch tubing is 1.125 inches. As previously stated, the outside diameters of all the pipe types are identical. This means you can use standard fitting with any type of copper tubing so long as the sizes correspond.

Tempers and Lengths. Copper tubing is made in hard-drawn and bending-tempered straight lengths of 20 feet, and also in an annealed or soft condition in lengths of 20 feet and coils of 60 and 100 feet. DWV is made only in hard-drawn lengths of 20 feet.

Tubing of all tempers can be soldered and brazed. Soft tubing can be bent with the help of a simple wire device that is slipped over the tubing. Hand pressure is all that is needed to effect a bend. Bending-tempered tubing requires a hand- or hydraulically powered, lever-type bending tool.

Hard-drawn tubing is almost never bent. Soft and bending-tempered tubing can be expanded to make a flare joint; the hard cannot.

ACR. This is a fifth type of copper tubing. It is made specifically for use in heating and air conditioning. It should *not* be used for plumbing.

Cutting. Copper tubing may be cut with a hacksaw, or a wheeled cutter. When you saw, be sure to remove the external burrs with a file. When you use the wheeled cutter, the diameter of the tubing is slightly reduced. Return the tubing to its original internal diameter by using a reamer. Most wheeled cutters have reamers attached to their frames.

Weight and Internal Friction. Type M copper tubing weighs 0.65 pounds per linear foot in the 1-inch size. The same diameter standard galvanized steel pipe weighs 1.68 pounds per linear foot.

Copper's internal resistance to the flow of water is much less than that of galvanized steel pipe, so much so that you can install copper tube one size smaller than galvanized and still get the same rate of water flow. For example, ¾-inch copper tubing will pass as much water as will 1-inch galvanized steel pipe.

Precautions. Nails are easily driven through copper tubing. If carpentry is to follow the installation of copper tubing, place metal plates on the studs, etc., so that there is no chance of driving a nail through an unseen tube.

Copper will corrode quickly (in a process called galvanic action) if it is in contact with iron and even more quickly with galvanized iron (zinc). The presence of water speeds up the galvanic action, and since all water-carrying pipes sweat, you must make sure never to use galvanized clips, clamps, etc., to hold or to make contact with copper tubing.

When it is necessary to connect copper tubing to galvanized pipe or a galvanized tank, always use a plastic transition fitting between them.

JOINING COPPER TUBING

Copper tubing is easily joined to itself, to fittings, valves, and other controls, and to other types of tubing. Several methods are used. They are discussed below more or less in the order of frequency of use.

Soldering. This is a heat process whereby one piece of metal—copper tube in this case—is joined to another piece of metal—a second copper tube or copper fitting—and is atomically bonded by means of an interposed piece of metal, called solder. Solder used for soldering copper consists of a fifty-fifty mixture of lead and tin. The more tin the lower the solder's melting point and the more easily the joint is effected.

The end of one tube cannot be successfully soldered to the end of another tube. Either a "fitting," which may be merely a slightly larger section of tubing, is used between them or the end of one tube is enlarged for a distance equal to the diameter of the tubing. Then the end of the second piece is slipped into the enlarged end of the first and is soldered in place.

The process of soldering is very simple. When done correctly, it takes only a few minutes per joint and results in a water- and gas-tight joint that is equally as strong as the pipes themselves and that will last as long as the pipe.

Before you can solder together two pipes you must make sure that the faying surfaces—the surfaces to be joined by solder—are brushed or sanded bright. Then apply flux, and heat the metal with a propane torch. Remove the torch and touch the tip of the solder to the faying surfaces. If the metal is hot enough the solder will flow and adhere to the copper. If it is not hot enough, you must remove the solder and again apply heat to the metal, preferably near the joint-to-be but not directly on the flux. Remove the torch and touch the solder to the hot metal (the solder should flow now). Then insert the tube within the fitting or the enlarged tube end, apply heat to the outside surface of the joint, and press the tip of the solder against the joint. The solder will melt and be drawn into the joint by capillary action. When the joint is filled with liquid solder, remove the heat and the solder. In a few minutes the solder will solidify and the joint will be completed.

Compression Fittings. Use this type of joint when you want to connect tubing to a fitting and know that you may have to open the joint sometime in the future. For example, you would use a compression joint to join a pipe end to a faucet; the fitting itself is a part of the faucet or valve. There are two types of compression fittings: metal and nonmetal.

To make a compression fitting, first cut the end of the tube square across

and remove all internal and external burrs. Slip the compression fitting nut and then the metal ring up on the tube end and insert the tube end into the fitting. Push the ring into place and tighten the nut until it's just a little more than finger tight. If the pipe has not been deformed by bending, the joint will hold pressure. When you take apart and reassemble this joint you must take care to replace the tube end and its ring in the exact same position as before. If you don't, the joint may leak.

The nonmetal compression joint consists of the same parts, but here the metal ring is replaced by a ring of plastic or rubber. Disassembly and reassembly are much less of a problem. So long as the ring is intact, the joint will hold water no matter how many times you take it apart and put it back together again.

Flare Fittings. For this you need a flaring tool. There are two kinds: one, a hand-held tool, the other, a vise-type tool. The vise is better.

This type of joint can be made only with annealed tubing. First cut the end of the tube straight and square and remove all internal and external burrs. Slip the flare nut up on the tube. Flare the end of the tube and place the flared end in the fitting. Then tighten the flare nut. This joint too can be taken apart and then reassembled. When it is done correctly, it holds beautifully, but the flared end must be perfectly smooth and round. Rough spots will produce leakage.

Brazing. This technique is identical to soldering except for two points: Brazing is done at a higher temperature; and the "solder" is called brazing filler. Soldering is accomplished at temperatures below 800°F. Brazing takes place at temperatures above 800°F, but lower than the melting point of the metals to be joined, which in the case of copper is 2,000°F. Brazing filler metals are usually a combination of silver, zinc, copper, and sometimes phosphorous and tin. Since brazing filler metal is much stronger than solder, brazing produces a much stronger joint than solder. But note that when done correctly, solder joints are all that are needed for ordinary plumbing.

Sweat Fittings. This is the more common name for soldered fittings. They are almost always made of copper tubing, and unless otherwise specified, the fitting is always the female. This means the pipe, which is the male, enters the fitting. The distance the pipe enters the fitting is generally equal to, or a fraction greater than, the diameter of the tubing involved.

STEEL PIPE

Sometimes called iron pipe, steel pipe is manufactured in two forms: galvanized and black. Except for cost and resistance to corrosion, the two types are, for all practical purposes, identical. Galvanized is made by dipping the pipe in a bath of molten zinc, thus coating its interior and exterior with this corrosion-reducing metal. Black pipe is simply painted black.

Application. Galvanized steel pipe is used for carrying water and heating gas. Black steel pipe is used for carrying steam and hot water for heating. Sometimes it is also used for carrying cooking gas. Black is used in place of galvanized because it is a bit less expensive.

Size. Steel pipe is made in a range of diameters starting with 1/16 of an inch and going on up to 5 or more inches. Steel pipe is sized by its approximate internal dimension. For example, a 1-inch steel pipe has an internal diameter of exactly 1.04 inches.

Weight and Internal Friction. Steel pipe weighs roughly two-and-one-half times more than copper tubing of an equal size. Half-inch steel pipe weighs 0.85 pounds per foot. Galvanized steel pipe has the greatest coefficient of internal friction of all the pipes used to carry water. The internal friction of black steel pipe is only slightly less.

Cutting. Steel pipe may be cut with a hacksaw or a wheeled cutter. Use a coarse-tooth blade in the saw. If you use the wheeled cutter, the pipe must be held in a vise. The most convenient to use is a pipe vise, but you can make do with an ordinary vise. Pieces of wood between the pipe and the vise jaws will keep the pipe from turning.

Powered pipe cutters consist of a motor-driven vise. The pipe is inserted in the vise, the cutter is positioned, and then the vise turns. Great care must be taken to keep one's hands and arms from being caught between the cutter and the vise.

Cutting Alternatives. Steel pipe is normally sold in 10- and 20-foot lengths, threaded at each end and accompanied by a coupling. It is also sold in much shorter lengths called nipples. These vary from a few inches to a few feet. When none of these prepared lengths will do, and you do not want to buy or rent equipment, find a plumbing supply shop or even a plumber who will cut the pipe for you. Many commercial supply houses offer this service for a fee.

JOINING STEEL PIPE

For plumbing work, steel pipe is joined to valves and fittings by means of threads. Pipe thread is cut on the outside of the pipe ends, which make them male. Pipe threads are cut on the inside of the valves and fittings, which make them female. The pipes are then screwed into the valves and fittings as necessary, making a permanent, watertight joint.

Pipe Thread Dimensions. There are two types of pipe thread is use. One, called water-hose thread, is very coarse. You find it only on the end of faucets to which water hoses are to be attached and on water-hose couplings and connectors.

The other is simply called pipe thread, and this is what is used on all water pipe. It is a fairly coarse thread, with the number of threads per inch decreasing as the diameter of the pipe increases. Five-inch pipe has 8 threads per inch; 1/16-inch pipe has 27 threads per inch. When the correct fitting or valve is used with a pipe, the threads match.

Pipe thread is unlike machine thread. Whereas the machine thread can run the entire length of a 5-foot bolt, pipe thread cannot. Pipe thread is cut at an angle of about 5 degrees. The end of a threaded pipe is tapered,

as is the threaded hole it is to enter. In other words, the pipe plugs the walls of the hole it must enter. This means there must be sufficient threads for the pipe to enter and hold properly but not so many the pipe cannot seat tightly.

Cutting Pipe Thread. The pipe end is reamed, and if an exterior burr has been formed, this may have to be ground or filed down. The proper size pipe cutting die is selected and locked in its handle, called a stock. Cutting oil or even automotive oil is placed on the pipe end. The die is positioned over the pipe end, pressed against the pipe, and given a half-turn. Then it is backed off a quarter-turn, then turned forward a half-turn. After a total of two full forward-turns have been made, more oil is placed on the end of the pipe. The entire routine is continued until two threads extend beyond the face of the die. Then the die is backed off and the thread is completed.

If you do not lubricate the die, the threads will be rough and even torn. If you do not back the die up every now and again, it may fill with metal particles and produce a poor thread.

The same motor-driven vise previously mentioned may also be used to cut thread. The pipe is locked in the vise, the die is pressed against the pipe end, and the motor turned on. Then the die is kept well lubricated as the pipe turns.

Assembling Pipe, Fittings, and Valves. This is called "making up" in plumbing parlance. It means simply screwing all the parts together. In doing so, there are two precautions to observe: Always place pipe dope on the pipe threads and never over-tighten.

Pipe dope is a lubricant, insulator, and sealant. It comes in paste, stick, and tape form. The paste is the easiest to use and the least expensive. Stick dope is more expensive but can be stored in one's toolbox for years without hardening. The tape is still more expensive and is a nuisance to use.

Pipe dope lubricates the joint so that the pipe easily enters all the way and won't get stuck or need to be forced. Dope insulates the pipe end from the fitting so that the two do not rust solid. Without dope, old threaded joints are very difficult to impossible to open. Dope also seals the tiny openings between pipe and fitting. In many instances a joint that will leak when made up dry will hold pressure when made with dope.

Overtightening a joint deforms its parts. Should an overtightened joint be taken apart and reassembled, chances are it will leak. When tightening up a joint, use just a little more pressure than is necessary to make it watertight.

STEEL PIPE FITTINGS
Since steel pipe is not bent, if you want bends and angles in a run of steel pipe, you must make them with the aid of preformed bends and angles that have female threads at their ends. When a pipe is to be connected to one or more other pipes, other types of fittings, called Ys, Ts, and crosses, are used. When the end of one pipe is to be connected in line with the end of another pipe, a fitting called a coupling is used.

There are dozens of different types and shapes of fittings to accommodate all possible piping requirements. When a single fitting won't accomplish the job, use two or more, with a nipple between them.

Specify the fitting you want by its size and function. For example, to carry a pipe around a right-angle turn, you need a 90-degree elbow. If the pipe you are running is ¾-inch, you need a ¾-inch, 90-degree elbow. If you are running drainpipe, you need a drain fitting. This differs from standard fittings in that there is no ledge within the fitting on which waste will catch and pile up.

BRASS PIPE
Brass pipe and fittings are manufactured in the same dimensions as galvanized and black steel pipe. In fact, if necessary, one can be used to replace the other. Since the metals are different, however, galvanic action is set up (see METAL) and the iron pipe alongside will corrode at a high rate. Thus the metals should be interchanged only as a temporary repair.

When replacing brass with brass, be sure to use the same "kind" of brass. Red brass has more copper than yellow, and when a mixture of the two brasses is used this will accelerate corrosion.

SOLDERABLE GALVANIZED STEEL
This is a fairly new type of pipe and fittings that can be joined by soldering. This pipe has the strength and rigidity of steel, but offers the convenience and speed of pipe that can be soldered. So far, not too many plumbing supply houses stock this pipe and its fittings.

THIN-WALL BRASS

This pipe is produced in comparatively short lengths and just a few diameters ranging from 1 inch through,
possibly, 1¾ inches. It is used almost
exclusively to connect the drain of a
sink, tub, or shower to the thicker-
walled pipe that follows. When and
where the pipe may be visible,
chrome-plated brass pipe is used.

Cutting. Thin-wall brass pipe may be
cut with a hacksaw and a medium-
tooth blade. The pipe is held in a
miter box or similar arrangement.
When just a little needs to be removed
from an end, it can also be cut with
compound-gear tin snips.

Joining. Preformed thin-wall brass
pipe made expressly for a specific
size and design of sink, tub, or
shower may have a small lip at one
end. In such cases that end of the pipe
is held in place with a large flange
nut that goes over the pipe and
screws onto the fixture. NOTE: When
there is a lip, the washer or compression ring, which may be of rubber or
plastic, goes between the lip and the
fixture.

When and where the no-lip end of
the thin-wall pipe enters a fitting, a
compression ring is placed over the
pipe end, and the flange nut screws
onto the fitting. In such cases the
flange nut compresses the ring, expanding it and locking it in place.

In some cases the no-lip end of the
thin-wall pipe will enter an expanded
end of another pipe. In such cases a
joint can be made by soldering or by
sealing with epoxy cement.

When the drain system beneath a
sink is complex—made up of many
pipes and fittings—the end of one or
more pieces of thin-wall pipe may be
threaded. Such joints are made by
screwing the pipe into the fitting. No
dope is needed between brass and
brass.

RIGID PLASTIC PIPE

Rigid plastic pipe is rapidly replacing almost all other types of pipe in
the construction of new homes and in
many repair and remodeling jobs.
The reasons are many. Rigid plastic
pipe costs less; is far easier to work
with because it weighs one twentieth
as much as metal pipe; and can be cut
and joined in less than one minute.
And since its inside is very smooth, it
can be used one size smaller than the
size of galvanized pipe that is
needed.

But, like everything else on earth,
plastic pipe is not perfect. It expands
considerably when heated, which
means supporting clips must be
loose. It also softens when heated,
which means you must support it
every few feet or in time it will hang
like spaghetti. And because it softens
with heat, it cannot be used for extremely hot weather. Up to 100°F, PVC
pipe can be used. Up until 180°F,
CPVC pipe may be used. When
higher temperatures are expected,
metal pipe is used. When plastic pipe
is used to carry hot water, the first few
feet of pipe leading from the water
heater are always made of metal.
After that, plastic can be used.

JOINING RIGID PLASTIC PIPE

Like galvanized and copper pipe and
tubing, plastic pipe is joined to other
pieces of plastic pipe by means of
plastic fittings. The fittings are "cement welded" to the pipe by means of
special cement. Very simply, use

CPVC cement for CPVC pipe and PVC cement for PVC pipe.

Sizing. In a pipe-to-fitting joint, the pipe is always the male, meaning it enters the fitting. Thus a 1-inch fitting is sized to accept 1-inch plastic pipe, which for plastic pipe is always its outside diameter. Proper fit is an interference fit, which means it is not loose and does not need to be forced.

Joining. Cut the pipe with a pipe cutter or hacksaw. Remove the shine from the end of the pipe with sandpaper, or apply a thin coating of pipe primer. Give the primer a minute to do its work. Then apply a thin layer of the cement to the end of the pipe, making the layer as wide as the depth to which the pipe will enter the fitting. Encircle the pipe end completely with the cement. Push the pipe end all the way into the fitting and give it a fraction of a turn to settle the cement. In one minute the joint will be hard enough for you to continue assembling the system. After several hours the joint will be watertight.

Take care when making these joints. They cannot be taken apart—ever. That is why they are called cement welded.

VALVES

Valves control the flow of water and gas. There are many kinds of valves, but they are easily divided into four main categories: compression, gate, faucet, and automatic. Do not attempt to further subdivide these categories; the list would be endless.

COMPRESSION VALVES
Valves differ from faucets only in that

they are found within a pipeline. Their repair is effected exactly the same way as suggested for compression faucets. Replacement is much easier, since all you need do is match the valve to the pipe type and size.

GATE VALVES
These differ in that they have a gate or slide that slides down within the valve body, effectively closing the valve. You can recognize them by their long bonnets and by the need to turn the handle half a dozen times or more until they are fully open or closed. It is not economical to repair a gate valve; it must be replaced. To extend the life of a gate valve, always make sure its gate is always either fully open or closed.

FAUCETS
A faucet is a valve positioned at the end of a pipe. When water passes through a faucet it enters into the air. There are many different types of faucets. There is the standard, old-fashioned faucet with its spout and handle directly visible. This is sometimes called a spigot. There are the dual faucets with two control knobs directing the flow of hot and cold water to a single spout. And there are lever faucets of various designs in which water temperature and flow rate are selected or controlled by the position of the lever.

Faucet repairs. The most common type of faucet problem is the drip. No amount of handle turning will cause the drip to cease. If the handle moves in toward the body of the faucet when you shut off the flow, you have a compression-type faucet (valve) in hand. Shut off the water. Open the faucet to let the system drain and then take the device apart. You will find a worn washer on the bottom of the stem—the rod that carries the handle. Replace the washer with an exact duplicate; nothing else will do. Then examine the faucet seat, the area that the washer contacts when it stops the water from flowing. If the seat is bright and shiny, or at least perfectly smooth, all is well. If there is a groove across the seat, it must be removed. (You will require a valve-seat removal tool.) Take the old seat to the plumbing shop and get an exact duplicate; again, nothing else will do. Reassemble the faucet and your problem should be solved.

If your faucet stem moves outward from the faucet body when you shut off the water, you have a reverse-compression faucet. Shut off the water in the system and drain it by letting the faucet remain open. Then take the faucet apart and take the entire assembly to the plumbing shop. All the washers and/or grommets must be replaced.

If you have a lever-type faucet, shut off the water and drain the system. Disassemble the control. Replace the grommets and/or pads you find. Be careful not to lose the little brass springs you may find.

Old-fashioned faucets that drip around their stems require packing around those stems. Just loosen the large nut under the handle and apply a turn or two of graphite packing.

Should the faucet leak around its stem and should the stem wobble, it is worn. Many shops carry stem replacement kits. Unfortunately, every faucet manufacturer not only makes his faucets slightly different from all others, but also changes the dimensions of his faucets from year to year. The result is that there are hundreds of slightly different faucets in use today. So don't be shocked if you cannot find replacement parts but must replace the entire faucet or faucet assembly.

FIXTURES

BATHTUBS

Bathtubs are made in a number of shapes and sizes and of three materials: cast iron, sheet steel, and fiberglass-reinforced polyester.

The old reliable iron tub is coated with fired-in-place ceramic perhaps 1/16 inch thick. It is very heavy, solid to the touch and underfoot, and is the longest lasting and most expensive of the three types. The sheet steel tub is also ceramic coated, but it sounds hollow to the touch and is slightly flexible underfoot. It weighs about half as much (or less) than the cast-iron tub. The plastic tub is half again as heavy. It is about as solid to the touch as the sheet metal tub, but it loses its shine much faster than either of the other two types of tubs. The reason is that plastic is not nearly as hard as china (ceramic). Whether it is cheaper than sheet metal depends on the price of oil, at the time, but it is easier to install.

Installing New Tubs. The tub always rests on the subfloor and against the bare studs (if it is not positioned clear of all walls). The floor joists must be strong enough to support it. If not, they must be reinforced before the tub is installed. There must be space beneath the tub's outlet for the drainpipe and trap. Adjoining wall surfaces and flooring are always installed after the tub is in place and connected.

Replacing a Tub. Since the wall tile and Sheetrock or plaster always overlap the rim of the tub, you must expect considerable damage in these areas when you remove the old tub. In addition you must consider the physical problems of interchanging the two tubs. In many instances the carpenters constructed the bathroom doorway after the tub was in place. This may mean you will have to disassemble the doorway to remove the old tub. You may also have to cut up the ceiling of the room below to get at the pipes.

To make sure your new tub is of the correct size and that the drain hole is properly positioned, it is advisable to hold off purchase until the old tub is out and you can make your measurements directly in the space the tub will occupy.

SHOWERS
There are two basic types of showers. One is constructed in place. First, a waterproof pan, fitted with a drain connection, is positioned, after which a close-fitting wall is constructed around the pan. The shower head and its valves are mounted on one wall, and then the necessary water pipes are connected to the valves and a drainpipe is connected to the drain fitting in the pan.

The second type is a prefabricated enclosure which comes complete with bottom pan, drain connection, shower head, and valves. All you need do with the second type is slide it into position and connect the pipes.

Check the manufacturer's litera-

ture before you start cutting the subfloor and walls. Allow a good inch of clearance around the drainpipe so that there is no weight on the pipe and you have clearance for future repairs.

SINKS
Sinks go in kitchens; lavatories are sinks that are found in bathrooms. Except for size and shape, that is the major difference between them, though modern sinks are never freestanding, while some lavatories are.

Sinks come in three basic styles, with a number of variations. One is the rim type, the second is the rimless type. The rim type is carried on a metal rim that fits into a hole cut into the counter top. The size of this hole is critical. It must be accurate to ¼ of an inch or less. The rimless type has a lip that rests on the counter top and the size of the hole it fits into is not critical. Critical or not, it is unlikely that any rim-type sink can be fitted into a rimless hole or vice versa. So order or cut your table- or counter top only after you have selected your sink.

Both types of sink are made either of porcelain, porcelain on cast iron and pressed steel, stainless steel, or fiberglass-reinforced polyester. Stainless steel is probably the toughest, but it has to be wiped perfectly dry if you want it to look perfectly clean.

The third style or variation of sink is determined by the placement of the faucet. In most, the faucet mounts in the center of the rear side of the sink itself. But in some, the faucets mount to one side of the rear side, and in still others the faucet mounts on the counter top, separate from the sink.

Sink Replacement. Obviously the dimensions of the replacement sink and its manner of mounting must be identical to those of the old sink. What is not obvious from the top of the sink is the number of holes provided for the faucet. There may be two, three, or four holes. Unless you are prepared to purchase a new faucet to go with the new sink, you have to duplicate the number of holes and their diameters and placement when selecting the new sink.

The position of the drain hole in a new sink is not too much of a problem, as you can usually change or alter the ·drainpipe to suit the new sink.

LAVATORIES

Lavatories are available in two designs: freestanding and vanity supported. The first may hang from a wall bracket, or it may stand on a pedestal or legs. The second is like a kitchen sink in that it is carried on a counter top that forms the top of the vanity. Vanity lavatories may have a rim or rimless washbasin, just like kitchen sinks.

Vanity and decor aside, the difference between the freestanding and the vanity type of lavatories is the matter of installation. The pipes leading to the freestanding lavatory are fully visible. They must be installed straight and square if the job is to look good. Therefore you are well advised to select a vanity when re-placing an old lavatory. You can make as many bends and turns connecting the old pipes to the new lavatory as you wish and your work will be out of sight.

Lavatories are made of porcelain on cast iron, of sheet steel, and completely of porcelain (usually called vitreous china). The latter can be had on a single porcelain pedestal in any of a number of colors. Some lavatories are also made of plastic composition that resembles marble.

TOILETS

Today toilets are always made of porcelain, except for the seat. They come in a multitude of colors and designs. Some use less water than others by virtue of their design. The best design is called a siphon jet. Next is the siphon whirlpool followed by the reverse trap. Last, and least effective, is the simple washdown.

Toilet replacement. What you have to watch for here is clearance between the seat and tank and the wall in relation to the toilet drain. The drain is not visible when the seat is in position. You can be certain of the drain only when you remove the seat. This may mean going without a toilet for a while, but the alternative is to show up with a toilet that won't fit the allotted space. You'll want the tank's cover to clear the nearest wall by about 1 inch or more.

PIPE DATA AT A GLANCE

TYPE OF PIPE	EASE OF WORKING	WATER FLOW EFFICIENCY FACTOR	TYPE OF FITTINGS NEEDED	MANNER USUALLY STOCKED	LIFE EXPECTANCY	PRINCIPAL USES	REMARKS
Brass, Threaded	No threading required. Cuts easily, but can't be bent. Measuring a job rather difficult	Highly efficient because of low friction	Screw on Connections	12 ft. rigid lengths. Cut to size wanted.	Lasts life of building	Generally for commercial construction	Required in some cities where water is extremely corrosive. Often smaller diameter will suffice because of low friction coefficient
Copper- Hard	Easier to work with than brass	Same as brass	Screw on or or Solder Connections	12 ft. rigid lengths. Cut to size wanted.	Same as brass	Same as brass	
Copper- Soft	Easier to work with than brass or hard copper because it bends readily by using a bending tool. Measuring a job not too difficult	Same as brass	Solder Connections	Coils - usually soft	Same as brass	Widely used in residential installations	
Copper Tubing, Flexible	Easier than soft copper because it can be bent without a tool. Measuring jobs is easy.	Highest of all metals since there are no nipples, unions, or elbows	Solder or Compression Connections	3 wall thicknesses: 'K'-Thickest 'L'-Medium 'M'-Thinnest 20 ft. lengths or 15 ft., 30 ft., or 60 ft. coils (Except 'M')	Same as brass	'K' is used in municipal and commercial construction. 'L' is used for residential water lines. 'M' is for light domestic lines only - check Code before using.	Probably the most popular pipe today. Often a smaller diameter will suffice because of low friction coefficient.
Wrought Iron (or galvanized)	Has to be threaded. More difficult to cut. Measurements for jobs must be exact.	Lower than copper because nipples unions reduce water flow.	Screw on Connections	Rigid lengths, up to 22 ft. Usually cut to size wanted.	Corrodes in alkaline water more than others. Produces rust stains.	Generally found in older homes	Recommended if lines are in a location subject to impact.
Plastic Pipe	Can be cut with saw or knife.	Same as copper tubing	Insert couplings, clamps; also by cement. Threaded & compression fittings can be used (Thread same as for metal pipe)	Rigid, semi-rigid & flexible. Coils of 100-400 ft.	Long life & it is rust & corrosion-proof.	For cold water installations. Used for well casings, septic tank lines, sprinkler systems. Check Codes before installing.	Lightest of all, weighs about 1/8 of metal pipe. Does not burst in below freezing weather.

Courtesy Hardware Retailing

Physical characteristics of copper tube
Types K, L, M and DWV

TYPE K

	Nominal Dimensions, inches			Calculated Values, Based on Nominal Dimensions			
Size, inches	Outside Diameter	Inside Diameter	Wall Thickness	Cross Sectional Area of Bore, sq inches	External Surface, sq ft per lin ft	Internal Surface, sq ft per lin ft	Weight, pounds per lin ft
¼	.375	.305	.035	.073	.098	.080	0.145
⅜	.500	.402	.049	.127	.131	.105	0.269
½	.625	.527	.049	.218	.164	.138	0.344
⅝	.750	.652	.049	.334	.196	.171	0.418
¾	.875	.745	.065	.436	.229	.195	0.641
1	1.125	.995	.065	.778	.294	.261	0.839
1¼	1.375	1.245	.065	1.22	.360	.326	1.04
1½	1.625	1,481	.072	1.72	.425	.388	1.36
2	2.125	1.959	.083	3.01	.556	.513	2.06

TYPE L

Size, inches	Outside Diameter	Inside Diameter	Wall Thickness	Cross Sectional Area of Bore, sq inches	External Surface, sq ft per lin ft	Internal Surface, sq ft per lin ft	Weight, pounds per lin ft
¼	.375	.315	.030	.078	.098	.082	0.126
⅜	.500	.430	.035	.145	.131	.113	0.198
½	.625	.545	.040	.233	.164	.143	0.285
⅝	.750	.666	.042	.348	.196	.174	0.362
¾	.875	.785	.045	.484	.229	.206	0.455
1	1.125	1.025	.050	.825	.294	.268	0.655
1¼	1.375	1.265	.055	1.26	.360	.331	0.884
1½	1.625	1.505	.060	1.78	.425	.394	1.14
2	2.125	1.985	.070	3.09	.556	.520	1.75

TYPE M

Size, inches	Outside Diameter	Inside Diameter	Wall Thickness	Cross Sectional Area of Bore, sq inches	External Surface, sq ft per lin ft	Internal Surface, sq ft per lin ft	Weight, pounds per lin ft
⅜	.500	450	.025	.159	.131	.118	0.145
½	.625	.569	.028	.254	.164	.149	0.204
¾	.875	.811	.032	.517	.229	.212	0.328
1	1.125	1.055	.035	.874	.294	.276	0.465
1¼	1.375	1.291	.042	1.31	.360	.338	0.682
1½	1.625	1.527	.049	1.83	.425	.400	0.940
2	2.125	2.009	.058	3.17	.556	.526	1.46

TYPE DWV

Size, inches	Outside Diameter	Inside Diameter	Wall Thickness	Cross Sectional Area of Bore, sq inches	External Surface, sq ft per lin ft	Internal Surface, sq ft per lin ft	Weight, pounds per lin ft
1¼	1.375	1.295	.040	1.32	.360	.339	.65
1½	1.625	1.541	.042	1.87	.425	.403	.81
2	2.125	2.041	.042	3.27	.556	.534	1.07
3	3.125	3.030	.045	7.21	.818	.793	1.69
4	4.125	4.009	.058	12.6	1.08	1.05	2.87
5	5.125	4.981	.072	19.5	1.34	1.30	4.43

Bending guide for copper tube

Tube Size	Tube Type	Temper	Minimum Bend Radius, Inches	Type of Bending Equipment
½	K, L	Annealed	2¼	Lever or gear type
			4½	None; by hand*
	K, L, M	Drawn	2½	Gear type
¾	K, L	Annealed	3	Lever or gear type
	K	Annealed	4½	None; by hand*
	L	Annealed	6	None; by hand*
	K	Drawn	3	Gear type
	K, L	Drawn	4	Heavy-duty gear type
1	K, L	Annealed	4	Gear type
			7½	None; by hand*
1¼	K, L	Annealed	9	None; by hand*

*When bending by hand, without the use of bending equipment, a circular wooden disc is used. The radius of the disc should be about ¼ to ½ inch less than the minimum bend radius shown.

Examples of minimum copper tube sizes for short branch connections to fixtures

Fixture	Copper Tube Size, inches
Drinking Fountain	⅜
Lavatory	⅜
Water Closet (tank type)	⅜
Bathtub	½
Dishwasher (home)	½
Kitchen Sink (home)	½
Laundry Tray	½
Service Sink	½
Shower Head	½
Sill Cock, Hose Bibb, Wall Hydrant	½
Urinal (tank type)	½
Washing Machine (home)	½
Kitchen Sink (commercial)	¾
Urinal (flush valve)	¾
Water Closet (flush valve)	1

Courtesy Copper Development Association

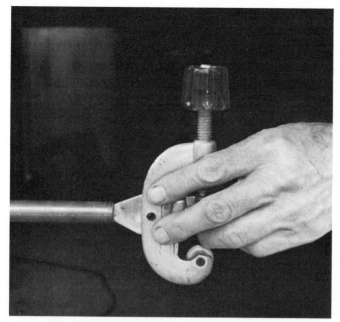

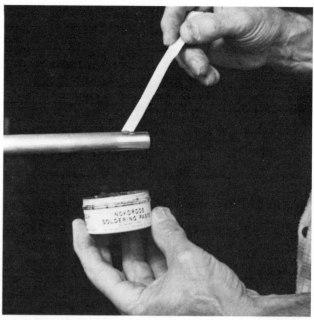

Steps in soldering copper tubing to a sweat valve. A. The pipe is cut. Its end is reamed free of burrs with the reamer on the tubing cutter.

B. The pipe end is cleaned bright with sandpaper or steel wool. Soldering flux is applied to the pipe end.

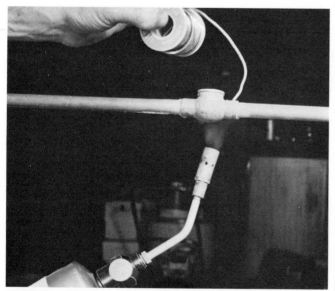

C. The pipe end is inserted into the sweat valve. Note that the valve has been disassembled. Heat is applied to the valve body. The tip of the solder is applied to the joint. When the metal has reached the proper temperature, the solder melts and is drawn into the joint by capillary action.

An example of a nonmetal compression joint. Here a plastic ring (white) will be compressed by the flange nut. The ring will expand and seal the chromium-plated, thin-wall drainpipe to the plastic fitting.

STANDARD PIPE SIZES AND THREADS

Nom'l. Pipe Size	Thrds. per inch	Out. Diam. (in.)	Inside Diam. (in.)	Thrd. Length (in.)	Thrd. in Fitting (in.)	Tap Drill Size (in.)
1/8	27	.405	.269	.2638	3/16	21/64
1/4	18	.540	.364	.4018	9/32	27/64
3/8	18	.675	.493	.4078	19/64	9/16
1/2	14	.840	.622	.5337	3/8	11/16
3/4	14	1.050	.824	.5457	13/32	29/32
1	11½	1.315	1.049	.6828	1/2	1⅛
1¼	11½	1.660	1.380	.7068	35/64	1 15/32
1½	11½	1.900	1.610	.7235	9/16	1 23/32
2	11½	2.375	2.067	.7565	37/64	2 9/16
2½	8	2.875	2.469	1.1375	7/8	2 9/16
3	8	3.500	3.018	1.2000	15/16	3 3/16
3½	8	4.000	3.548	1.2500	1	3 11/16
4	8	4.500	4.026	1.3000	1 1/16	
5	8	5.563	5.047		1 5/32	
6	8	6.625	6.065		1¼	

Extracted from USA Standard Pipe Threads—USAS B2.1—1968 Now an ANSI Standard.

Courtesy Atlas Minerals and Chemicals, Inc.

To achieve the highest degree of success when using Plumber Seal, here are a few tips that are worthwhile heeding. Be sure Plumber Seal is thoroughly mixed before applying. A simple operation like wetting a cloth or finger and running it gently over in-place Plumber Seal to obtain a smooth finish can add to the completion of a better job.

PUSH OUT inner cartridge **CUT OFF** equal portions **MIX** until all white

1. **Clean area to be repaired.** Thoroughly remove all grease, loose particles, rust. Roughen surface slightly with sandpaper.

2. **Press Epoxybond firmly into damaged area.** For running leaks, use wooden plug to halt dripping. Mold EPOXYBOND around leak, covering plug.

3. **Wrap Epoxybond repair with tape** where necessary to hold repair in position until Plumber Seal hardens.

4. **Use light bulb to speed hardening.** When temperature is below 60°F., hang light bulb near repaired area.

What to do when even the best-made joints leak. *Courtesy Atlas Minerals and Chemicals, Inc.*

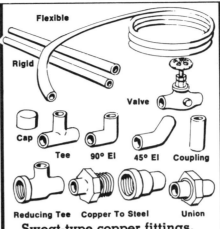

Cap **Tee** **90° El** **45° El** **Coupling**

Reducing Tee **Copper To Steel** **Union**

Sweat-type copper fittings. *Courtesy Hardware Retailing*

Tee **90° El** **45° El** **Street El**

Reducer Tee **Reducer** **Coupling** **Bushing**

Cap **Plug** **Hose Adapter** **Valve**

These Hubs For WATER and VENT PIPE ONLY

A few standard steel pipe fittings. *Courtesy Hardware Retailing*

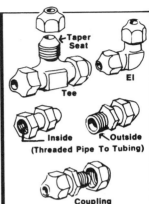

Taper Seat **El** **Tee**

Inside **Outside** (Threaded Pipe To Tubing)

Coupling

Flare-type copper fittings. *Courtesy Hardware Retailing*

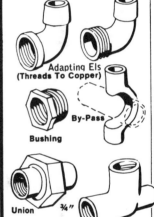

Adapting Els (Threads To Copper)

By-Pass

Bushing

Union **¾″**

¾″ Reducing Tee

Special steel pipe fittings. *Courtesy Hardware Retailing*

Globe Valve **Globe Stop and Drain** **Check**

Angle **Lavatory Straight** **Gate** **Swing Check**

Valve types often used with steel pipe. *Courtesy Hardware Retailing*

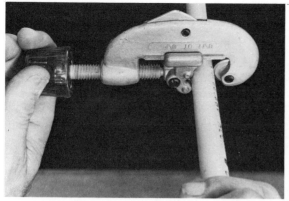

Joining plastic pipe to a plastic fitting. A. Pipe cutter is used to sever pipe. Pipe end is reamed. (Reamer is folded into cutter.)

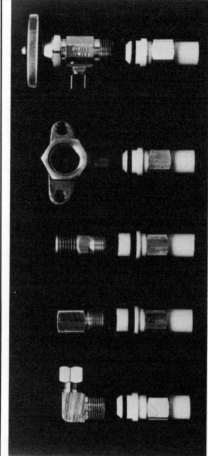

Plastic pipe and fittings.

Transition fittings. They are used to connect plastic pipe to threaded pipe and to copper tubing.

←

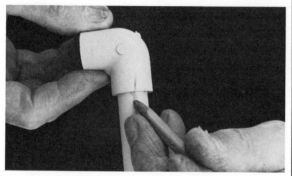

B. The fitting is positioned "dry." Its desired relation to the pipe is carefully indicated with a pencil mark.

↓ Examples of plastic pipe fittings.

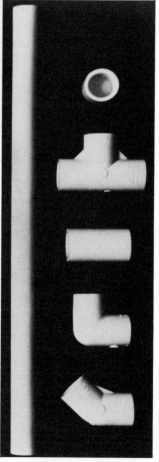

C. The fitting is removed. The end of the pipe is cleaned with sandpaper or primer. A band of suitable cement is applied to the end of the pipe. The fitting is replaced, given a fraction of a turn, and lined up with the pencil mark.

Typical sweat-type compression valve disassembled. Notice the washer and the machine bolt that normally holds it in place.

How a transition fitting is used to join plastic pipe to steel pipe.

Typical gate valve. You can recognize it by its long bonnet and the fact that a dozen turns are required to fully open or close it.

A clamp-on valve and tap. When this device is clamped to a copper tube, it automatically pierces the tube. Turning handle controls the flow of liquid through the fitting. Copper tubing joint is made with a metal ring compression fitting.

A. Disassembling a diaphragm-type faucet. The bolt that holds the handle in place is under the cap, which can be pried off.

B. The diaphragm assembly itself. When the little rubber cap is worn, the valve cannot be completely closed. When any of the O rings are worn, the water leaks out from around the handle when the valve or faucet is in its open position.

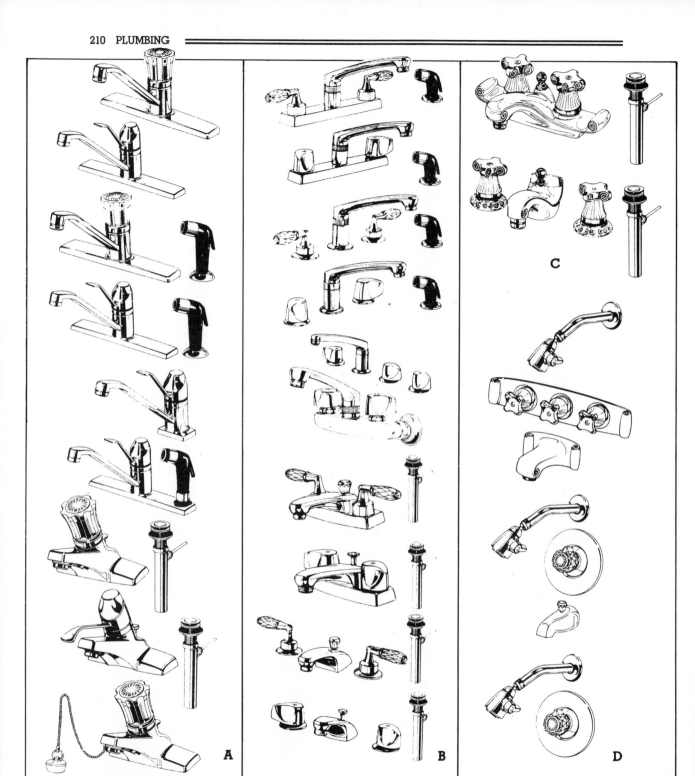

A few of the many faucets available.
A. Single-lever types. B. Dual-valve types. C. Ornamental lavatory types. D. Shower valves, shower heads, and tub spigots. *Courtesy Bradly Corp.*

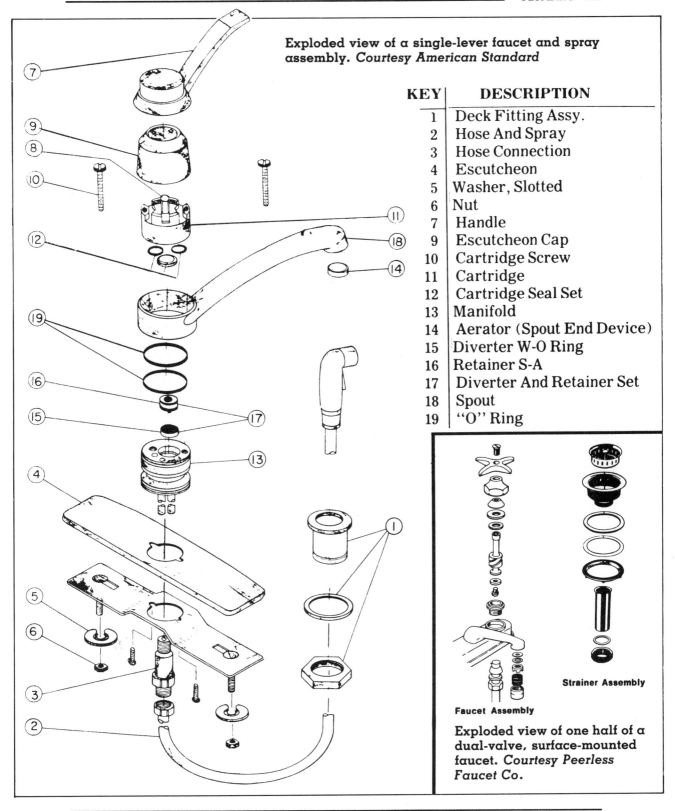

Exploded view of a single-lever faucet and spray assembly. *Courtesy American Standard*

KEY	DESCRIPTION
1	Deck Fitting Assy.
2	Hose And Spray
3	Hose Connection
4	Escutcheon
5	Washer, Slotted
6	Nut
7	Handle
9	Escutcheon Cap
10	Cartridge Screw
11	Cartridge
12	Cartridge Seal Set
13	Manifold
14	Aerator (Spout End Device)
15	Diverter W-O Ring
16	Retainer S-A
17	Diverter And Retainer Set
18	Spout
19	"O" Ring

Strainer Assembly

Faucet Assembly

Exploded view of one half of a dual-valve, surface-mounted faucet. *Courtesy Peerless Faucet Co.*

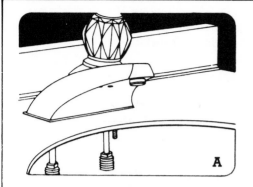

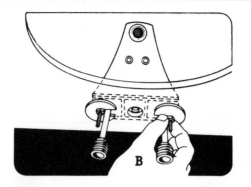

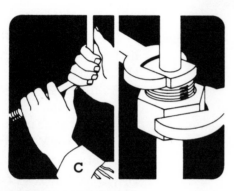

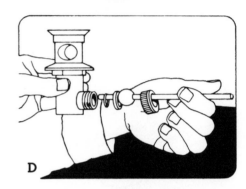

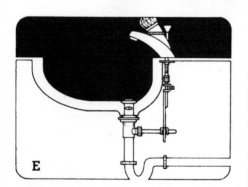

Steps in installing a single-lever lavatory faucet. A. The faucet is positioned. B. The washers are positioned and the nuts are made snug. C. If the feed pipes have to be bent, they are bent very carefully. The supply pipes are bolted to the feed pipes. D. The pop-up valve is assembled and installed. E. The pop-up valve control arm is connected and adjusted to the control lever position. *Courtesy Peerless Faucet Co.*

HOW TO SELECT THE RIGHT SIZE WATER HEATER

Gas

Number of people in family		1	1½	2	3
				Number of Bathrooms	
No Home	2	30-gal.	30-gal.	30-gal.	40-gal.
Laundering	3	30-gal.	30-gal.	40-gal.	40-gal.
	4	30-gal.	50-gal.	50-gal.	50-gal.
	5	40-gal.	50-gal.	50-gal.	50-gal.
	6 or more	50-gal.	50-gal.	50-gal.	50-gal.
With	2	40-gal.	40-gal.	40-gal.	50-gal.
Automatic	3	40-gal.	50-gal.	50-gal.	50-gal.
Washer	4	50-gal.	50-gal.	50-gal.	50-gal.
	5	50-gal.	50-gal.	50-gal.	50-gal.
	6 or more	50-gal.	50-gal.	50-gal.	50-gal.

Electric

Number of people using hot water*	With washer	Without washer
3	66-gal.	52-gal.
5	82-gal.	66-gal.
7	82-gal.	82-gal.

*Count each child under 7 as two persons.
Note: In homes with more than one bathroom, order high speed model or one size larger.

Courtesy Hardware Retailing

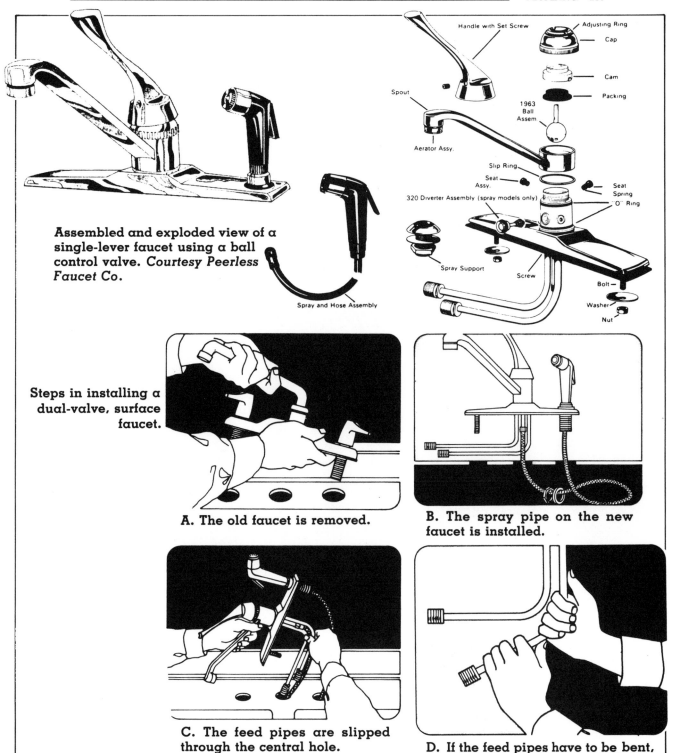

Assembled and exploded view of a single-lever faucet using a ball control valve. *Courtesy Peerless Faucet Co.*

Handle with Set Screw

Adjusting Ring

Cap

Cam

Packing

1963 Ball Assem

Spout

Aerator Assy.

Slip Ring

Seat Assy.

Seat Spring

"O" Ring

320 Diverter Assembly (spray models only)

Spray Support

Screw

Bolt

Washer

Nut

Spray and Hose Assembly

Steps in installing a dual-valve, surface faucet.

A. The old faucet is removed.

B. The spray pipe on the new faucet is installed.

C. The feed pipes are slipped through the central hole.

D. If the feed pipes have to be bent, they are bent very gently in a large radius arc to preclude kinking.

Courtesy Peerless Faucet Co.

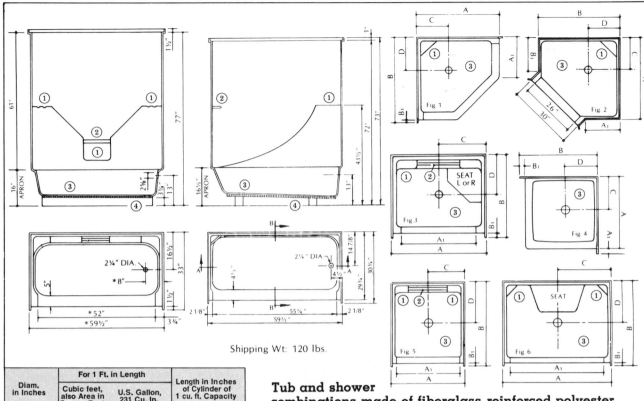

Shipping Wt: 120 lbs.

Tub and shower combinations made of fiberglass reinforced polyester. *Courtesy Efron Corp.*

Fig.	A	A¹	B	B¹	C	D	Curbs	Walls	Height	Wt. Lbs.
4	32"	1½"	33½"	1½"	14½"	14½"	2	2	76"	80
5	32"	28"	35½"	1½"	16"	17"	1	3	78½"	80
5	32"	28"	37½"	1½"	16"	18"	1	3	78½"	85
5	36"	30"	37½"	1½"	18"	18"	1	3	78½"	96
2	36"	14¾"	36"	14¾"	18"	18"	1	4	78½"	110
1	38"	18"	39½"	1½"	14½"	14½"	3	2	80"	88
5	42"	36"	37½"	1½"	21"	16"	1	3	78½"	100
3	42"	36"	37½"	1½"	21"	18"	1	3	78½"	105
5	48"	41"	37½"	1½"	24"	18"	1	3	78½"	105
6	48"	41"	37½"	1½"	24"	18"	1	3	78½"	110
6	60"	53"	37½"	1½"	30"	18"	1	3	78½"	120

Shipping Wt: 130 lbs. 110 lbs.
Optional Dome:
① Soap Ledge ③ Slip resistant safety floor
② Integral Grab Bar ④ Drainage through floor or wall

Diam. in Inches	For 1 Ft. in Length		Length in Inches of Cylinder of 1 cu. ft. Capacity
	Cubic feet, also Area in Square Feet	U.S. Gallon, 231 Cu. In.	
12"	.7855	5.875	15.276
12½	0.8522	6.375	14.080
12⅝	0.8693	6.503	13.800
12¾	0.8866	6.632	13.530
12⅞	0.9041	6.763	13.270
13	0.9218	6.895	13.020
13⅛	0.9395	7.028	12.780
13¼	0.9575	7.163	12.530
13⅜	0.9757	7.299	12.300
13½	0.994	7.436	12.070
13⅝	1.013	7.578	11.850
13¾	1.031	7.712	11.640
13⅞	1.051	7.855	11.420
14	1.069	7.997	11.230
14⅛	1.088	8.139	11.030
14¼	1.107	8.281	10.840
14⅜	1.127	8.431	10.650
14½	1.147	8.578	10.460
14⅝	1.167	8.730	10.280
14¾	1.187	8.879	10.110
14⅞	1.207	9.029	9.940
15	1.227	9.180	9.780
15⅛	1.248	9.336	9.620
15¼	1.268	9.485	9.460
15⅜	1.289	9.642	9.310
15½	1.310	9.801	9.160
15⅝	1.332	9.964	9.010
15¾	1.353	10.121	8.870
15⅞	1.374	10.278	8.730
16	1.396	10.440	8.600
16¼	1.440	10.772	8.330
16½	1.485	11.11	8.081
16¾	1.530	11.45	7.843
17	1.576	11.79	7.511
17¼	1.623	12.14	7.394
17½	1.670	12.49	7.186
17¾	1.718	12.85	6.985
18	1.768	13.22	6.787
18¼	1.817	13.59	6.604
18½	1.867	13.96	6.427
18¾	1.917	14.34	6.259
19	1.969	14.73	6.094
19¼	2.021	15.12	5.938

Toilet Tank Sizes

Contents in cubic feet and U.S. Gallons, of Pipe and Cylindrical Tanks of various diameters and 1 foot in length, when completely filled.

Courtesy Atlas Minerals and Chemicals, Inc.

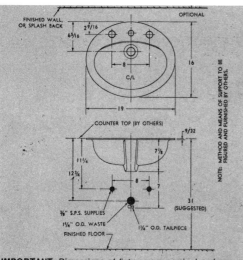

Enameled Cast Iron Oval Lavatory (with pop-up drain).
←

Roughing-in data for lavatory and toilet.

Courtesy American Standard Inc.

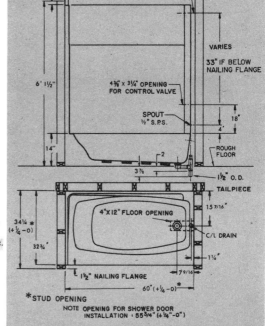

PLUMBER NOTE: THIS COMBINATION IS DESIGNED TO ROUGH-IN AT MINIMUM DIMENSION OR 12" FROM FINISHED WALL TO C/L OF OUTLET.

IMPORTANT: Dimensions of fixtures are nominal and may vary within the range of tolerances established by ANSI Standards—A112.19.1.

These measurements are subject to change or cancellation. No responsibility is assumed for use of superseded or voided leaflets.

→

Vitreous China Toilet (close-coupled combination).

IMPORTANT: Dimensions of fixtures are nominal and may vary within the range of tolerances established by ANSI Standards—A112.19.2.

These measurements are subject to change or cancellation. No responsibility is assumed for use of superseded or voided leaflets.

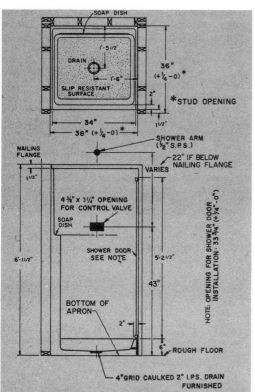

36" Shower (fiberglass reinforced polyester).
←

Roughing-in data for shower and tub.

Courtesy American Standard Inc.

→

Integral Tub and Surround (fiberglass reinforced polyester).

IMPORTANT: Dimensions of fixtures are nominal and may vary within the range of tolerances established by Industry Standards ANSI—Z124.2.

These measurements are subject to change or cancellation. No responsibility is assumed for use of superseded or voided leaflets.

IMPORTANT: Dimensions of fixtures are nominal and may vary within the range of tolerances established by Industry Standards ANSI—Z124.1.

These measurements are subject to change or cancellation. No responsibility is assumed for use of superseded or voided leaflets.

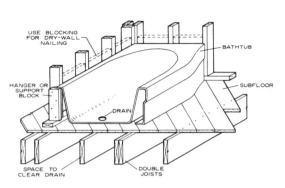

Framing a bathtub.

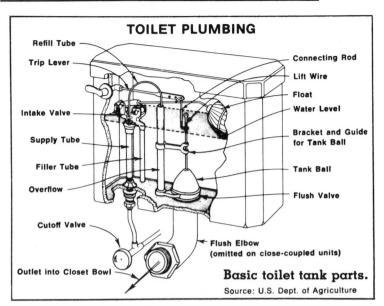

TOILET PLUMBING

Refill Tube
Trip Lever
Intake Valve
Supply Tube
Filler Tube
Overflow
Cutoff Valve
Outlet into Closet Bowl

Connecting Rod
Lift Wire
Float
Water Level
Bracket and Guide for Tank Ball
Tank Ball
Flush Valve
Flush Elbow (omitted on close-coupled units)

Basic toilet tank parts.

Source: U.S. Dept. of Agriculture

USE BLOCKING FOR DRY-WALL NAILING
BATHTUB
HANGER OR SUPPORT BLOCK
SUBFLOOR
DRAIN
SPACE TO CLEAR DRAIN
DOUBLE JOISTS

How to Solve Common Household Plumbing Problems

Problem	Solution
Leaking faucet	Has a worn washer. Shut off water, dismantle faucet and replace worn washer. Spout leak needs new faucet washer; under stem cap, bibb washer; handle stem, cone bonnet packing or "O" ring.
Leaking pipes	Plumbing joints may be parted. Copper plumbing joints are not threaded and can be permanently soldered or brazed if accidental bending or a hard blow causes a leak. Threaded joints of other metals may have to be reconnected, adding waterproof compound to threads.
Dripping pipes	Warm, moist air condenses when it strikes cold pipe. Wrap with pipe insulation.
Too much water in toilet tank	If water in tank flows off through overflow tube, replace supply cock. If water leaks past rubber ball stopper through outlet valve, replace valve.
Toilet tank ball does not fit (humming sound)	Outlet pipe is corroded or covered with grit and makes irregular seat for stopper ball. Smooth with emery cloth or replace outlet pipe.
Whistling when toilet tank fills	Increase flow of water into tank by adjusting float valve.
Hammering noise when faucet is turned off rapidly	Generally a simple do-it-yourself job to install air chambers, shock absorbers or pressure-reducing valves. If system already has air chambers, unclog them by shutting off water supply and opening all faucets.
Water rushes down drain with sucking noise	Means non-existent, improper or clogged vent. Depending on local plumbing codes, can be cured with anti-siphon trap.
General noises in pipes	Almost always caused by underestimating the overall size of the plumbing system; pipes (or tubing) are too small. Accumulation of rust or deposits in old lines can also reduce the operating size of pipes. Installation of larger pipes, a pressure reducing valve, expansion loops or water-hammer arrester will correct most noises. A "creaking" noise is caused by expansion and contraction of piping which was incorrectly installed in direct contact with walls and floors instead of against sound-deadening devices. Urge customers, in initial installation, to allow for their own maximum use of plumbing, rather than always go by the minimum permitted by some plumbing codes. It will be less expensive in the long run.
Rumbling noise near water heater	Water may be too hot. Re-adjust thermostat to 140° to 160°
Sluggish drains	Drain piping must be of correct size and sloped uniformly; one quarter of an inch to the foot is best. Local codes prevail, but it is possible to oversize as well as undersize drain pipe. Piping that is too big may not allow water to completely remove material clinging to its walls. The result—clogging.
Low water pressure	Undersize plumbing or clogged pipes or both. A major plumbing job, by contractor, may be the only solution.

Courtesy Hardware Retailing

32

PLYWOOD

Wide boards of solid wood have always been a problem. Early carpenters countered the tendency of wide boards to split, warp, and shrink by carefully seasoning the lumber before they used it and working mainly with lumber less likely to cause problems. Sometimes they would force iron rods through the width of the boards and sometimes they would use wood dowels for the same purpose.

As glue was developed over the centuries and saws improved, another technique came into use. Wide boards were sawn into strips, the strips turned around and glued to one another, side to side. In this way the tendency of one board to twist in one direction was countered by the tendency of another board to twist in the opposite direction. This technique is still used today. You will see it in many modern solid (but glued) tabletops.

Plywood did not come into common use until sometime in the 1800s. Veneers have been used since Egyptian times. But a veneer is simply a layer of wood, metal, or bone glued atop another piece of wood for ornamentation. True plywood is wood made of two or more plies, or sheets, of wood. The purpose, of course, is to make a single wide sheet of wood that will not crack, split, or warp. True plywood did not become practical until the development of power sources and machines that could peel wood from a log in the same way toilet paper is removed from a roll.

DIMENSIONS

The standard sheet of plywood is 4 × 8 feet in size. This amounts to a surface containing 32 square feet. The figure is mentioned here merely to point out that some plywood bargains are advertised at a per-square-foot rate. The full sheet price is not obvious until you stop to multiply it out. To a much smaller extent plywood is also manufactured in sizes of 4 × 6 and 4 × 12 feet. Few yards stock these sizes. The size of the foreign-made sheets may differ, so always check before lugging them home.

THICKNESSES AND PLIES

Plywood is manufactured in thicknesses ranging from ⅛ of an inch to 1¼ inches. Ply count ranges from two to a dozen and possibly more. Obviously the thicker the sheet, the more plies it has, and the stronger and more costly the plywood.

BASIC CATEGORIES

There are two types of plywood; the division is based on the glue that is used. One is called interior. It cannot be exposed to the weather. Should interior plywood be exposed to the elements, the glue will dissolve and the plies will separate. When this happens, the wood has, of course, lost its strength and becomes useless.

Obviously, interior plywood may get wet. If you are using this grade to build either your home or a chicken coop—and this is the grade or type that is always used for construction that will be protected by a roof and siding—don't worry about a little rain. It will do no harm. But do worry about the wood remaining wet or being stored in a damp area. When storing plywood outdoors always raise the boards a foot or more above the earth, and always cover the sheets completely with a plastic tarp.

The second type of plywood is classed as exterior. This is the type or grade that you use when you want the exterior of the building to be of plywood (not covered by siding or shingles). While standard grades of exterior plywood can be used this way, do not depend on the wood to protect itself against moisture. Exterior plywood must be varnished and/or thoroughly painted just like ordinary wood or it will disintegrate and rot.

There are stronger, more water-resistant grades of exterior plywood made that need less protection. These are classified as marine grades. They are tough and expensive and are used for making boats.

SURFACES

When making plywood a manufacturer has not only a choice of wood, but also a choice of the types of wood he is going to join, and a choice of finishings to use on the faces of the exposed, surface plies. This opportunity has not been overlooked. The variety of plywood surface layers and finishes is tremendous: It easily runs into the hundreds.

GOOD ONE SIDE OR TWO
When only one side of the plywood sheet is to be exposed, there is no point for paying the price of two highly sanded, good-quality layers of wood. When both surfaces are to be visible, there is no alternative but to purchase the more expensive sheet.

CHOICE OF SURFACES
Here are just a few of the many surfaces available:

    Rough sawn, with open knotholes
    Rough sawn with patched
      knotholes
    Sanded
    Brushed
    V-grooved, equal spacing
    V-grooved, random spacing
    Natural wood—dozens of species
    Natural wood, clear finish
    Natural wood-stained, clear finish
    Striated
    Channel-grooved
    Texture enhanced

CUTTING

When hand-sawing use a saw with 10 to 15 points per inch. Keep the good side of the panel up, and place a piece of scrap lumber beneath the panel to prevent splitting on the underside.

When working with a radial power saw or a table power saw, keep the good side up, and make sure the saw blade is sharp. A fine-tooth saw is best, and do not let the saw teeth project more than a small fraction of an inch beyond the surface of the plywood.

When working with a portable power saw, keep the good face of the plywood down; make sure the blade is very sharp and don't "push" the saw, meaning let the saw blade rotate at full speed.

When working with a saber saw, use a very sharp, fine-tooth blade.

FASTENING

Mastic is probably the best material to use to fasten very thin sheets of plywood to their supports. Finishing nails or casing nails can be used with ⅜-inch and thicker plywood. Keep the nails well in from the edge. If you have to place them closer to the edge than a half inch, it is advisable to drill pilot holes to avoid splitting the panel. (You might also try the nails on some scrap lumber first.)

APPLICATION GUIDE

Thickness	Application	Fastening method
under ¼ inch	Decorative panels furniture	Mastic on a solid wall or studs, furring strips, no more than 16 inches on center in any direction
¼ inch	Decorative panels non-load-bearing walls furniture	Nails or mastic 16 inches on center studs or furring strips
⅜ inch	Subflooring sheathing roofing	Mastic or nails 16 inches on center studs, joists
½ inch	Subflooring sheathing roofing furniture	Mastic or nails 16 inches on center studs, joists; 24 inches on center non-load-bearing wall
¾ inch	Single-layer flooring furniture	Mastic, plus nails plus clips. Up to 48 inches on center studs and joists (see manufacturer's literature, local building code).

HOW TO ESTIMATE PANELING

1. Determine perimeter of room (total of widths of all walls).

2. Use following conversion table to figure number of panels needed:

(All figures based on rooms with 8' or less ceiling height.)

3. Allow for windows, doors, fireplaces, etc. as follows:

Door	1/3 panel
Window	1/4 panel
Fireplace	1/2 panel

Example: Assume a room 16' long by 14' wide with two doors, two windows and a fireplace. Perimeter is 60' requiring 15 panels; subtracting for the doors, windows and fireplace reduces number to 13 panels. Always use highest number of panels when perimeter total is between ranges shown in table.

Courtesy Hardware Retailing

Perimeter	No. of 4x8 Panels
36'	9
40'	10
44'	11
48'	12
52'	13
56'	14
60'	15
64'	16
68'	17
72'	18
92'	23

Applying plywood panels. Note that the blocking rests flush with the studs. When using plywood less than ¼-of-an-inch thick, spacing between studs and block should be no less than 16 inches on centers. If this was an interior wall, there would be no need for the vapor barrier.

Guide to Appearance Grades of Plywood

(1) SPECIFIC GRADES AND THICKNESSES MAY BE IN LOCALLY LIMITED SUPPLY. SEE YOUR DEALER BEFORE SPECIFYING.

	Grade Designation (2)	Description and Most Common Uses	Typical (3) Grade-Trademarks	Face	Inner Plies	Back	Most Common Thicknesses (inch)				
Interior Type	N-N, N-A N-B INT-APA	Cabinet quality. For natural finish furniture, cabinet doors, built-ins, etc. Special order items.	NN GT IN APA PS 174 000 / NA G2 INT APA PS 174 000	N	C	N,A, or B					3/4
	N-D-INT-APA	For natural finish paneling. Special order item.	ND G2 INT APA PS 174 000	N	D	D	1/4				
	A-A INT-APA	For applications with both sides on view, built-ins, cabinets, furniture, partitions. Smooth face; suitable for painting.	AA G2 INT APA PS 174 000	A	D	A	1/4	3/8	1/2	5/8	3/4
	A-B INT-APA	Use where appearance of one side is less important but where two solid surfaces are necessary.	AB GT INT APA PS 174 000	A	D	B	1/4	3/8	1/2	5/8	3/4
	A-D INT-APA	Use where appearance of only one side is important. Paneling, built-ins, shelving, partitions, flow racks.	A-D GROUP 1 INTERIOR PS 1 000 APA	A	D	D	1/4	3/8	1/2	5/8	3/4
	B-B INT-APA	Utility panel with two solid sides. Permits circular plugs.	BB G2 INT APA PS 174 000	B	D	B	1/4	3/8	1/2	5/8	3/4
	B-D INT-APA	Utility panel with one solid side. Good for backing, sides of built-ins, industry shelving, slip sheets, separator boards, bins.	B-D GROUP 2 INTERIOR 000 APA	B	D	D	1/4	3/8	1/2	5/8	3/4
	DECORATIVE PANELS—APA	Rough-sawn, brushed, grooved, or striated faces. For paneling, interior accent walls, built-ins, counter facing, displays, exhibits.	DECORATIVE BD G1 INT APA PS 174	C or btr.	D	D	5/16	3/8	1/2	5/8	
	PLYRON INT-APA	Hardboard face on both sides. For counter tops, shelving, cabinet doors, flooring. Faces tempered, untempered, smooth, or screened.	PLYRON INT APA 000	C & D					1/2	5/8	3/4
Exterior Type	A-A EXT-APA	Use where appearance of both sides is important. Fences, built-ins, signs, boats, cabinets, commercial refrigerators, shipping containers, tote boxes, tanks, ducts. (4)	AA GT EXT APA PS174 000	A	C	A	1/4	3/8	1/2	5/8	3/4
	A-B EXT-APA	Use where the appearance of one side is less important. (4)	AB GT EXT APA PS174 000	A	C	B	1/4	3/8	1/2	5/8	3/4
	A-C EXT-APA	Use where the appearance of only one side is important. Soffits, fences, structural uses, boxcar and truck lining, farm buildings. Tanks, trays, commercial refrigerators. (4)	A-C GROUP 1 EXTERIOR PS 1 000 APA	A	C	C	1/4	3/8	1/2	5/8	3/4
	B-B EXT-APA	Utility panel with solid faces. (4)	BB G2 EXT APA PS174 000	B	C	B	1/4	3/8	1/2	5/8	3/4
	B-C EXT-APA	Utility panel for farm service and work buildings, boxcar and truck lining, containers, tanks, agricultural equipment. Also as base for exterior coatings for walls, roofs. (4)	B-C GROUP 2 EXTERIOR PS 1 000 APA	B	C	C	1/4	3/8	1/2	5/8	3/4
	HDO EXT-APA	High Density Overlay plywood. Has a hard, semi-opaque resin-fiber overlay both faces. Abrasion resistant. For concrete forms, cabinets, counter tops, signs, tanks. (4)	HDO 6060 PLYFORM EXT APA PS174	A or B	C or C plgd	A or B		3/8	1/2	5/8	3/4
	MDO EXT-APA	Medium Density Overlay with smooth, opaque, resin-fiber overlay one or both panel faces. Highly recommended for siding and other outdoor applications, built-ins, signs, displays. Ideal base for paint. (4)(6)	MDO BB G2 EXT APA PS174 000	B	C	B or C		3/8	1/2	5/8	3/4
	303 SIDING EXT-APA	Proprietary plywood products for exterior siding, fencing, etc. Special surface treatment such as V-groove, channel groove, striated, brushed, rough-sawn and texture-embossed MDO. Stud spacing (Span Index) and face grade classification indicated on grade stamp.	303 SIDING 6-S GROUP 1 24 oc SPAN EXTERIOR PS 1 IN 000 APA	(5)	C	C		3/8	1/2	5/8	
	T 1-11 EXT-APA	Special 303 panel having grooves 1/4" deep, 3/8" wide, spaced 4" or 8" o.c. Other spacing optional. Edges shiplapped. Available unsanded, textured and MDO.	303 SIDING 6-S/W T 1 11 GROUP 1A oc SPAN EXTERIOR PS 1 IN 000 APA	C or btr.	C	C			19/32	5/8	
	PLYRON EXT-APA	Hardboard faces both sides, tempered, smooth or screened.	PLYRON EXT APA 000		C				1/2	5/8	3/4
	MARINE EXT-APA	Ideal for boat hulls. Made only with Douglas fir or western larch. Special solid jointed core construction. Subject to special limitations on core gaps and number of face repairs. Also available with HDO or MDO faces.	MARINE AA EXT APA PS174 000	A or B	B	A or B	1/4	3/8	1/2	5/8	3/4

(1) Sanded both sides except where decorative or other surfaces specified.
(2) Can be manufactured in Group 1, 2, 3, 4 or 5.
(3) The species groups, Identification Indexes and Span Indexes shown in the typical grade-trademarks are examples only.
(4) Can also be manufactured in Structural I (all plies limited to Group 1 species) and Structural II (all plies limited to Group 1, 2, or 3 species).

(5) C or better for 5 plies. C Plugged or better for 3 plies.
(6) Also available as a 303 Siding.

Courtesy Georgia-Pacific Corp.

Guide to Engineered Grades of Plywood

Courtesy Georgia-Pacific Corp.

	Grade Designation	Description and Most Common Uses	Typical Grade-trademarks (1)	Face	Inner Plies	Back	Most Common Thicknesses (inch)				
Interior Type	C-D INT-APA	For wall and roof sheathing, subflooring, industrial uses such as pallets. Most commonly available with exterior glue (CDX). Specify exterior glue where construction delays are anticipated and for treated-wood foundations. (7)	C-D 32/16 APA INTERIOR PS1-74 000; C-D 24/0 APA INTERIOR PS1-74 000 EXTERIOR GLUE	C	D	D	5/16	3/8	1/2	5/8	3/4
	STRUCTURAL I C-D INT-APA and STRUCTURAL II C-D INT-APA	Unsanded structural grades where plywood strength properties are of maximum importance: structural diaphragms, box beams, gusset plates, stressed-skin panels, containers, pallet bins. Made only with exterior glue. See (6) for species group requirements. Structural I more commonly available. (7)	STRUCTURAL I C-D 24/0 APA INTERIOR PS1-74 000 EXTERIOR GLUE	C(3)	D(3)	D(3)	5/16	3/8	1/2	5/8	3/4
	STURD-I-FLOOR INT-APA	For combination subfloor-underlayment. Provides smooth surface for application of resilient floor covering. Possesses high concentrated- and impact-load resistance during construction and occupancy. Manufactured with exterior glue only. Touch-sanded. Available square edge or tongue-and-groove. (7)	STURD-I-FLOOR 24oc T&G 23 32 INCH INTERIOR 000 EXTERIOR GLUE NRB-108	C Plugged	(4)	D				19/32 5/8	23/32 3/4
	STURD-I-FLOOR 48 O.C. (2-4-1) INT-APA	For combination subfloor-underlayment on 32- and 48-inch spans. Provides smooth surface for application of resilient floor coverings. Possesses high concentrated- and impact-load resistance during construction and occupancy. Manufactured with exterior glue only. Unsanded or touch-sanded. Available square edge or tongue-and-groove. (7)	STURD-I-FLOOR 48oc 2-4-1 T&G 118 INCH INTERIOR 000 EXTERIOR GLUE NRB-108	C Plugged	C(5) & D	D	1-1/8				
	UNDERLAYMENT INT-APA	For application over structural subfloor. Provides smooth surface for application of resilient floor coverings. Touch-sanded. Also available with exterior glue. (2)(6)	UNDERLAYMENT GROUP 1 INTERIOR PS1-74 000	C Plugged	C(5) & D	D		3/8	1/2	19/32 5/8	23/32 3/4
	C-D PLUGGED INT-APA	For built-ins, wall and ceiling tile backing, cable reels, walkways, separator boards. Not a substitute for Underlayment or Sturd-I-Floor as it lacks their indentation resistance. Touch-sanded. Also made with exterior glue. (2)(6)	C-D PLUGGED GROUP 2 INTERIOR PS1-74 000	C Plugged	D	D		3/8	1/2	19/32 5/8	23/32 3/4
Exterior Type	C-C EXT-APA	Unsanded grade with waterproof bond for subflooring and roof decking, siding on service and farm buildings, crating, pallets, pallet bins, cable reels, treated-wood foundations. (7)	C-C 42/20 EXTERIOR PS1-74	C	C	C	5/16	3/8	1/2	5/8	3/4
	STRUCTURAL I C-C EXT-APA and STRUCTURAL II C-C EXT-APA	For engineered applications in construction and industry where full Exterior type panels are required. Unsanded. See (6) for species group requirements. (7)	STRUCTURAL I C-C 32/16 APA EXTERIOR PS1-74	C	C	C	5/16	3/8	1/2	5/8	3/4
	STURD-I-FLOOR EXT-APA	For combination subfloor-underlayment under resilient floor coverings where severe moisture conditions may be present, as in balcony decks. Possesses high concentrated- and impact-load resistance during construction and occupancy. Touch-sanded. Available square edge or tongue-and-groove. (7)	STURD-I-FLOOR 20oc 5 8 INCH EXTERIOR 000 NRB-108	C Plugged	C(5)	C				19/32 5/8	23/32 3/4
	UNDERLAYMENT C-C PLUGGED EXT-APA	For application over structural subfloor. Provides smooth surface for application of resilient floor coverings where severe moisture conditions may be present. Touch-sanded. (2)(6)	UNDERLAYMENT C-C PLUGGED GROUP 2 EXTERIOR PS1-74 000	C Plugged	C(5)	C		3/8	1/2	19/32 5/8	23/32 3/4
	C-C PLUGGED EXT-APA	For use as tile backing where severe moisture conditions exist. For refrigerated or controlled atmosphere rooms, pallet fruit bins, tanks, box car and truck floors and linings, open soffits. Touch-sanded. (2)(6)	C-C PLUGGED GROUP 2 EXTERIOR PS1-74 000	C Plugged	C	C		3/8	1/2	19/32 5/8	23/32 3/4
	B-B PLYFORM CLASS I & CLASS II EXT-APA	Concrete form grades with high reuse factor. Sanded both sides. Mill-oiled unless otherwise specified. Special restrictions on species. Available in HDO and Structural I. Class I most commonly available. (8)	B B PLYFORM CLASS I APA EXTERIOR PS1-74 000	B	C	B				5/8	3/4

(1) The species groups, Identification Indexes and Span Indexes shown in the typical grade-trademarks are examples only. See "Group," "Identification Index" and "Span Index" for explanations and availability.
(2) Can be manufactured in Group 1, 2, 3, 4, or 5.
(3) Special improved grade for structural panels.
(4) Special veneer construction to resist indentation from concentrated loads, or other solid wood-base materials.
(5) Special construction to resist indentation from concentrated loads.
(6) Can also be manufactured in Structural I (all plies limited to Group 1 species) and Structural II (all plies limited to Group 1, 2, or 3 species).
(7) Specify by Identification Index for sheathing and Span Index for Sturd-I-Floor panels.
(8) Made only from certain wood species to conform to APA specifications.

PUTTY

(ALSO SEE CAULK)

Putty is used to hold window glass within a window frame. The putty seals the joint between the glass and the wood or metal and also provides a cushion that permits the glass to expand without cracking.

Ordinary putty is made of a combination of powdered whiting and boiled linseed oil. If you wish to mix your own, use a mixture of 16 ounces of powder to 9 liquid ounces of oil. For a harder mixture add up to 5 ounces of white lead. More lead than that produces a putty that will, eventually, become rock hard, which makes its removal almost impossible.

Ordinary putty should not be used on bare wood. First the wood should be given a coat of paint or shellac. Otherwise, the wood soaks the oil out of the putty, making it crack.

GLAZING COMPOUNDS

Many of the companies manufacturing glazing compounds, which are an improved form of putty, produce three grades. The least expensive grade is made for primed (painted) wood or metal. The middle quality compound can be used with unpainted metal. The best grade, sometimes called flexible, forms a more flexible, watertight seal. It does not shrink and can be used with metal, primed wood, glass, porcelain, and other materials. The first two grades are made in white and gray. The flexible grade comes only in aluminum gray.

SPECIAL PUTTIES

Putties have been classified as special because they have no general classification. They are not true putties, but they are used like putty to fill holes and the like.

WATER PUTTY

Sometimes called wood putty, this is a powder that is mixed with water to form a puttylike dough. It sets in about fifteen minutes, at which time you can shave it like soap. It becomes hard in another thirty minutes, but if you want to be able to sand its woodlike surface, you must give it eight hours to set completely.

Left as is it dries to a cream color. If you want a different color, tint it with vinyl or latex paint or "color." Do not use paint or color containing oil.

PLASTIC WOOD

This is a premixed combination of wood fibers, cement, and a volatile solvent made for use with or on wood only. It can be had in a number of colors and it takes stains and paint.

AUTO BODY FILLER

This is used for filling dents and scratches in metal. It dries fast, but should not be used in cold weather, which slows the drying, or applied in layers more than $\frac{1}{8}$ inch thick.

PLASTIC FILLER

This is a two-part filler that can be used on metal and plastic. It can be used to rebuild automotive and marine hulls and body sections.

RE-SIDING

(ALSO SEE SIDING)

Re-siding is the term most often used to describe siding that can be—and is—used in the conventional way, which is atop sheathing, but is most often used atop in-place siding. In other words, if you are going to re-side your home, these are the materials you will use.

AVAILABLE RE-SIDING

Three types of re-siding materials are most often used: aluminum, vinyl, and steel. In overall, nationwide quantities, aluminum is the most often used, with vinyl somewhat less popular, and steel least used of all.

ALUMINUM

This is the most expensive of the three. For all practical purposes, it is fireproof, rot-proof, and corrosion-proof. It is unaffected by temperature, and depending on its manufacturer, its paint may be warrantied for as many as forty years. It is, however, relatively soft and easily dented with a baseball bat or similar object.

VINYL

This is somewhat cheaper than aluminum, fire-resistant but not fireproof. When it does burn—it has an ignition temperature 255°F higher than paper—it produces noxious and poisonous gases. It is not easily dented, but can be cracked with a light blow at sub-zero temperatures. Exposed to very hot weather it may sag, producing ripples in the horizontal lines. Plastic siding is not available in as many colors as aluminum, and its colors are solid through and through, but they do fade in time.

STEEL

Galvanized steel siding is the least expensive of all. It is, of course, fire- and rot-proof, but it is not completely rust-proof. Its colors last as long as any of the other re-siding materials. It is more difficult to install, however, simply because it is steel and is tougher and more difficult to cut.

SYSTEM OF APPLICATION

The re-siding materials discussed are known as formed-strip sidings. Whereas clapboard, for example, is a strip of wood with a wedge-shaped end, formed-strip siding is a long channel with weep holes in its folded bottom edge and oval holes in its top lip. A portion of the bottom and the top curve inward and out to form "lips." The upper lips "hook" into the panel above. The lower lips hold the lower panel in place. In this way all the panels covering a wall form a continuous, tied-together but flexible surface.

If the first installed panel is perfectly horizontal (or vertical), perforce all following panels must be equally accurately positioned.

The ends of each panel fit into a channel about 1 inch deep. This permits the panel to expand and contract without its end being exposed and also permits a ⅜-inch latitude in cut length. Panels are joined end to end simply by overlapping them.

As you can readily visualize, the application of formed-strip siding is a great deal faster and easier than the application of shingles or clapboard siding.

SHAPES AND DIMENSIONS

All formed-strip siding is made in somewhat similar shapes and dimensions, but few if any products are interchangeable even if their materials, colors, and overall dimensions are the same. Deliberately or not, formed-strip sidings by two different manufacturers are rarely, if ever, interchangeable.

ALUMINUM SHAPES AND SPECIFICATIONS

Horizontal siding is generally made in 8-inch and double-4-inch siding panels that simulate equal-width clapboard siding. The double-4 is a bit stiffer because of its center fold. To a lesser degree aluminum panels are also made with 5 inches of exposure and 9 inch with two folds to simulate a panel with two beveled edges.

Vertical aluminum siding is made in 10-, 12-, and 16-inch-wide panels. The 10-inch panels are shaped to simulate either board-and-batten or V-grooved wood panels. The 12-inch is available with a V groove; the 16-inch with a double-V, and in board-and-batten as a triple-5-inch or with five 3-inch indentations.

Aluminum panels are available with a smooth finish or textured surface that simulates wood grain.

Siding is sold on the basis of expo-

sure. Horizontal siding is usually 12½ or 13 feet long, packed in a box marked "two squares," meaning the box contains sufficient paneling to cover 200 square feet. Vertical siding is usually cut to the same lengths but packed one square to a box. Note that reliable dealers will accpet clean and uncut returns.

TRIM (ACCESSORIES)

Formed-strip siding is held in place not only by nails driven into the building but also by a variety of metal shapes, called trim. The channels that hold the ends of the panels may be a part of an outside corner or an inside corner. The sides of the panels may he held in place by J channels, starter strips, channel runners, vertical joiner strips, L channels, undersill trim, and more.

Unfortunately, all siding supply houses and all siding manufacturers do not use the same terminology. But you can identify the trim you want by its position in relation to the preformed panels and by the task it performs in relation to the panels.

MAKING YOUR OWN

In addition to the trim you'll need to hold the panels in place or to hide edges, you may also want to apply trim over the wood trim of the building (the house trim). In some instances you may be able to find channels and angles that can be adapted to the job. In most instances, you will have the option either of just painting the house trim or of bending flat coil stock to fit over it. This is easy to do if you have a sheet metal brake, which is a large bending tool, but is difficult or even impossible to do without the tool. One alternative is to hire a siding company (which, of course, has the tool) to bend it for you. Another is to locate a panel supplier that has a brake on the premises and that will let you use it for nothing or for a small fee. When using the brake, first bend a few sample pieces to learn just how much metal is "lost" going around the bend.

INSULATION

Aluminum siding applied directly over a wall has, by itself, an R factor of only 0.6. When breather (perforated) foil is added beneath the panel, the total R is increased to 1.1. When aluminum siding is backed with fiberboard and used alone it rates an R of 1.5. When the aluminum panel is backed with a layer of polystyrene and foil, the R rises to 2.5 to 3.0. When a bare aluminum panel is laid atop a sheet of either ½-inch-thick isocyanurate or ¾-inch-thick polystyrene, the figure rises to between 4.7 and 5 R. To bring the figure up to a possible rating of 5.5 to 6.0, polystyrene backer board is used on the panel, and two layers of breather foil are installed within a ¾-inch air space, created by fastening the panels to 1-×-2-inch furring strips.

NOTE: To secure maximum results when using foil, the reflective side must face the air space. When two layers of foil are used they should not touch each other. When the panels are supported on furring strips, the open spaces between the ends of the strips should be closed with more furring strips. In this way dead air spaces are created.

When the panels are fastened atop sheets of polystyrene or isocyanurate, small spaces should be left between the sheets, or holes should be punched in the sheets to permit the passage of air.

CUTTING ALUMINUM SIDING

Aluminum siding may be cut with a tin snips, hacksaw, razor knife, or power saw. The trouble with tin snips is that it is difficult to cut a straight line with them and they crease the lip of the panel, which then must be opened with the point of a screwdriver. The hacksaw is slow. The razor knife can be used only for lengthwise cuts; the metal is scored, then folded back and forth until it breaks. The power saw is best, but it must have a blade made for cutting aluminum. When using the saw, set up a jig consisting of a plank and some scrap lumber to guide the saw. This makes for accuracy and speed.

INSTALLATION OF ALUMINUM FORMED-STRIP PANELS

The usual sequence for applying aluminum formed-strip panels is as follows: first the fascia and soffit, then the house trim, if it is to be covered, and then the sides of the building.

INSTALLING THE SOFFIT
Where there is no soffit, but there are exposed roof rafters, nail a fascia runner to the building, flange up, on a line horizontal with the bottom ends of the rafters. Cut the soffit panels as

necessary. Slip one end of the panels into the channel in the fascia runner. Lift the other end and face-nail with aluminum nails to the ends of the rafters or the bottom edge of the fascia. Use a number of perforated soffit panels to allow the movement of air.

When there is a soffit, remove the wood soffit molding. Nail a soffit J channel in its place or a quarter-round molding, which combines a metal molding and a J channel. Then proceed as before.

COVERING THE FASCIA
Install a wide fascia cap atop the fascia. If necessary, follow with a narrow angle fitted into the corner formed by the fascia and the underside of the shingles. Cut and bend around the corners as necessary.

PREPARING THE WINDOWS AND DOORS
With a saw, cut all window- and doorsills flush with the sides of their frames.

Measure the distance from the front surface of the window trim to the topmost surface of the existing house siding. Record this figure. If this figure is less than the *total* thickness of the panels plus the materials (furring strips, insulation), that you plan to fasten atop the existing siding, you must build out the window and doorframes an equal or slightly greater amount. Use boards of equal width and suitable thickness. Simply nail them atop the trim. Generally the sills and tops of the frames do not have to be built out.

COVERING THE HOUSE TRIM
Cover the sill first. Use one or two pieces of metal. Use preformed an-

gles or bend the needed metal covering from 0.019 aluminum strip. Then cover the sides of the frame and, last, the top of the frame using a few 1-inch aluminum nails.

APPLYING THE HORIZONTAL PANELS
If you are going to use reflective foil, staple the foil over the wall, reflective side in. If you are going to use furring strips, now is the time to nail them in place. If you are going to use sheet insulation, it goes on next. Next, the corners are nailed in place. Make sure they are vertical and the nails are *not* driven home. Next, install the starter strip. This should not touch the corner posts and its bottom edge should be flush with the old siding. Use 2-inch aluminum nails every 16 inches or so. Butt the ends of starter strips together if one piece is not long enough.

Slip the end of one panel into the channel in a corner post. Lift the panel up until its lower lip engages the lip of the starter strip. If there is an insulator behind the panel, you must cut it clear of the panel ends by several inches. Put the panel in place, one end clear of the bottom of the channel by ¼ of an inch, and then nail it in place. Use nails long enough to go ¾ of an inch into the house sheathing. Make sure the nails go straight in, and leave 1/32 of an inch of space beneath the nailheads. The panels hang on the nails.

When you near the top of the wall, you fasten a J channel in place, channel down, and slip the top edge of the panel into the slot. When you reach the underside of a window or door, you fasten a J channel or a section of utility trim in place. The panel edge enters the channel or trim. The same is done at the sides of the window- and doorframes. The top of the frame is covered by another piece of trim and the panel fits into it and continues on upward.

APPLYING THE VERTICAL PANELS

The same procedure is followed, as above, the only difference being that you start on one side with the starter strip in a vertical position.

INSTALLATION OF VINYL SIDING

Vinyl panels are made in more or less the same sizes and shapes as the aluminum, formed-strip siding. The panels can be cut the same way. However, it is much easier to cut the plastic with tin snips, but the temperature of the plastic must be well above freezing or it will shatter. The same method of application is used, with only two major differences. While plastic is available in strip form and can be bent to shape, the plastic must be at 70°F or more. If the plastic is bent while cold, it will crack. It is also more difficult to bend the plastic to small radii (very sharp bends). As a result, it is common to use aluminum trim covering with plastic formed-strip siding.

Nails should not be driven through the plastic while it is cold; it may crack. To be safe, first drill holes for the nails.

Plastic has a much greater coefficient of expansion than metal. Therefore you must be certain to leave ¼ of an inch of clearance between each end of the panel and the bottom of whatever channel it fits into. When you join panel ends by overlapping them, be certain to cut the nailing flange back two inches on each panel.

When the edge of a panel is to be inserted in utility trim, it is advisable to use a snap-lock punch on the cut edge. This expands the edges of the panel so that it makes the tighter fit in the utility trim.

SHAPES AND DIMENSIONS

Formed-strip plastic siding is available in practically as many trim shapes, panel shapes, and sizes as formed-strip aluminum siding. Panel lengths and weights, however, are a bit different. Plastic panels for vertical application are usually 12 feet 6 inches long. They are packed in boxes containing two squares (enough exposure to cover 200 square feet). Altogether the weight is close to 100 pounds per box. Vertical panels are only 10 feet long. They are made in one thickness only and do not come with attached backer boards or insulation.

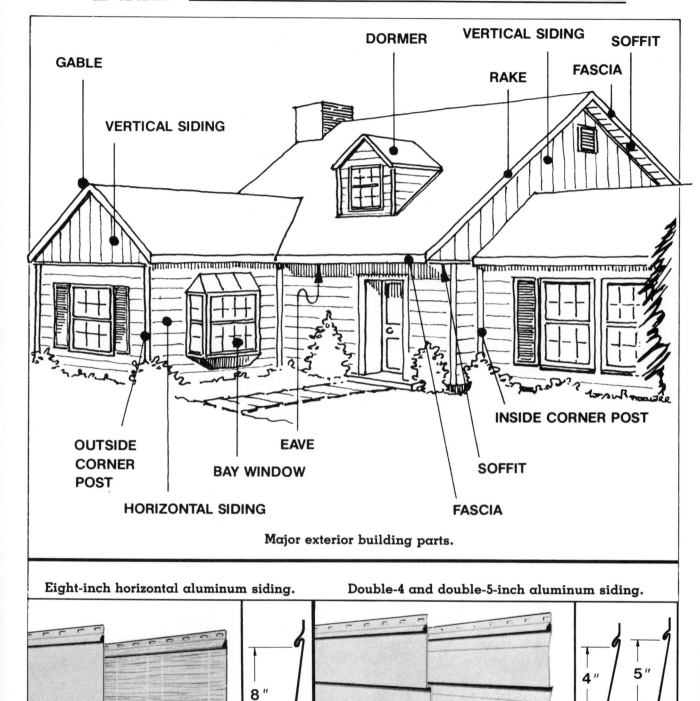

GABLE

VERTICAL SIDING

DORMER

VERTICAL SIDING

SOFFIT

RAKE

FASCIA

OUTSIDE CORNER POST

EAVE

BAY WINDOW

SOFFIT

INSIDE CORNER POST

HORIZONTAL SIDING

FASCIA

Major exterior building parts.

Eight-inch horizontal aluminum siding.

8"

Double-4 and double-5-inch aluminum siding.

4"

4"

5"

5"

Courtesy The Aluminum Association

	Aluminum	Steel	Vinyl Plastic
Weather and pollution resistant	Yes	Yes	Yes
Affected by sunlight	Finish only	Finish only	Yes
Fade-resistance	Good	Good	Good
Quality control of color	Excellent	Excellent	Fair
Dent resistance	Medium	Medium	High
Becomes brittle with age	No	No	Yes
Can crack or break in cold weather	No	No	Yes
Need periodic cleaning	Yes	Yes	Yes
Colors available	Wide range	Wide range	White & pastel only
Textures and patterns available	Smooth, embossed, & heavy textures and patterns	Heavy textures & embossed	Smooth finish & shallow textures
Matching & coordinating accessories (shutters, downspouts & gutters, window trim, soffit, etc.)	Aluminum accessories available	Aluminum trim generally used	Aluminum trim generally used
Rot resistance	Excellent	Excellent	Excellent
Warp resistance	Excellent	Excellent	Fair
Termite resistance	Excellent	Excellent	Excellent
Fire resistance	Excellent	Excellent	Can burn
Red rust resistance	Excellent	Fair	Excellent
Magnifies unevenness of wall	Very little	Very little	More than others
Warranties available	Generally 20-40 years	Generally 20-30 years	Generally 20-30 years
Moisture resistance	Excellent	Can rust if not properly coated	Excellent
Needs to be grounded	No	No	No
Attracts lightning	No	No	No
Can cause TV interference	Not a problem	Not a problem	Not a problem
Nails recommended for installing	Aluminum	Galvanized steel	Aluminum
Appearance of joints	Good	Good	Fair
Can be recycled	Always	Sometimes	Never

Note: The above chart summarizes the best information available to us. Products obviously vary from manufacturer to manufacturer, and local regulations may affect the use or installation of certain products.

A comparison of formed-strip siding.

Insulated siding.

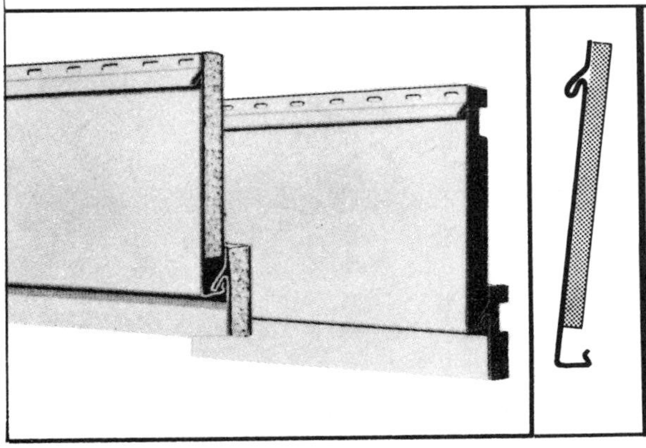

Vertical aluminum siding.

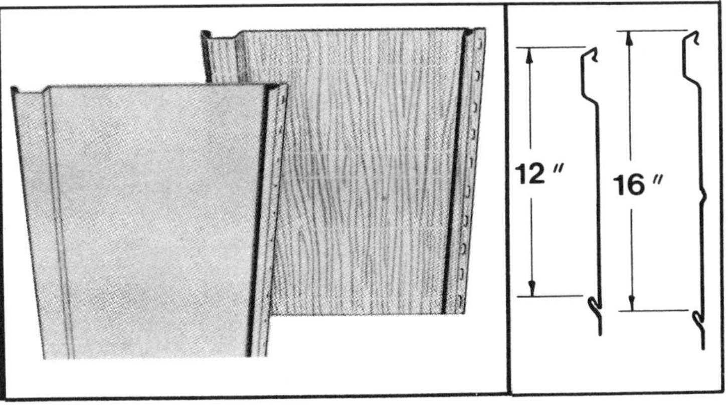

12 "   16 "

Aluminum siding accessories and trim. *Courtesy Bendix Corp.*

Vertical Starter

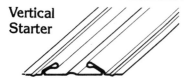

color: 01 only
length per piece: 10'
pieces per package: 10
lineal feet per package: 100'

Under Sill Trim

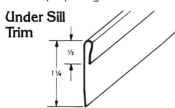

color: all
length per piece: 12'
pieces per package: 50
lineal feet per package: 600'

Casing Trim

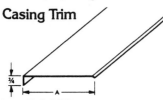

sizes: 4", 5-5/8"
color: 01 only
length per piece: 12'
pieces per package: 30
lineal feet per package: 360'

Rake Edge Cover

Rake Edge Cover 5
length per piece: 10'
pieces per package: 50
lineal feet per package: 500'
dimensions: (A) 3", (B) 1", (C) 1"
color: 01

Rake Edge Cover 6
length per piece: 10'
pieces per package: 50
lineal feet per package: 500'
dimensions: (A) 3", (B) 1-1/2", (C) 1"
color: 01

Casing Trim Recessed

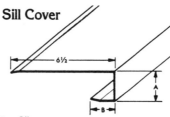

size: 5/8"
colors: all
length per piece: 12'
pieces per package: 20
lineal feet per package: 240'

Sill Cover

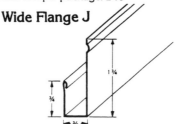

size: 2"
color: 01 only
length per piece: 12'
pieces per package: 20
lineal feet per package: 240'

Wide Flange J

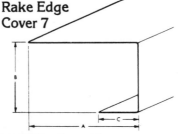

colors: 01, 08, 09, 11
length per piece: 12'
pieces per package: 25
lineal feet per package: 300'

Rake Edge Cover 7

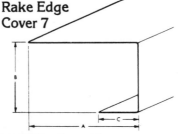

Rake Edge Cover 7
length per piece: 10'
pieces per package: 50
lineal feet per package: 500'
dimensions: (A) 3", (B) 2", (C) 1"
color: 01

Drip Cap

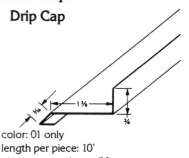

color: 01 only
length per piece: 10'
pieces per package: 50
lineal feet per package: 500'

Backer Strips

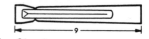

color: 01 only
pieces per package: 200

Brick Moulding

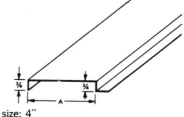

size: 4"
color: 01 only
length per piece: 12'
pieces per package: 10
lineal feet per package: 120'

Rake Angle

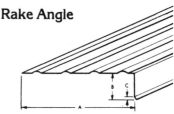

Rake Angle 2"
length per piece: 10'
pieces per package: 100
lineal feet per package: 1000'
dimensions: (A) 2", (B) 1", (C) 1/4"
color: 01

Rake Angle 4"
length per piece: 10'
pieces per package: 50
lineal feet per package: 500'
dimensions: (A) 4", (B) 1", (C) 1/4"
color: 01

Drip Edge

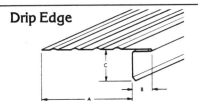

Drip Edge 2
length per piece: 10'
pieces per package: 50
lineal feet per package: 500'
dimensions: (A) 3", (B) 3/4", (C) 7/8"
color: 01

Drip Edge 3
dimensions: (A) 3", (B) 3/4", (C) 1-1/8"
color: 01, 08

Drip Edge 5
dimensions: (A) 2-1/2", (B) 3/4", (C) 7/8"
color: 01

Drip Edge 8
dimensions: (A) 3", (B) 3/4", (C) 1-3/4"
color: 01

Gravel Stop

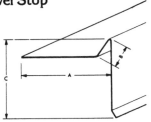

Gravel Stop 500
length per piece: 10'
pieces per package: 50
lineal feet per package: 500'
dimensions: (A) 2-1/2", (B) 5/8", (C) 2-1/4"
color: 01

Gravel Stop 900
length per piece: 10'
pieces per package: 10
lineal feet per package: 100'
dimensions: (A) 4", (B) 1", (C) 4"
color: 01

Soffit patterns, colors.
10" exposure, solid or louvered, in white, seal brown, desert tan, black.
16" exposure, solid or louvered, in white.

Fascia patterns, colors.
4", white only
6", white, seal brown, black, desert tan
8", white, seal brown, black, desert tan
10", white only

Soffit systems.
10" Soffit

color: 01, 08, 09, 11
length per piece: 12'
pieces per package: 20
lineal feet per package: 240'

16" Soffit
color: 01 only
length per piece: 12'
pieces per package: 12
lineal feet per package: 144'

Soffit system accessories.

Wide Flange J Channel
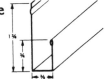
colors: 01, 08, 09, 11
length per piece: 12'
pieces per package: 25
lineal feet per package: 300'

Tapered Soffit Channel
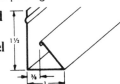
color: 01, 08, 09, 11
length per piece: 12'
pieces per package: 25
lineal feet per package: 300'

Recess Crown Moulding
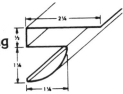
color: 01 only
length per piece: 12'
pieces per package: 25
lineal feet per package: 300'

Double Channel Runner
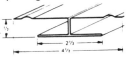
color: 01 only
length per piece: 10'
pieces per package: 10
lineal feet per package: 100'

Fascia Runner FR 1-19
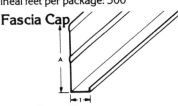
color: 01, 08
length per piece: 12'
pieces per package: 25
lineal feet per package: 300'

Fascia Cap

Fascia Cap - 4"
color: 01 only
length per piece: 12'
pieces per package: 25
lineal feet per package: 300'

Fascia Cap - 6"
color: 01, 08, 09, 11
length per piece: 12'
pieces per package: 25
lineal feet per package: 300'

Fascia Cap - 8"
color: 01, 08, 09, 11
length per piece: 12'
pieces per package: 25
lineal feet per package: 300'

Fascia Cap - 10"
color: 01 only
length per piece: 12'
pieces per package: 25
lineal feet per package: 300'

lengths: 50', 150'
widths: 10.3", 12", 14", 16", 18", 24"
finish: emulsion acrylic finish, both sides.
colors: 12" and 18" available colored one side, white on reverse.
All other sizes white both sides.

J-Channel

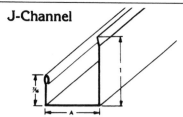

sizes: 1/2", 5/8", 3/4", 1"
color: 1/2" - all
   5/8" - white only
   3/4" & 1" - all
length per piece: 12'
pieces per package: 50 pieces (white)
         25 pieces (colors)
lineal feet per package: 600' (white)
          300' (colors)

L Moulding

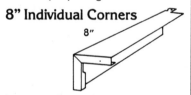

sizes: 5/8", 1"
color: 5/8" - 01 only
   1" - 01 only
length per piece: 12'
pieces per package: 25
lineal feet per package: 300'

8" Individual Corners

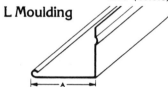

sizes: smooth, rough sawed
color: smooth and rough sawed - all
pieces per package: 100

Outside Corner Post

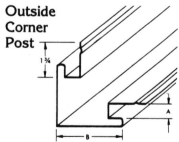

sizes: 5/8" smooth and rough sawed
   1" smooth and rough sawed.
color: 5/8" and 1" smooth and rough
   sawed - all
length per piece: 10'
pieces per package: 10
lineal feet per package: 100'

Inside Corner Post

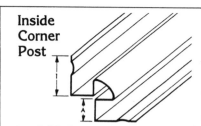

sizes: 5/8", 1"
color: all
length per piece: 10'
pieces per package: 10
lineal feet per package: 100'

Nu-Clip Outside Corner Post

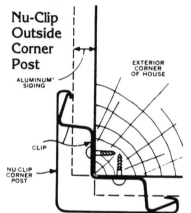

sizes: smooth, rough sawed
color: smooth, 01 only
   rough sawed - 01, 02, 03 only
length per piece: 10'
pieces per package: 20
lineal feet per package: 200'

Horizontal Starter

length per piece: 12'
pieces per package: 50
lineal feet per package: 600'

Correct Use Of Aluminum Reflector Foil

WITH FURRING STRIPS

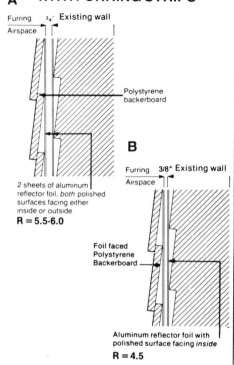

A

2 sheets of aluminum reflector foil, *both* polished surfaces facing either *inside* or *outside*
R = 5.5-6.0

B

Foil faced Polystyrene Backerboard

Aluminum reflector foil with polished surface facing *inside*
R = 4.5

WITHOUT FURRING STRIPS

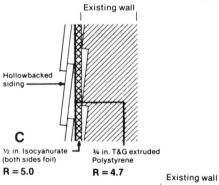

C

½ in. Isocyanurate (both sides foil)
R = 5.0

¾ in. T&G extruded Polystyrene
R = 4.7

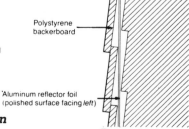

D R = 2.5-3.0

Use "breather" (i.e., perforated) aluminum reflector foil except on backerboard, to vent wall vapor through siding vent holes.

Courtesy The Aluminum Association

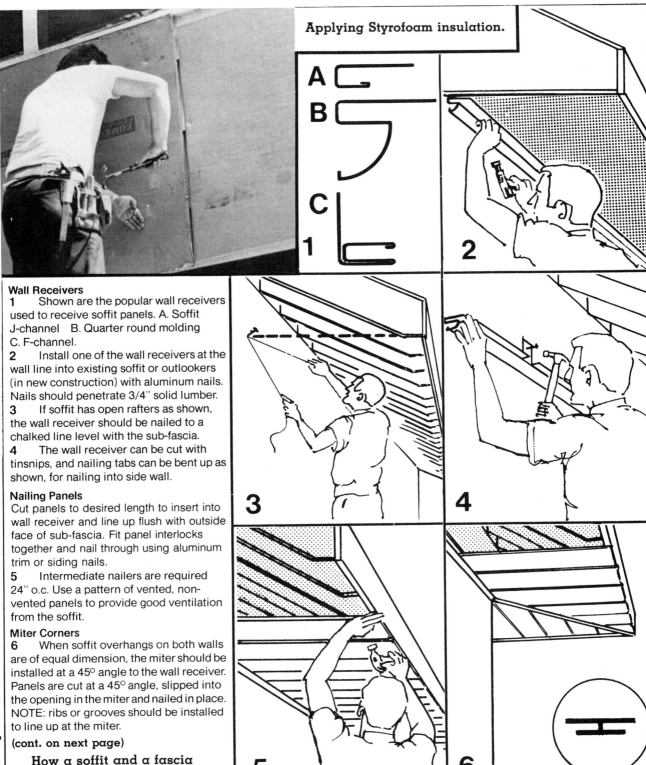

Applying Styrofoam insulation.

Wall Receivers
1   Shown are the popular wall receivers used to receive soffit panels. A. Soffit J-channel   B. Quarter round molding C. F-channel.
2   Install one of the wall receivers at the wall line into existing soffit or outlookers (in new construction) with aluminum nails. Nails should penetrate 3/4" solid lumber.
3   If soffit has open rafters as shown, the wall receiver should be nailed to a chalked line level with the sub-fascia.
4   The wall receiver can be cut with tinsnips, and nailing tabs can be bent up as shown, for nailing into side wall.

Nailing Panels
Cut panels to desired length to insert into wall receiver and line up flush with outside face of sub-fascia. Fit panel interlocks together and nail through using aluminum trim or siding nails.
5   Intermediate nailers are required 24" o.c. Use a pattern of vented, non-vented panels to provide good ventilation from the soffit.

Miter Corners
6   When soffit overhangs on both walls are of equal dimension, the miter should be installed at a 45° angle to the wall receiver. Panels are cut at a 45° angle, slipped into the opening in the miter and nailed in place. NOTE: ribs or grooves should be installed to line up at the miter.

(cont. on next page)

How a soffit and a fascia may be covered.

Courtesy The Aluminum Association

(cont. from previous page)

Square Corners

7   When overhang dimensions are not equal on both sides, install the miter molding parallel with the largest dimensions. Ribs or grooves will not line up on this application.

Fascia

Various styles and height dimensions are available.

8   Never face nail the fascia. Face nailing can result in a wavy or buckled appearance during thermal expansion cycles. Always use a drip edge, gutter, or all-purpose trim to receive cut top edge of fascia.

9   Nail underside of fascia as shown. Keep nails lined up with soffit V-grooves for best appearance. Nail every 24 inches, but do not nail too tight.

Many times it is necessary to use trim sheet bent on a portable brake to the special fascia shapes. Nail the special fascia the same way. Nails should penetrate a minimum of ¾-inch.

Outside Corner Fascia

10   Bend one-inch flange on the first fascia piece, 90 degrees around corner. Cut overlapping fascia at 45 degree angle. Nail with white aluminum soffit nails.

Inside Corner Fascia

11   Use the same technique as for outside corner.

Courtesy
The Aluminum Association

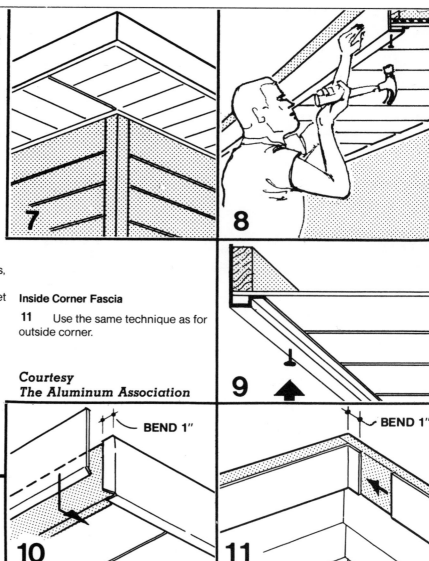

All sills are cut flush with the sides of their frames.
Courtesy The Aluminum Association

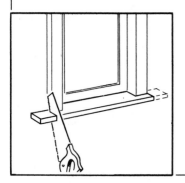

Thermal resistance values (**R** values) for aluminum siding systems.

Type of Aluminum Siding	R Value (The higher the better)
Aluminum siding with polystyrene backer, two layers of reflector foil and ¾-in. furring airspace	5.5-6.0
Hollowbacked aluminum siding with ½-in. Isocyanurate or ¾-in. extruded Polystyrene	4.7-5
Insulated aluminum siding, with polystyrene backer and foil	2.5-3.0
Hollow-backed aluminum siding with fiberboard backer	1.5
Aluminum siding with breather foil	1.1
Aluminum siding (plain)	0.6

Courtesy The Aluminum Association

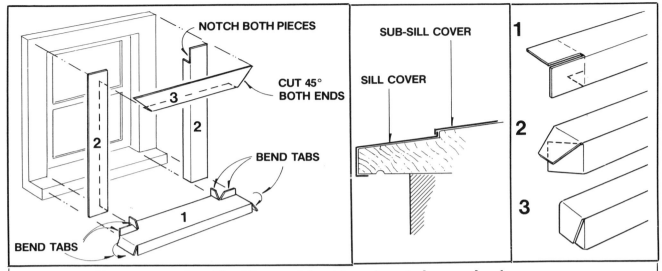

How to cover the sill, sides, and front top of a window- or doorframe.

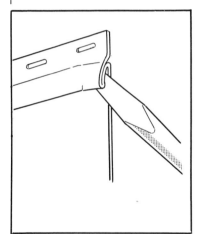

When a panel is cut with tin snips the lip on the panel must be opened.

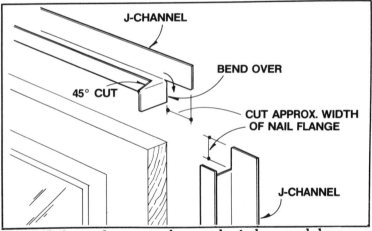

How J channels are used around window- and door-frames. Panel ends and edges fit into the channels. *Courtesy The Aluminum Association*

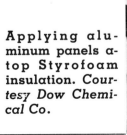

Applying aluminum panels atop Styrofoam insulation. *Courtesy Dow Chemical Co.*

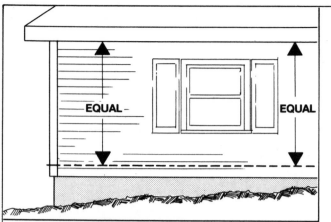

When the height of a wall is not equal at both ends and you do not want to cut the topmost panel at an angle, nail a 4-inch-wide strip of plywood across the bottom of the wall. Make the board parallel with the top of the wall.

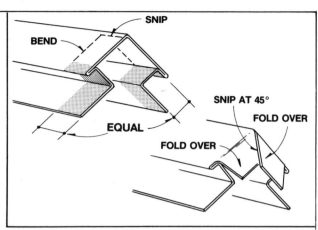

How the bottom of a corner post may be cut and folded to make a neat termination. *Courtesy The Aluminum Association*

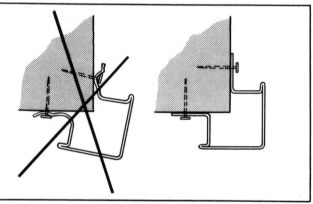

The right and wrong way to fasten a corner post. *Courtesy The Aluminum Association*

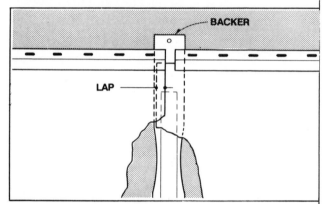

How aluminum panel ends are joined by lapping. Only the plain, 8-inch panels need the backer strip shown here. *Courtesy The Aluminum Association*

	Horizontal	Vertical
Length of Panel (feet)	12'6"	10'0"
Depth of Panel (in.)		
(including nailing flange)	9"	11"
Average Approx.		
Wt. Per Square (lbs.)	45	43
Squares Per Carton	2	2
Panels Per Carton	24	24
Panels Per Square	12	12
Exposure (in.)	8 or double 4	10
Top Lap (in.)	1"	—
Side Lap (in.)	—	1"

Courtesy GAF

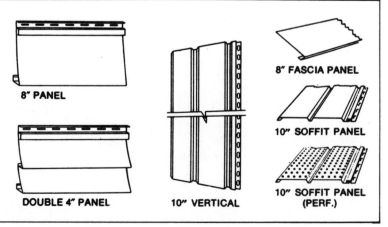

8" PANEL

DOUBLE 4" PANEL

10" VERTICAL

8" FASCIA PANEL

10" SOFFIT PANEL

10" SOFFIT PANEL (PERF.)

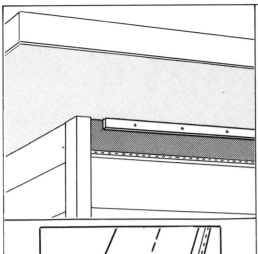

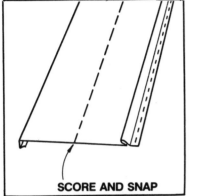

SCORE AND SNAP

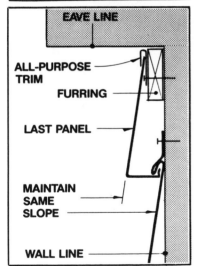

EAVE LINE

ALL-PURPOSE TRIM

FURRING

LAST PANEL

MAINTAIN SAME SLOPE

WALL LINE

How a furring strip may be used beneath an eave to space a panel's cut edge the proper distance from a wall. *Courtesy The Aluminum Association*

Colors.

Horizontal: white, gold, avocado, yellow, light green
Vertical: white only

Vinyl siding accessories

Vinyl Horizontal Starter

color: 21
length per piece: 10'
pieces per package: 40
lineal feet per package: 400'

Vinyl Finishing Trim

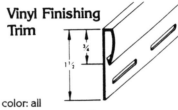

color: all
length per piece: 12'
pieces per package: 25
lineal feet per package: 300'

J-Channel 3/4"

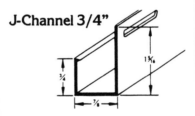

color: all
length per piece: 12'
pieces per package: 25
lineal feet per package: 300'

J-Channel 1-1/8"

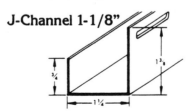

color: all
length per piece: 12'
pieces per package: 25
lineal feet per package: 300'

Courtesy GAF

Outside Post for Non-Insulated 3-1/2" Face

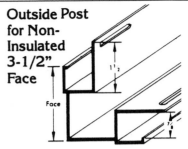

color: all
length per piece: 10'
pieces per package: 10
lineal feet per package: 100'

Outside Post for Insulated 3-1/2" Face

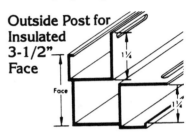

Inside Corner Post Non-Insulated

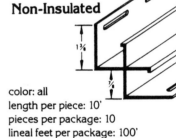

color: all
length per piece: 10'
pieces per package: 10
lineal feet per package: 100'

Inside Corner Post Insulated

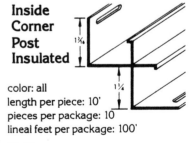

color: all
length per piece: 10'
pieces per package: 10
lineal feet per package: 100'

Patterns.

Horizontal: 8", Double 4"
Vertical: Non-Perforated, 7"
Perforated, 7"

Textures.

Horizontal: Embossed only
Vertical: Smooth only

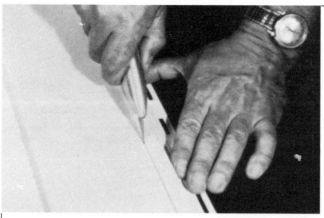

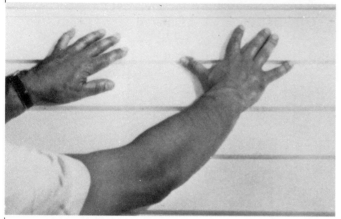

Eave Treatment

To insure a proper fit for the top or finishing course, first cut the vinyl siding panel so that it will cover the remaining open section.

Using a snaplock punch, punch the vinyl siding along the cut edge every 16 inches to 24 inches so that the raised ear or lug is on the outside face.

Push the siding into the finish or undersill trim that has been nailed in place along the top ot the wall. (Furring may be needed to maintain the face of the panel at the desired angle.) The raised ears will catch and hold the siding firmly in place.
Courtesy The Society of the Plastics Industry, Inc.

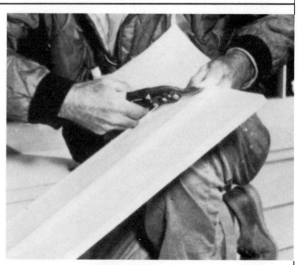

Time Savers

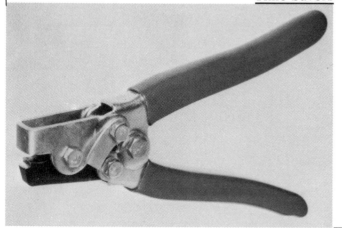

AVIATION TINSNIPS: Some applicators prefer the cam-action aviation type tinsnips for forming end joints for lapping the siding. Avoid completely closing the snips at the end of the cut to minimize danger of cracking vinyl. Always keep cutting tools sharp.

SNAPLOCK PUNCH: It is used to punch ears or lugs in the cut edges of siding to be used for the top or finishing course. The punched edge will engage and lock in the installed undersill trim or finish trim.

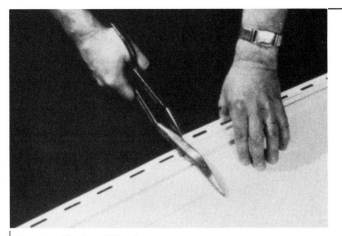

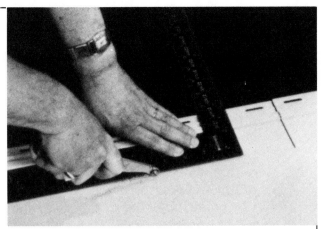

Fitting Under Windows

Mark the section to be cut out. Cut the sides with snips and score lengthwise with a utility knife or scoring tool.

Bend section back and forth along scored line to separate from main panel.

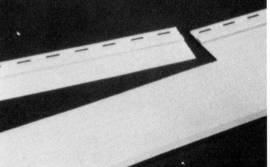

Cut panel is ready for installation under window. Undersill trim may be used along the horizontal cut edge. Furr if necessary.

End Joint Spacing

LAPPING END JOINTS: Since the vinyl siding moves as the temperature changes, overlap the vinyl panels approximately one-half of the factory notched cut-outs.

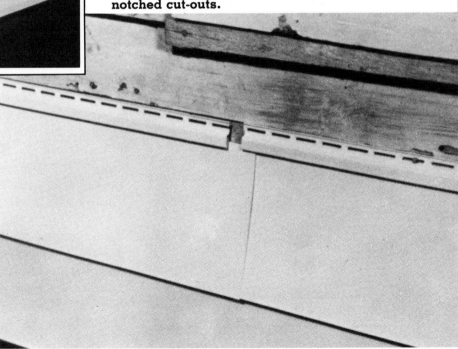

ROOFING

The standard framed roof consists of roof joists, which are timbers positioned on edge, covered by roof sheathing, which may be boards or plywood nailed over the joists. Together, the joists and sheathing form the roof-deck. Roofing is the material placed on top of the roof-deck to keep water from penetrating into the building and to improve its appearance.

SELECTING ROOFING

The pitch of your roof will determine the type of roofing that can be used. When the pitch of the roof is between 4 and 8 inches in 12, you can use shingles on top of 15-pound felt, laid dry. When the roof's pitch is between 2 and 4 inches in 12, you can use shingles if you lay them on top of sealed, (cemented joint) coated felt. If the pitch of the roof is less than 2 inches in 12, but more than 1 inch in 12, you can use coated felt with well-sealed joints. Shingles are never used on a roof that is almost flat. If the pitch is 1 inch in 12 or less, the roof is flat for all practical purposes and only built-up roofing will keep the water out. Built-up roofing consists of several layers of saturated or coated felt that has been completely sealed. This means that the first layer of roofing is completely covered with a layer of roofing cement before the second layer is applied.

PURCHASING ROOFING MATERIALS

Roofing materials can be purchased from your local lumber or masonry supplier. However, try your local roofing products distributor first. Many of them will sell directly to the consumer. You'll find them listed in the phone book.

ASPHALT ROOFING

Asphalt roofing is made from asphalt, various fibers, stabilizing chemicals, and particles of stone pressed into a sheet and then cut to various shapes. When the sheets ae left as they are, the roofing is called saturated felt. When the felt is coated with an asphalt compound, it is called coated roofing. When mineral granules are forced to adhere to the coated roofing, the product is called mineralized roofing.

Asphalt roofing is the least expensive roofing available today both in terms of initial cost and labor and in years of service. The heavier grades of roofing will remain watertight and attractive for twenty or more years.

Asphalt roofing is fire-resistant. Graded by the Underwriter's Laboratories as A, B, and D (descending resistance), asphalt roofing is not easily ignited, will not readily spread flames, and will not create flaming brands that could spread fire to adjacent structures. Asphalt roofing can be used on homes with wood-burning fireplaces. Most building codes prohibit the use of wood shingles for roofing on such homes.

Asphalt roofing bearing the UL "wind resistant" label can withstand

60-mile-per-hour winds for at least two hours without a tab lifting.

Asphalt roofing is easily nailed in place on new roof-decks and over old asphalt shingles or old wood shingles. (Wedge spacers must be used on wood shingles to present a flat supporting surface for the new shingles.)

GRADES

Asphalt roofing is not graded in the ordinary sense, but grades are produced by manufacturing. The thicker and heavier the roofing, the more desirable it is, as it will last that much longer than the thinner, lighter roofing. Thus 30-pound felt is better than 20- or 15-pound felt.

EFFECTIVE DIMENSION

Roofing is measured by the "square" it will properly cover. A square is exactly 100 square feet. Thus weights, such as those stated above, for example, always refer to the weight of that particular "grade" of roofing necessary to cover a square. Since roofing always includes a certain amount of overlap, the actual weight of the material necessary to cover a square is always greater than the weight per square of the roofing.

ROLL ROOFING

This is roofing material generally cut into 36-inch-wide strips and formed into a roll. Roll roofing ranges from lightweight, saturated felt, usually called tar paper, through coated roll, to mineralized roll weighing 90 pounds per square. In addition there is a special grade of mineral roll weighing upward of 200 pounds per square that is meant to be walked on. Some manufacturers call this "traffic

top." It is used for a porch that is also the roof of an understructure.

SHINGLE ROOFING

Shingles are made from partially mineralized stock cut into strips 12 inches wide and then recut into 36-inch-long pieces. The shingles are packed in bundles, so many bundles to the square. The more bundles the heavier the shingles. Some of the shingles are flat, some styles have been pressed to simulate wood shingles. Some styles have notches, some don't. There are also shingles designed to lock one another down. They require a little more care to install but resist wind much better.

COLOR

This is a matter of taste, but two points are worth mentioning. The blended colors are easier to install because their uneven coloring tends to hide installation inaccuracies. Light-colored shingles last as long as do dark shingles, but the dark shingles look better for many more years. Since the shingle itself is black, loss of mineral particles does not result in as great a color change. Also the new black shingles contain mica, which reflects sunlight just about as well as does the white shingle; thus the black is just as cool in the summer. In the winter, black absorbs and holds more heat than the white.

INSTALLING ROLL ROOFING

NEW DECK

The deck is swept clean and inspected to make certain all nails have been driven down. A single sheet of tar paper (15-pound felt) is laid flush to the edge of the eave. It is nailed down with roofing nails. A second sheet is laid parallel to the first, the second overlapping the first sheet by 2 inches or more. Successive sheets are laid down the same way, the higher overlapping the lower. If there is a ridge, the highest sheet is folded over the ridge. This accomplished, the mineralized sheet is laid down atop the first sheet. The lower edge of the mineralized sheet should extend beyond the edge of the roof deck by 1 inch all around. The second mineralized sheet is laid down so as to overlap the first by 2 to 4 inches. The overlapped area is given a coating of roofing cement to seal the joint. Successive sheets of roofing are laid down the same way until the roof is covered. If there is a ridge, the last sheet is brought over the ridge and sealed in place with cement and roofing nails. One nail every foot is plenty.

OVER OLD ROOFING

Make certain all the old nails are either removed or driven home. Slit bubbles, seal with a little cement, and nail down. Make the edges of the new roofing flush with the old.

INSTALLING SHINGLES

NEW DECK

Cover the deck with tar paper as described above. Start with 1-foot-wide, mineralized roll roofing. Or alter shingles by cutting 3 inches from the tabs and removing the non-mineralized portion of the shingle. Start with shingle or roll, mineralized side up, ¼ of an inch past the rake (side) of the roof and either flush with the metal drip edge or 1 inch beyond

the wood deck. End the first course (row) ¼ of an inch beyond the other end of the roof. Start the second course with a full shingle, flush with the in-place roofing at either end of the roof. Continue across. Start the third course with shingle from which a half tab has been cut. Start the fourth course with a shingle from which a full tab has been cut. Repeat until the entire roof is covered. Limit shingle exposure to 5 inches. Vary exposure as you near the ridge in order not to finish the roofing with a fraction of a shingle. Cap the ridge with shingles cut into squares.

OVER OLD SHINGLES

Drive all the nails home. Start with a row of shingles cut in half lengthwise. Then start with a full, right-side and edge-up shingle and work across the roof. Do not cover a roof with a third set of shingles, but strip it down to the bare wood, then treat like a new deck.

OVER WOOD SHINGLES

Nail strips of wood with narrow, triangular cross sections, called feathers, atop the old shingles. This produces a fairly level surface for the asphalt shingles. If you do not do this, the asphalt shingles will slump down and present a very rough, uneven surface.

DRIP EDGES

For a better job, the rake and eave edges of a roof are covered with metal angles. Use nothing but aluminum for the drip edges. Galvanized iron will rust with time and stain the building. For the rake edge use an angle tht is 1½ × 2 to 3 inches wide. The wide portion goes on the roof-deck or atop the old shingles. The narrow portion goes against the house trim. For the eave, use metal that is 1 × 3 inches, with the wider portion of the metal resting on the roof. Let the eave edging project 1 inch beyond the roof-deck, then make the following shingles flush with the metal. Use aluminum nails with the edging. One nail every 3 feet is plenty.

FIBERGLASS ROOFING SHINGLES

These roofing shingles are similar in appearance and application to standard asphalt shingles. Manufactured with a good percentage of glass fibers, these shingles have a UL Class A fire rating, the highest rating for shingles containing any percentage of asphalt.

Supposedly, they last one third longer than standard asphalt shingles. In any case, the 235-pound shingle carries a fifteen-year limited warranty. The 275-pound shingle is warranted for twenty-five years.

ALUMINUM ROOFING SHINGLES

These shingles have the look of hand-split wooden shakes. Exposure is a nominal 12 × 24 inches. The visible shingle butt is 1⅛ inch thick. The exposed side of the shingle is treated to retain its color for a warranted twenty years.

The shingles can be nailed in place on a wood roof-deck or slipped into metal purlins that are nailed to the deck. This saves considerable time and assures a straight line across the roof.

For sheds and similar buildings, it is possible to eliminate the normal roof-deck and just use metal purlins into which the metal roof shingles fit.

FLASHING

Flashing is the name given to the materials and the methods used to prevent rain from entering joints between roof sections, between chimneys and roofs, and between roofs and walls. The flashing does not seal the opening, but it provides a kind of roof or series of small roofs that leads the water away. Flashing is used where the opening is too large to be sealed with caulking or when movement is expected, movement that would eventually crack time-hardened caulking and permit the entrance of water.

METAL FLASHING
Copper is preferred, in thicknesses of .01 inch or more, but aluminum is used more often today because of its lower cost. Both metals will last many decades when used in sufficient thicknesses. Copper turns green with age, aluminum turns gray.

Metal flashing is sold in two forms: 6-×-6- and 8-×-8-inch squares, which are then bent to the required shape; and rolls. Roll widths are usually 6, 8, and 12 inches. The strip of metal is then cut to the required size.

MINERALIZED ROLL ROOFING FLASHING
You can use the 1-foot-wide starter-roll felt, or cut the 36-inch-wide standard roll down to the width you need. Generally, the 90-pound mineralized felt is used for flashing.

METALIZED PAPER

This is the least desirable flashing. The layer of metal is so thin that any mishandling leads quickly to rips and tears. Even when successfully installed, its life-span is compara-tively short. It is used to give the appearance of standard-thickness copper, as its copper coating does turn green with time, just as full-thickness copper does.

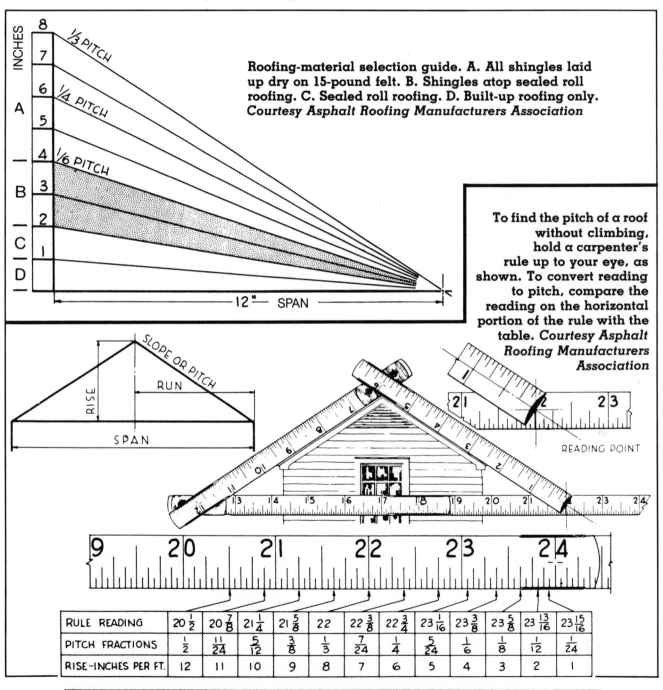

Roofing-material selection guide. A. All shingles laid up dry on 15-pound felt. B. Shingles atop sealed roll roofing. C. Sealed roll roofing. D. Built-up roofing only. *Courtesy Asphalt Roofing Manufacturers Association*

To find the pitch of a roof without climbing, hold a carpenter's rule up to your eye, as shown. To convert reading to pitch, compare the reading on the horizontal portion of the rule with the table. *Courtesy Asphalt Roofing Manufacturers Association*

RULE READING	$20\frac{1}{2}$	$20\frac{7}{8}$	$21\frac{1}{4}$	$21\frac{5}{8}$	22	$22\frac{3}{8}$	$22\frac{3}{4}$	$23\frac{1}{16}$	$23\frac{3}{8}$	$23\frac{5}{8}$	$23\frac{13}{16}$	$23\frac{15}{16}$
PITCH FRACTIONS	$\frac{1}{2}$	$\frac{11}{24}$	$\frac{5}{12}$	$\frac{3}{8}$	$\frac{1}{3}$	$\frac{7}{24}$	$\frac{1}{4}$	$\frac{5}{24}$	$\frac{1}{6}$	$\frac{1}{8}$	$\frac{1}{12}$	$\frac{1}{24}$
RISE-INCHES PER FT.	12	11	10	9	8	7	6	5	4	3	2	1

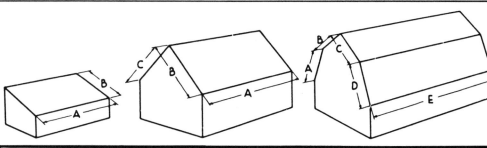

To determine the roof area of a building, multiply and add the areas shown. *Left*: A times B. *Center*: A times B plus C. *Right*: E times A plus B plus C plus D.

Underwriters' Laboratories, Inc.
®
LISTED
ROOFING MATERIAL
WIND RESISTANT

SHINGLES   CLASS C

When applied in Accordance with
Instructions included with this Roofing

ISSUE No. C-00000

All packages of wind-resistant shingles carry this label.

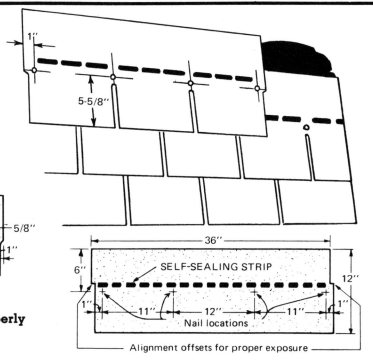

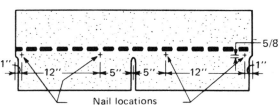

5/8"

1"   12"   5"   5"   12"   1"

Nail locations

How various types of shingles are properly nailed. *Courtesy Asphalt Roofing Manufacturers Association*

36"

6"   SELF-SEALING STRIP   12"

1"   11"   12"   11"   1"

Nail locations

Alignment offsets for proper exposure

Application of roll roofing by the concealed-nail method. *Courtesy Asphalt Roofing Manufacturers Association*

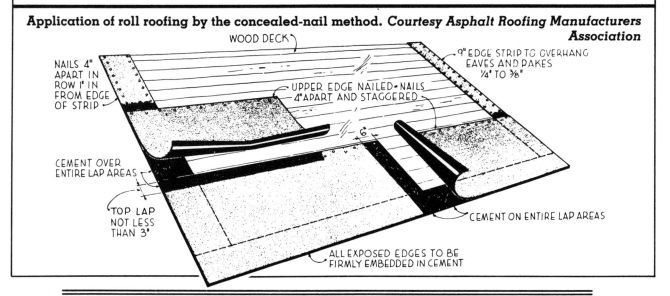

WOOD DECK

NAILS 4" APART IN ROW 1" IN FROM EDGE OF STRIP

UPPER EDGE NAILED-NAILS 4" APART AND STAGGERED

9" EDGE STRIP TO OVERHANG EAVES AND RAKES ¼" TO ⅜"

6"

CEMENT OVER ENTIRE LAP AREAS

TOP LAP NOT LESS THAN 3"

CEMENT ON ENTIRE LAP AREAS

ALL EXPOSED EDGES TO BE FIRMLY EMBEDDED IN CEMENT

1	2	3		4		5	6
		Per Square		Size			
PRODUCT	Configuration	Approximate Shipping Weight	Shingles	Bundles	Width	Length	Exposure	Underwriters' Listing
Wood Appearance Strip Shingle More Than One Thickness Per Strip Laminated or Job Applied	Various Edge, Surface Texture & Application Treatments	285# to 390#	67 to 90	4 or 5	11-1/2" to 15"	36" or 40"	4" to 6"	A or C - Many Wind Resistant
Wood Appearance Strip Shingle Single Thickness Per Strip	Various Edge, Surface Texture & Application Treatments	Various 250# to 350#	78 to 90	3 or 4	12" or 12-1/4"	36" or 40"	4" to 5-1/8"	A or C - Many Wind Resistant
Self-Sealing Strip Shingle	Conventional 3 Tab	205#- 240#	78 or 80	3	12" or 12-1/4"	36"	5" or 5-1/8"	A or C - All Wind Resistant
	2 or 4 Tab	Various 215# to 325#	78 or 80	3 or 4	12" or 12-1/4"	36"	5" or 5-1/8"	
Self-Sealing Strip Shingle No Cut Out	Various Edge and Texture Treatments	Various 215# to 290#	78 to 81	3 or 4	12" or 12-1/4"	36" or 36-1/4"	5"	A or C - All Wind Resistant
Individual Lock Down Basic Design	Several Design Variations	180# to 250#	72 to 120	3 or 4	18" to 22-1/4"	20" to 22-1/2"	-	C - Many Wind Resistant

Typical asphalt roofing shingle data.
Courtesy Asphalt Roofing Manufacturers Association

1	2		3	4		5		6	7
PRODUCT	Approximate Shipping Weight		Sqs. Per Package	Length	Width	Side or End Lap	Top Lap	Exposure	Underwriters' Listing
	Per Roll	Per Sq.							
Mineral Surface Roll	75# to 90#	75# to 90#	One	36' 38'	36" 36"	6"	2" 4"	34" 32"	C
			Available in some areas in 9/10 or 3/4 Square rolls.						
Mineral Surface Roll Double Coverage	55# to 70#	55# to 70#	One Half	36'	36"	6"	19"	17"	C
Coated Roll	50# to 65#	50# to 65#	One	36'	36"	6"	2"	34"	None
Saturated Felt	60# 60# 60#	15# 20# 30#	4 3 2	144' 108' 72'	36" 36" 36"	4" to 6"	2"	34"	None

Typical asphalt roll roofing data.
Courtesy Asphalt Roofing Manufacturers Association

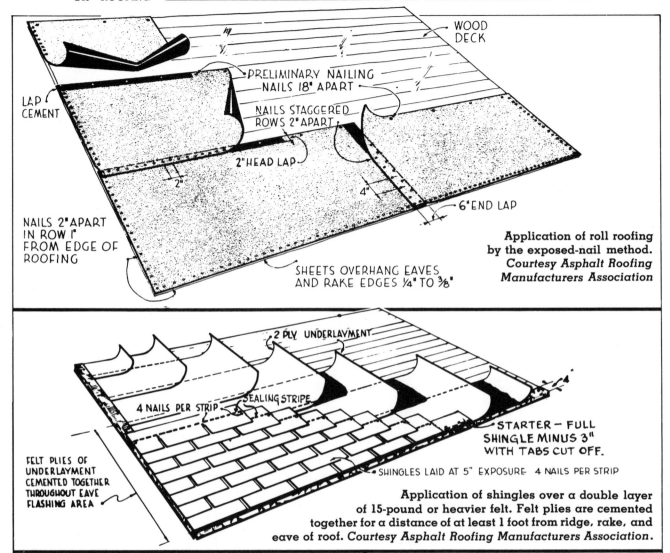

WOOD DECK

PRELIMINARY NAILING
NAILS 18" APART

NAILS STAGGERED
ROWS 2" APART

LAP CEMENT

2" HEAD LAP

2"

4"

6" END LAP

NAILS 2" APART
IN ROW 1"
FROM EDGE OF
ROOFING

SHEETS OVERHANG EAVES
AND RAKE EDGES ¼" TO ⅜"

Application of roll roofing
by the exposed-nail method.
*Courtesy Asphalt Roofing
Manufacturers Association*

2 PLY UNDERLAYMENT

4 NAILS PER STRIP

SEALING STRIPE

STARTER — FULL
SHINGLE MINUS 3"
WITH TABS CUT OFF.

FELT PLIES OF
UNDERLAYMENT
CEMENTED TOGETHER
THROUGHOUT EAVE
FLASHING AREA

SHINGLES LAID AT 5" EXPOSURE 4 NAILS PER STRIP

Application of shingles over a double layer
of 15-pound or heavier felt. Felt plies are cemented
together for a distance of at least 1 foot from ridge, rake, and
eave of roof. *Courtesy Asphalt Roofing Manufacturers Association.*

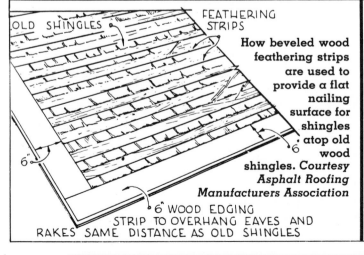

OLD SHINGLES

FEATHERING
STRIPS

How beveled wood
feathering strips
are used to
provide a flat
nailing
surface for
shingles
atop old
wood
shingles. *Courtesy
Asphalt Roofing
Manufacturers Association*

6"

6"

6" WOOD EDGING
STRIP TO OVERHANG EAVES AND
RAKES SAME DISTANCE AS OLD SHINGLES

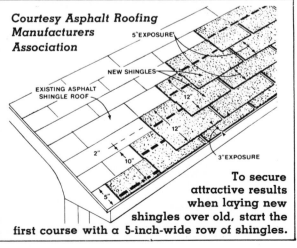

*Courtesy Asphalt Roofing
Manufacturers
Association*

5" EXPOSURE

NEW SHINGLES

EXISTING ASPHALT
SHINGLE ROOF

12"

12"

2"

10"

3" EXPOSURE

5"

To secure
attractive results
when laying new
shingles over old, start the
first course with a 5-inch-wide row of shingles.

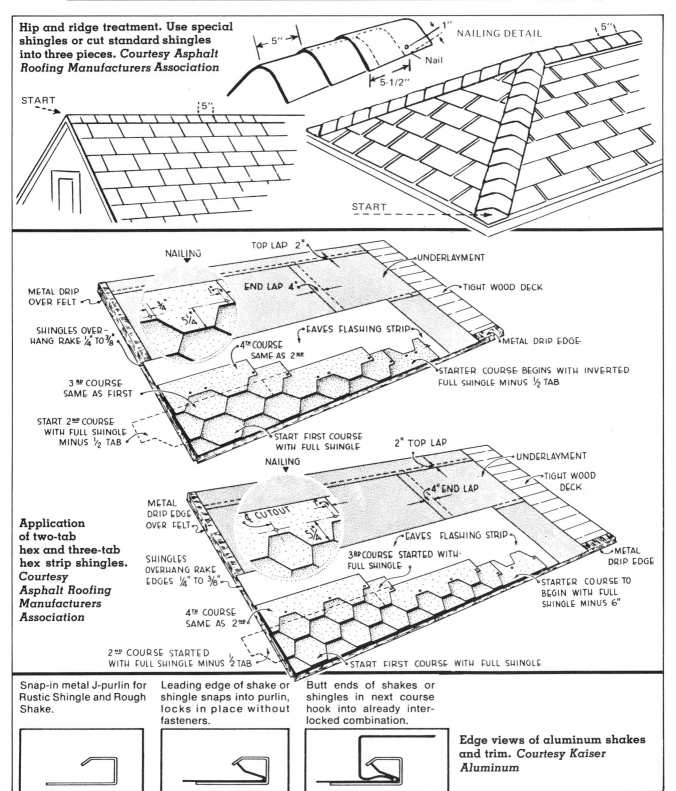

Hip and ridge treatment. Use special shingles or cut standard shingles into three pieces. *Courtesy Asphalt Roofing Manufacturers Association*

NAILING DETAIL

START

Application of two-tab hex and three-tab hex strip shingles. *Courtesy Asphalt Roofing Manufacturers Association*

Snap-in metal J-purlin for Rustic Shingle and Rough Shake.

Leading edge of shake or shingle snaps into purlin, locks in place without fasteners.

Butt ends of shakes or shingles in next course hook into already interlocked combination.

Edge views of aluminum shakes and trim. *Courtesy Kaiser Aluminum*

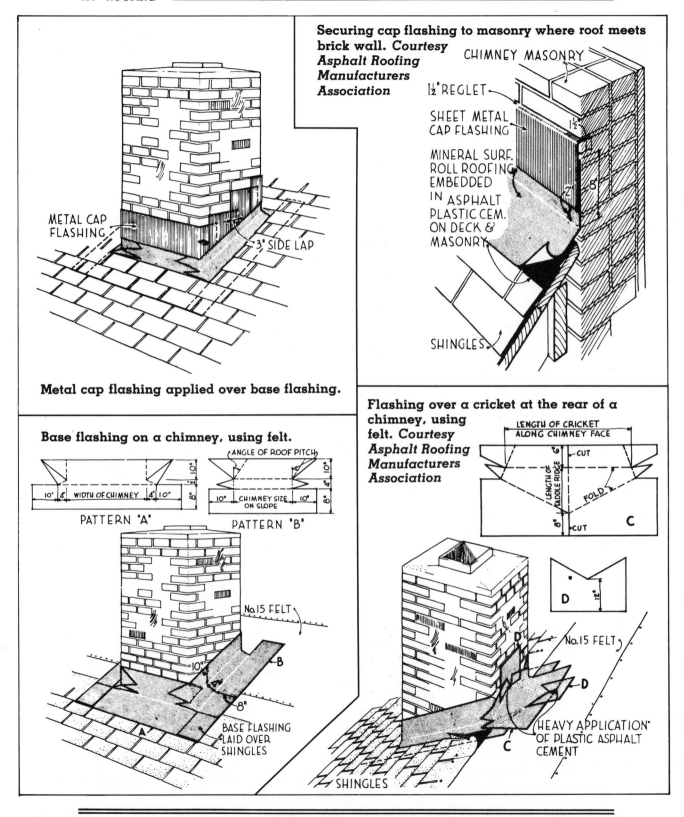

METAL CAP FLASHING

3" SIDE LAP

Metal cap flashing applied over base flashing.

Securing cap flashing to masonry where roof meets brick wall. *Courtesy Asphalt Roofing Manufacturers Association*

CHIMNEY MASONRY

1½" REGLET

SHEET METAL CAP FLASHING

1½"

8"

2"

MINERAL SURF. ROLL ROOFING EMBEDDED IN ASPHALT PLASTIC CEM. ON DECK & MASONRY

SHINGLES

Base flashing on a chimney, using felt.

ANGLE OF ROOF PITCH

10"
2"
4"
8"
10" 4" WIDTH OF CHIMNEY 4" 10"

PATTERN "A"

10"
4"
8"
10" CHIMNEY SIZE ON SLOPE 10"

PATTERN "B"

No.15 FELT

10"

B

8"

A

BASE FLASHING LAID OVER SHINGLES

Flashing over a cricket at the rear of a chimney, using felt. *Courtesy Asphalt Roofing Manufacturers Association*

LENGTH OF CRICKET ALONG CHIMNEY FACE

6"

CUT

LENGTH OF SADDLE RIDGE

FOLD

8"

CUT

C

D

12"

No.15 FELT

D

D

C

HEAVY APPLICATION OF PLASTIC ASPHALT CEMENT

SHINGLES

Two-hundred-sixty-pound, shake-type shingle roof with a UL Class C rating. *Courtesy Owens-Corning Fiberglas*

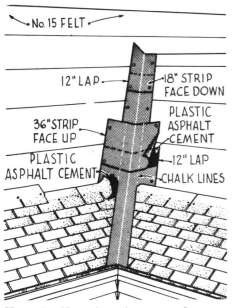

No. 15 FELT

12" LAP

18" STRIP FACE DOWN

36" STRIP FACE UP

PLASTIC ASPHALT CEMENT

PLASTIC ASPHALT CEMENT

12" LAP

CHALK LINES

Use of roll roofing for typical open-valley flashing. *Courtesy Asphalt Roofing Manufacturers Association*

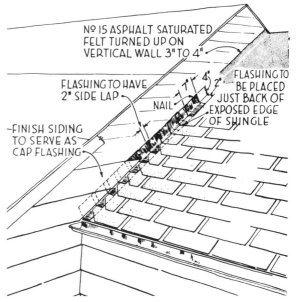

Nº 15 ASPHALT SATURATED FELT TURNED UP ON VERTICAL WALL 3" TO 4"

FLASHING TO HAVE 2" SIDE LAP

NAIL

FINISH SIDING TO SERVE AS CAP FLASHING

1"   4"   2"

FLASHING TO BE PLACED JUST BACK OF EXPOSED EDGE OF SHINGLE

Use of squares of metal flashing to protect joint between sloping roof and vertical wall. *Courtesy Asphalt Roofing Manufacturers Association*

The first wire screening to be made in this country was manufactured in 1857. It isn't difficult to imagine the cussin', slapping, and waving that went on before there were screens to keep the bugs out. Today there are few—if any—homes without screened windows. Even back-packers' tents incorporate screening.

AVAILABLE SCREENING

Four materials are commonly used for screening: bronze, aluminum, galvanized steel, and plastic. Each has its advantages, disadvantages, and limitations.

BRONZE
This is the most durable of all types of wire screening. Bright-finished screening has a natural bronze or golden color that turns a dull brown after the weather hits it. Antique-finished bronze screening is a deep, dark brown.

Bronze is tough and corrosion-resistant, but when water drips down the bronze screen after a rain, it will wash off the copper salts. The resulting solution can stain much of what it may contact.

Both the bright-finished and the antiqued-finished screening come with a coating of factory-applied varnish. This will prevent copper wash-off for a few years, but eventually the varnish wears off. If you plan on applying a coating of varnish or lacquer, be certain to "thin" it out so that the spaces in the screen mesh are not

filled. It's best to wait a season or two before doing this, since neither lacquer nor varnish will stick very well to brand-new screening.

ALUMINUM
Slightly lower in cost than bronze and not quite as strong, aluminum screening is nonstaining and does not require either varnish or lacquer. To provide strength, the wire used for screening is made of a central core of a hard aluminum alloy coated with a more weather-resistant alloy. In smoggy areas the screening will turn a dark gray. This does not affect its strength. You can remove this grime with soap and water. When used near salt water, aluminum oxidizes more rapidly than bronze.

GALVANIZED
Lower in cost than the two previously mentioned types, galvanized screening is far shorter-lived than the others; the zinc wears off or flakes off and the underlying steel wires rust out very quickly. It is, however, stronger to some degree than aluminum screening. It is important to note that when rain washes down galvanized screening and falls on an oak floor, the rainwash will very quickly stain the floor a dark color.

PLASTIC
Made from fine strands of plastic, this screening has greater impact resistance than either bronze or aluminum. It doesn't corrode, but it can be melted by the lighted end of a cigarette. Plastic is a very stable ma-

terial, so rainwash produces no stains and it is, of course, impervious to corrosion. It costs about as much as aluminum screening and has only one major drawback: It is difficult to frame tightly. You must double-fold all edges before you staple or tack them. The plastic wires are of a larger gauge than those used for equal size wire screening, so less light and air will pass through the plastic screen.

MESH

Standard insect-wire screening is manufactured in three mesh sizes. They are 16 × 16, 16 × 18, and 18 × 18. The higher the number the more wires per square inch and the smaller the openings between them. While all three mesh sizes will keep mosquitoes outside, if you are particularly worried about these pests, it is best to purchase the 18-×-18-gauge mesh screening.

SCREEN DIMENSIONS

Screening is sold by the square foot and is manufactured in rolls 24, 26, 28, 30, 32, 36, 42, and 48 inches wide. The total length of a standard roll is 100 feet, but the screening may be in two shorter pieces rather than a single long one. Some dealers sell screening by the linear foot, having computed the square footage per line foot beforehand.

INSTALLATION

The major consideration here is galvanic action: If you fasten metal screening with incompatible metals, you will drastically reduce the life of the screen. Use only copper tacks to fasten bronze screening. Use only aluminum tacks with aluminum screening and only galvanized tacks with galvanized screening. For more information on galvanic corrosion see METAL.

TENSION SCREENING

In addition to being sold in rolls, screening is also sold precut and bound along its edges. Metal or plastic strips are fastened to the screen's ends and the sides are reinforced with additional wires. To install, merely stretch the screen across the window opening and hold in place with screws. Held down by the screws, the ends of the screen make firm contact with the support surfaces (the door or window frame). The sides of the screen are held against the frame by the tension on the screen.

Tension screening is easily installed and quickly removed, but when there is a wind, insects can slip between the sides of the screen and the window frame or door opening.

SHAKES & SHINGLES

(ALSO SEE ROOFING AND SHINGLES—ASBESTOS CEMENT)

Shakes and shingles are alike in that both are made of wood and almost always of cedar. Shakes differ from shingles only in surface texture. Shakes have a rough texture on one side or both, produced when the shake was split apart from the balance of the log. Shingles have machine-cut surfaces. One surface may be sanded. With the exception of one type of shake, both shakes and shingles may be used for roofing and sidewalls. The exception is the machine-grooved shake, which has a striated surface and parallel edges. Its use is limited to sidewall applications.

CEDAR

Cedar, found mainly on the northwest coast of the United States, is one of the most durable woods known. The first white men to see these towering trees, named them *Arborvitae* ("tree of life"). A cedar may live as long as eight-hundred years and grow to a height of more than 200 feet. The wood is very light in weight and is easily split. It has a fine grain filled with countless air spaces, which makes it a good insulator. It has no pitch or resin, but exudes an aromatic odor when first cut. Most important is its resistance to decay. Evidence shows that red cedar lying on the ground has resisted decay for more than two-hundred-and-fifty years.

LIMITATIONS

As a roofing and sidewall material, cedar does have certain limitations. Most building codes prohibit the use of a cedar shingle roof when the structure includes a wood-burning fireplace. Those that do permit the use of wood shingles usually require special placement of the chimney or special protective devices to preclude the possibility that sparks from the fire might ignite the wood shingle roof.

Red cedar shingles vary from blond to red-brown in color. When exposed to the weather, the color tends to darken. The rate and the extent of darkening depend literally on the amount of smog in the area. But even away from the city, the shingles will darken with time.

Shingles shaded from the sun provide a home for fungus and other small green plants. Nonwood shingles do not "green" up nearly as fast under similar conditions.

PAINTING AND STAINING

Painting reduces the rate of moss and fungus growth on shaded wood shingles. Bare wood shingles absorb copious quantities of paint, however. To produce a "solid" layer of color, you will find it necessary to give the shingles at least three coats. And when you have painted the shingles, you have negated the major reason for using red cedar shingles in the first place—their color, naturalness, and the avoidance of painting.

Stain takes to wood shingles much more easily than paint and it will replace some of the lost color without hiding the wood itself.

PREPAINTED SHINGLES

Grooved red cedar sidewall shakes are given one or two coats of paint by the manufacturer. The single-coated shingles have a more natural look and cost less. Since the first coat acts to seal the wood, subsequent paint goes on more easily and smoothly.

GRADES AND DIMENSIONS

As the table on page 00 illustrates, shingles and shakes are manufactured in several grades. The difference between the grades is mainly appearance, with one exception. You can use No. 3 shingles, which have some tight knots, by intermixing them with a few No. 2 shingles, which have no knots. But No. 4 shingles, which have loose knots, can only be used as an undercourse.

Shingle lengths range from 16 to 24 inches. Shakes also come in lengths of 15 inches. From a labor point of veiw the longer shingles and shakes require less work. Whether there is also a financial saving will depend on the relative costs of the shingles. See the table to compute the quantity needed.

APPLICATION

Use aluminum or hot-dipped galvanized nails of the paper length. When shingling a roof, start by laying a 36-inch-wide strip of 15- pound mineral felt. The first course of shingles should be doubled for appearance. After you have laid a course of shingles or shakes, cover the upper portion of the course with a layer of 15-pound or heavier mineral felt. Then lay the second course.

See that joints do not line up vertically. Leave a ½-inch space between shakes to allow for expansion. Do not lay shingles or shakes on roofs with a pitch of less than 4 inches in 12. Maximum recommended weather exposure is 10 inches for 24-inch shakes and 7½ inches for 18-inch shakes.

Use no more than two nails to a shake. Place them 1 inch in from the sides and high enough up so that their heads are covered by the next higher course of shakes or shingles.

CERTIGRADE RED CEDAR SHINGLES

GRADE	Length	Thickness (at Butt)	No. of Courses Per Bundle	Bdls/Cartons Per Square		Description
No. 1 BLUE LABEL	16" (Fivex) 18" (Perfections) 24" (Royals)	.40" .45" .50"	20/20 18/18 13/14	4 bdls. 4 bdls. 4 bdls.	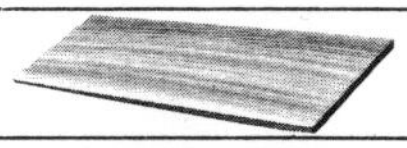	The premium grade of shingles for roofs and sidewalls. These top-grade shingles are 100% heartwood. 100% clear and 100% edge-grain.
No. 2 RED LABEL	16" (Fivex) 18" (Perfections) 24" (Royals)	.40" .45" .50"	20/20 18/18 13/14	4 bdls. 4 bdls. 4 bdls.		A good grade for many applications. Not less than 10" clear on 16" shingles, 11" clear on 18" shingles and 16" clear on 24" shingles. Flat grain and limited sapwood are permitted in this grade.
No. 3 BLACK LABEL	16" (Fivex) 18" (Perfections) 24" (Royals)	.40" .45" .50"	20/20 18/18 13/14	4 bdls. 4 bdls. 4 bdls.		A utility grade for economy applications and secondary buildings. Not less than 6" clear on 16" and 18" shingles, 10" clear on 24" shingles.
No. 4 UNDER-COURSING	16" (Fivex) 18" (Perfections)	.40" .45"	14/14 or 20/20 14/14 or 18/18	2 bdls. 2 bdls. 2 bdls. 2 bdls.		A utility grade for undercoursing on double-coursed sidewall applications or for interior accent walls.
No. 1 or No. 2 REBUTTED-REJOINTED	16" (Fivex) 18" (Perfections) 24" (Royals)	.40" .45" .50"	33/33 28/28 13/14	1 carton 1 carton 4 bdls.	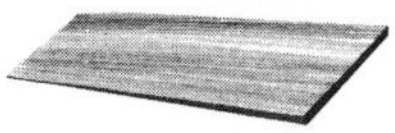	Same specifications as above for No. 1 and No. 2 grades but machine trimmed for parallel edges with butts sawn at right angles. For sidewall application where tightly fitting joints are desired. Also available with smooth sanded face.

	Maximum exposure recommended for roofs:								
PITCH	NO. 1 BLUE LABEL			NO. 2 RED LABEL			NO. 3 BLACK LABEL		
	16"	18"	24"	16"	18"	24"	16"	18"	24"
3 IN 12 TO 4 IN 12	3¾"	4¼"	5¾"	3½"	4"	5½"	3"	3½"	5"
4 IN 12 AND STEEPER	5"	5½"	7½"	4"	4½"	6½"	3½"	4"	5½"

LENGTH AND THICKNESS	Approximate coverage of one square (4 bundles) of shingles based on following weather exposures																										
	3½"	4"	4½"	5"	5½"	6"	6½"	7"	7½"	8"	8½"	9"	9½"	10"	10½"	11"	11½"	12"	12½"	13"	13½"	14"	14½"	15"	15½"	16"
16" x 5/2"	70	80	90	100*	110	120	130	140	150‡	160	170	180	190	200	210	220	230	240†	....	....	....	....	....	....	....	....
18" x 5/2¼"	....	72½	81½	90½	100*	109	118	127	136	145½	154½‡	163½	172½	181½	191	200	209	218	227	236	245½	254½†	....	....	....	....
24" x 4/2"	....	....	....	....	....	80	86½	93	100*	106½	113	120	126½	133	140	146½	153‡	160	166½	173	180	186½	193	200	206½	213†

NOTES: * Maximum exposure recommended for roofs. ‡ Maximum exposure recommended for single-coursing No. 1 and No. 2 grades on sidewalls.
† Maximum exposure recommended for double-coursing No. 1 grades on sidewalls.

CERTIGROOVE GROOVED RED CEDAR SIDEWALL SHAKES

GRADE	Length	Thickness (at Butt)	No. Courses Per Carton	Cartons Per Square*		Description
No. 1 BLUE LABEL	16" 18" 24"	.40" .45" .50"	16/17 14/14 12/12	2 ctns. 2 ctns. 2 ctns.		Machine-grooved shakes are manufactured from shingles and have striated faces and parallel edges. Used exclusively double-coursed on sidewalls.

NOTE: *Also marketed in one-carton squares.

CERTI-SPLIT RED CEDAR HANDSPLIT SHAKES

GRADE	Length and Thickness	18" Pack**			Description
		‡ Courses Per Bdl.	‡ Bdls. Per Sq.		
No. 1 HANDSPLIT & RESAWN	15" Starter-Finish 18" x ½" Mediums 18" x ¾" Heavies 24" x ⅜" 24" x ½" Mediums 24" x ¾" Heavies	9/9 9/9 9/9 9/9 9/9 9/9	5 5 5 5 5 5		These shakes have split faces and sawn backs. Cedar logs are first cut into desired lengths. Blanks or boards of proper thickness are split and then run diagonally through a bandsaw to produce two tapered shakes from each blank.
No. 1 TAPERSAWN	24" x ⅝" 18" x ⅝"	9/9 9/9	5 5	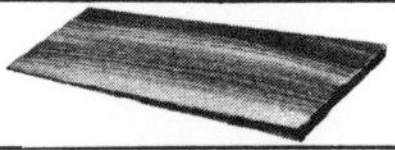	These shakes are sawn both sides.
No. 1 TAPERSPLIT	24" x ½"	9/9	5		Produced largely by hand, using a sharp-bladed steel froe and a wooden mallet. The natural shingle-like taper is achieved by reversing the block, end-for-end, with each split.
No. 1 STRAIGHT-SPLIT	18" x ⅜" True-Edge* 18" x ⅜" 24" x ⅜"	20" Pack			Produced in the same manner as tapersplit shakes except that by splitting from the same end of the block, the shakes acquire the same thickness throughout.
		14 Straight 19 Straight 16 Straight	4 5 5		

NOTE: * Exclusively sidewall product, with parallel edges.
** Pack used for majority of shakes.

Courtesy Red Cedar Shingle and Handsplit Shake Bureau

SHAKE TYPE, LENGTH AND THICKNESS	Approximate coverage (in sq. ft.) of one square, when shakes are applied with ½" spacing, at following weather exposures, in inches (h):					
	5½	7½	8½	10	11½	16
18" x ½" Handsplit-and-Resawn Mediums (a)	55(b)	75(c)	85(d)	100	. . . .	. . . .
18" x ¾" Handsplit-and-Resawn Heavies (a)	55(b)	75(c)	85(d)	100	. . . .	. . . .
18" x ⅝" Tapersawn	55(b)	75(c)	85(d)			
24" x ⅜" Handsplit	. . . .	75(e)	85	100(f)	115(d)	. . . .
24" x ½" Handsplit-and-Resawn Mediums	. . . .	75(b)	85	100(c)	115(d)	. . . .
24" x ¾" Handsplit-and-Resawn Heavies	. . . .	75(b)	85	100(c)	115(d)	. ·. . .
24" x ⅝" Tapersawn		75b	85	100(c)	115(d)	
24" x ½" Tapersplit	. . . .	75(b)	85	100(c)	115(d)	
18" x ⅜" True-Edge Straight-Split	. . . .	. . . .	. . . .	. . . .	. . . .	112(g)
18" x ⅜" Straight-Split	65(b)	90	100(d)	. . . .	. . . .	. . . .
24" x ⅜" Straight-Split	. . . .	75(b)	85	100	115(d)	. . . .
15" Starter-Finish Course	Use supplementary with shakes applied not over 10" weather exposure.					

(a) 5 bundles will cover 100 sq. ft. roof area when used as starter-finish course at 10" weather exposure; 6 bundles will cover 100 sq. ft. wall area at 8½" exposure; 7 bundles will cover 100 sq. ft. roof area at 7½" weather exposure; see footnote (h).

(b) Maximum recommended weather exposure for 3-ply roof construction.

(c) Maximum recommended weather exposure for 2-ply roof construction.

(d) Maximum recommended weather exposure for single-coursed wall construction.

(e) Maximum recommended weather exposure for application on roof pitches between 4-in-12 and 8-in-12.

(f) Maximum recommended weather exposure for application on roof pitches of 8-in-12 and steeper.

(g) Maximum recommended weather exposure for double-coursed wall construction.

(h) All coverage based on ½" spacing between shakes.

Begin with a double thickness of shingles at bottom edge of roof

Let shingles protrude over edge to assure proper spillage into eave-trough or gutter.

Proper application of shingles at the roof's eave. *Courtesy Red Cedar Shingle and Handsplit Shake Bureau*

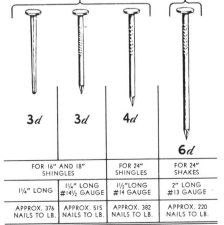

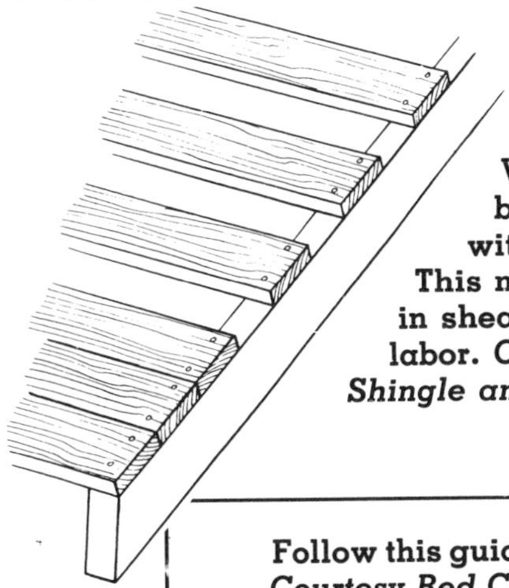

Wood shingles may be applied to a roof with open sheathing. This makes for a savings in sheathing, weight, and labor. *Courtesy Red Cedar Shingle and Handsplit Shake Bureau*

A square of shingles may consist of four bundles, enough to cover 100 square feet of roofing surface. Exact area covered depends upon shingle dimensions and exposure. (See table.)

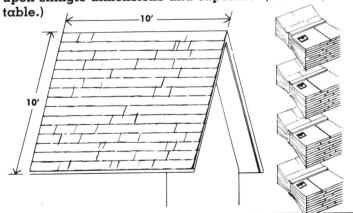

Follow this guide for nail selection. *Courtesy Red Cedar Shingle and Handsplit Shake Bureau*

FOR SHINGLE ROOF CONSTRUCTION		FOR SHAKE ROOF CONSTRUCTION	
3d	3d	4d	6d
FOR 16" AND 18" SHINGLES		FOR 24" SHINGLES	FOR 24" SHAKES
1¼" LONG	1¼" LONG #14½ GAUGE	1½" LONG #14 GAUGE	2" LONG #13 GAUGE
APPROX. 376 NAILS TO LB.	APPROX. 515 NAILS TO LB.	APPROX. 382 NAILS TO LB.	APPROX. 220 NAILS TO LB.

SQUARE CUT NAILS OF SAME LENGTH WILL ALSO GIVE SATISFACTORY SERVICE. STANDARD "BOX" NAILS OF THE SIZES GIVEN WILL PROVE SATISFACTORY IF PROPERLY ZINC COATED OR MADE RUST-RESISTANT.

Use of 15-pound felt between shingle courses. *Courtesy Red Cedar Shingle and Handsplit Shake Bureau*

It's easy to use a board as a straight-edge to line up rows of shingles

Tack board temporarily in place for guide

Makes work faster, results professional

How to align shingles. *Courtesy Red Cedar Shingle and Handsplit Shake Bureau*

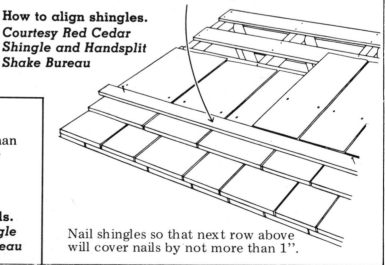

Nail shingles so that next row above will cover nails by not more than 1".

Place nails no further than ¾″ from edge of shingle

Correct placement of nails. *Courtesy Red Cedar Shingle and Handsplit Shake Bureau*

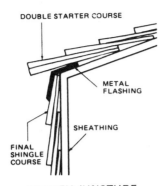

DOUBLE STARTER COURSE

METAL FLASHING

SHEATHING

FINAL SHINGLE COURSE

CONVEX JUNCTURE

After applying final course of shingles at top of wall, install metal flashing (26 gauge galvanized iron, 8" wide) to cover top 4" of wall surface and bottom 4" of roof slope. Bend flashing carefully to avoid fracturing. Make sure flashing covers nails which affix final course. Then apply a double starter course at eave, allowing for 1½" overhang of wall surface, and complete roof in normal manner.

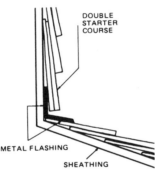

DOUBLE STARTER COURSE

METAL FLASHING

SHEATHING

CONCAVE JUNCTURE

After applying final course of shingles, install metal flashing to cover last 4" of roof slope and bottom 4" of wall surface. Make sure flashing covers nails which affix final course. Then apply a double starter course at bottom of wall surface, and complete shingling.

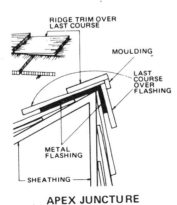

RIDGE TRIM OVER LAST COURSE

MOULDING

LAST COURSE OVER FLASHING

METAL FLASHING

SHEATHING

APEX JUNCTURE

Before applying final course of shingles, install 12" wide flashing to cover top 8" of roof and bend remaining 4" to cover top portion of wall. Complete roof shingling to cover flashing, allowing shingle tips to extend beyond juncture. Complete wall shingling, trimming last courses to fit snugly under protecting roof shingles. Apply molding strip to cover topmost portion of wall. Roof shingles then are trimmed even with outer surface of molding. Finally, apply conventional shingle "ridge" across top edge of roof in a single strip without matching pairs.

How shingle junctures should be constructed and flashed. *Courtesy Red Cedar Shingle and Handsplit Shake Bureau*

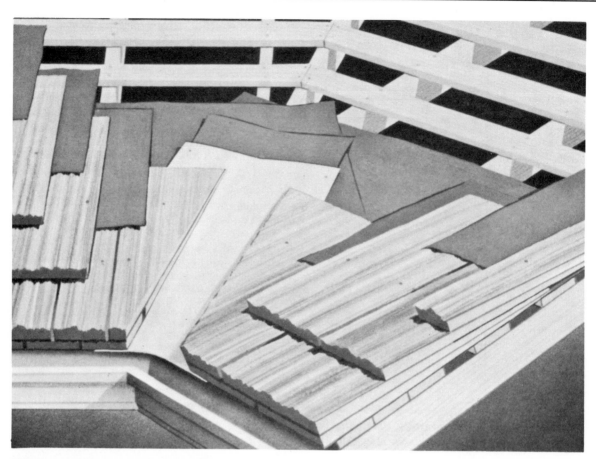

How an open valley is made. *Courtesy Red Cedar Shingle and Handsplit Shake Bureau*

Proper hip and ridge construction. *Courtesy Red Cedar Shingle and Handsplit Shake Bureau*

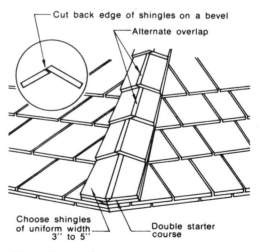

Cut back edge of shingles on a bevel

Alternate overlap

Choose shingles of uniform width 3'' to 5''

Double starter course

The alternative overlap type hip and ridge can be built by selecting uniform-width shingles and lacing as shown.

Sheathing is the name given the material nailed directly onto the wood studs forming the frame of a building. Sheathing serves several purposes: It provides a solid wall; it strengthens and stiffens (braces) the building; it insulates the building's interior. In many instances, but not all, sheathing also serves as the support and nailing base for the siding, which is a second layer of material that covers the sheathing and is exposed to the weather.

TYPES OF SHEATHING

A number of materials are used. Each has its special advantages and limitations. Choice of material is usually based on cost, ease of installation, insulating value, bracing effectiveness, fire resistance, and nailing support for siding.

BOARDS

Yellow pine (also called southern pine) is most often used because it is strong and hard and not particularly attractive, which helps hold down its cost. The boards should be tongued and grooved. The wider boards are better because there is less waste, but the narrow boards are just as strong.

Sheathing boards can be nailed horizontally across the studs or at an angle. The latter method provides much greater frame rigidity and bracing, but the waste is considerably higher, probably running to 10 percent where there are a lot of windows and doors.

When boards are used as sheathing, no additional stud bracing is required. Boards will take all kinds of nails and siding without problem.

PLYWOOD

Construction-grade plywood is used. The sheets are never less than ⅜ inch thick, and rarely thicker than ½ inch unless there is some special need for additional sheathing strength. When designing a frame for plywood, it is important to bear in mind the size of the sheets, which is 4 × 8 feet. When building dimensions are not even multiples of these dimensions or when fenestrations are not correctly placed, the use of plywood can result in considerable waste.

GYPSUM BOARD

Sometimes called black top, sometimes called exterior Sheetrock, sheathing-core gypsum board is rot- and fireproof and can withstand water for a considerable length of time. Sheathing-core gypsum board is commonly manufactured in 2- × -8-foot sheets, ½ inch thick, tongued and grooved along its long edges. It is the least expensive of all the sheathing materials and is easily installed. Sheathing-core gypsum board has a low insulating value. Its biggest drawback is that it won't hold nails. If you plan to use shingles as siding atop sheathing-core gypsum board, you must use special split nails. These nails penetrate the gypsum board and then split apart. At best they have low holding power. When you use sheathing-core gypsum board, frame corners must always be braced.

FIBERBOARD

Made of either cane or wood fibers impregnated with a waterproof compound and then coated on both sides with a layer of asphalt, fiberboard has three times the insulating value of yellow pine. While some authorities state that fiberboard has greater strength than wood, many building codes insist upon corner bracing when the fiberboard is less than an inch thick.

Commonly manufactured in sheets 4 × 8 and 4 × 9 feet in size and in thicknesses of ½ and 25/32 of an inch, the boards are light in weight, easily cut, and easily nailed. The ½-inch board has an R value of 1. The thicker board has an R value of 2.

INSULATING SHEATHING

Polystyrene, polyurethane, isocyanurates, and Styrofoam are used to make insulating sheathing with R ratings from 3 to 8. Their dimensions and special characteristics are listed in the accompanying table. While not inexpensive, they are light in weight, easily applied, and over the long run can pay off their costs and then some in energy savings.

In addition to their costs they do have other drawbacks or limitations. *Insulating sheathing products are combustible and present a potential fire and smoke hazard if not properly installed.* Make certain you follow the manufacturer's instructions carefully and that you meet all the requirements of your local building department. Remember, they are there for your protection.

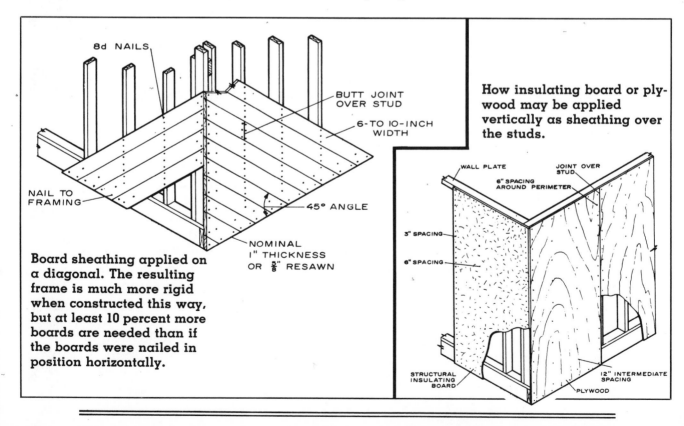

8d NAILS

BUTT JOINT OVER STUD

6-TO 10-INCH WIDTH

NAIL TO FRAMING

45° ANGLE

NOMINAL 1" THICKNESS OR ⅝" RESAWN

Board sheathing applied on a diagonal. The resulting frame is much more rigid when constructed this way, but at least 10 percent more boards are needed than if the boards were nailed in position horizontally.

How insulating board or plywood may be applied vertically as sheathing over the studs.

WALL PLATE

JOINT OVER STUD

6" SPACING AROUND PERIMETER

3" SPACING

6" SPACING

STRUCTURAL INSULATING BOARD

12" INTERMEDIATE SPACING

PLYWOOD

Applying high R insulating sheathing. *Courtesy Owens-Corning Fiberglas*

		INSULATION PROPERTIES		PHYSICAL PROPERTIES				MOISTURE PROPERTIES		PANEL SIZES
		R-Factor[1] (R-Value)	Available in Tongue & Groove	Density (Lbs. Per Cubic Foot)	Resistance To Abuse (Hammer Blows, Etc.)	Corner Bracing Required	Storage Requirements	Water Vapor Permeance[2] (Perm Inches)	Water Absorption (Maximum (Volume by %)[3]	
R GUARD 1	FIBERBOARD ½" REGULAR ASPHALT IMPREGNATED	R-1	No	17 to 20	High	Yes	Outside (Raise off ground)	High 20-50	High 7%	4x8 4x9
R GUARD 2	FIBERBOARD 25/32" ASPHALT IMPREGNATED	R-2	No	20 to 23	High	No	Outside (Raise off ground)	High 20-50	High 7%	4x8 4x9
R GUARD 3	POLYSTYRENE ¾" MOLDED	R-3	Yes	1.0 to 1.5	Low (Medium with Foil Skin)	Yes	Outside (Protect from Sunlight)	Low 2.0	Low (Less than 2%)	2x8, 13½x4, 4x8, 4x9 4x10, 4x12
R GUARD 4	POLYSTYRENE 1" MOLDED	R-4	Yes	1.0 to 1.5	Low (Medium with Foil Skin)	Yes	Outside (Protect from Sunlight)	Low 2.0	Low (Less than 2%)	2x8, 13½x4, 4x8, 4x9 4x10, 4x12
	STYROFOAM* ¾" EXTRUDED	R-4	Yes	2.1	Medium	Yes	Outside (Protect from Sunlight)	Vapor Barrier 0.6	Very Low 0.02%	2x8 4x8, 4x9, 4x12
	POLYURETHANE OR ISOCYANURATES ½" & ⅝" WITH FOIL	R-4	No	2.0	Medium	Yes	Outside (Protect from moisture)	Foil Vapor Barrier 0	Low Less than 1.0% to 1.2%	2x8 4x8, 4x9, 4x12
R GUARD 5	STYROFOAM* 1" EXTRUDED	R-5	Yes	2.1	Medium	Yes	Outside (Protect from Sunlight)	Vapor Barrier 0.6	Very Low 0.02%	2x8 4x8, 4x9, 4x12
	POLYURETHANE OR ISOCYANURATES ¾" WITH FOIL	R-5	No	2.0	Medium	Yes	Outside (Protect from moisture)	Foil Vapor Barrier 0	Low Less than 1.0% to 1.2%	2x8 4x8, 4x9, 4x12
R GUARD 6	POLYURETHANE OR ISOCYANURATES ⅞" WITH FOIL	R-6	No	2.0	Medium	Yes	Outside (Protect from moisture)	Foil Vapor Barrier 0	Low Less than 1.0% to 1.2%	4x8, 4x9, 4x10, 4x12
R GUARD 7	POLYURETHANE OR ISOCYANURATES 1" WITH FOIL	R-7	No	2.0	Medium	Yes	Outside (Protect from moisture)	Foil Vapor Barrier 0	Low Less than 1.0% to 1.2%	4x8, 4x9, 4x10, 4x12
R GUARD 8	POLYURETHANE OR ISOCYANURATES 1⅛" WITH FOIL	R-8	No	2.0	Medium	Yes	Outside (Protect from moisture)	Foil Vapor Barrier 0	Low Less than 1.0% to 1.2%	4x8, 4x9, 4x10, 4x12

NOTES: [1]R-Values shown are based on ASTM test C-518 or C-177 at 75° F. mean temperature.

[2]Water vapor permeance values based on ASTM test C-355.

[3]Maximum water absorption % based on ASTM test C-272.

*Styrofoam is a Registered Trademark of The Dow Chemical Company.

Major characteristics of insulating sheathing. Courtesy Georgia-Pacific Corp.

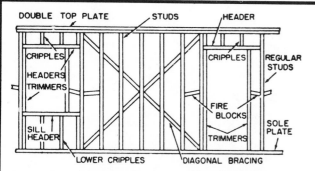

Typical wall-frame details. Upper frame rests on wood soleplate and has let-in diagonal bracing. Lower frame is bolted directly to concrete slab foundation. If plywood or board sheathing is used, studs need not be braced.

39 SHINGLES— ASBESTOS CEMENT

Asbestos cement shingles are often called siding shingles because they are not used for roofing. They are much too brittle to be stepped on, something that can't be avoided in the application of roofing shingles.

As the name implies, asbestos cement shingles are a combination of asbestos and cement. They are durable, reasonably attractive, and have a long service life. The common size is 12 × 24 inches and 5/32 inch thick. They are generally applied with a lap of 1½ inches and are butted side to side. It is advisable to use the tar paper strips supplied with the shingles behind each of these vertical joints. Given the recommended 10½ inches of exposure, 57 shingles will cover 100 square feet of wall area.

Asbestos cement shingles have almost no insulating properties, but they are fireproof and comparatively inexpensive. Application requires the renting of a special shingle cutter—no other device is practical. Care must be used when nailing, as the shingles crack very easily.

The shingles come in a number of pastel colors with smooth and striated surfaces. The color is impregnated into the shingle, but with time the color fades and the shingle becomes soiled. You can clean the shingles with soap, water, and a scrub brush. You can't revive the color, but clean, dry shingles take paint very well.

Siding is literally the material placed on the outside of a structure to finish it. Traditionally, siding was made of wood. The reason is, of course, that when tradition began wood was the least expensive material to be had. Today a number of other materials have been developed for use as siding with a number of advantages other than price.

WOOD SIDING

Wood siding is never applied directly over a structure's frame but always over sheathing. Since the wood is in the form of strips or boards, there is no problem in nailing. The nails can almost always be driven into the studs, so gypsum and fiberboard sheathing may be used beneath wood siding.

Wood siding is made from any number of species of wood including white pine, ponderosa pine, spruce, western red cedar, cypress, redwood, tight-knoted southern yellow pine, Douglas fir, and hemlock. There is nothing wrong with knots so long as they are small and tight. But when you go to paint, give the knots a coat of shellac first or they will "bleed" through.

Wood siding for horizontal application is manufactured in two general styles: bevel and drop or rabbeted. When you install bevel siding you control the overlap, which is helpful when you get close to the eave. The other general type of siding must be lapped for the full width of the bevel.

Other than these two considerations, choice between the two general types is a matter of style. Siding width is not only a matter of taste, but also of cost and labor. You need more board feet for coverage when you apply narrow-width siding and, of course, there is more labor. The wider boards cost more, however.

Vertical wood siding is made from straightedge boards. They are nailed in a vertical position with ¼ inch spacing between them. The spaces are covered with narrow boards. The entire arrangement is called board-and-batten siding. There is much less waste and the cost of the lumber is much less for vertical siding than traditional strip siding.

Naturally, the insulating value of wood siding is equal to that of the wood plus whatever air spaces may be formed underneath.

PLYWOOD

In an effort to reduce the cost of building, plywood siding was developed. It reduces cost two ways: When plywood siding is used there is no need for sheathing; and the large sheets go up much faster than the boards.

Plywood siding is made in thicknesses of ⅜ to 19/32 of an inch and in panel sizes of 4 × 8, 9, and 10 feet. A number of different species of wood are used for the surfaces of the panels including fir, redwood, cedar, softwood (species unidentified), and MDO. The latter is the description used by Georgia-Pacific to identify their medium-density overlaid plywood. It differs from the other types of plywood in that the topmost layer consists of a permanently bonded, resin-impregnated sheet of medium-density wood. The purpose of the overlay is to provide a better surface for painting.

The application of single-layer plywood siding is straightforward. Plywood sheets are marked 16 in. O.C. (on center) or 24 in. O.C., indicating whether the sheet can be used on studs with 16- or 24-inch stud spacing.

Building paper is not required when the siding is applied over sheathing, when the joints are shiplapped, or when the joints are covered by battens. When the panels are applied directly to the studs, using square butt joints, building paper must be used.

The panels are usually applied vertically. Panel length must be such as to allow a 1-inch lap over the foundation wall and 1½ inches over the top plate. A space of 1/16 of an inch should be left between all ends and edges of the panels to allow for expansion. All panel edges must be backed by solid lumber framing or blocking.

No caulking is necessary for shiplapped joints or joints backed by sheathing or building paper. But all butt joints at inside and outside corners should be caulked. Any polyurethane or silicone caulk, or a polysulfide rubber sealant such as Thiokol, may be used.

In addition to the various species of wood used for surfacing plywood siding, any number of surface treatments are used, including reverse board-and-batten, plain, V-grooved (regularly spaced and random), channel-grooved, rough-sawn, and touch-sanded.

HARDBOARD SIDING

Like the hardboard discussed in the "Hardboard" chapter, hardboard siding is also made from chips of wood that have been reduced to fibers and molded into a board under high pressure. And like plywood siding discussed above, hardboard siding was developed to reduce the cost and labor of home construction.

DIMENSIONS

Hardboard siding is manufactured in lap (board) and panel form. Both range in thicknesses from ⅜ through 9/16 of an inch. The lap strips are 16 feet long and come in widths of 6, 8, and 9 inches. The panels are 4 × 8 and 9 feet in size.

SURFACE TEXTURES

The lap siding comes in smooth, imitation wood lap surfaces, grained wood lap surfaces, V-grooved, and imitation wood shakes—to mention just a few surface styles. The panels come in smooth, rough-sawn, V-grooved, channel-grooved pecky cypress, and imitation stucco surfaces.

Lap and panel hardboard comes unpainted, primed, and painted in a number of colors. The paint is guaranteed to a limited degree for five years. The board itself is similarly guaranteed for twenty-five years.

APPLICATION

Lap siding may be applied over sheathed or unsheathed walls with studs no more than 16 inches apart on centers. When there is no wood or plywood sheathing, or when foam sheathing is used, the wall must be properly braced.

Grooved panels or panels joined by shiplap joints can be applied directly to unbraced studs when they are no more than 16 inches on center. When the panels are not grooved and when the joints are made by butting the square edges of the panels together, stud spacing can be extended to 24 inches.

In all cases it is advisable to cover the inside of the studs with a continuous moisture barrier to prevent moisture from collecting in the spaces between the studs. In some instances it may be advisable to provide limited ventilation for these enclosed spaces.

Triple-4-inch lap hardboard siding used to side a small frame house. *Courtesy Masonite Corp.*

Hardboard panel finished to resemble stucco. *Courtesy Masonite Corp.*

Hardboard nailing data. *Courtesy Masonite Corp.*

NAIL CHART	
NAIL SIZE*	NAIL SPACING
Panel Siding 8d (2½" nominal) when applied over existing siding or furring strips.	**Panel Siding** Edges Intermediate Locations 6" o.c. 12" o.c. Note: When nailing across the panel from edge to intermediate locations, nail spacing should not exceed 16" o.c.
Lap Siding 8d (2½" nominal) when applied direct to furring strips. 10d (3" nominal) when applied over existing siding. *Use galvanized nails with a head at least ³/₁₆" in diameter. Checkered head nails are preferred with textured siding.	**Lap Siding*** Nails must be spaced no more than 16" o.c. *For installation instructions of Masonite brand CountrySide° lap siding see Technical Bulletin 204L. If installing Masonite brand Beaded Lap siding see Technical Bulletin 210.

SPACE 16" OR 24"

SECOND STUD

NAIL TO CORNER POST

END WALL

SIDE WALL

PANEL - SIDING

16" OR 24"

Plywood siding applied directly over frame studs. Note corner detail.

To estimate how much siding is needed to cover a house you must first calculate its total surface area. Multiply the length by the height of each side. To calculate the area of a gable, multiply the length by the height and then divide the result in half. Add these square foot figures together plus the areas of any other elements that will be sided such as dormers, bays and porches.

You now have the total surface area of the house. But since the windows and doors will not be covered, their surface areas must be allowed for. To do this multiply the width by the height of each opening. Add the results together. Since some waste is involved in cutting the siding to fit around these openings, the total area of the openings is divided in half. This figure is then subtracted from the total area of the house to arrive at the total square footage of siding required to cover the house.

Here's an example:

House Area

Front Wall	40′ x 9′ =	360 sq. ft.
Back Wall	40′ x 9′ =	360 sq. ft.
Left Side Wall	22′ x 9′ =	198 sq. ft.
Right Side Wall	22′ x 9′ =	198 sq. ft.
Left Gable	$\dfrac{22′ \times 6′}{2}$ =	66 sq. ft.
Right Gable	$\dfrac{22′ \times 6′}{2}$ =	66 sq. ft.
Total House Area		1248 sq. ft.

Opening Area

10 Windows 3′ x 4′	=	120 sq. ft.
2 Windows 2′ x 4′	=	16 sq. ft.
2 Doors 3′ x 7′	=	42 sq. ft.
Total Opening Area	=	178 sq. ft.

$\dfrac{178 \text{ sq. ft.}}{2}$ = 89 sq. ft.

Total house area minus $\dfrac{\text{opening area}}{2}$ = required siding.

1248 sq. ft. minus 89 sq. ft. = 1159 sq. ft.

How to estimate hardboard siding requirements.
Courtesy Masonite Corp.

Panel Siding Surface Coverage
4′ x 8′ siding covers 32 sq. ft. per piece.
4′ x 9′ siding covers 36 sq. ft. per piece.

Lap Siding Surface Coverage

Siding Width	Exposure	Quantity To Cover 1000 sq. ft.
12″	11″	1,150 Square Feet
12″	10½″	1,200 Square Feet
9″	8″	1,185 Square Feet
9″	7½″	1,260 Square Feet

Average use of accessories per 1,000 sq. ft.

Nails	15 lbs.
Caulking	3 tubes

Lap siding accessories per 1,000 sq. ft.

Outside Corners—12″	60 pcs.
Outside Corners—9″	80 pcs.
Joint Moldings—12″	60 pcs.
Joint Moldings—9⅜″	80 pcs.

USE SHEATHING PAPER OVER LUMBER SHEATHING

NO SHEATHING PAPER REQUIRED FOR PLYWOOD OR FIBERBOARD SHEATHING

FLASHING

SIDING TO CLEAR DRIP CAP

BUILDING PAPER AROUND AND UNDER FRAME

SIDING FLUSH WITH BOTTOM OF SILL

BUTT JOINTS MADE OVER STUD

STARTING STRIP

Wood lap siding over various types of wood sheathing. *Courtesy American Plywood Association*

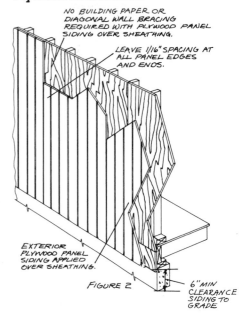

Plywood siding panel over plywood sheathing. *Courtesy American Plywood Association*

NO BUILDING PAPER OR DIAGONAL WALL BRACING REQUIRED WITH PLYWOOD PANEL SIDING OVER SHEATHING.

LEAVE 1/16″ SPACING AT ALL PANEL EDGES AND ENDS.

EXTERIOR PLYWOOD PANEL SIDING APPLIED OVER SHEATHING.

FIGURE 2

6″ MIN CLEARANCE SIDING TO GRADE

Grades & Finishing

There are four basic APA plywood siding classifications:

Class	Patches
303-0	none
303-6	maximum 6
303-18	maximum 18
303-NL	no limit

Within the 303-0 class, three grades are defined:

303-0/C*	clear
303-0/L	overlaid (e.g. MDO siding)
303-0/R	rustic (permits open knotholes, etc.)

Within the other classes, grades are further designated:

-W (e.g. 303-6-W)	wood repairs only
-S (e.g. 303-6-S)	synthetic repairs only
-S/W (e.g. 303-6-S/W)	both wood and synthetic repairs

Table 1 summarizes repair limitations for the new 303 face grades.

Table 1

Grade	Wood	Type of Patch	Synthetic
303-0/C	Not permitted		Not permitted
303-0/L		Not applicable for overlays	
303-0/R	Not permitted		Not permitted
303-6-W	Limit 6		Not permitted
303-6-S	Not permitted		Limit 6
303-6-S/W		Limit 6—any combination	
303-18-W	Limit 18		Not permitted
303-18-S	Not permitted		Limit 18
303-18-S/W		Limit 18—any combination	
303-NL-W	No limit		Not permitted
303-NL-S	Not permitted		No limit
303-NL-S/W		No limit—any combination	

All panels except 303-0/R allow restricted minor repairs such as shims. These and such other face appearance characteristics as knots, knotholes, splits, etc., are limited by both size and number in accordance with panel grades, 303-0/C being most restrictive and 303-NL being least. Multiple repairs are permitted only on 303-18 and 303-NL panels.

303 Series Plywood Siding Grades		Stains		Paints
		Semi-Transparent (oil)	Opaque (oil or latex)	Minimum 1 primer plus 1 topcoat (acrylic latex)
303	-0/C	✔	✔	✔
	-0/L	Not Recommended	Not Recommended	✔
	-0/R	✔	✔	✔
303	-6-W	✔	✔	✔
	-6-S	*	✔	✔
	-6-S/W	*	✔	✔
303	-18-W	*	✔	✔
	-18-S	*	✔	✔
	-18-S/W	*	✔	✔
303	-NL-W	*	✔	✔
	-NL-S	*	✔	✔
	-NL-S/W	*	✔	✔

✔Recommended with provisions given in text.
*Finish may be semi-transparent oil stain if color contrast, especially between repairs and surrounding wood, is acceptable.

Typical new APA 303 Siding grade-trademarks:

Siding face grade

303 SIDING 6-S

GROUP 1
24 oc SPAN
EXTERIOR
PS 1-74 000

Mill number

303 SIDING 6-S/W

GROUP 2
24 oc SPAN
EXTERIOR
PS 1-74 000

303 SIDING 18-S/W

GROUP 4
16 oc SPAN
EXTERIOR
PS 1-74 000

Species Group Number
Maximum stud spacing, siding direct-to-studs
Designates the type of plywood
Product Standard governing manufacture

APA plywood siding grading and designation. *Courtesy American Plywood Association*

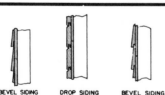

Standard types of wood lap siding.

BEVEL SIDING (LAP)
DROP SIDING (TONGUE & GROOVE)
BEVEL SIDING (SHIP LAP)

STANDARD SIZES IN SIDING LUMBER

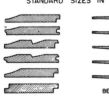

4" BEVEL SIDING
5" BEVEL SIDING
6" BEVEL SIDING
8" BEVEL SIDING (SHIP LAP)
10" BEVEL SIDING

BEVEL SIDING

DROP SIDING

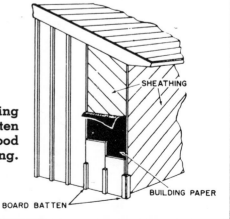

Applying board-and-batten siding over wood sheathing.

SHEATHING
BUILDING PAPER
BOARD BATTEN

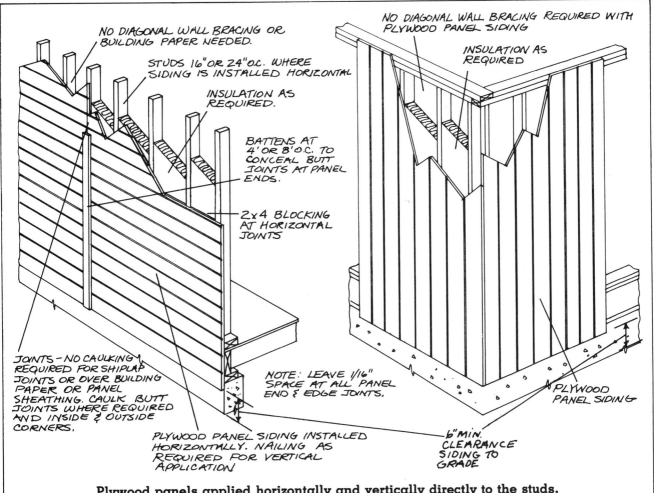

NO DIAGONAL WALL BRACING OR BUILDING PAPER NEEDED.

STUDS 16" OR 24" O.C. WHERE SIDING IS INSTALLED HORIZONTAL

INSULATION AS REQUIRED.

BATTENS AT 4' OR 8' O.C. TO CONCEAL BUTT JOINTS AT PANEL ENDS.

2x4 BLOCKING AT HORIZONTAL JOINTS

NO DIAGONAL WALL BRACING REQUIRED WITH PLYWOOD PANEL SIDING

INSULATION AS REQUIRED

JOINTS – NO CAULKING REQUIRED FOR SHIPLAP JOINTS OR OVER BUILDING PAPER OR PANEL SHEATHING. CAULK BUTT JOINTS WHERE REQUIRED AND INSIDE & OUTSIDE CORNERS.

PLYWOOD PANEL SIDING INSTALLED HORIZONTALLY. NAILING AS REQUIRED FOR VERTICAL APPLICATION

NOTE: LEAVE 1/16" SPACE AT ALL PANEL END & EDGE JOINTS.

PLYWOOD PANEL SIDING

6" MIN. CLEARANCE SIDING TO GRADE

Plywood panels applied horizontally and vertically directly to the studs. Courtesy American Plywood Association

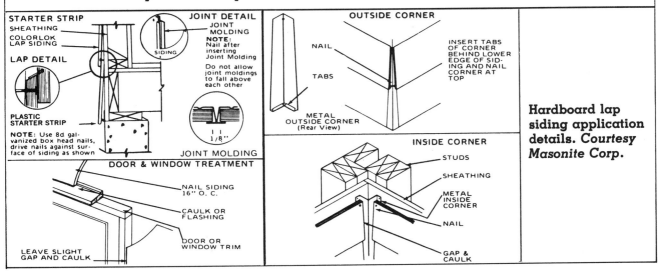

STARTER STRIP
SHEATHING
COLORLOK LAP SIDING

LAP DETAIL

PLASTIC STARTER STRIP

NOTE: Use 8d galvanized box head nails, drive nails against surface of siding as shown

JOINT DETAIL
JOINT MOLDING
NOTE: Nail after inserting Joint Molding
Do not allow joint moldings to fall above each other

SIDING

1/8"

JOINT MOLDING

DOOR & WINDOW TREATMENT

NAIL SIDING 16" O. C.

CAULK OR FLASHING

DOOR OR WINDOW TRIM

LEAVE SLIGHT GAP AND CAULK

OUTSIDE CORNER

NAIL

TABS

METAL OUTSIDE CORNER (Rear View)

INSERT TABS OF CORNER BEHIND LOWER EDGE OF SIDING AND NAIL CORNER AT TOP

INSIDE CORNER

STUDS

SHEATHING

METAL INSIDE CORNER

NAIL

GAP & CAULK

Hardboard lap siding application details. Courtesy Masonite Corp.

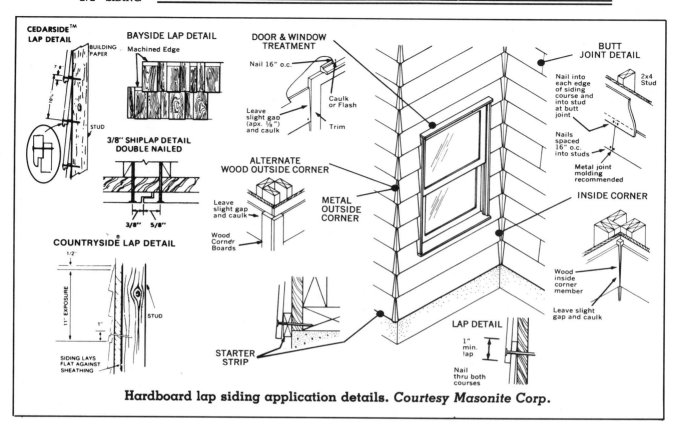

Hardboard lap siding application details. *Courtesy Masonite Corp.*

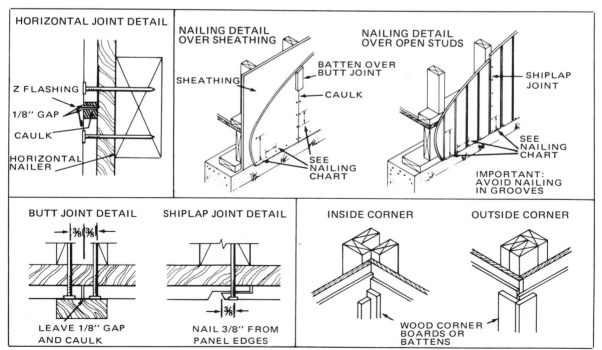

Hardboard panel siding application details. *Courtesy Masonite Corp.*

41 STAIN

Stain differs from paint in that stain is formulated to penetrate the pores of the wood to which it is applied and to stain or "dye" the wood a different color. Paint is formulated to seal the surface of the wood to which it is applied and to hide the wood from sight. Thus stained wood continues to look like wood. Painted wood no longer looks like wood—it looks like paint. Once it's smoothly covered by paint you cannot tell whether the material that has been painted is wood, metal, plastic, hardboard, plaster, Sheetrock, or whatever it may be.

Chemically, the difference between paints and stains is small; in a sense, stain is thinned paint. If you need stain in a hurry for an unimportant staining job, you can improvise with paint: Double the volume of the paint with linseed oil and turpentine or a cheap paint thinner and you will have a stain. If you are working with water-based paint, you can do the job with plain water. Many old-timers make their own exterior stain from creosote oil and oil color.

TYPES OF STAIN

There are, actually, three types of stain on the market (although most books on the subject mention only two). They are pure stain; semiopaque or semitransparent stain; and opaque or solid color stain.

PURE STAIN

This is, literally, a dye. It has no body—no pigment or solid particles.

You can make your own by mixing oil-soluble dyes with turpentine. The depth or strength of the color depends on the quantity of dye you mix with the turpentine. To get the results you want, try the mixture on some scrap lumber first. For an evenly colored job, make several applications rather than a single heavily dyed application. Use a brush or rag and apply with the grain.

SEMITRANSPARENT STAIN

This class or group of stains combines pigment and a vehicle (liquid). To speed drying, a drier such as Japan drier may be included, and to combat fungus growth, an antifungal compound such as pentachlorophenol or tributyltin oxide may be added. The oil-based stains will include linseed oil. The water-based stains will include alkyd resins, latex, or vinyl—just like water-based paints.

Semitransparent stain seals the wood and protects it from moisture. The pigment or color hides the color of the wood to some extent and stains it to some extent, but does not hide the grain or the texture of the wood.

OPAQUE OR SOLID STAIN

These stains differ from the others mainly in that they contain more pigment. They hide much more of the wood, and act very much like thin paint. In fact, if you have purchased opaque stain and find it too opaque for your taste, thin it out with turpentine or water, depending on the solvent used.

ADVANTAGES

Stains in general offer a number of distinct advantages over paint but only in limited situations.

EASE OF APPLICATION

Stains are more quickly and easily applied than paints. Pure stain is the easiest, the semiopaque next, and the opaque a little more difficult. This is because while paint must be applied evenly and spread over every portion of the wood, the stain is thinner, flows into cracks and crevices, and is in a great sense, self-distributing. Whereas you can apply pure stain and semiopaque stain with a rag, you need careful, consistent brushwork for a beautiful paint job.

ONLY PRACTICAL MATERIAL

When you are faced with protecting or changing the color of shingles, shakes or rough-sawn siding, stain is the only practical material you can use. Painting over rough-sawn lumber is physically difficult. In addition, three or four coats of paint are necessary to "cover," or achieve a solid, single-color surface. Usually, rough-surface woods soak up huge quantities of paint—much more than the same wood with a smooth, sanded surface.

Stain won't blister, peel, or crack the way paint will. Neither will it chalk. And it will last as long as paint.

COSTS

Depending upon type, stains cost one third to one half as much as equal quantities of paint.

DISADVANTAGES

Stain will not cover defects in the wood. Even the opaque stain will show defects, old paint, and the like. If the wood is not perfectly clean and dry (free of all paint and varnish) the stain will not cover. The ads that urge you to apply stain over paint are leading you on. If you apply stain over a solid coat of paint, you'll end up with a bastard color with uneven spots or areas unless you use the opaque stain and apply it with tremendous care. Apply stain over old, partially worn-off paint and you will end up with an uneven—and unsightly— job.

If you have used a creosote-based stain, you must wait two years before applying paint. If you have used a semitransparent or solid stain, subsequent coats will not actually stain the wood; they will only cover what is already present.

PURCHASING STAIN

Most authorities in the home maintenance field favor oil-based stain, believing it provides deeper penetration of the wood and more protection. But with an oil-based solution, you must use an oil solvent to wash your brush or pad.

Modern stains contain fungicides, sometimes called wood preservatives. If the product offered doesn't contain a fungicide, don't buy it. Fungicides are very important, especially in the Southeast, where warm, wet weather is common.

MAKING YOUR OWN STAIN

Two formulas have already been mentioned. One is simply to thin out whatever paint you wish to use. The second is to add whatever color you wish to creosote. (Some people add a little wood preservative to the mixture.) Make sure to stir the creosote and color formula almost constantly because if you don't the color will quickly settle to the bottom of the pail or can.

For a better wood sealer—but one that will not take a second coat of stain—mix together the following formula:

Raw linseed oil	36 fl. oz.
Creosote	16 fl. oz.
Turpentine	16 fl. oz.
Japan drier	8 fl. oz.
Fungicide	(Follow manufacturer's instructions)
Color	(Depends on desired opacity)

42

STAIRS

There are three ways in which you can get yourself a staircase if you don't consider hiring a carpenter to do the job for you. One is to construct the entire staircase yourself. This is often done with cellar and back porch stairs. The other is to construct and install the stringers yourself and then purchase the treads and railings cut to size, which you install yourself. The third and easiest way is to hire a local stair-maker to fit a complete and finished staircase into the opening you provide. The last method is the one most used by experienced carpenters. Stair-makers have the experience and tools to do the job quickly and comparatively inexpensively. Most important, the responsibility of making everything fit is theirs.

PURCHASING STAIR PARTS

Local lumberyards sell stair treads, which are 1-inch-thick boards with one rounded edge. The yard will cut these stair boards into whatever lengths you need and want, or you can cut them yourself. Local yards also stock a limited number of different styles of handrails and balusters and can also get stair parts from national stair-system manufacturers, so altogether you have lots of styles and materials from which to choose.

GETTING IT RIGHT

The important point in all this is that you must construct the supporting risers properly and you must order the correct parts. Most of the large stair-system manufacturers offer small brochures that detail stair design and measurements as well as stair-system parts. You are well advised to get hold of one such instruction booklet and study it well before you begin to construct your stairs. If you are refurbishing an old set of stairs, you will, of course, have to work with what is already there.

CHOICE OF MATERIAL

First choice for the treads is oak or hemlock or a similar hardwood. Second choice is fir. When the treads are to be completely covered, yellow pine is satisfactory. NOTE: The risers and the stringer coverings usually are not supplied by the stair-system manufacturers. You will have to furnish and cut these parts to fit yourself. Generally, number 2 pine is used here. Number 1 is too rare and expensive.

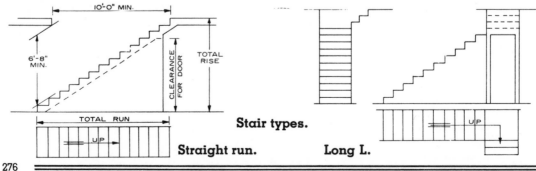

Stair types.

Straight run.

Long L.

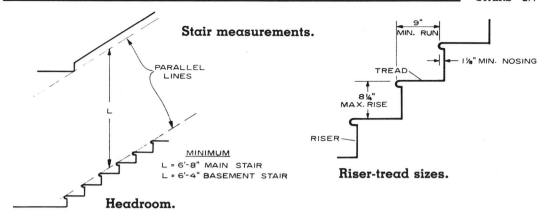

Stair measurements.

PARALLEL
LINES

L

MINIMUM
L = 6'-8" MAIN STAIR
L = 6'-4" BASEMENT STAIR

Headroom.

9"
MIN. RUN

1⅛" MIN. NOSING

TREAD

8¼"
MAX. RISE

RISER

Riser-tread sizes.

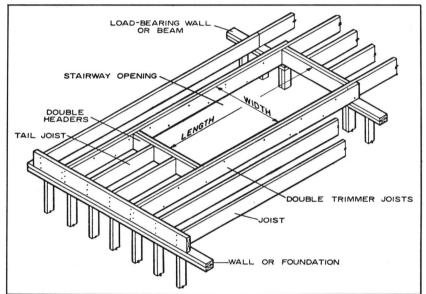

LOAD-BEARING WALL
OR BEAM

STAIRWAY OPENING

WIDTH

DOUBLE
HEADERS

LENGTH

TAIL JOIST

DOUBLE TRIMMER JOISTS

JOIST

WALL OR FOUNDATION

**Framing when stairwell is
parallel to the joists.**

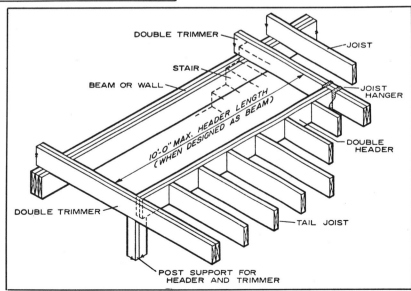

DOUBLE TRIMMER

JOIST

STAIR

BEAM OR WALL

JOIST
HANGER

10'-0" MAX. HEADER LENGTH
(WHEN DESIGNED AS BEAM)

DOUBLE
HEADER

DOUBLE TRIMMER

TAIL JOIST

POST SUPPORT FOR
HEADER AND TRIMMER

**Framing when the stairwell is
at right angles to the joists.**

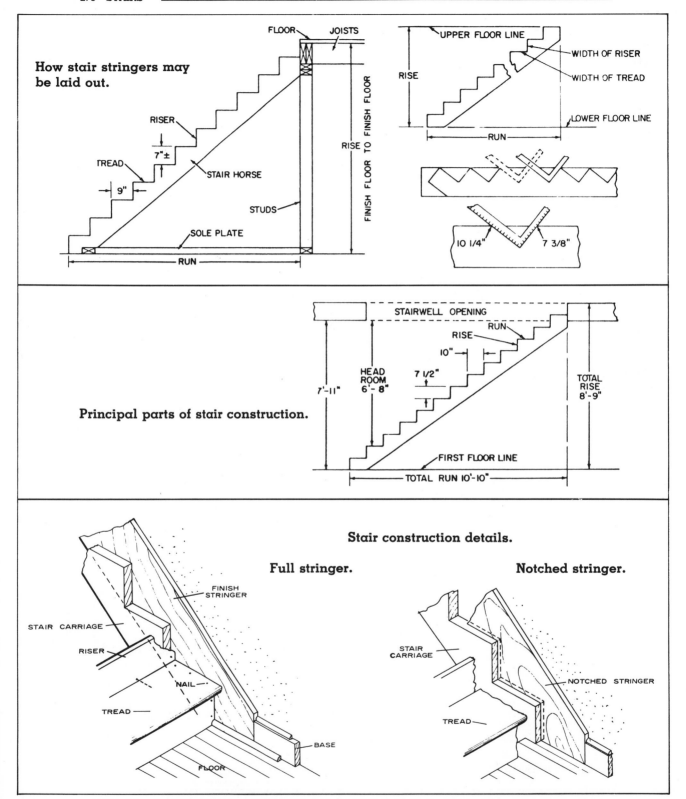

How stair stringers may be laid out.

FLOOR
JOISTS
RISER
7"±
TREAD
9"
STAIR HORSE
STUDS
SOLE PLATE
RUN
RISE FINISH FLOOR TO FINISH FLOOR

UPPER FLOOR LINE
WIDTH OF RISER
WIDTH OF TREAD
RISE
LOWER FLOOR LINE
RUN
10 1/4" 7 3/8"

Principal parts of stair construction.

STAIRWELL OPENING
RISE
RUN
10"
7 1/2"
HEAD ROOM 6'- 8"
7'-11"
TOTAL RISE 8'-9"
FIRST FLOOR LINE
TOTAL RUN 10'-10"

Stair construction details.

Full stringer.

Notched stringer.

FINISH STRINGER
STAIR CARRIAGE
RISER
NAIL
TREAD
BASE
FLOOR

STAIR CARRIAGE
NOTCHED STRINGER
TREAD

PLANNING TECHNIQUES

HEAD ROOM

FIG 15

Head room is the distance or clearance above a stair measured from outside corner of the tread and riser directly underneath the lowest point of the soffit or ceiling overhead. If two or more flights of stairs are arranged one above the other in the same stair well (for example, cellar stairs under, or attic stairs over, the main staircase), the question of adequate head room underneath the upper stair is introduced into the planning problem and must be considered most carefully. It has been found from studies of the dimensions of the average man or woman that this head room, measured vertically from top of tread at face of riser up to the under side of the stair above, varies with the steepness of the stair, but is generally from 7 feet 4 inches to 7 feet 7 inches. This allows for the arm to be swung up over the head without hitting anything. While the minimum required by F.H.A. is 6 feet 8 inches it is not sufficient for the main stair which, as stated above, should be from 7 feet 4 inches to 7 feet 7 inches.

RISE AND RUN

It is of vital importance that the stairway be built with the proper rise and run. If one of the three rules described below is used, the stairway will be easy to ascend and safe to descend.

If the rise is too steep the person ascending the stairs will be subjected to unnecessary strain. This is a very serious matter for elderly persons, and also for others who may be physically handicapped.

The stairway should definitely be built to provide the maximum ease in both ascending and descending. Such a stairway is easy to build with Morgan stock parts and at the same time it will be graceful and charming because Morgan stair parts are correctly designed and precision-made to fit together perfectly.

Fig. 16—Tread too wide, riser too short.

Fig. 17—Tread too narrow, riser too high.

Fig. 18—Correct tread width 10", correct riser height 7½".

HOW TO DETERMINE RISER HEIGHT AND TREAD WIDTH.

First determine the height from floor to floor in inches. This height is divided by 8 inches and usually gives a whole number and a fraction. Example: if floor to floor height is 9 feet (108 inches) divided by 8 inches, the result is 13½. The next largest whole number (14) will be the total number of risers required.

Dividing the floor to floor height (108 inches) by 14 gives a riser height of 7⅝".

Knowing the riser height, the tread width (from face to face of risers) can be determined by applying one or all of the three rules.

Note: The number of treads in each flight of stairs is always one less than number of risers. This does not include landing tread if used.

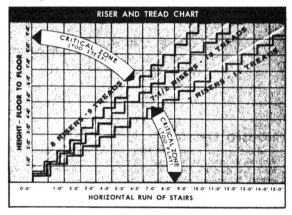

RULE NO. 1

The sum of 2 risers and 1 tread should be between 24 and 25. Acceptable therefore would be a riser 7" to 7½" and tread 10" to 11". (Example: 7½" + 7½" + 10).

RULE NO. 2

The sum of 1 riser and 1 tread should equal between 17 and 18. (Example: 7½" + 10").

RULE NO. 3

The product obtained by multiplying the height of the riser by width of tread should be between 70" and 75".

For the main staircase in a house, risers should not be higher than 7⅝" and not less than 7", combined with a tread width of 10" to 11" (not including nosing).

Portion of a stair-design brochure. Courtesy C. E. Morgan

newel posts

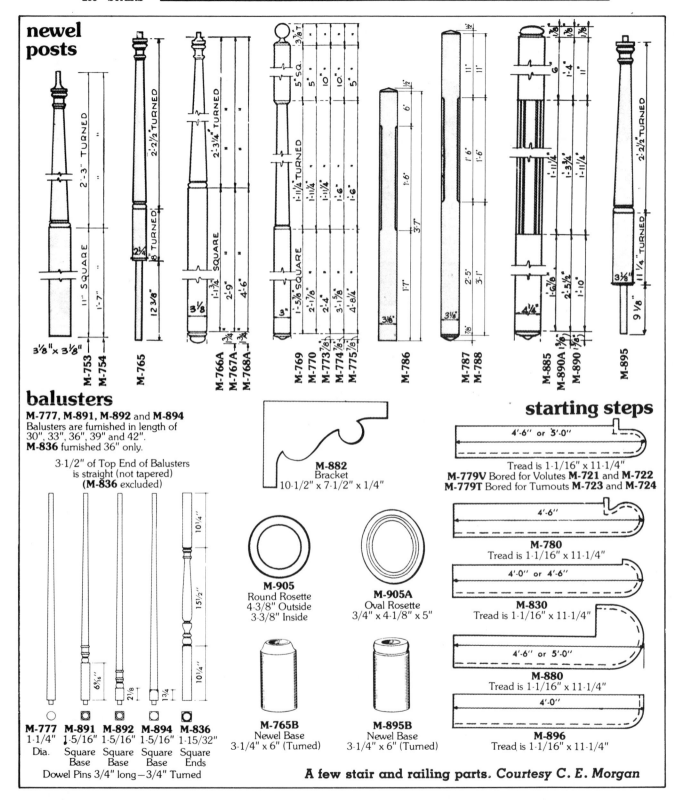

M-753 M-754

M-765 12 3/8"

M-766A M-767A M-768A

M-769 M-770 M-773 M-774 M-775

M-786

M-787 M-788

M-885 M-890A M-890

M-895

balusters

M-777, M-891, M-892 and **M-894**
Balusters are furnished in length of 30", 33", 36", 39" and 42".
M-836 furnished 36" only.

3-1/2" of Top End of Balusters is straight (not tapered) **(M-836 excluded)**

M-777 1-1/4" Dia.
M-891 1-5/16" Square Base
M-892 1-5/16" Square Base
M-894 1-5/16" Square Base
M-836 1-15/32" Square Ends

Dowel Pins 3/4" long — 3/4" Turned

M-882
Bracket
10-1/2" x 7-1/2" x 1/4"

M-905
Round Rosette
4-3/8" Outside
3-3/8" Inside

M-905A
Oval Rosette
3/4" x 4-1/8" x 5"

M-765B
Newel Base
3-1/4" x 6" (Turned)

M-895B
Newel Base
3-1/4" x 6" (Turned)

starting steps

4'-6" or 5'-0"
Tread is 1-1/16" x 11-1/4"
M-779V Bored for Volutes **M-721** and **M-722**
M-779T Bored for Turnouts **M-723** and **M-724**

4'-6"
M-780
Tread is 1-1/16" x 11-1/4"

4'-0" or 4'-6"
M-830
Tread is 1-1/16" x 11-1/4"

4'-6" or 5'-0"
M-880
Tread is 1-1/16" x 11-1/4"

4'-0"
M-896
Tread is 1-1/16" x 11-1/4"

A few stair and railing parts. *Courtesy C. E. Morgan*

Stairwork Fittings

For use with **M-720** Rail (illustrated at right). For complete measurements see page 11. Necessary rail bolt and wood plug packed with each fitting.

Stairwork fittings. *Courtesy C. E. Morgan*

in natural birch and red oak

Use with
Starting
Step
M-780

Use with
Starting
Step
M-779V

M-724
Turnout Easement with
Newel Cap, Right

M-723
Turnout Easement with
Newel Cap, left

M-718
Volute with Easement
Fitted, Left
M-719
Volute with Easement
Fitted, Right (illustrated)

M-721
Volute with Easement
Fitted, Left (illustrated)
M-722
Volute with Easement
Fitted, Right

Use with Starting Step **M-779T**

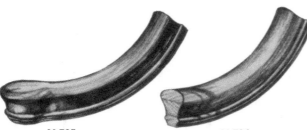

M-727
Concave Easement,
90 degrees

M-728
Convex Easement

M-725
Easement with Newel Cap

M-726
Concave Easement

M-751
Starting Rail Drop

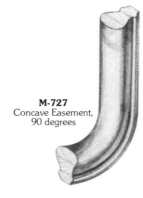

M-733
Goose Neck with
Newel Cap (1 Riser)

M-734
Goose Neck with
Newel Cap (2 Risers)

M-734 Natural Birch Only

M-730
Goose Neck without
Newel Cap (1 Riser)
M-731
Goose Neck without
Newel Cap (2 Risers)

M-750
Vertical Volute

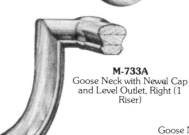

M-733A
Goose Neck with Newel Cap
and Level Outlet, Right (1
Riser)

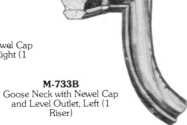

M-733B
Goose Neck with Newel Cap
and Level Outlet, Left (1
Riser)

M-733C
Goose Neck with Newel Cap
and Level Outlet, Straight
(1 Riser)

43

STONE

Stone is a lot easier to cut and work with than most nonmasons would imagine. Used as is, or cut and shaped, stone can be laid up dry or with mortar. A lot of physical work may be involved, but there is no need to rush the job—the stone will wait. You can take your time so that it is not unpleasant. As for technical skill, you needn't worry too much, because stone is very forgiving. Its very weight will hold it in place in most applications, and its appearance is such that only gross errors look bad.

FIELDSTONE

Any and all stones found lying about are classified as fieldstones. Some are easily split by way of a good hard rap with a sledgehammer. Others can be pried apart or split with a mason's chisel and a small sledgehammer. Look for the grain and align your chisel with it.

Fieldstones can be used for walls, borders, and even walks. For the latter, find stones with one relatively flat side, or split round stones to produce the desired level walking surface.

QUARRY STONES

Stones cut from mother earth are classified as quarry stones. The type of stone—granite, sandstone, etc.—depends on the quarry. The price of the stone depends on the labor expended to secure, and possibly shape, the stone, the type of stone—marble fetching a better price than sandstone—and transportation.

Obviously, if you care to lug the stone from the quarry yourself, the cost per stone will be considerably less than if the stone is hauled for you.

Each quarry has its own method of classification. Thus the following types can serve only as a guide, but it will help you to know in advance the relative cost of the quarry stone you select.

RUBBLE

These are the odds and ends left after the better stones have been removed. This is the least expensive quarry stone you can purchase. It is sold by the square yard. Since the rubble is merely dumped into the back of a truck, an 8-yard truck, for example, will contain only about 60 percent stone. The balance will be voids or air spaces between the stones.

QUARRY RUN

These are unselected stones, sold untrimmed and unsorted—or, as is—after being blasted loose from the face of the quarry wall. Size and shape will depend on the nature of the quarry. In some areas the quarry stone comes in natural 4- to 6-inch-thick layers. Thus quarry run stones will have two fairly parallel sides. In some quarries the stone is more or less solid, and blasted pieces have no regular shapes or parallel or even flat sides.

SELECT

These are hand-selected stones, picked out according to your specifications. But each stone will be only approximately the size and shape you ask for. The value of such stones is that they require much less cutting to be used. They are usually sold by weight.

VENEER

These stones fall within a specified thickness. For example, if you wanted 4-inch veneer, no stone would be thicker than 5 inches at any point, nor thinner than possibly 3 inches. Such stones could be used as is for walks, borders, edging, and walls. These stones are sold by the square foot.

TRIMMED

These are veneer stones that are trimmed to specified dimensions. Whereas you might receive a triangular veneer stone if you order veneer, such a stone would be excluded from an order for trimmed stones. These stones are sold by the square foot. Their overall dimensions fall within specifications and are never exact.

SIZED STONES

These are selected and trimmed stones, but held to closer tolerances than merely trimmed stones.

SAWN AND POLISHED

Only stones cut with a saw will have dimensions as exact as those of standard lumber. Saw-cut stones cost a good deal more and polishing pushes the price up even higher.

MORTARING STONE

The mortar generally used with all types of stone contains no lime. It is a mixture of cement and water, generally in the ratio, by volume, of two or three parts sand to one part cement.

No special care need be taken to lay up stone in mortar, with the single exception that the stone must be perfectly clean. Fieldstone, for example, should be washed and scrubbed free of all dirt.

See MORTAR for more information on same.

PAVING STONES

This is a general term used to denote types of stones that are most often used for paving. The reason they are so popular for this application is that these stones occur in nature in layers of suitable thickness.

FLAGSTONE

This is a type of sandstone ranging in color from pale brown to a kind of greenish brown. Common thicknesses are a nominal 1 inch and 2 inches. But be advised that the 1-inch may vary in thickness from ¾ of an inch to 1¼ inches. The 2-inch stone may vary from 1½ inches to 2½ inches.

Most masonry yards and some garden supply shops stock flagstone in several sizes starting with 12 × 12 inches and increasing in both one and two directions by 6-inch jumps. This permits you to lay down the flagstones in patterns if you wish. Some yards will cut the stones to your sketch.

Cutting Flagstone. The desired line of cut is scratched across the stone and the stone is placed atop a 2 × 4 or similar board so that the line of cut is supported by the piece of wood. Then, with a mason's chisel and a small sledgehammer, the line is deepened into a shallow groove. The stone is turned over and a second groove is cut into the stone directly above the first. The wood support is moved so that the groove is just beyond the edge of the support. Now, with hand pressure alone the flagstone is snapped into two pieces.

This method results in a snap cut, which leaves the exposed edges of the stone rough. For a smooth edge the stone has to be cut with a saw. This can be done with a power saw equipped with a diamond- or carbide-tipped blade. Naturally, if you order saw-cut stone your cost per cut will be much higher than snap-cut stone.

BLUESTONE

This is a harder form of sandstone. Its color ranges from a deep blue through a lighter green-blue. Bluestone may be cut exactly as flagstone is cut.

SLATE

Slate is a still-harder form of sandstone. It is found in many more colors than are either bluestone or flagstone. Slate colors include gray, green, dark blue, slate blue, red, purple, and a near black. The reds and purples cost the most.

Not all slate has a smooth, flat surface. Much of the slate commonly found has a somewhat wavy or rippled surface. Slate thickness is generally under 1 inch; thus slate is rarely placed directly on the earth as is 2-inch and thicker pieces of flag- and bluestone. Slate is most often used as a decorative surface for concrete; when this is done it's called "flagging" the concrete. Slate is slippery when wet and should not be used on steep walks and the like.

Cutting Slate. Slate cannot be snap-cut. Instead it must either be sawn or crushed. The edge of the slate is placed on a flat stone and then gently pounded with a hammer. This crushes the edge and in this way the size of the stone is reduced. The resulting edge is never straight or smooth.

Cut and Polished Slate. Saw-cut and partially polished slate is often used for windowsills in brick and stone walls and doorsills leading to pools, bathrooms, and the like. The great advantage of using slate, is that it is frost- and waterproof. The term *partially polished* means that the slate is not polished until it gleams like the front of a tombstone; it is merely made very flat and smooth. Cut and polished slate is available in dimensions suited to standard windows and doorways.

BELGIUM BLOCK

No one remembers where the name comes from, but these are hand-cut blocks of gray granite generally 6 × 6 × 16 inches in size. They are used for borders and paving.

BUYING STONE

Stone can be purchased at lumberyards, masonry yards, quarries, and some garden supply shops. None of these sources stocks more than a few types, and generally in a limited number of dimensions.

Lumberyards and garden supply shops usually carry no more than an assortment of flagstones, slate, and sometimes Belgium blocks. The flagstones will range in sizes of multiples of 6 inches, less ⅜ of an inch in each direction. Thus they may stock pieces they call 1 × 1s, 1 × 1½s, 1 × 3s, and so on possibly up to 2 × 3 feet, and in thicknesses of 1 and 2 inches, which will vary from ¾ of an inch to 2½ inches. But each piece of stone will be shorter and narrower then its designation to allow for mortar between the stones. Thus the 1-×-1-foot stone will actually be about 11⅝ × 11⅝ inches. The garden shops will stock fewer sizes, but they often will also stock circular pieces of flagstone.

The slate these two sources usually stock has not been cut to size; they are random pieces, some with rough surfaces.

Masonry yards stock a greater range of sizes and some will also carry sawn slate, which is used for window- and doorsills. They may also stock some quarry stone and

generally will order special stone—limestone, sandstone, granite, etc.—cut and even polished to your specifications, if you are willing to pay.

For quarry stone your best bet is to visit the quarry, assuming that this is feasible. In this way you will save the middleman's cost. But our quarries are scattered all over the map, so what you save by eliminating the middleman you may spend in getting to the quarry that has the stone you want.

If they quarry flagstone, bluestone, or slate, or if they wholesale these stones and just call themselves a quarry or stone supplier, they will cut these stones to your sketch. This means that if you have a special design for your garden walks or patio, you can draw what you want and they

MAJOR PROPERTIES OF STONE USED IN CONSTRUCTION

Type	Name	Principal ingredient	Weight/ cu. ft.	Color	Major use
Igneous	Black granite (traprock)	Silica	163 lbs.	Black	Building veneer, walls, construction
	Granite	Silica	163 lbs.	White, pink, black	Monuments, veneer
Sedimentary	Bluestone	Calcium carbonate	150 lbs.	Blue-gray	Sills, flooring, walks
	Limestone	Calcium carbonate	165 lbs.	Buff-gray	Coping, sills, flooring
	Flagstone	Calcium carbonate	160 lbs.	Blue, gray, brown	Flooring, walks
Metamorphic	Slate	Calcium carbonate	173 lbs.	Blue, gray, green, red	Blackboards, sills, counter tops
	Marble	Calcium carbonate	165 lbs.	Range of colors	Flooring, counter tops, sills, artwork

will cut the pieces to fit. In most cases you can save money by hauling the stones home yourself.

FREE STONE

In the process of excavating for roads, cellars, and the like, a great deal of stone has to be blasted free and hauled away. Generally, you can get permission to remove whatever stones you want. There is a lot of labor involved, since you have to do the pushing and moving to free the stones you want, but the price is unbeatable. Be sure to wear leather-palmed gloves because freshly blasted stone has many knife-sharp edges.

Another source of free stone is a demolished house. The rubble foundations used in years past is easily pried apart to free the individual stones. And many front and rear walks were paved with blue- and flagstone.

Building a retaining wall of flat fieldstones.

Splitting fieldstone. Note the white grain in the stone.

Mason constructing stone veneer wall of veneer-grade quarry stone, in this case granite.

Belgium block arranged in patterns and set in mortar.

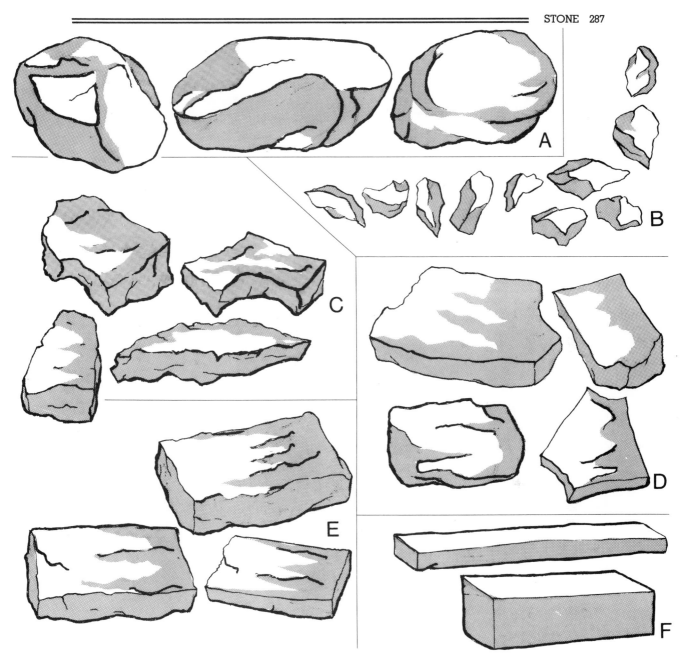

Major forms of building stone and their usual designations. A. Boulders or fieldstones. These are stones that have been rounded by nature and are to be found literally in the field. B. Rubble. The lowest grade of quarry stone; the broken pieces and odds and ends produced by blasting. Usually sold by the truckload or by weight. C. Select quarry stones. Stones with one or two good (relatively flat) sides that can be used with a minimum of cutting. D. Veneer. Selected stones that are reasonably flat on one side and not more than 4 or 5 inches thick. Sold by weight or by square foot. (Stones are spread over the earth and priced by the area they cover.) E. Trimmed veneer. Veneer, hand cut, and almost ready to be used without further cutting. Used for walk edging, building veneer, etc. Sold by the piece. F. Cut stone or dimensioned stone. Sold by the piece with price depending on type of stone; method of cutting (chisel or saw) and accuracy of cutting and polishing, if any. Called ashlar when cut into brick proportions.

Building a patio simply by laying 2-inch flagstones atop cut grass. The string acts as a guide.

Sand is brushed between flagstones to produce a level surface.

First step in cutting flagstone.

Slate must be either sawn or crushed as shown.

Mason selecting a piece of "veneer" from a pile of White Plains granite.

Wall made from cut or "dimensioned" stone. Stones started as "select" at the quarry and were then hand cut to specifications at the quarry or by a mason on the job site.

Modern ceiling tiles are made of fire-retardant fibers without asbestos. They have an insulating rating of approximately 2.40 R per inch of thickness, plus the R value of whatever air becomes trapped behind them. Fiber ceiling tiles also absorb between 55 and 75 percent of the sound that strikes them. This is why fiber ceiling tiles are sometimes called acoustical tile. Tiles designed mainly for noise suppression are pierced by a multitude of small holes.

Two types of fiber ceiling tiles are currently being manufactured. Both are available in a number of pale colors, including white, and in a large variety of surfaces ranging from smooth through deeply textured and patterned.

The difference between the two types of fibrous ceiling tile is mainly in their shape and in the manner in which they may be fastened to a ceiling. The older type, simply called ceiling tile, has tongue-and-groove edges that permit the tiles to be locked together. They are designed to be either cemented directly to a ceiling or nailed or stapled to furring strips fastened to a ceiling or bare ceiling joists. Ceiling tiles are most often available in the 12-×-12-inch size. Some supply houses also stock 16-×-16-inch and 16-×-32-inch tiles. Tile thickness varies from ⅝ of an inch through 1 inch, depending on grade and manufacturer. The thicker tile is easier to work with.

The second type is called hanging ceiling panels. These have straight edges and are designed to be supported by a special, light, metal grid that hangs from wires fastened either to an existing ceiling or to bare ceiling joists. The height of the finished ceiling varies with the length of the wires used. The ceiling panels simply rest on the supporting frame. They can be lifted up, removed, and replaced anytime you wish. The most common panel size is 2 × 4 feet. The most common thickness is 1 inch.

Fibrous ceiling tiles and panels are used to reduce noise level in a room; improve its acoustics; alter the appearance of an existing ceiling; hide cracks and other damage in a gypsum board (Sheetrock) or plaster ceiling; lower a ceiling; or as an alternative to a gypsum board or plaster ceiling.

INSTALLING CEILING TILE

There are several precautions to bear in mind. Tiles are easily soiled. Many professional installers wear clean white cotton gloves when handling tile. Tile dimensions vary a little from tile to tile and box to box. It is therefore advisable to open all the boxes and use one tile from each box in turn. In this way dimensional variations are minimized.

Few rooms have perfectly squared walls. If you rush the job and start at one wall, you may find yourself cutting a large number of tiles at an angle.

Few ceilings are even multiples of either of your tile's two major dimensions. So if you don't want to end up with a sliver of tile at one or more walls, take the time necessary to start applying the tile in the center of the ceiling, at a point that will permit you to end up with either a whole tile at the walls or at least half a tile.

To facilitate the cutting and installing of the tiles that terminate the ceiling's edges, use a wide cover molding to hide these joints. For example, if you use a 2-inch-wide cover molding, you can end up with a 1¾-inch gap between the tile edge and the wall and still have an attractive job. The molding hides the opening.

Old ceilings are rarely flat. Cover a bumpy ceiling with tile and you will have a bumpy tiled ceiling. To produce a perfectly level ceiling, you have to cover the existing ceiling with furring strips, which are made perfectly flat with the aid of shims, and fasten the tile to the strips.

To check a ceiling for bumps, hold a long straightedge up against it. Note that gypsum board (Sheetrock) ceilings are never perfectly flat. They always have gentle ridges up to ¼ inch high over the joints.

CEMENTING TILE IN PLACE

Wash the ceiling carefully with alcohol or lots of strong soap and hot water. All traces of dust, grease, and oil must be removed or the adhesive won't stick.

Divide the ceiling into four, approximately equal, squares by snapping two chalk lines across the ceiling. Your starting point will be where the lines cross, and as stated previously, the first tile must be positioned so that you will not end up with a sliver of a tile at any of the four walls.

Apply four or five gobs of tile cement to the underside of one tile. Align the tile with any of the two lines. Press it firmly in place. Apply cement to a second tile. Slip its tongue into the groove of the in-place tile. Press the second tile firmly against the ceiling. Do not force the tongue into the groove. Just make it snug. Continue applying tile, following the chalk-line guides.

When you come to a wall and have to cut a tile, use a razor knife. Hide the joint between the tile and wall with cove molding.

NAILING OR STAPLING TILE IN PLACE

Use No. 17, flathead brads, or staples of an equal size. Drive the nails through the thickest portion of the tongue, taking care not to mar the surface of the tile or to mash the tongue with the hammer. One nail every 4 inches on the two sides of the tile that can be nailed is sufficient. If you have to face-nail, use nails with matching-color heads.

NAILING TO FURRING STRIPS

Furring strips can be nailed to existing ceilings. Use 10d common nails. Run the strips across the joists (tap or break the ceiling to locate the joists). One nail through each strip where it crosses a joist is sufficient. Space the strips so that they run with the length of the tile (if the tile is not square) and so that the tile edge centers on the strip. In the case of 12-×-12-inch tiles, the strips would be positioned 12 inches on center.

If there is no existing ceiling, you can use 8d common nails to hold the strips in position.

In either case, check the flatness of the in-place furring strips by stretching a line temporarily along the length of each strip and then across the strips. Since a taut length of string is always perfectly straight, you can immediately spot dips and bends in the furring strips. Where necessary, force shims between the strips and the ceiling or the joists. Then use small nails to lock the shims in place. In some spots you may have to cut the old ceiling or the joists back a little to make the furring strips perfectly level.

Now you can nail the ceiling tile to the furring strips, or if you wish, you can cement them in place.

INSTALLING HANGING CEILINGS

Start by measuring the width of the ceiling. Divide this dimension by the given width of the panels you plan to hang. If you are lucky and it comes out evenly, no problem. If not, decide on whether to cut the first and last line of panels lengthwise or only the last one.

INSTALLING THE SUPPORT MOLDING

Decide on the height of your ceiling. Mark this height on any wall. Snap four perfectly horizontal chalk lines on the four sides of the room, all lines to be at exactly the decided and marked ceiling height. Nail the metal support molding to the walls, making sure that the bottom of the molding is perfectly flush with the chalk lines. If necessary, butt the end of the one piece of molding up against the next. The molding can be a half inch or so shy of the corners.

INSTALLING THE RUNNERS

The runners are metal strips with a T-shaped cross section. The tee is positioned upside down, and is hung by wires through screw eyes from the joists. To properly locate the screw eyes, measure out from the wall exactly the width of the panel you are going to hang, plus whatever clearance is suggested by the panel manufacturer. Mark each spot on the joist and then drive a pilot hole into the joist. You can do this with a nail. Then screw the eyes in place. One eye every second joist is sufficient.

When you have positioned the first row of screw eyes, install the second, third, and so on until they are all in. Bear in mind that you must measure from the wall or your mark each time, and not from the side of the screw eye, as its thickness will alter your measurements.

Now, using short pieces of wire, you can hang the main runners. Just fold the ends of the wires over at this time. Next, check the hung runners to make certain they are all parallel, the correct distance apart, and are all on the same level. If not, adjust the wires, and then lock them with a few twists.

INSTALLING THE CROSS TEES

These are short pieces of metal that go from runner to runner. The tees have tabs that engage slots in the runners.

POSITIONING THE PANELS

The panels are lifted at an angle, slipped through the openings in the supporting grid, and then lowered gently in place. Nothing more needs to be done.

FLUSH ILLUMINATION

Lighting fixtures that are positioned above the hanging ceiling are available. One or more ceiling panels are removed and replaced by a translucent plastic panel. The result is an evenly dispersed source of illumination that is flush with the hanging ceiling.

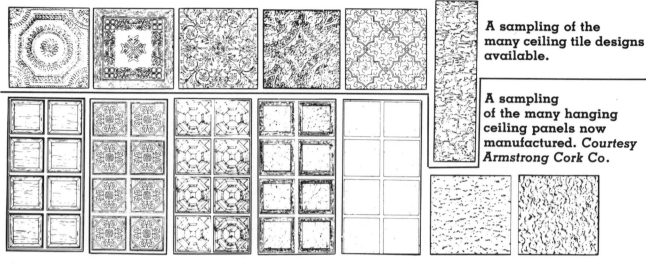

A sampling of the many ceiling tile designs available.

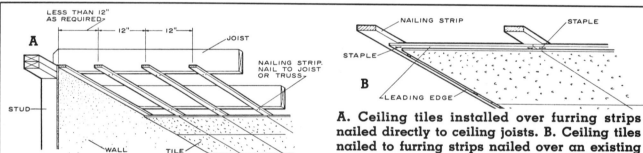

A sampling of the many hanging ceiling panels now manufactured. *Courtesy Armstrong Cork Co.*

A. Ceiling tiles installed over furring strips nailed directly to ceiling joists. B. Ceiling tiles nailed to furring strips nailed over an existing ceiling.

An electrical fixture is installed above the metal grid that supports the ceiling panels.

The fixture installed, a plastic panel is now positioned below. The panel passes and diffuses the light. Note that this panel could just as well be positioned beneath a skylight. *Courtesy Armstrong Cork Co.*

Using adhesive to fasten ceiling tile in place. *Courtesy Armstrong Cork Co.*

Installing hanging ceiling panels. A. The first step in installing a suspended or hanging ceiling is to decide the height at which you want the ceiling and then nail the support molding at that height. B. The T supports are installed by hanging them from wires. One wire every two joists is plenty. Don't tighten the wire yet, as you may have to adjust it. C. Next, install the cross tees.

Tees have tabs that fit into slots in the main runners or T supports. D. If all the metal supports are at one height and properly positioned, all you need do is tighten the wires and then slip the panels into place. E. A view of another ceiling, showing a different panel design being installed. *Courtesy Armstrong Cork Co.*

Ceramic tile is made by firing a plain flat piece of clay. In this form it is unglazed; its surface has no shine. When the little slab of clay is covered with glaze before it is fired, the result is glazed tile. In all respects glazed tile is similar to porcelain; it is covered with a thin layer of glass. When colors different from those that can be secured with clay alone are desired, the tile can be painted with a ceramic color, after which it is glazed and fired. In this way the paint is locked into the tile. When further decoration is desired, the tile can be painted in patterns or with pictures. This is then followed with a coating of glaze and the entire piece fired.

For all practical purposes a piece of fired clay is a piece of stone with or without a glaze—a construction material that can last—and has lasted—thousands of years.

MODERN TILE

Modern tile is made in hundreds of different colors, sizes, and shapes; in addition, individual tiles are often painted in a way that when they are laid together they form a pattern or even a scene. Just visit any tile specialty shop to see the range available.

FLOOR TILE

Floor tile differs from wall tile in one major respect: Glazed tiles never are—or never should be—used for floors. No matter how careful one may be, foot traffic quickly wears through the glaze, most often unevenly. The result is an unattractive floor. Unglazed tile is one color and texture all the way through, and no amount of foot traffic will wear through unglazed tile—even over several hundred years.

Floor tile is sold in sheets and in pieces. Small circles, squares, octagons, and other shapes are pasted to a heavy paper backer. Sheet tile is installed by laying it paper side up on the prepared floor. After the mortar or the mastic has hardened, water is used to remove the paper. Thus the task of aligning several hundred small pieces of tile is made simple and easy.

Individual tiles range in size from 3 × 3 to 12 × 12 inches and in thicknesses from 3/16 to ⅝ of an inch, including the bosses that are to be found on the bottoms of some tile. The larger, unglazed tiles are generally called quarry tiles, but they are made of clay and are not stone.

WALL TILE

Wall tiles, which can be glazed or unglazed, range in size from 3¼ × 3¼ to as much as 12 × 12 inches. Some are rectangular in shape.

TILE SELECTION

To reduce cutting to a minimum, find the tile size that is an even multiple of the given area that will be tiled. If the cuts to be made will be straight across the tile, the labor involved will be reduced if you select the largest tile. If the cuts across the tiles are not square across, it is better to work with small tiles. Then a little inaccuracy in each cut is not as visible. If the wall is not or cannot be made perfectly flat, it is better to work with small tiles, as small tiles will not make a bump as obvious as large ones will.

We have assumed so far that the tiles have no pattern. If they do, you must either select tiles of a size that will not require cutting, or surround the patterned tile with a border of plain tile. For example, if each large tile has a picture of a rose, it would not look nice to have that rose cut in half. If you purchased a set of tiles, that together depicts a village scene or what have you, you would not want part of that scene cut off by a wall.

TRIM

Most American tile manufacturers provide trim with their tile. Most English, French, Spanish, and Italian companies do not. Trim is the tiles you use to go around corners, edge, or terminate the top and sides of tiles that do not stop at a wall. Trim is used to round off corners between one tile wall and another, and between a tile wall and a tub or sink.

Most American tile manufacturers supply accessories with their tiles. These include towel hangers, soap dishes, grab bars, toilet paper holders, and the like. Matching accessories have matching colors and are of a size to be fitted into a tile wall without cutting any tile.

INSTALLING TILE FLOORS

Tile floors are installed after the tub is in place and after the toilet and lavatory plumbing are in place, but before the toilet has been installed. The toilet bowl rests on top of the tile.

USING MORTAR

The floor molding and baseboard are removed. The wood floor is covered with a layer of 15-pound tar paper. A layer of wire lath is nailed atop the paper. The lath is now covered with a layer of mortar ½ to 1¼ inches thick. A long straightedge board and guides are used to make the mortar perfectly smooth. The mortar is a mixture of one part cement and three parts sand with just enough water to permit the mix to be formed into a nondripping ball. The tiles are now laid in place, paper side up (if they have been pasted to paper). If you are working with individual tiles and they have no side nibs, use toothpicks or something similar to space them. When the tiles are in place, tamp them down lightly using a 2×4 and a small sledgehammer.

Let three days pass and then use water to remove the paper, or if you used toothpicks, remove them. Mix enough water with white cement to make a thick cream, called grout. With a sponge, spread the grout over the tile and into the spaces. When the grout no longer shines with water, use a clean sponge to wipe off the excess. Follow a little while later with a clean, damp sponge.

USING MASTIC

Remove the baseboard and molding. Cover the floor with a layer of mastic made for the purpose. Use a notched trowel designed for the purpose. Position the tiles and tamp them down lightly using a 2×4 and a small sledgehammer to make them all level (but don't bash them). If you are laying paper-backed small tiles, the paper will hold the tiles in alignment. If you are laying individual tiles, it is best to start in the center. See FLOORING, RESILIENT for the procedure to follow.

Grouting is the same with mastic-supported tile as with mortar-supported tile. Many artisans perfer a mastic grout, however, believing the mastic grout will give a little as the tiles move.

CUTTING TILE

Place the tile, glazed side up, on the workbench. Using a glass cutter, score a groove across the tile along the desired line of cut. Then place the tile, glazed side up, over a sharp, metal edge. Position the edge beneath the score mark, push down on the ends of the tile, and it will break along the line.

To make a large hole in a tile, cut it in two more or less across the center of the desired hole. Now outline the edges of the hole with the glass cutter. Using a pair of pliers, nibble away at the tile until you have broken off as much as necessary to produce the semicircular opening in each tile.

When the pieces of tile are then positioned, the crack will be invisible.

INSTALLING WALL TILES

Most tile mechanics apply the tile to standard, ½-inch gypsum board walls that have been properly taped and sanded (see GYPSUM BOARD). Some give the board a coat or two of paint before applying the tile. When and where there will be a high degree of moisture more or less constantly in the room, waterproof gypsum board or waterproof plywood may be used.

USING MASTIC

Wall tiles are no longer set in plaster or mortar as they used to be—they are always set in mastic.

The mastic is spread over the wall using a notched trowel made specifically for the job (the notches are of the correct depth). The tiles are then simply pressed into place. NOTE: American tiles have little nibs along their edges, which take care of the necessary spacing. Many foreign tiles do not. With these you have to use toothpicks or something similar to provide spacing.

The same grout suggested for grouting floors is used on walls.

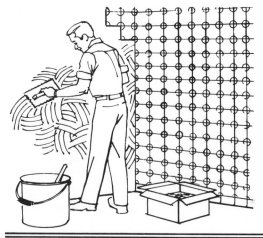

Applying wall tile.
Courtesy H. B. Fuller Co.

Because of climatic temperature changes, all structures must be ventilated. If they are not, moisture collecting inside any given structure will encourage rot. Excessive moisture within a wood-frame building will saturate the siding with water and cause the paint to blister and peel. In addition, buildings are often ventilated for summer comfort. Not only is this a quieter and more economical way of cooling a home's interior, but many people also prefer fan cooling to the refrigeration offered by an air conditioner.

PROTECTIVE VENTILATION

Minimum attic ventilation can be calculated from the table below.

EXPLANATION OF TERMS

Obviously, when there is an entrance for the ventilating air as well as an exit, ventilation is accomplished all the more easily. The word *inlet* in the table simply means the opening or openings cut into the building to admit venting air. The word *outlet* means exactly that.

LOSS AT VENT

The figures for vent dimensions given in the table assume that there will be no obstructions. This is never actually so. There is usually an insect screen covering the ventilator and sometimes there is a metal louver. Screening cuts the passage of air in half, and louvers reduce airflow by some 40 percent. When you protect the vent opening with both, you must increase the area of the opening four times.

VENT PLACEMENT

Inlet vents are usually placed in the soffits of a house when the soffits are sealed to the outside air but open to the attic. When there is no soffit, the inlet vents are usually cut into the frieze board.

Outlets are placed as high as possible, generally in the top section of a gable. In some cases outlet vents are positioned on the roof itself. These are either fixed vents or wind-driven vents made expressly for the purpose.

CRAWL-SPACE VENTILATION

The soil within all crawl spaces should be sealed with concrete or, better yet, blacktop, a mixture of asphalt and small stones. The underside of the structure should be sealed

MINIMUM PREVENTIVE VENTILATION

Type of roof	Inlet	Outlet
Gable roof with outlet ventilators only		1/300 of attic area
Gable roof with both inlet and outlet ventilators	1/900	1/900 of attic area
Hip roof with inlet and outlet ventilators (distributed)	1/900	1/900 of attic area
Flat or low-slope roofs with ventilators in soffit or eave area only (located at each side of house)		1/250 of attic area

with a vapor barrier and also insulated. But even with all these moisture protectors, it is advisable to vent the crawl space. Venting can be accomplished with small metal vents that replace a few foundation-wall concrete blocks or that are set into poured concrete walls. A few square feet of ventilation is usually adequate for an average-sized, sealed crawl space. For best results, place the vents directly opposite on both sides of the building.

RECOMMENDED MINIMUM CRAWL-SPACE VENTILATION

Sealed earth   1/1,600 of the ground area
Bare earth   1/160 of the ground area
Ventilation must be provided by at least two vents.

COMFORT VENTILATION

The forced movement of air through a residence is termed *comfort ventilation*. It isn't necessary for the well-being of the structure, just for its inhabitants.

Forced-air ventilation or cooling is less expensive than air conditioning and is also less noisy. Forced-air cooling is very effective when the air outside is cool, for example, in the evening after the sun has gone down. But when the outside air is uncomfortably warm, forced-air cooling is effective only when there is actually a breeze. While fresh air moving through one's home is much healthier than stagnant air-conditioned air, many people find even a light breeze uncomfortable. Few ventilating fans have speed controls. They are either on or off. However, airflow can be controlled by opening and closing windows and doors. Should you want, for example, a gale blowing through your bedroom, you would close all other windows and doors in the house. All air movement would then be through your bedroom.

FAN SIZE

In warm climates the attic exhaust fan that provides the cooling flow of air through the entire house (when all the windows are open) should be capable of changing all the air every minute. Above the Mason-Dixon line, a complete change of air every minute and a half is sufficient.

To compute the total volume of air in your home, add up the floor areas, excluding the basement. Subtract 10 percent for the closets. Then multiply by room height, which is almost always 8 feet. Having determined this figure, you can find the fan size, given in fan diameter, from the manufacturer's literature.

The manufacturer's literature will also provide you with the size of the opening necessary for the fan. You will need at the minimum the same size opening at your gable ends. Larger openings would be even more desirable. This figure or figures will enable you to select the louvers and vents necessary. Bear in mind that it is unwise to install two sets of automatic vents in the airflow system. The reason is, of course, that the fan wastes twice as much power opening two vents as one.

ROOM VENTING

For comfort and the elimination of odors, many homeowners power-ventilate their kitchens, baths, and laundry rooms. Again, the rate of air exchange has been established by testing. To determine fan power requirements, use the following formulas and select a fan size that is suitable.

Kitchen	2 × floor area in sq. ft. = CFM* for fifteen changes of air per hour
Bath	1.07 × floor area in sq.ft. = CFM* for eight changes of air per hour
Laundry	0.80 × floor area in sq. ft. = CFM* for six changes of air per hour
Example:	Kitchen is 10 × 12 feet = 120; 120 × 2 = 240. A fan with a capacity of 240 CFM* would change the air in this kitchen eight times an hour.

*CFM = cubic feet per minute

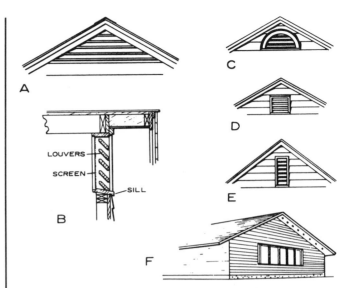

Outlet ventilators. A. Triangular. B. Section through louvers. C. Semicircular. D. Square. E. Rectangular. F. Vented overhanging gable.

Screened openings in frieze boards provide ventilation.

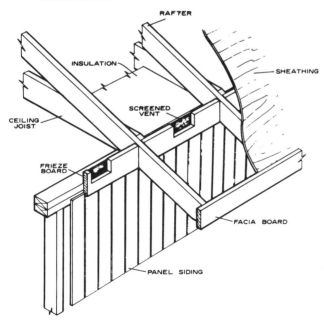

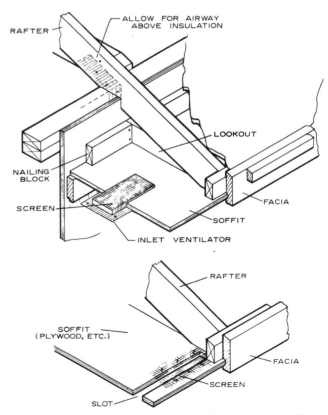

Two ways to provide inlet ventilation in a soffit.

Section Length	Sq. Ft. Louver Ventilates	No. Per Ctn.	Wt. Per Ctn.
4'	160	10 sect. or 40'	28½
10'	412	10 sect. or 100'	46

*AVAILABLE IN **BROWN, BLACK** AND **WHITE** BAKED ENAMEL FINISHES

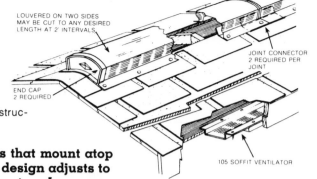

LOUVERED ON TWO SIDES MAY BE CUT TO ANY DESIRED LENGTH AT 2' INTERVALS

JOINT CONNECTOR 2 REQUIRED PER JOINT

END CAP 2 REQUIRED

105 SOFFIT VENTILATOR

VARI-PITCH RIDGE-LINE LOUVERS HAVE THE FOLLOWING FEATURES

- Maintenance free all Aluminum Construction, .019 thickness
- Built-in Inter-lock Connector
- Adjustable from 4/12 to 10/12 Without Build-up
- Built-in Baffle for increased weather Protection
- Complete Installation Instructions Included

Ridge-line louvers that mount atop a roof ridge. This design adjusts to any roof pitch. *Courtesy Lomanco*

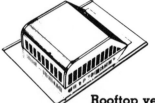

Rooftop ventilators. *Courtesy Lomanco*

Overall Size (Including flange)	Diameter Circular Opening	Sq. Ft. Louver Ventilates
12-3/16"x17-3/4"x4"	6¼"	63
14-7/16"x20-5/16"x5"	8"	104
14-7/16"x20-5/16"x5"	8"	104
16-5/8"x22-3/8"x6"	9½"	146
32-1/2"x22-3/8"x6"	Two 9½"	292

C.F.M. AT WIND VELOCITY OF

5 mph	8 mph	11 mph	15 mph
95	172	250	329
188	310	432	560
350	528	714	947
350	528	714	947
431	677	935	1215
431	677	935	1215
578	870	1181	1540
578	870	1181	1540
768	1175	1604	2075
771	1155	1570	2036
1033	1550	2099	2692
1015	1535	2088	2710

Interior- and exterior-braced turbine louvers. As the accompanying table indicates, their effectiveness increases with increasing wind speed. *Courtesy Lomanco*

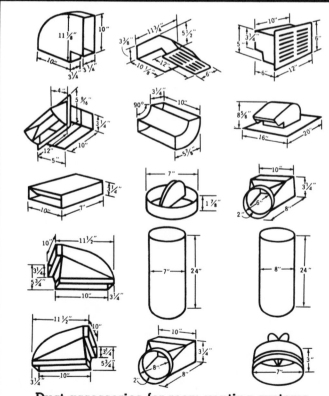

Duct accessories for room venting systems. *Courtesy Nutone*

MODEL 106

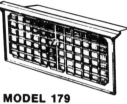

MODEL 106L

MODEL 179

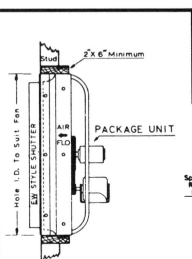

MODEL 189

MODEL 142

MODEL 2711

MODEL 2712

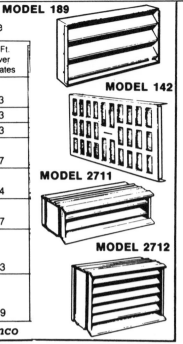

• Equipped with 8 x 8 mesh insect scre

Model No.	Size	Description	Sq. Ft. Louver Ventilates
106	16x8	Die-cast aluminum, 8-mesh screen, aluminum damper	133
106L	16x8	Same as 106, with 1½" lintel	133
106S	16x8	Same as 106, without damper	133
179	16x8	Die-cast aluminum, 8-mesh screen, 3-slide shutter	117
189	16x8	All alum. const. 8x8 mesh screen, 3-hinged louver	154
142	16x8	2 slide, die stamped alum. self-framed on all sides	87
2711	1 brick	Extruded aluminum, overlapping top & bottom, mortar ribs 2-3/8x7-7/8x3-5/8	23
2712	2 brick	Extruded aluminum, overlapping top & bottom, mortar ribs 5-1/16x7-7/8x3-5/8	49

Typical foundation vents. *Courtesy Lomanco*

Circle louvers used for ventilating walls. *Courtesy Maurice Franklin Manufacturing Co.*

Louver Size	Dimension In Inches			D Screen Diameter	E No. Fins	Approximate Free Area In Square Inches	
	A	B	C			RS	Regular
1"	0.985	1.219	13/32"	7/8"	5	0.376	0.185
1½"	1.485	1.813	9/16"	1-3/8"	5	1.030	0.399
2"	1.980	2.391	5/8"	1-15/16"	6	1.846	0.803
2½"	2.485	2.907	5/8"	2-11/32"	6	2.610	1.210
3"	2.980	3.530	11/16"	2-7/8"	6	4.064	1.735
4"	3.980	4.625	3/4"	3-7/8"	9	7.380	3.500
6"	5.990	6.688	13/16"	5-7/8"	8	16.970	5.490

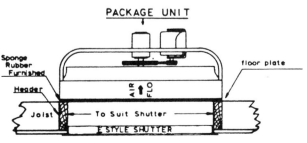

Ceiling- and wall-mounted building ventilators. *Courtesy Fasco*

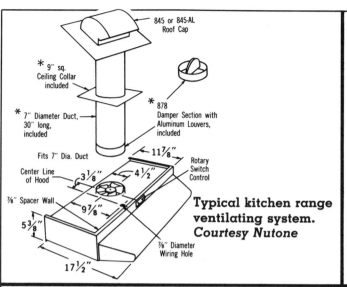

Typical kitchen range ventilating system.
Courtesy Nutone

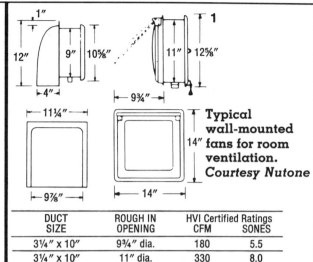

Typical wall-mounted fans for room ventilation.
Courtesy Nutone

DUCT SIZE	ROUGH IN OPENING	HVI Certified Ratings CFM	SONES
3¼" x 10"	9¾" dia.	180	5.5
3¼" x 10"	11" dia.	330	8.0

Beginning with just the thickness of the stock (A) it pushes the board up to 5/32", (B) just enough to provide airflow under the lap siding and keep the wood dry; yet, not too much to cool off the house.

By using the special tool, (below) designed for installation, all the vents are evenly distributed and with the spurs (C) locking in, a permanent installation is effected.

To determine the rough opening for installing any model Vari-Pitch louver, just measure down from the peak of the roof, along the roof line, the length of the frame. The louver quickly adjusts to the opening perfectly, and can be installed in a matter of minutes.

• Adjustable from 2-1/2 to 9 roof pitch.

• Blades pivot as they adjust, allowing maximum ventilating capacity and weather protection.

• All aluminum construction.

• 8 x 8 mesh aluminum screen.

• Completely assembled, easy to install.

• All sizes available in baked white acrylic enamel finish.

Large adjustable triangular louvers.
Courtesy Lomanco

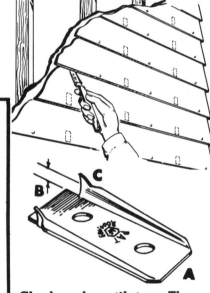

Clapboard ventilators. They are slipped between the boards to vent the walls and prevent paint from blistering.
Courtesy Maurice Franklin Manufacturing Co.

Model No.	Frame Length	Adjustable Base Length	Sq. Ft. Lvr. Ventilates
904	21-1/4"	45-1/8" - 34-1/4"	71 to 144
*905	26-1/4"	54-3/4" - 42-3/8"	119 to 243
906	31-1/4"	64-1/2" - 50-1/4"	179 to 377
*907	36-1/4"	73-1/2" - 58-3/8"	254 to 531
908	41-1/4"	84-1/2" - 66-1/2"	340 to 710
*909	46-1/4"	94-1/8" - 74-5/8"	440 to 915
910	51-1/4"	103-1/8" - 82-1/2"	548 to 1142
911	56-1/4"	113-1/2" - 90-1/2"	667 to 1392

BAKED WHITE ACRYLIC ENAMEL FINISH:

Model No.	Frame Length	Adjustable Base Length	Sq. Ft. Lvr. Ventilates
904-W	21-1/4"	45-1/8" - 34-1/4"	71 to 144
*905-W	26-1/4"	54-3/4" - 42-3/8"	119 to 243
906-W	31-1/4"	64-1/2" - 50-1/4"	179 to 377
*907-W	36-1/4"	73-1/2" - 58-3/8"	254 to 531
908-W	41-1/4"	84-1/2" - 66-1/2"	340 to 710
*909-W	46-1/4"	94-1/8" - 74-5/8"	440 to 915
910-W	51-1/4"	103-1/8" - 82-1/2"	548 to 1142
911-W	56-1/4"	113-1/2" - 90-1/2"	667 to 1392

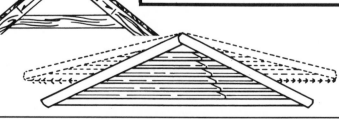

47 WINDOWS

Over the centuries various types of windows have been developed along with type and part names. Each type has its own specific application along with a number of advantages and disadvantages in relation to other types. To facilitate the purchase of replacement window parts and windows, you need to know the nomenclature. To select the window types best for your new home or addition, you need to know something about their characteristics.

TYPES OF WINDOWS

Windows are named by their function and also their material of construction.

FIXED SASH

Many, many years ago, lights, as windows were called then, were placed directly in the frame of the building. This led to problems and the early cracking of the then-, relatively, very-high-priced glass. It was learned that the better way to mount windowpanes in a wall was first to mount the glass in a frame, then place the frame in the wall. In this way less wall movement was transmitted to the glass, and the glass was less likely to break. This method of mounting also permitted the glass some movement of its own.

The frame in which the glass is positioned is called a sash. The sash can be of any size, from 1 × 1 foot to 10 × 20 feet. When the sash normally is immobile it is called a fixed sash.

A fixed sash is often used in basements, attics, pantry walls, and as a part of a larger window assembly.

DOUBLE-HUNG

This type of window consists of two sash placed within a vertical track. The sash moves up and down, leaving a full half of the window open when both sash are up or down.

The double-hung window is the most frequently used window, at least in this country. It is not the least expensive, but it is the most reliable so far as sealing and service life are concerned. Modern, double-hung windows ride on aluminum tracks that are spring-loaded to provide a tight seal. Ropes and weights have been replaced by counterbalancing springs. Most double-hung windows of wood have been chemically treated against rot. A few companies make double-hung windows with easily removable sash, which makes cleaning the outsides of the window easy.

Double-hungs come in single, double, and triple glazing. Since the window always presents a flat exterior surface, there is no problem in fitting them with combination storm and screen windows.

SLIDERS

Two sash are positioned in two pairs of channels, side by side in the top and bottom of a frame. The sash are free to be moved from side to side. In some designs, one sash is fixed within the frame. In either case, the window can be opened to one half of the total window area.

Sliders are made of metal and of wood, with the metal being the least expensive of the two and the least expensive, as a type, of all the movable-sash windows.

Sliders suffer from a number of problems arising from their very design. Dust, dirt, leaves, and other debris tend to gather in the slide. If you do not keep it clean, the window, or rather the movable sash, can jam. This tendency is compounded by the use of tall sash—sash that are much taller than they are wide. The result is a sash that easily cocks in its frame.

Another problem is that the two slides do not make as tight a seal with each other as do the sash in a double-hung window. And the track or channel tends to collect and hold water for a long time.

Sliders are also used for doors. The major difference between the two is size and glass thickness. When you purchase a sliding door it is wise to go the full route and spend the extra money for ⅜-of-an-inch-thick saftey glass. Double-weight window glass will not do at all, and ordinary plate glass, even ¼ inch thick or more, will shatter into flying knives when struck hard enough.

Sliders are made of wood and metal, the latter almost always aluminum. Aluminum can be had in anodized finishes in many colors. Anodizing provides a hard, glossy ceramic finish that lasts a long time. Unfinished, or bare, aluminum turns a pale gray, but will withstand the weather for centuries if nothing but aluminum or stainless steel nails and screws are used to hold it in place. Some companies sheath their aluminum window- and doorframes in vinyl; some sheath their wood in vinyl.

Sliders can be had with single, double, and triple glazing. All are, or can be, fitted with insect screens. Normally, sliders are not designed to accept storm windows.

CASEMENT WINDOWS

A casement window consists of a sash in a frame. The sash is hinged on one side and swung inward or outward (most often outward) under the control of some sort of mechanism. In the fully open position, the entire window is open; thus twice as much air will flow through a casement window as will pass through a slider or double-hung window. That is the casement's one practical advantage over the two aforementioned window types. The remaining advantage is aesthetic. Since many people connect casement windows with castles and mansions, casement windows lend a touch of grace or class—if you will—to a structure.

On the negative side, the top surfaces of casement windows are exposed to rain and snow when the sash is in its open position. Thus when casement windows are made of materials identical to those used for double-hung windows, the casements do not last nearly as long.

In any case, casement windows are made of plain wood, treated wood, wood encased in vinyl, and of metal, which may be iron, aluminum, or brass (the last being the best). But note that not all casement windows are designed to be opened all the way and not all control arms will open these windows all the way.

Screens for casement windows go on the inside of the window frame. Casements are available with double glazing. For triple glazing, the third pane of glass is positioned within a sash that is snapped into place over the moving sash. Actually, this is not triple glazing but a storm window arrangement.

AWNING WINDOWS

Whereas casement windows have sashes that are hinged at their sides, awning windows have sashes that are hinged at their tops. The major difficulty with awning windows is that they tend to catch and hold snow and water when they are open, although none of them are designed to be fully opened, meaning the sash cannot be swung into a fully horizontal or higher position.

Awning windows are made of plain wood, treated wood, wood sheathed in vinyl, and metal. Generally they may be arranged vertically in a series of two or three windows. More often they are used beneath larged fixed-sash windows. The fixed sash admits the larger quantity of light, the awning sash admits the air.

Like the casement windows, awning windows have their insect screens fitted inside the frame. And like casement windows, they come single- and double-glazed. For that third pane, the glass is fitted to a frame that is snapped in place.

HOPPER WINDOWS

A hopper window is literally an awning window turned upside down. They were used fairly extensively years ago to ventilate cellars.

CLERESTORY WINDOWS

These may be fixed or movable sash windows that are named by their position in a structure and not by their design. They are positioned vertically within a roof. For this to be so, one portion or half of the roof must be higher than another.

SKYLIGHTS

These windows are also positioned within the roof, but are parallel with the roof. Generally, fixed- or awning-sash windows are used here.

BOW WINDOWS

A bow window differs from all previously described windows in that it projects beyond the surface of the building. If you don't care about cost, you could make one from a large sheet of curved glass and fit it into a curved sash. Where cost is a factor—and cost is a factor just about everywhere—the bow window is constructed of three of more ordinary windows, which may be any of the types previously described or any combination thereof.

Generally, the top of the window will not extend beyond the soffit, which then acts as the window's roof. The bottom of the bow window is generally "floored" with lumber cut and fitted at the job site. Generally, the floor does not extend much below the bottom of the bow window.

BAY WINDOWS

These differ from bow windows only in that they project farther from the side of the structure and the angles between windows are sharper and more clearly defined. There is no attempt to produce a curved front with a bay window; it is angular. Bay windows usually reach beyond the soffit and have little roofs of their own.

Often the floor of the bay window is lowered so that its inside is flush with the floor in the room, making this useful indoor floor space.

PICTURE WINDOWS

Any larger-than-ordinary window may be termed a picture window. Generally, this is a flat frame with a large fixed sash in the center and smaller movable windows at the sides.

INSTALLING A WINDOW

The following suggestions are very general. Each window design or structure has its own requirements. There is, however, a basic approach to window installation, which if followed will greatly lessen the chance of difficulties.

NEW FRAME

Select your window or windows at the same time you or your architect are planning your building, addition, or remodeling job. Determine how the window will fit into the wall. When the wall is of wood, most windows are fastened atop the sheathing, with the inner edge of the window frame flush with the surface of the Sheetrock or plaster. In the case of the standard, wood-frame window, the frame is face-nailed to the sheathing. The siding is then butted to the side of the frame. In some designs the frame is nailed through its top and sides to the wall framing.

The depth of the standard wood-frame, double-hung window is such that it projects into the room to a depth that will make it flush with the surface of the Sheetrock or plaster to be installed. In other designs another frame, called an extension jamb, must be added to the frame to make its interior-edge surface flush with the finished wall. The window trim is then nailed atop the edge of the extension jamb or the frame itself.

Most window data includes window dimensions plus rough opening dimensions. The latter usually allows for ½ inch of clearance all around. This permits you to make the window perfectly horizontal without troubling to make the rough opening perfectly horizontal and square. But most published window data does not include frame depth, and this is a crucial dimension, as necessary depth will vary with the thickness of your interior wall.

OLD FRAME

Remove the interior trim and the old sash. Reach through the window opening and pull the face nails with a "cat's-paw" nail puller. Unless the previous carpenter has added more nails, the window frame should now be removable. If it isn't, look for more nails. With the old window removed, the new window can be slipped into place and nailed.

NEW WINDOWS IN MASONRY STRUCTURES

Windows are fitted into slightly larger masonry openings and are locked in place either with a little mortar or with screws driven through the window frame and into the masonry. In the latter case, caulking may be used to seal the small openings between the window frame and the masonry opening. As you can see, this method requires careful control of the window opening. Very often this is accomplished with a window buck. A temporary frame is constructed of timbers and the masonry is built to the frame. Then the frame is removed and the window installed.

An alternate method, used when a wide band of mortar around the window frame is acceptable, consists of leaving a larger-than-necessary opening in the masonry wall. Next, the window, and it should be of metal, is positioned with the aid of wood braces and the like. Mortar is then troweled into the spaces between the masonry and the window's metal frame. The result is a smooth, tight, permanent joint.

ENERGY CONSERVATION

Windows can work not only to conserve energy within one's home, but also to permit energy to enter and hold it there. This is, of course, the well-known "greenhouse effect."

The subject can be mentioned only by way of introduction here. Essentially, in cold areas, the majority of the windows in terms of exposed glass should face south. In this way, heat from the sun, such as there may be in the winter, can enter the house and reduce the artificial and expensive heat requirements. At the same time, few windows should be exposed to the northern skies. There is little or no sun there in the winter, and windows are the greatest single source of heat loss in the average home.

In southern climates, the reverse is true. The largest percentage of your window glass should face north, with a bare minimum facing south. So far as east–west orientation is concerned, it is best to minimize the number and size of the windows on the western side of the house; this is where the setting sun will hit when the house has already been baked by summer heat. If you need light, place the windows on the eastern wall. Whatever summer sun enters, it will, at least, do so when the building is comparatively cool.

INSULATION
Refer to the section on INSULATION for information on window insulation.

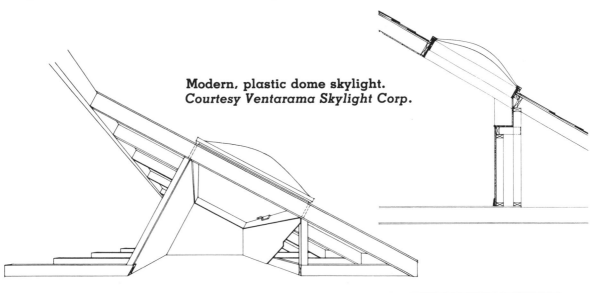

Modern, plastic dome skylight.
Courtesy Ventarama Skylight Corp.

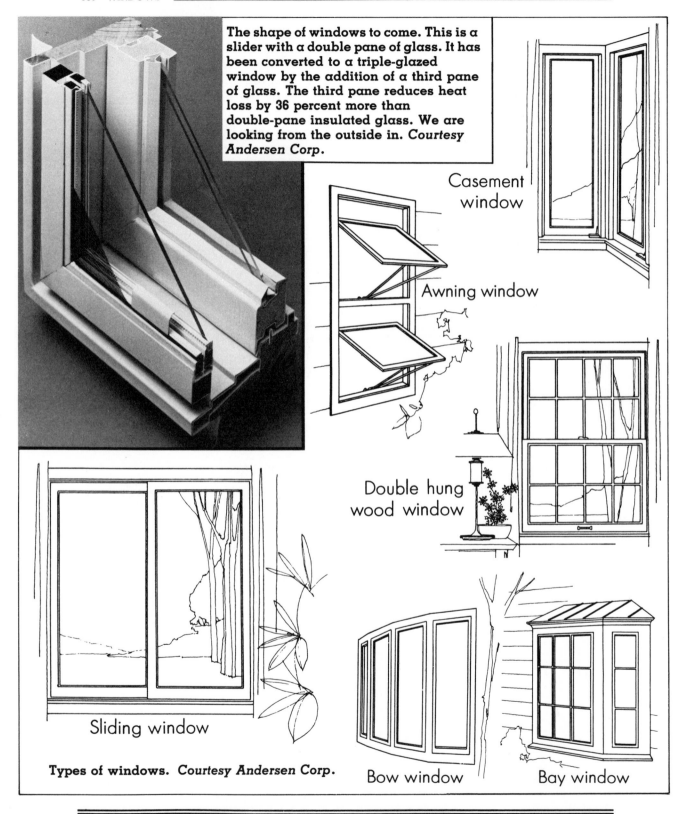

The shape of windows to come. This is a slider with a double pane of glass. It has been converted to a triple-glazed window by the addition of a third pane of glass. The third pane reduces heat loss by 36 percent more than double-pane insulated glass. We are looking from the outside in. *Courtesy Andersen Corp.*

Casement window

Awning window

Double hung wood window

Sliding window

Types of windows. *Courtesy Andersen Corp.*

Bow window

Bay window

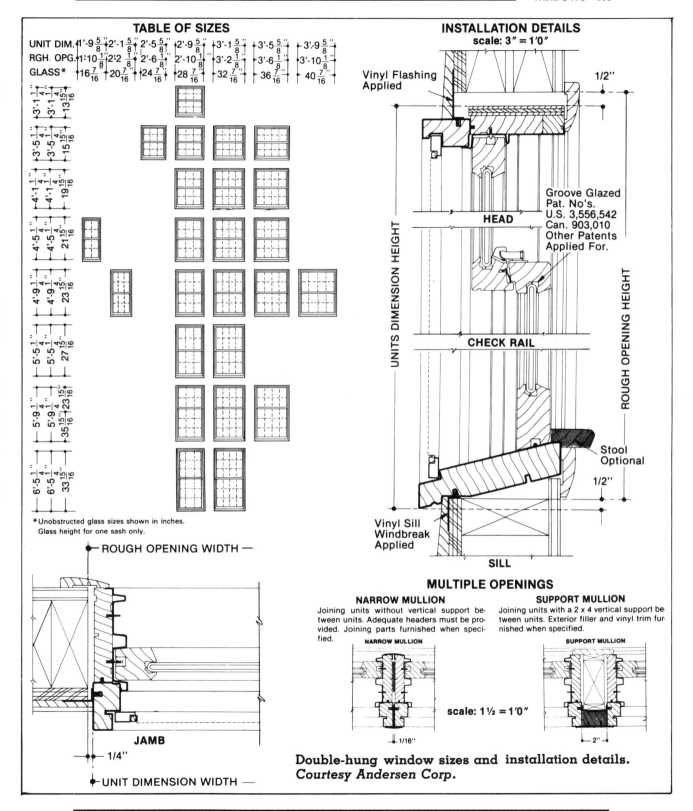

Double-hung window sizes and installation details. Courtesy Andersen Corp.

BASIC SIZES

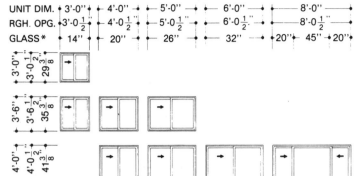

*Unobstructed glass sizes shown in inches. Glass width for one sash only.

VERTICAL DETAIL

Arrows indicate operation of left-hand sash with right-hand stationary. Picture windows have left and right venting flanking sash. All venting indicated as viewed from the exterior.

TYPICAL COMBINATION
(Narrow Mullion)

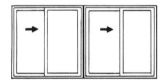

3-5/8"

1/2"

Prefinished Ext. Jambs

HEAD

UNIT DIMENSION HEIGHT

1-1/8"

4-1/2"

SILL

MULTIPLE OPENINGS
NARROW MULLION

Joining units without vertical support between units. Adequate headers must be provided. Joining parts furnished when specified.

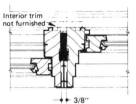

Interior trim not furnished

3/8"

Overall Unit Dimension Width—Sum of individual unit dimensions plus ³⁄₈″ for each unit joining.

scale: 1½′0″

SUPPORT MULLION

Joining units with a 2 x 4 vertical support between units. Exterior filler and vinyl trim furnished when specified.

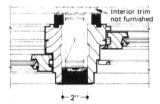

Interior trim not furnished

2"

Overall Unit Dimension Width—Sum of individual unit dimensions plus 2″ for each unit joining.

Overall Rough Opening Width—Add ½″ to Overall Unit Dimension Width when using either narrow or support mullion.

HORIZONTAL DETAIL

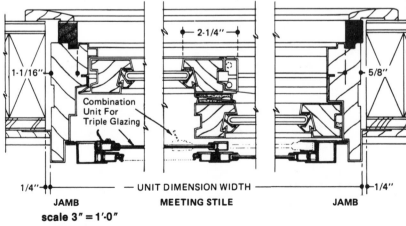

2-1/4"

1-1/16"

5/8"

Combination Unit For Triple Glazing

1/4"

UNIT DIMENSION WIDTH

1/4"

JAMB   **MEETING STILE**   **JAMB**

scale 3″ = 1′-0″

Sliding window sizes and installation details. *Courtesy Andersen Corp.*

FRAME / BRICK VENEER

Awning unit installed in brick veneer wall construction with ½" sheathing and interior wall. Unit secured to wall by nailing through vinyl flanges into sheathing.

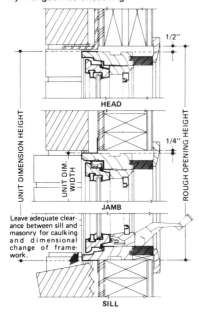

SOLID MASONRY / STUCCO

Casement unit installed in solid 8" masonry wall with ½" dry wall on furring strips and stucco exterior.

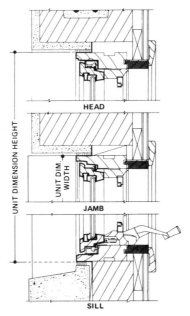

PRECAST MASONRY

Casement unit installed in a pre-cast masonry wall with interior wall on furring strips. Metal trim and extension jambs used on interior. Unit secured in opening with side jamb clips nailed to furring strips.

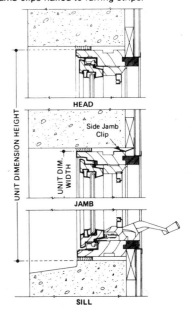

12" MASONRY WALL

Casement unit installed in 12" masonry wall. Unit secured through side jambs into metal wall plugs located in masonry joints.

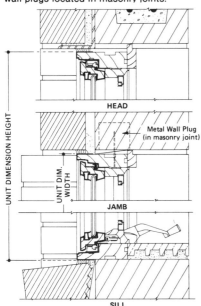

FRAME / BRICK VENEER AND AUXILIARY CASING

Detail showing Andersen Auxiliary Casing applied for a wider casing appearance or for remodeling to arrive at larger unit sizes.

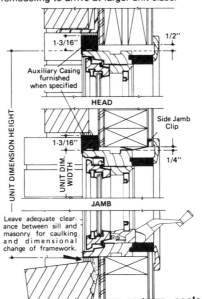

scale—1½" = 1'0"

2" x 6" WALL

Detail showing unit installed in 2 x 6 stud wall. Note special width extension jambs furnished by others.

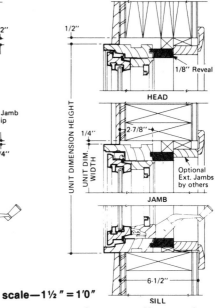

CAUTION: In masonry wall construction leave adequate clearance between sill and masonry for caulking and dimensional change of framework.

Awning and casement window installation details.
Courtesy Andersen Corp.

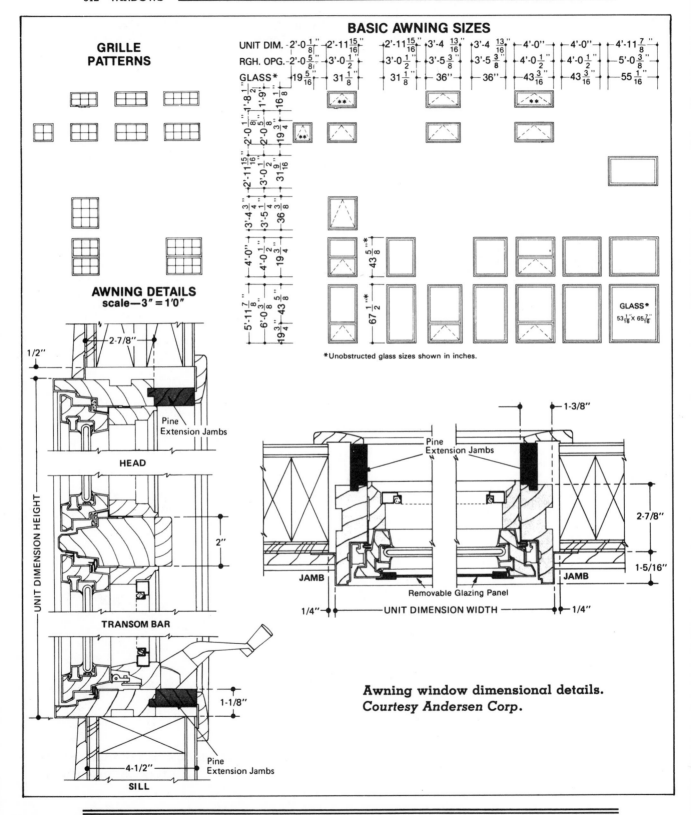

Awning window dimensional details.
Courtesy Andersen Corp.

STATIONARY PICTURE WINDOW UNITS

UNIT DIM. | 4'-5 5/8" | 5'-1 5/8" | 5'-9 5/8"
RGH. OPG. | 4'-6 1/8" | 5'-2 1/8" | 5'-10 1/8"
GLASS* | 48 3/16" | 56 3/16" | 64 3/16"

4'-5 1/4" | 4'-5 1/4" | 45"

4'-9 1/4" | 4'-9 1/4" | 49"

5'-5 1/4" | 5'-5 1/4" | 57"

PICTURE WINDOW UNITS COMBINED WITH 1-8 FLANKING UNITS

UNIT DIM. | 8'-1" | 8'-9" | 9'-5"
RGH. OPG. | 8'-1 1/2" | 8'-9 1/2" | 9'-5 1/2"

4'-5 1/4" | 4'-5 1/4"

4'-9 1/4" | 4'-9 1/4"

PICTURE WINDOW UNITS COMBINED WITH 2-0 FLANKING UNITS

UNIT DIM. | 8'-9" | 9'-5" | 10'-1"
RGH. OPG. | 8'-9 1/2" | 9'-5 1/2" | 10'-1 1/2"

4'-5 1/4" | 4'-5 1/4"

4'-9 1/4" | 4'-9 1/4"

5'-5 1/4" | 5'-5 1/4"

A few of the many possible windows that can be made from a combination of fixed and movable sash. *Courtesy Andersen Corp.*

FRAME
STUD
CALKING
10d GALV. NAILS SPACE 12" APART
CASING
PANEL SIDING
SILL
USE CARPENTER'S LEVEL TO PLUMB CASING AND LEVEL SILL
USE 1/4 ROUND UNDER SILL OVER CALKING FOR TIGHT JOINT

Installation of a double-hung window frame.

Courtesy Architectural Aluminum Manufacturing Association

"U-VALUE" IMPROVEMENT FROM ADDING STORM WINDOWS*

PRIME WINDOW TYPE	"U-VALUE" WITHOUT STORM	"U-VALUE" WITH STORM
Old Wood Single-Glazed	1.36	0.77
New Aluminum Single-Glazed	1.21	0.73
New Wood Single-Glazed	1.12	0.58
New Aluminum Insulating-Glass	0.86	0.62
Thermalized Aluminum	0.59	0.49

45° ANGLE BAY UNIT SIZES

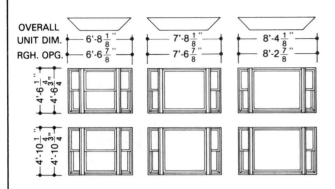

OVERALL UNIT DIM.	6'-8 1/8"	7'-8 1/8"	8'-4 1/8"
RGH. OPG.	6'-6 7/8"	7'-6 7/8"	8'-2 7/8"

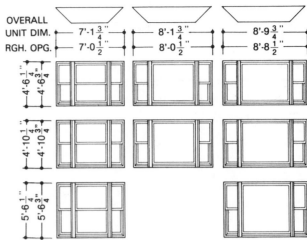

OVERALL UNIT DIM.	7'-1 3/4"	8'-1 3/4"	8'-9 3/4"
RGH. OPG.	7'-0 1/2"	8'-0 1/2"	8'-8 1/2"

VERTICAL SECTION

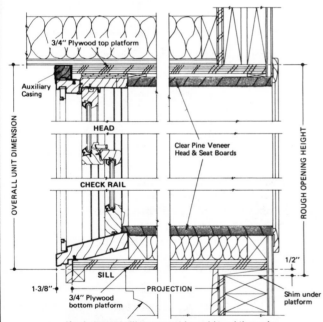

Auxiliary Casing

3/4" Plywood top platform

HEAD

Clear Pine Veneer Head & Seat Boards

CHECK RAIL

OVERALL UNIT DIMENSION

ROUGH OPENING HEIGHT

SILL

1/2"

1-3/8"

PROJECTION

3/4" Plywood bottom platform

Shim under platform

If adequate nailing cannot be achieved through top platform into roof lookout members, use additional support at bottom of unit.

45° ANGLE BAY PLAN SECTION
scale: 1½" = 1'0"

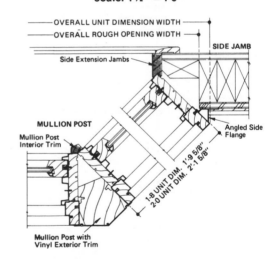

OVERALL UNIT DIMENSION WIDTH

OVERALL ROUGH OPENING WIDTH

Side Extension Jambs

SIDE JAMB

MULLION POST

Mullion Post Interior Trim

Angled Side Flange

1-8 UNIT DIM. 1'-9 5/8"
2-0 UNIT DIM. 2'-1 5/8"

Mullion Post with Vinyl Exterior Trim

DEGREE OF ANGLE	UNIT WIDTH NUMBER	PROJECTION
45°	1-8 Flankers	16 15/16"
45°	2-0 Flankers	19 9/16"

Bay window sizes and installation details. *Courtesy Andersen Corp.*

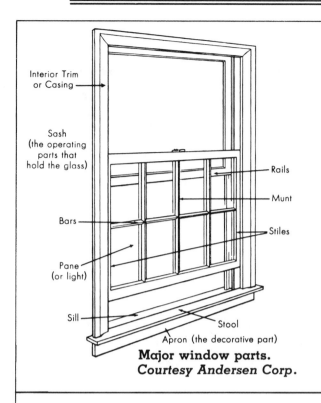

**Major window parts.
Courtesy Andersen Corp.**

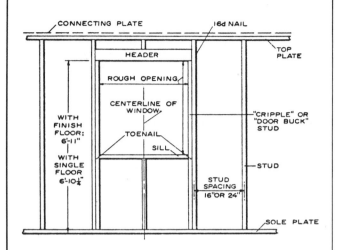

**Window framing details and opening
dimensions.**

*Frame opening sizes for double
hung windows*

Window glass size (each sash)		Rough frame opening size	
Width *Inches*	Height *Inches*	Width *Inches*	Height *Inches*
24	16	30	42
28	20	34	50
32	24	38	58
36	24	42	58

**Window trim. A. With stool and apron. B. Wood
casing of window. C. Metal casing of window.**

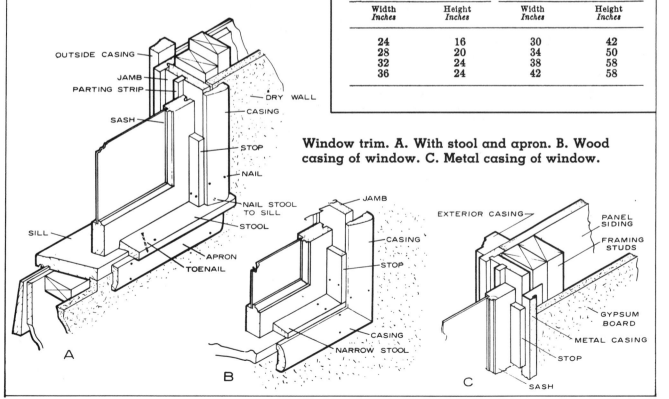

WOOD

Up until World War II, or thereabouts, wood was the most frequently used material for building homes and small commercial structures. Since that time concrete, in poured and block form, has surpassed wood as a building material. While the overall, quantitative use of wood has declined in relation to concrete, however, the number of forms into which wood is now fashioned has proliferated; so while it is now more likely that you can purchase wood in a form you can use with a minimum of fabrication, finding and selecting the wood product you want has become correspondingly complicated. There is now so much more from which to choose.

CONSIDERATIONS

When selecting wood there are many factors to consider: strength, workability, appearance, weather and wear resistance, finishing characteristics, dimensions, cost.

All these factors vary with specie, cutting method, seasoning, and post-seasoning treatment, if any.

HARDWOODS VS. SOFTWOODS

Trees divide into two categories. Hardwoods are trees having broad leaves that fall off with the coming of winter. They grow comparatively slowly. Softwood trees are conifers (evergreens). They have needlelike leaves that remain in place throughout the year. They grow comparatively quickly.

While wood characteristics vary tremendously with individual specie, you can generalize on the characteristics of the two broad categories of wood. The slow-growing hardwoods are denser, heavier, and harder than the softwoods. Some of the hardwoods are so heavy they will not float and you will have difficulty cutting them with a knife. Two beautiful examples are teak and ironwood. They burn better than the softwoods and produce more heat when burned. Generally the BTUs (heat output) of a burning log correspond in a direct ratio to its weight.

Hardwoods resist wear and weather better than most, but not all, softwoods. But there are exceptions. Locust and teak will not rot, but maple, a hardwood, will rot quickly in the presence of wet earth. Cedar, which is an easily split softwood, and cypress resist rot very well. Cedar shingles have been known to last for a century or more.

Most of the softwoods are pale in color, and while they do take paint well, they are unsuited to the clear finishes. The finish adheres well, but, because the wood is so soft, the finish is easily dented and cracked.

Most of the hardwoods have beautiful grain and color. Some are so hard and shiny that they need very little finishing. Some, like oak, have open pores that must be filled in order to provide a perfectly smooth supporting surface for the finish.

CUTTING

There are any number of ways in

which a log can be cut into boards. To secure a maxium quantity of boards, the log is simply sawn into a number of parallel slices. This makes for a flat grain. Such boards have a tendency to warp. A better method is to cut the log into quarters and then slice the quarters. These boards are called quartered. The grain crosses these boards at a slight angle. Still another method consists of cutting the boards so that the grain runs almost straight across the thickness of the board. This is called a rift cut and is used to "tame" wild grain. Wild grain occurs when a softwood such as fir is sawn so that its grain is flat— parallel with the width of the board. The grain tends to rise and form ridges and sometimes splinters. Cut rift, the grain remains in place. In this way it is possible to use comparatively cheap lumber such as fir and even yellow pine to make acceptable flooring.

SEASONING

This is the process of reducing the water content of wood. Depending on specie and time of year, the weight of a newly felled tree may be as much as two-thirds water. In this condition the wood is called green, and green lumber is almost useless for the ordinary purposes for which wood is used. Green lumber is difficult to cut and saw, it holds nails poorly, and sometimes water will squirt out when you drive a nail into it. Green lumber shrinks and warps and has a much greater tendency to rot than the same specie when it has been properly seasoned.

Seasoning can be accomplished in a few months simply by exposing the rough-sawn planks to the air; it can

be done in a few days with the aid of a kiln, which is basically a giant oven.

Properly seasoned lumber has a moisture content of some 12 to 18 percent. It is lighter than green lumber and also much stronger. It is more easily cut and otherwise shaped when seasoned and it also holds nails much more tightly. (But even properly seasoned lumber may warp and even shrink a little, sometimes as much as 2 percent.)

If you purchase your lumber from a local yard, you need not worry about seasoning: All commercial lumber is seasoned. It is only when you purchase lumber directly from a small mill that you have to check on its moisture content. Small mills depend on air drying, and air drying can vary with the weather.

NOTE: Excessive drying can also cause problems, because the wood is drier and, therefore, smaller than normal. When the applied wood absorbs moisture from the air it swells and causes trouble. This is a problem limited mainly to flooring. Therefore, it's advisable to let any bundles of flooring you'll be using remain in the room a few days before you lay them. During this period the wood will stabilize, absorbing or losing just enough moisture to balance with the moisture content of the air, and any dimensional changes following application of the flooring will be minimized.

COMMON SOFTWOODS

WHITE PINE

This wood weighs 25 pounds per cubic foot. It is soft, comparatively weak, easily worked. It takes nails and screws very well, has good stability, and holds glue and paint well. It is used mainly for millwork, shelving, and inexpensive furniture. Though pine takes finish very well, it is so soft it doesn't support the finish; therefore the finish is easily marred and chipped.

White pine is generally available in four grades:

Clear—completely knot-free; scarce and expensive

Number 1—some very small, tight knots

Number 2—a number of medium-sized, tight knots

Number 3—sometimes called shelving; large loose knots

NOTE: To hide the knots, cover them with shellac prior to painting. Otherwise they will "bleed" through.

YELLOW PINE
Hard and strong, this wood weighs 38 pounds per cubic foot. It is difficult to cut, tends to split, and has prominent, raised or wild grain. Glue holds it fairly well, but it takes nails and screws poorly. It is used mainly for house construction.

POPLAR
This is a soft, weak wood, excellent for glueing and nailing; very stable dimensionally. Since it is a fast-growing wood and comparatively inexpensive, it is being used increasingly in building construction. However, most building codes insist that roughly 20 percent more lumber be used when poplar is used in place of fir. NOTE: It neither weathers nor resists rotting very well. It weighs only 29 pounds per cubic foot, and takes paint and other finishes very poorly.

FIR
This is a hard, strong, comparatively heavy wood weighing 41 pounds per cubic foot. It is dimensionally very stable, and when rift cut can be used for flooring and even trim. Flat cut, its grain rises visibly. It's used mainly for house construction, takes nails and screws well, but cannot be easily shaped, as it tends to split.

CEDAR
This is a soft, light, red-colored wood (there is also a white cedar). It weighs 24 pounds per cubic foot and it resists rot very well. Since it is easily split it is used mainly for shingles. It's also used as a liner for closets and hope chests, because its resinous fragrance reputedly keeps the moths away.

REDWOOD
A soft, moderately strong, light-weight wood weighing 29 pounds per cubic foot, it takes nails and glue very well. Redwood is easily cut but not easily shaped because it tends to split; not as readily as cedar but much more readily than white pine. Moderately scarce and expensive, it is used mainly for outdoor furniture, decks, and similar construction, since it is highly resistant to rot. It is (obviously) red in color, and since it doesn't need protection against the weather it's rarely painted.

CYPRESS
This is another soft, moderately strong, lightweight wood that weighs 29 pounds per cubic foot and takes nails and glue very well. Its color is a beautiful red-brown and it is often used for wall covering without paint or varnish. The boards cut from the

outer surface of the tree are called pecky cypress. They are marked by indentations and holes, some of which may be as large as 1 inch across and which may pierce the board all the way through.

COMMON HARDWOODS

BEECH
Weiging 39 pounds per cubic foot, this is a hard, moderately strong, light-colored wood that takes neither glue nor nails well. It is not the wood of first choice for turning and otherwise shaping. It is beautiful, however, and is often used as a top-surface veneer for plywood.

BIRCH
Also light in color and beautiful when properly finished, this wood weighs 40 pounds per cubic foot, takes glue a little better than beech, accepts nails well, and is excellent for turning and carving and other forms of shaping. It is often used in solid form for furniture and railings.

BUTTERNUT
A soft, weak wood, light in color, weighing only 25 pounds per cubic foot, it takes stain beautifully and is often used to imitate the much more expensive walnut.

HICKORY
One of the hardest, strongest, and densest woods of North America, it weighs 42 pounds per cubic foot. Light in color, ash was one of the most popular woods of days gone by for first choice for handles, wheels, etc. It doesn't take nails too well, but it can be glued without problem.

ASH
Light in color, ash was one of the most popular woods of days gone by for making tools and building wagons and wagon wheels. Moderately strong and weighing 35 pounds per cubic foot, it takes nails well and can be shaped, but not easily. It is tougher than its density would make it appear and hard to work with hand tools.

OAK
Red oak is pale red to brown in color, is cheaper than white oak, weighs 39 pounds per square foot. White oak weighs 40 pounds per square foot. Both woods are hard and strong, and are weather- and wear-resistant. Both take nails, paint, and other finishes very well; white oak is easily shaped, while red responds poorly to shaping. Red is more easily split. Both types of oak have open pores, which means the wood must be treated with a filler before it is varnished, and both are excellent for furniture.

MAHOGANY
There are many mahoganys, some light in color, some red, some dark brown. All are excellent for furniture-making, as they can be easily shaped, take paint and stain well, and are dimensionally very stable. On the average mahogany weighs 35 pounds per cubic foot, is medium-hard and strong, and can be very solidly glued.

MAHOGANY, PHILIPPINE
Actually, this is Luan, a comparatively soft, light wood of reddish color. It has coarse grain and partially open pores. It weighs 33 pounds

per cubic foot and is often passed off as real mahogany and is used mainly as a veneer on plywood.

WALNUT

This is the best and by far the most beautiful native American furniture wood. Light to dark brown in color, it is equal in every way to mahogany. Unfortunately, it is scarcer and even more expensive than true mahogany. So valuable have these trees become that they are sometimes stolen from people's front lawns.

FANCY HARDWOODS

As things work out in much of life, the hardest, most beautiful woods are the scarcest and the most expensive. You will not find them at ordinary lumberyards and do-it-yourself shops. You can find them by asking at the yards, looking in the phone book under exotic lumber and the like, and by reading through the various crafts magazines. Many of these fancy hardwood specialists sell through mail order.

PRESSURE-PRESERVATIVE-TREATED LUMBER

Over the past twenty years the construction industry has developed and put to use an all-weather wood-foundation system (AWWF) of materials and construction that eliminates the need for a concrete foundation beneath a residential building or similar structure.

Very simply, the basement or crawl space is excavated, leveled, and covered with a layer of crushed stone or gravel several inches thick. Then stud walls are erected resting on a 2-×-8-inch or wider board. Plywood is nailed to the studs, and covered with a plastic vapor barrier; then the excavation is backfilled.

At present more than 27,000 buildings have been erected this way without problems and with the approval of many government agencies, lending agencies, and local building departments.

The lumber and plywood used for such construction must be specially treated. The treated wood must extend 6 or 8 inches above grade and only type 304 or 316 stainless steel fasteners can be used with it. All lumber should be treated before it is cut, but if cutting is necessary, the cut ends can be treated at the building site.

The lumber used must be treated according to the American Wood Preservers Bureau. The plywood must be American Plywood Association (APA) grade-trademarked C-D or better.

For more information write the American Wood Preservers Bureau, P.O. Box 6085, Arlington, Virginia 22206, or the American Plywood Association, P.O. Box 11700, Tacoma, Washington 98411.

DIMENSIONS

Originally trees were sawn into boards at the mill and sold that way to the local carpenter and cabinetmaker. Today, the only way you can secure rough-sawn lumber is either to go directly to the mill yourself or to special order it from a lumberyard. The wood commonly used to build structures and cabinets is planed—made smooth—before it is sold at the lumberyard or do-it-yourself shop. This has caused some confusion in the sizing of wood, making it necessary to develop a sizing system with both nominal dimensions and true or actual dimensions.

Originally, a piece of wood designated as a 2 × 4, meaning it had a cross section of 2 inches by 4 inches, really was that size or close enough to it so it did not matter. Today a 2 × 4 is actually 1⅝ inches by 3⅝ inches in cross section. Two by four is its nominal designation, and the smaller figures are its actual dimensions.

The loss of ⅜ of an inch in two directions in all wood ranging from a nominal 2 × 3 to 4 × 14 is normal throughout the industry. The wood is lost when the rough-sawn boards are made smooth. (Just why the boards must be made smooth is a question many people have asked.)

Wood nominally designed as 1-inch thick is close to ¾ inch thick. The same holds true for its width. Some thinner pieces of wood are much closer to their nominal dimensions, but the actual figure may vary from mill to mill. If you want a piece of wood to be exactly 1 inch or 1½ inches thick, you must special order it. Few yards stock anything but standard-dimension lumber, meaning lumber in widths and thicknesses as produced by the mill.

NOMENCLATURE

If you are polite you will get what you want even if you ask for a piece of wood "this big," and demonstrate the size with your hands. But you will save a lot of time—both yours and the yardman's—if you ask for the wood you want by its correct name.

• Boards. Lumber less than 2 inches thick and at least 8 inches wide is called a board.

• Strip. This is any board less than 8 inches wide.

• Dimension Lumber. This is lumber more than 2 inches thick but less than 5 inches thick, any width. It's usually designated as 2 by 3, 4, 5, 6, 8, 10, 12, and 14; 3 × 3, 4, and so on.

• Timber. All lumber that is more than 4 × 4 in cross section is called timber.

• Balk Timber. All lumber more than 8 × 8 in cross section is called balk timber.

ORDERING

Since an order for various types and sizes of lumber can involve a lot of numbers, a standard ordering system has evolved through the years. If you follow this system you will avoid errors and ending up with the wrong materials: *Designate the material first, the dimensions second, the number of pieces last.*

For example: construction grade fir, 2 × 4s, each 8 feet long, 23 pieces. (Not: 23, 8-foot, 2 × 4s, construction-grade fir.)

PRICING

Lumber is sold by the *nominal* board foot. A board foot is a board 1 foot wide, 1 foot long, and 1 inch thick. Thus a 1 × 12, 8 feet long is charged as 8 board feet, although the board is only 11⅝ inches wide and ¾ inch thick. A 3 × 12 that is 10 feet long works out to 30 board feet.

To find the board feet in any piece of lumber, multiply its thickness in inches by its width in inches by its length in inches, and then divide by 144.

Example: We have a 3×8, 12 feet long.

$$\frac{3 \times 8 \times 144\ (12\ \text{feet} \times 12\ \text{inches})}{144}$$

= 24 board feet

CATCH NUMBER 2

The first catch is that you pay by the nominal dimensions of the lumber you purchase. The second catch is that because the boards are smaller than their nominal dimensions you need more than you may think. For example, you want to build a 10-×-10-foot frame and cover it with 2-inch boards. It would seem that you could accomplish this very neatly with 60 boards, each 10 feet long. But it doesn't work out this way, since each board is only 1¾ inches wide. Thus you need 68.57 boards, meaning you will have to purchase 69 boards and cut one lengthwise.

CATCH NUMBER 3

The lengths of construction boards and lumber available begin at 6 feet and increase in even 2-foot multiples. This is convenient for most construction work. However, if you plan to use pieces of wood less than 6 feet long, you must take into consideration the wood that will be lost during cutting. This will be at least ⅛ of an inch to each cut, and more likely ¼ of an inch when a power saw is used. Thus you cannot cut any board into exact, even multiples of its length. For example, if you try to cut a 12-foot board into six 2-foot lengths, the last piece, the sixth piece, will be at least ⅝ of an inch short and even as much as 1¼ inches short—something to

bear in mind when designing a wood structure.

BUYING WOOD

If you take the time and trouble to follow these buying suggestions you will undoubtedly save enough money to make the extra effort worth your time.

LUMBERYARDS VS. DO-IT-YOURSELF SHOPS

To some extent these two sources of supply are competitive. But generally, you will do better at the yard. They do, of course, deal with professional builders, but they will charge the small purchaser no more than they will charge their professional accounts. Generally they are farther out of town and have fewer salespeople, which tends to lower their prices. At the same time they do not have the time or the patience to "fuss" with a customer. You have to know pretty much what you want when you buy at a yard.

The do-it-yourself shops often go through a delivery of lumber, and separate the cleaner, better pieces from the rest; they tend to call these boards select and charge more for them. A lumberyard will let you do your own selection, if you're careful not to knock the piles down.

Yards usually include delivery with their prices, if the load is so big you cannot possibly cart it home by yourself. Do-it-yourself shops often charge extra for delivery. Yards will often give you the courtesy of an end-of-the-month bill; shops will rarely extend credit.

Yards will do some cutting to size

for free. Do-it-yourself shops usually charge for every cut.

Yards will bid on big jobs. You can show them your building plan and receive a flat bid for all the lumber. (They usually charge for the bid.) In this way you can get the best total price in the area. If you are able to purchase the millwork directly from the mill, you can save even more money, as the markup on millwork is far greater than the markup on yard lumber.

SELECTION

If you are constructing a building and you need 2 × 4s, you order 2 × 4s of the proper length and grade. Some of the lumber will be perfect, some near perfect, and a few pieces will be badly knotted and warped. This is par for the course. However, when you are going to use more than a couple of dozen pieces of lumber, chances are that you will have to cut a number of them; thus, there will be no real waste.

If you need just a couple of boards, you want them to be sound and straight. In such cases you have a right to refuse defective lumber, and not pay a premium for so-called select lumber. Loose knots are, of course, obvious, as are bad warpages. To find slight warpages, you have to sight down the length of the board. Warped boards and timbers can be used if they are to be fastened in such a way that the board is straightened. But note that a free-standing board such as a fence rail or handrail that is warped will not straighten out in time; it will remain warped. Do not accept a warped

board unless you are charged only for the straight portion of the board.

AGED LUMBER

Untreated wood that is exposed to the weather develops a light gray patina. This in no way weakens the board or reduces its ability to hold paint. If the board has rested on the ground, however, and has developed some black spots, rot has set in. The damaged areas must be cut away and discarded. If rot has permeated much of the wood, then, to be safe, the entire piece should be discarded.

USED LUMBER

The trouble with used lumber is that it is full of nails. Even if you or the seller pull all the nails in sight, there is always a good chance that your saw will encounter a nail, which means the saw has to be sharpened or the power blade discarded. Lumber strength remains high over long periods of time, and unless the wood has rotted, used lumber still retains most of its strength. Of course, if you are planning on making a violin from the lumber, the older it is the better.

GRADES

Many species of wood and building products are manufactured in grades. Generally the top grade is merely the best-looking grade, or considered to be the best-looking grade. For example, number 1 oak flooring has no knots, number 2 has some, and number 3 has even more. There is nothing wrong with knots; in fact many people believe that the knots make the floor look more attractive. The knotty flooring is the least expensive.

In the case of choosing between building grades of framing timbers, you would have to determine whether or not the additional lumber you might require in the lower grade would offset the savings in cost. In such cases going to a lower grade might not result in a savings.

JOIST AND RAFTER SELECTION GUIDE

Figures are based on the use of number 2 lumber with a Modulus of Elasticity (E) of 800,000, which is a relatively weak wood. To make certain you are not overdesigning and wasting money, check with your building department as to the dimensions of the wood that may be available to you.

FLOOR JOISTS

Forty psi, residential loading, joists spaced 16 inches on center, diagonally braced every 6 feet or less.

MAXIMUM SPANS

2 × 6	8'–0"	3 × 6	13'–0"
2 × 8	10'–7"	3 × 8	17'–8"
2 × 10	13'–6"	3 × 10	22'–3"
2 × 12	15'–0"	3 × 12	24'–8"

ROOF RAFTERS

Fifteen psi dead load, plus 20 psi live load (snow, etc.). Compute on the basis of rafter span. (See table)

MAXIMUM RAFTER SPANS

2 × 6	9'–0"
2 × 8	13'–0"
2 × 10	16'–0"
2 × 12	20'–0"

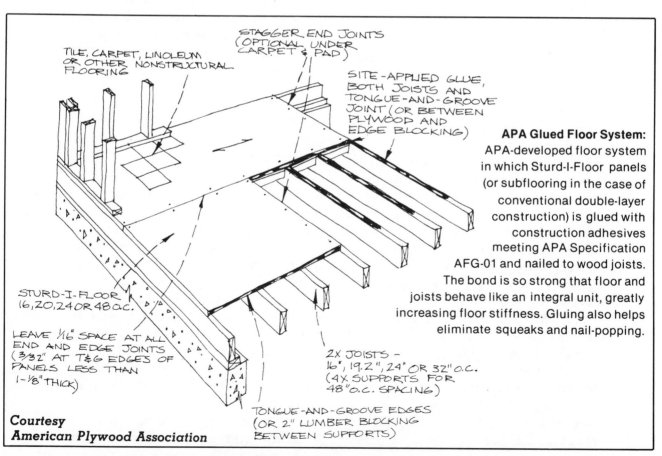

STAGGER END JOINTS (OPTIONAL UNDER CARPET & PAD)

TILE, CARPET, LINOLEUM OR OTHER NONSTRUCTURAL FLOORING

SITE-APPLIED GLUE, BOTH JOISTS AND TONGUE-AND-GROOVE JOINT (OR BETWEEN PLYWOOD AND EDGE BLOCKING)

STURD-I-FLOOR 16, 20, 24 OR 48 o.c.

LEAVE 1/16" SPACE AT ALL END AND EDGE JOINTS (3/32" AT T&G EDGES OF PANELS LESS THAN 1-1/8" THICK)

2X JOISTS – 16", 19.2", 24" OR 32" O.C. (4X SUPPORTS FOR 48" O.C. SPACING)

TONGUE-AND-GROOVE EDGES (OR 2" LUMBER BLOCKING BETWEEN SUPPORTS)

APA Glued Floor System: APA-developed floor system in which Sturd-I-Floor panels (or subflooring in the case of conventional double-layer construction) is glued with construction adhesives meeting APA Specification AFG-01 and nailed to wood joists. The bond is so strong that floor and joists behave like an integral unit, greatly increasing floor stiffness. Gluing also helps eliminate squeaks and nail-popping.

Courtesy
American Plywood Association

WORKING PROPERTIES OF COMMON WOODS

Name of Wood	Weight Per Cubic Foot (1)	Hardness	Strength (2)	Stability (3)	Gluing	Nailing (4)	Steam Bending	Planing and Jointing (5)	Turning (6)	Sanding (7)	Shaping	Mortising (8)	Remarks
Ash	35	Med.	Med.	Best	Fair	Good	Good	Good 10-25	Fair	Best 2/0	Best	Fair	Tough—Hard to work with hand tools
Basswood	24	Soft	Weak	Good	Best	Best	Poor	Good 20-30	Poor	Poor 4/0	Poor	Fair	Excellent for toys, drafting boards, corestock
Beech	39	Hard	Med.	Poor	Poor	Poor	Good	Fair 10-20	Fair	Good 4/0	Fair	Best	Not durable outside. Hard on tools because of mineral deposits in cells
Birch	40	Hard	Strong	Good	Fair	Poor	Good	Good 15-20	Good	Fair 4/0	Best	Best	Excellent for furniture, turning, dowels, handles
Butternut	25	Soft	Weak	Best	Good	Fair	Poor	Good 10-25	Good	Fair 4/0	Fair	Fair	Furniture—Perfect for walnut imitation
Cherry	36	Med.	Med.	Good	Best	Fair	Poor	Best 10-25	Best	Best 4/0	Best	Best	Furniture, boat trim, novelties
Chestnut	27	Soft	Weak	Best	Best	Good	Fair	Good 15-20	Best	Best 3/0	Good	Good	Stains badly in contact with wet iron. Very dusty in all machining operations
Cottonwood	27	Soft	Weak	Fair	Best	Best	Poor	Poor 5-20	Poor	Poor 4/0	Poor	Fair	Excellent for boxes and other nailing jobs. Wears very well for a soft wood
Cypress	29	Soft	Med.	Good	Fair	Fair	Poor	Good 15-25	Fair	Fair 2 0	Poor	Poor	Tends to splinter. Most durable of American woods for outdoor and soil exposure
Elm (Southern)	34	Med.	Med.	Poor	Fair	Best	Good	Poor 15-20	Poor	Good 2 0	Poor	Good	Very durable under paint. A good furniture wood despite difficulties in machining
Gum (Red)	33	Med.	Med.	Poor	Best	Good	Fair	Fair 10-20	Best	Fair 4/0	Fair	Fair	One of the most used furniture woods for imitations of walnut and mahogany
Hickory	42	Hard	Strong	Good	Good	Poor	Good	Good 10-25	Good	Best 2/0	Fair	Best	Excellent for furniture and long a favorite for steam bending, tool handles, wheels
Magnolia	30	Soft	Weak	Fair	Best	Best	Best	Good 5-15	Fair	Good 4/0	Good	Poor	Excellent for steam bending, although little used as such. Often marketed as poplar
Mahogany	35	Med.	Med.	Best	Best	Good	Poor	Good 5-25	Best	Good 4/0	Best	Best	One of the best furniture woods
Mahogany (Phil.)	33	Med.	Med.	Best	Best	Good	Poor	Good 5-25	Good	Poor 3/0	Fair	Fair	Generally coarser and softer than true mahogany. Furniture, boat planking, trim
(9) Maple (Hard)	41	Hard	Strong	Good	Fair	Poor	Fair	Fair 15-20	Good	Good 4/0	Best	Best	Fine furniture, flooring, turnings, bowling pins. One of the best hardwoods
Maple (Soft)	31	Med.	Med.	Fair	Good	Fair	Fair	Poor 10-15	Fair	Good 4/0	Fair	Good	Same uses as hard maple but an inferior wood. Difficult to machine smooth
Oak (Red)	39	Hard	Strong	Best	Good	Good	Best	Best 10-25	Good	Best 2/0	Fair	Best	Substitute for white oak in cheaper work
Oak (White)	40	Hard	Strong	Best	Good	Good	Best	Best 10-20	Good	Best 2 0	Good	Best	Interior trim, floors, furniture. One of the most used American woods
Pine (White)	25	Soft	Weak	Good	Best	Best	Poor	Good 10-25	Good	Fair 2 0	Good	Fair	Best all around soft wood. Excellent for paint
Pine (Yellow)	38	Hard	Strong	Fair	Fair	Poor	Poor	Good 10-25	Poor	Fair 2 0	Good	Good	Main uses: House construction, trim, floors
Poplar	29	Soft	Weak	Good	Best	Best	Fair	Good 5-20	Good	Poor 4 0	Poor	Fair	Excellent for carvings, toys, corestock
Redwood	29	Soft	Med.	Best	Best	Good	Poor	Good 10-25	Fair	Poor 2 0	Good	Poor	Excellent for outdoor furniture, window sills, etc
Sycamore	35	Med.	Med.	Poor	Good	Best	Poor	Poor 5-15	Good	Poor 3 0	Poor	Best	Interior trim, furniture. Difficult to machine, but excellent appearance
Walnut	36	Med.	Strong	Best	Best	Fair	Good	Good 15-20	Best	Best 4 0	Good	Best	Has every good feature for furniture and cabinet work

NOTES

Data in this chart is largely from extensive tests made by U. S. Forest Products Laboratory, with some additions.

1. Pounds per cubic foot, dry. All woods vary in weight, even in the same tree from trunk to top. A variation of 10% over or under average should be allowed.
2. Composite strength value. Woods rated weak are strong enough for all average work.
3. Rated on unrestrained warp. Most woods are quite stable if properly seasoned and cared for.
4. Rated on ability to take nails near end without splitting.
5. All flat grain stock, shallow cut. Rating is average from runs at 15, 20 and 25-degree cutting angles. Bottom figure is best knife angle for smooth cutting.
6. Rated on smooth cutting and ability to hold detail. Not much difference between best and good.
7. Rated on freedom from fuzz. Bottom figure is coarsest abrasive grit which can be used without scratching.
8. Rated on smoothness of cut. Work speed decreases with hardness of wood and this factor might be of more importance than smoothness in production work.
9. Sugar, white or hard maple. Should be distinguished from silver, red, big-leaf or soft maple, which is an inferior machining wood although often marketed simply as "maple."

STANDARD SIZES OF LUMBER

TYPE OF LUMBER	NOMINAL SIZE (in inches)		ACTUAL SIZE S4S AT COMM. DRY SHP. WT. (in Inches)		TYPE OF LUMBER	NOMINAL SIZE (in inches)		ACTUAL SIZE S4S AT COMM. DRY SHP. WT. (in Inches)	
	Thickness	Width	Thickness	Width		Thickness	Width	Thickness	Width
Dimension	2	4	1⅝	3⅝	Shiplap Boards	1	4	25/32	* 3⅛
	2	6	1⅝	5⅝		1	6	25/32	* 5⅛
	2	8	1⅝	7½		1	8	25/32	* 7⅛
	2	10	1⅝	9½		1	10	25/32	* 9⅛
	2	12	1⅝	11½		1	12	25/32	*11⅛
Timbers	4	6	3⅝	5½	Tongued and Grooved Boards	1	4	25/32	* 3¼
	4	8	3⅝	7½		1	6	25/32	* 5¼
	4	10	3⅝	9½		1	8	25/32	* 7¼
	6	6	5½	5½		1	10	25/32	* 9¼
	6	8	5½	7½		1	12	25/32	*11¼
	6	10	5½	9½					
	8	8	7½	7½					
	8	10	7½	9½					
Common Boards	1	4	25/32	3⅝					
	1	6	25/32	5⅝					
	1	8	25/32	7½					
	1	10	25/32	9½					
	1	12	25/32	11½					

*—Width at face   *Courtesy Weyerhaeuser Sales Co.*

Board Feet

Nominal size (in.)	Actual length in feet								
	8	10	12	14	16	18	20	22	24
1 x 2		1 2/3	2	2 1/3	2 2/3	3	3 1/2	3 2/3	4
1 x 3		2 1/2	3	3 1/2	4	4 1/2	5	5 1/2	6
1 x 4	2 3/4	3 1/3	4	4 2/3	5 1/3	6	6 2/3	7 1/3	8
1 x 5		4 1/6	5	5 5/6	6 2/3	7 1/2	8 1/3	9 1/6	10
1 x 6	4	5	6	7	8	9	10	11	12
1 x 7		5 5/8	7	8 1/6	9 1/3	10 1/2	11 2/3	12 5/6	14
1 x 8	5 1/3	6 2/3	8	9 1/3	10 2/3	12	13 1/3	14 2/3	16
1 x 10	6 2/3	8 1/3	10	11 2/3	13 1/3	15	16 2/3	18 1/3	20
1 x 12	8	10	12	14	16	18	20	22	24
1 1/4 x 4		4 1/6	5	5 5/6	6 2/3	7 1/2	8 1/3	9 1/6	10
1 1/4 x 6		6 1/4	7 1/2	8 3/4	10	11 1/4	12 1/2	13 3/4	15
1 1/4 x 8		8 1/3	10	11 2/3	13 1/3	15	16 2/3	18 1/3	20
1 1/4 x 10		10 5/12	12 1/2	14 7/12	16 2/3	18 3/4	20 5/6	22 11/12	25
1 1/4 x 12		12 1/2	15	17 1/2	20	22 1/2	25	27 1/2	30
1 1/2 x 4	4	5	6	7	8	9	10	11	12
1 1/2 x 6	6	7 1/2	9	10 1/2	12	13 1/2	15	16 1/2	18
1 1/2 x 8	8	10	12	14	16	18	20	22	24
1 1/2 x 10	10	12 1/2	15	17 1/2	20	22 1/2	25	27 1/2	30
1 1/2 x 12	12	15	18	21	24	27	30	33	36
2 x 4	5 1/3	6 2/3	8	9 1/3	10 1/3	12	13 1/3	14 2/3	16
2 x 6	8	10	12	14	16	18	20	22	24
2 x 8	10 2/3	13 1/3	16	18 2/3	21 1/3	24	26 2/3	29 1/3	32
2 x 10	13 1/3	16 2/3	20	23 1/3	26 2/3	30	33 1/3	36 2/3	40
2 x 12	16	20	24	28	32	36	40	44	48
3 x 6	12	15	18	21	24	27	30	33	36
3 x 8	16	20	24	28	32	36	40	44	48
3 x 10	20	25	30	35	40	45	50	55	60
3 x 12	24	30	36	42	48	54	60	66	72
4 x 4	10 2/3	13 1/3	16	18 2/3	21 1/3	24	26 2/3	29 1/3	32
4 x 6	16	20	24	28	32	36	40	44	48
4 x 8	21 1/3	26 2/3	32	37 1/3	42 2/3	48	53 1/3	58 2/3	64
4 x 10	26 2/3	33 1/3	40	46 2/3	53 1/3	60	66 2/3	73 1/3	80
4 x 12	32	40	48	56	64	72	80	88	96

Floor Joists

DOUGLAS FIR—COAST REGION

Nominal size (inches)	Spacing (inches o. c.)	Association Lumber Grades									
		Select Structural	Dense Construction	Construction	Standard	Utility	Select Structural	Dense Construction	Construction	Standard	Utility
		1950 f	1700 f	1450 f	1200 f	(1)	1950 f	1700 f	1450 f	1200 f	(1)
		30 LB. LIVE LOAD					40 LB. LIVE LOAD				
		Ft. In.	Ft. In.	Ft. In.	Ft. In.	Ft. In.	Ft. In.	Ft. In.	Ft. In.	Ft. In.	Ft. In.
2 x 6	12	11 4	11 4	11 4	11 4	8 4	10 6	10 6	10 6	10 6	7 4
	16	10 4	10 4	10 4	10 4	7 2	9 8	9 8	9 8	9 8	6 4
	24	9 0	9 0	9 0	9 0	5 10	8 4	8 4	8 4	8 2	5 2
2 x 8	12	15 4	15 4	15 4	15 4	12 4	14 4	14 4	14 4	14 4	11 0
	16	14 0	14 0	14 0	14 0	10 8	13 0	13 0	13 0	13 0	9 6
	24	12 4	12 4	12 4	12 4	8 8	11 6	11 6	11 6	11 0	7 10
2 x 10	12	18 4	18 4	18 4	18 4	16 10	17 4	17 4	17 4	17 4	15 2
	16	17 0	17 0	17 0	17 0	14 8	16 2	16 2	16 2	16 2	13 0
	24	15 6	15 6	15 6	15 6	12 0	14 6	14 6	14 6	14 0	10 8
2 x 12	12	21 2	21 2	21 2	21 2	19 8	20 0	20 0	20 0	20 0	17 8
	16	19 8	19 8	19 8	19 8	17 0	18 8	18 8	18 8	18 8	15 4
	24	17 10	17 10	17 10	17 10	14 0	16 10	16 10	16 10	16 10	12 6

1 Denotes grade is not a stress grade.

SOUTHERN YELLOW PINE—MEDIUM GRAIN

Nominal size (inches)	Spacing (inches o. c.)	Association Lumber Grades							
		No. 1 Dense K. D. 2" Dimension	No. 2 Dense K. D. 2" Dimension	No. 1 Dense 2" Dimension	No. 2 Dense 2" Dimension	No. 1 Dense K. D. 2" Dimension	No. 2 Dense K. D. 2" Dimension	No. 1 Dense 2" Dimension	No. 2 Dense 2" Dimension
		1700 f	1500 f	1450 f	1200 f	1700 f	1200 f	1450 f	1200 f
		30 LB. LIVE LOAD				40 LB. LIVE LOAD			
		Ft. In.	Ft. In.	Ft. In.	Ft. In.	Ft. In.	Ft. In.	Ft. In.	Ft. In.
2 x 6[1]	12	11 4	11 4	11 4	11 4	10 6	10 6	10 6	10 6
	16	10 4	10 4	10 4	10 4	9 8	9 8	9 8	9 8
	24	9 0	9 0	9 0	9 0	8 4	8 4	8 4	8 2
2 x 8	12	15 4	15 4	15 4	15 4	14 4	14 4	14 4	14 4
	16	14 0	14 0	14 0	14 0	13 0	13 0	13 0	13 0
	24	12 4	12 4	12 4	12 4	11 6	11 6	11 6	11 0
2 x 10	12	18 4	18 4	18 4	18 4	17 4	17 4	17 4	17 4
	16	17 0	17 0	17 0	17 0	16 2	16 2	16 2	16 2
	24	15 6	15 6	15 6	15 6	14 6	14 6	14 6	14 0
2 x 12	12	21 2	21 2	21 2	21 2	20 0	20 0	20 0	20 0
	16	19 8	19 8	19 8	19 8	18 8	18 8	18 8	18 8
	24	17 10	17 10	17 10	17 10	16 10	16 10	16 10	16 10

1 Spans for 2"x6" lumber having actual dressed size of 1⅝"x5⅝" may be increased 2½ percent.

Notes: (a) Spans may be increased 5 percent from those shown for rough lumber or lumber surfaced two edges (S2E).

(b) Spans shall be decreased 5 percent from those shown for lumber more than 2 percent but not more than 5 percent scant from American Lumber Standards sizes measured at a moisture content of 19 percent or less. Lumber scant more than 5 percent will not be acceptable.

Table of floor joist sizes and their spans.

Ceiling Joists

DOUGLAS FIR, COAST REGION—ASSOCIATION LUMBER GRADES

Nominal size (inches)	Spacing (inches o. c.)	Select Structural 1950 f		Dense Construction 1700 f		Construction 1450 f		Standard 1200 f		Utility (¹)		Select Structural 1950 f		Dense Construction 1700 f		Construction 1450 f		Standard 1200 f		Utility (¹)	
		NO ATTIC STORAGE										LIMITED ATTIC STORAGE									
2 x 4²	12	11	10	..	..	11	8	8	10	..	..	9	6	..	..	8	2	6	4	..	..
	16	10	10	..	..	10	0	7	8	..	..	8	6	..	..	7	2	5	6	..	..
	24	9	6	..	..	8	2	6	4	..	..	7	6	..	..	5	10	4	6	..	..
2 x 6	12	17	2	17	2	17	2	17	2	13	6	14	4	14	4	14	4	14	4	9	6
	16	16	0	16	0	16	0	16	0	11	8	13	0	13	0	13	0	12	10	8	4
	24	14	4	14	4	14	4	14	4	9	6	11	4	11	4	11	4	10	6	6	8
2 x 8	12	21	8	21	8	21	8	21	8	20	2	18	4	18	4	18	4	18	4	14	4
	16	20	2	20	2	20	2	20	2	17	6	17	0	17	0	17	0	17	0	12	4
	24	18	4	18	4	18	4	18	4	14	4	15	4	15	4	15	4	14	4	10	0
2 x 10	12	24	0	24	0	24	0	24	0	24	0	21	10	21	10	21	10	21	10	19	6
	16	24	0	24	0	24	0	24	0	22	6	20	4	20	4	20	4	20	4	16	10
	24	21	10	21	10	21	10	21	10	19	6	18	4	18	4	18	4	18	0	13	10

¹ Denotes grade is not a stress grade.
² Denotes light framing grade. (Not Industrial Light Framing)
Notes:
(a) Spans may be increased 5 percent from those shown for rough lumber or lumber surfaced two edges (S2E).

(b) Spans shall be decreased 5 percent from those shown for lumber more than 2 percent but not more than 5 percent scant from American Lumber Standards sizes measured at a moisture content of 19 percent or less. Lumber scant more than 5 percent will not be acceptable.

SOUTHERN YELLOW PINE—(MEDIUM GRAIN)—ASSOCIATION LUMBER GRADES

Nominal size (inches)	Spacing (inches o. c.)	No. 1 K. D. 2″ Dimension 1700 f		No. 2 K. D. 2″ Dimension 1500 f		No. 1 2″ Dimension 1450 f		No. 2 2″ Dimension 1200 f		No. 1 K. D. 2″ Dimension 1700 f		No. 2 K. D. 2″ Dimension 1500 f		No. 1 2″ Dimension 1450 f		No. 2 2″ Dimension 1200 f	
		NO ATTIC STORAGE								LIMITED ATTIC STORAGE							
2 x 4	12	11	10	11	10	11	10	11	10	9	6	9	6	9	6	9	6
	16	10	10	10	10	10	10	10	10	8	6	8	6	8	6	8	6
	24	9	6	9	6	9	6	9	6	7	6	7	6	7	6	6	10
2 x 6¹	12	17	2	17	2	17	2	17	2	14	4	14	4	14	4	14	4
	16	16	0	16	0	16	0	16	0	13	0	13	0	13	0	12	10
	24	14	4	14	4	14	4	14	4	11	4	11	4	11	4	10	6
2 x 8	12	21	8	21	8	21	8	21	8	18	4	18	4	18	4	18	4
	16	20	2	20	2	20	2	20	2	17	0	17	0	17	0	17	0
	24	18	4	18	4	18	4	18	4	15	4	15	4	15	4	14	4
2 x 10	12	24	0	24	0	24	0	24	0	21	10	21	10	21	10	21	10
	16	24	0	24	0	24	0	24	0	20	4	20	4	20	4	20	4
	24	21	10	21	10	21	10	21	10	18	4	18	4	18	4	18	0

¹ Spans for 2″x6″ lumber having actual dressed size of 1⅝″x5⅝″ may be increased 2½ percent.
Notes: (a) Spans may be increased 5 percent from those shown for rough lumber or lumber surfaced two edges (S2E).

(b) Spans shall be decreased 5 percent from those shown for lumber more than 2 percent but not more than 5 percent scant from American Lumber Standards sizes measured at a moisture content of 19 percent or less. Lumber scant more than 5 percent will not be acceptable.

Ceiling joist sizes and spacings

RAFTERS
(Roof Slope over 3 in 12)
DOUGLAS FIR—COAST REGION—ASSOCIATION LUMBER GRADES

Nominal size (inches)	Spacing (inches o. c.)	Select Structural 1950 f		Dense Construction 1700 f		Construction 1405 f		Standard 1200 f		Utility (1)		Select Structural 1950 f		Dense Construction 1700 f		Construction 1450 f		Standard 1200 f		Utility (1)	
		LIGHT ROOFING										**HEAVY ROOFING**									
2 x 4[2]	12	11	6	..	..	9	6	7	4	..	..	10	4	..	..	8	2	6	4	..	..
	16	10	6	..	..	8	4	6	4	..	..	9	6	..	..	7	2	5	6	..	..
	24	9	2	..	..	6	10	5	2	..	..	8	4	..	..	5	10	4	6	..	..
2 x 6	12	16	10	16	10	16	10	16	10	11	2	15	6	15	6	15	6	14	10	9	6
	16	15	8	15	8	15	8	15	0	9	8	14	4	14	4	14	0	12	10	8	4
	24	13	10	13	10	13	6	12	2	7	10	12	6	12	6	11	6	10	6	6	8
2 x 8	12	21	2	21	2	21	2	21	2	16	8	19	8	19	8	19	8	19	8	14	4
	16	19	10	19	10	19	10	19	10	14	4	18	4	18	4	18	4	17	6	12	4
	24	17	10	17	10	17	10	16	8	11	10	16	6	16	6	15	8	14	4	10	0
2 x 10	12	24	0	24	0	24	0	24	0	22	10	23	6	23	6	23	6	23	6	19	6
	16	23	8	23	8	23	8	23	8	19	8	21	10	21	10	21	10	21	10	16	10
	24	21	4	21	4	21	4	21	0	16	2	19	8	19	8	19	8	18	0	13	10

[1] Denotes grade is not a stress grade.
[2] Denotes light framing grade. (Not Industrial Light Framing)
Notes:
(a) Spans may be increased 5 percent from those shown for rough lumber or lumber surfaced two edges (S2E).

(b) Spans shall be decreased 5 percent from those shown for lumber more than 2 percent but not more than 5 percent scant from American Lumber Standards sizes measured at a moisture content of 19 percent or less. Lumber scant more than 5 percent will not be acceptable.

(Roof slope over 3 in 12)
SOUTHERN YELLOW PINE—MEDIUM GRAIN—ASSOCIATION LUMBER GRADES

Nominal size (inches)	Spacing (inches o.c.)	No. 1 K. D. 2" Dimension 1700 f		No. 2 K. D. 2" Dimension 1500 f		No. 1 2" Dimension 1450 f		No. 2 2" Dimension 1200 f		No. 1 K. D. 2" Dimension 1700 f		No. 2 K. D. 2" Dimension 1500 f		No. 1 2" Dimension 1450 f		No. 2 2" Dimension 1200 f	
		LIGHT ROOFING								**HEAVY ROOFING**							
2 x 4	12	11	6	11	6	11	6	11	4	10	4	10	4	10	4	9	8
	16	10	6	10	6	10	6	9	10	9	6	9	6	9	4	8	6
	24	9	2	9	0	8	10	8	0	8	2	7	8	7	6	6	10
2 x 6[1]	12	16	10	16	10	16	10	16	10	15	6	15	6	15	6	14	10
	16	15	8	15	8	15	8	15	0	14	4	14	4	14	0	12	10
	24	13	10	13	8	13	4	12	2	12	6	11	8	11	6	10	6
2 x 8	12	21	2	21	2	21	2	21	2	19	8	19	8	19	8	19	8
	16	19	10	19	10	19	10	19	10	18	4	18	4	18	4	17	6
	24	17	10	17	10	17	10	16	8	16	6	16	0	15	8	14	4
2 x 10	12	24	0	24	0	24	0	24	0	23	6	23	6	23	6	23	6
	16	23	8	23	8	23	8	23	8	21	10	21	10	21	10	21	10
	24	21	4	21	4	21	4	21	0	19	8	19	8	19	8	18	0

[1] Spans for 2"x6" lumber having actual dressed size of 1⅝"x5⅝" may be increased 2½ percent.
Notes: (a) Spans may be increased 5 percent from those shown for rough lumber or lumber surfaced two edges (S2E).

(b) Spans shall be decreased 5 percent from those shown for lumber more than 2 percent but not more than 5 percent scant from American Lumber Standards sizes measured at a moisture content of 19 percent or less. Lumber scant more than 5 percent will not be acceptable.

Rafter sizes and spacings.

CONVERSION DIAGRAM FOR RAFTERS

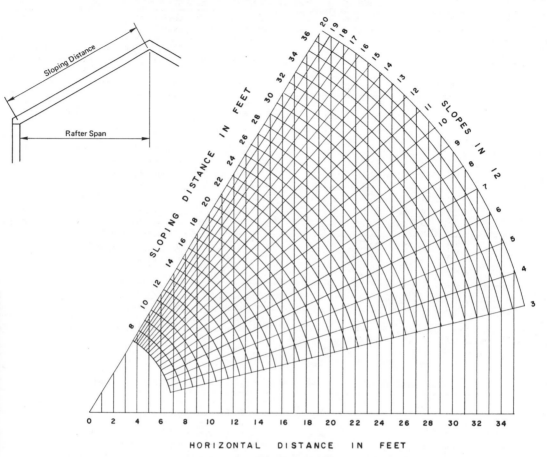

To use the diagram select the known horizontal distance and follow the vertical line to its intersection with the radial line of the specified slope, then proceed along the arc to read the sloping distance. In some cases it may be desirable to interpolate between the one foot separations. The diagram also may be used to find the horizontal distance corresponding to a given sloping distance or to find the slope when the horizontal and sloping distances are known.

Example: With a roof slope of 8 in 12 and a horizontal distance of 20 feet the sloping distance may be read as 24 feet.

Courtesy National Forest Products Association

C-D
32/16 (APA)
INTERIOR
PS 1-74 000
EXTERIOR GLUE
Typical APA Grade-Trademark

Rapid Calculation of Board Measure.

Width	Thickness	Board feet
3″	1″ or less	1/4 of the length
4″	1″ or less	1/3 of the length
6″	1″ or less	1/2 of the length
9″	1″ or less	3/4 of the length
12″	1″ or less	Same as the length
15″	1″ or less	1 1/4 of the length

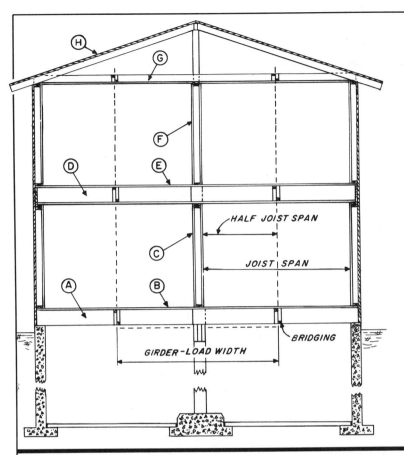

(A) DEAD LOAD OF FIRST FLOOR = 10 LBS PER SQ FT. DEAD LOAD OF FIRST FLOOR WITH BASEMENT CEILING PLASTERED = 20 LBS PER SQ FT.

(B) LIVE LOAD ON FIRST FLOOR = 40 LBS PER SQ FT UNLESS OTHERWISE SPECIFIED BY LOCAL BUILDING CODE REQUIREMENTS.

(C) DEAD LOAD OF PARTITIONS = 10 LBS PER SQ FT UNLESS OTHERWISE SPECIFIED.

(D) DEAD LOAD ON SECOND FLOOR = 20 LBS PER SQ FT.

(E) LIVE LOAD ON SECOND FLOOR = 40 LBS PER SQ FT UNLESS OTHERWISE SPECIFIED BY LOCAL BUILDING CODE REQUIREMENTS.

(F) DEAD LOAD OF PARTITIONS = 10 LBS PER SQ FT UNLESS OTHERWISE SPECIFIED.

(G) LIVE LOAD ON ATTIC FLOOR = 20 LBS PER SQ FT WHEN USED FOR STORAGE ONLY. DEAD LOAD OF ATTIC FLOOR NOT FLOORED = 10 LBS PER SQ FT. DEAD LOAD OF ATTIC FLOOR WHEN FLOORED = 20 LBS PER SQ FT WHEN USED FOR STORAGE ONLY.

(H) ROOF OF LIGHT CONSTRUCTION, INCLUDING BOTH LIVE AND DEAD LOADS = 20 LBS PER SQ FT. ROOF OF MEDIUM CONSTRUCTION WITH LIGHT SLATE OR ASBESTOS ROOFING, INCLUDING BOTH LIVE AND DEAD LOADS = 30 LBS PER SQ FT. ROOF OF HEAVY CONSTRUCTION WITH HEAVY SLATE OR TILE ROOFING, INCLUDING BOTH LIVE AND DEAD LOADS = 40 LBS PER SQ FT. NOTE: LOCAL BUILDING CODE REQUIREMENTS SHOULD BE CONSULTED AS THEY MAY SPECIFY OTHER MINIMUM LOAD VALUES.

LOAD PER LINEAR FOOT OF GIRDER	LENGTH OF SPAN				
	6'-0''	7'-0''	8'-0''	9'-0''	10'-0''
	NOMINAL SIZE OF GIRDER REQUIRED				
750	6x8 in.	6x8 in.	6x8 in.	6x10 in.	6x10 in.
900	6x8	6x8	6x10	6x10	8x10
1050	6x8	6x10	8x10	8x10	8x12
1200	6x10	8x10	8x10	8x10	8x12
1350	6x10	8x10	8x10	8x12	10x12
1500	8x10	8x10	8x12	10x12	10x12
1650	8x10	8x12	10x12	10x12	10x14
1800	8x10	8x12	10x12	10x12	10x14
1950	8x12	10x12	10x12	10x14	12x14
2100	8x12	10x12	10x14	12x14	12x14
2250	10x12	10x12	10x14	12x14	12x14
2400	10x12	10x14	10x14	12x14	
2550	10x12	10x14	12x14	12x14	
2700	10x12	10x14	12x14		
2850	10x14	12x14	12x14		
3000	10x14	12x14			
3150	10x14	12x14			
3300	12x14	12x14			

Sizes of built-up wood girders for various loads and spans based on Douglas Fir 4-Square Guide—Line Framing deflection not over 1/360 of span—allowable fiber stress 1,600 lbs. per sq. in.

The 6-in. girder is figured as being made with three pieces 2 in. dressed to 1-5/8 in. thickness.

The 8-in. girder is figured as being made with four pieces 2 in. dressed to 1-5/8 in. thickness.

The 10-in. girder is figured as being made with five pieces 2-in. dressed to 1-5/8 in. thickness.

The 12-in. girder is figured as being made with six pieces 2 in. dressed to 1-5/8 in. thickness.

Note—For solid girders multiply above loads by 1.130 when 6-inch girder is used; 1.150 when 8-in. girder is used; 1.170 when 10-in. girder is used and 1.180 when 12-in. girder is used.

Courtesy American Plywood Association

APPENDIX

Should you require information about a particular type or brand of material, the following compendium of manufacturers, manufacturing associations, and selected distributors will lead you to it. The list is arranged alphabetically by the type of material.

ADHESIVES

Adhesives Manufacturers
  Association
One Illinois Center
111 East Wacker Drive
Chicago, IL 60601

Arrow Adhesive Co.
5457 Spalding Drive, Building A
Norcross, GA 30071

Borden, Inc.
Dept. CP
Columbus, OH 43215

H. B. Fuller Co.
315 South Hicks Road
Palatine, IL 60067

Loctite
999 N. Mountain Road
Newington, CT 06111

BLOCK—CONCRETE

Art Stone Cement Co., Inc.
120 Old Boston Road
Wilbraham, MA 01095

Kissam Builders Supply Co.
Box 7819
Orlando, FL 32854

Lockstone Corp.
161 Forbes Road
P.O. Box 921
Braintree, MA 02184

Maier, Inc.
4700 Annapolis Road
Bladensburg, MD 20710

National Concrete Masonry
  Association
2302 Horse Pen Road

P.O. Box 781
Herndon, VA 22070

North American Stone Co.
2 Charlton Avenue
Suite 720
Toronto, Canada M5B 1J3

Plasticrete Block
  and Supply Co.
99 Stoddard Avenue
North Haven, CT 06473

BRICK

Babcock and Wilcox
P.O. Box 1126
Wall Street Station
New York, NY 10017

Brick Institute of America
1750 Old Meadow Road
MacLean, VA 22102

Frame Brick and Tile Co.
705 Quintard Avenue
Annistone, AL 36202

Reliance Clay Products Co.
9995 Monroe
P.O. Box 20237
Dallas, TX 75220

St. Louis Brick Co.
1338 South Kingshighway
St. Louis, MO 63110

Stark Ceramics, Inc.
584 West Church Street
Canton, OH 44730

Structural Clay
  Products Institute
1520 18th Street, N.W.
Washington, DC 20036

CABINETS

Ampco Products, Inc.
7797 West 20th Avenue
Hialeah, FL 33014

Gamble Bros., Inc.
4666 Almond Avenue
Louisville, KY 40209

Haas Cabinet Co.
625 West Utica Street
Sellersburg, IN 47172

Kroh-Wagner, Inc.
2335 North Pulaski Road
Chicago, IL 60639

National Kitchen Cabinet
  Association
136 St. Matthews Avenue
Louisville, KY 40207

Nierborg Co.
200 Lexington Avenue
New York, NY 10016

Samson Roll-Formed
  Products Co.
1816 North Lorel Avenue
Chicago, IL 60639

CAULK

H. B. Fuller Co.
315 South Hicks Road
Palatine, IL 60067

Glouster Co., Inc.
235 Cottage Street
Franklin, MA 02036

Goodyear Tire and Rubber Co.
Chemical Division
P.O. Box 9115
Akron, OH

Johns-Manville Corp.
Ken-Caryl Ranch
Denver, CO 80217

Lake Chemical Co.
270 North Washington Avenue
Chicago, IL 60612

Weather Guard/Marbleloid
  Prod., Inc.
2515 Newbold Avenue
Bronx, NY 10462

Fred. A. Wilson Co.
Box 7-TRA
Lathrup Village, MI 48076

CEMENT

Ash Grove Cement Co.
1000 Ten Main Center and High
Kansas City, MO 64105

Atlas Minerals and
  Chemicals Co.
121 Norman Street
Mertztown, PA 19539

Lone Star Industries, Inc.
1 Greenwich Plaza
Greenwich, CT 06830

Marten Marietta Cement
Cross Keys
2 Hamilton Road
Baltimore, MD 21220

Peerless Cement Co.
933 Dearborn Street
Detroit, MI 48209

Portland Cement Association
5420 Old Orchard Road
Skokie, IL 60077

Portland Cement Co. of Utah
615 West Eighth Street
Salt Lake City, UT 84110

CONCRETE

American Concrete Institute
Box 19150
22400 West Seven Mile Road
Detroit, MI 45219

National Concrete Masonry
  Association
2302 Horse Pen Road
P.O. Box 781
Herndon, VA 22070

DOORS

Andersen Corp.
Bayport, MN 55003

Door and Hardware Institute
1815 N. Fort Myer Drive
Arlington, VA 22209

Eggers Hardware Products Co.
164 North Lake Street
Neenah, WI 55121

C. E. Morgan, Inc.
523 Oregon Street
Oshkosh, WI 54903

Overhead Door Corp.
P.O. Box 222285
6250 LBJ Freeway
Dallas, TX 75222

Pella Windows and Doors
Rollscreen Co.
Pella, IA 50219

Raynor Manufacturing Co.
East River Road
Dixon, IL 61021

Rowe Manufacturing Co.
614 West Third Street
Galesburg, IL 61401

ELECTRICAL

Daburn Electronics and
  Cable Corp.
70 Oak Street
Norwood, NJ 07648

Gilbert Manufacturing Co.
45-20 Astoria Blvd.
Long Island City, NY 11103

Hubbell Electric Corp.
State Street
Bridgeport, CT 06602

Leviton Manufacturing Co., Inc.

59-25 Little Neck Parkway
Little Neck, NY 11362

Nutone Corp.
Madison and Red Bank Roads
Cincinnati, OH 45227

Tivoli Industries, Inc.
1513 East Street
Gertrude Place
P.O. Box 11523
Santa Ana, CA 92711

Trimtrac Lighting Corp.
1001 N.W. 159th Drive
Miami, FL 33169

FASTENERS

American Screw
Third and Marshall Streets
Wytheville, VA 24382

D.R.I. Industries, Inc.
6864 Washington Avenue, South
Eden Prairie, MN 55344

Eaton Corp.
Dept. 16 AE
P.O. Box 6688
Cleveland, OH 44101

Jacobson Manufacturing Co.
Box J
Kenilworth, NJ 07033

Mil-Spec Fastener Corp.
450 West McNab Road
Fort Lauderdale, FL 33309

P & R Fasteners, Inc.
897 South Avenue
Middlesex, NJ 08846

United Bolt and Screw Co., Inc.
Capital Drive
Moonochie, NJ 07074

FIBERBOARD

Aetna Plywood, Inc.
1733 North Elston Avenue
Chicago, IL 60622

Georgia-Pacific Corp.
900 S.W. Fifth Avenue
Portland, OR 97204

Grand Rapids Fabricators
200 Graham S.W. at Viaduct
Grand Rapids, MI 49503

Grillian Corp.
191 First Street
Brooklyn, NY 11215

Louisiana-Pacific Corp.
1300 S.W. Fifth Street
Portland, OR 97201

Masonite Corp.
29 North Wacker Drive
Chicago, IL 60606

FLOORING—RESILIENT

A-1 Plastic Moulders, Inc.
618 West Bradley Avenue
El Cajon, CA 92020

Armstrong World Industries, Inc.
P.O. Box 3001
Lancaster, PA 17604

Art-Craft Inc.
Box 318
Berlin, WI 54923

Artcrest Products, Inc.
403 West Ontario Street
Chicago, IL 60610

Congoleum Nair, Inc.
195 Belgrove Drive
Kearny, NJ 07032

Goodyear Tire and Rubber Co.
P.O. Box 9154
Akron, OH 44305

Kentile Floors, Inc.
58 Second Avenue
Brooklyn, NY 11215

Vinyl Plastics, Inc.
3123 South 9th Street
Sheboygan, WI 53081

FLOORING—SEAMLESS

Dur-A-Flex, Inc.
102 Meadow Street
Norwalk, CT 66114

Flecto Company, Inc.

1000-02 45th Street
Oakland, CA 94608

General Polymers, Inc.
2923 Houston Avenue
Cincinnati, OH 45212

Hill Brothers Chemical Co.
15017 East Clark Street
City of Industry, CA 91745

Masonite Corp.
29 West Wacker Drive
Chicago, IL 60606

Weatherguard/Marbleloid
Products, Inc.
2515 Newbold Avenue
Bronx, NY 10462

FLOORING—WOOD

Blue Ridge Flooring Co.
Huges Road
Darlington, MD 21034

Emerson Hardwood Co.
2279 N.W. Front Street
Portland, OR 97209

Kentucky Wood Floors, Inc.
7761 National Turnpike
Louisville, KY 40214

Maple Flooring Manufacturing
Association
2400 East Devon Avenue
Des Plains, IL 60018

National Oak Flooring
Manufacturers Association
804 Sterick Blvd.
Memphis, TN 38103

Riverside Millwork Company,
Inc.
77 Merrimack Street
Penacock, NH 03301

Wood and Synthetic Flooring
Institute
400 East Devon Avenue
Des Plains, IL 60018

FRAMING HARDWARE

Simpson Co.

1450 Doolittle Drive
P.O. Box 1568
San Leandro, CA 94577

Truss Plate Institute
2400 East Devon Avenue
Des Plains, IL 60018

GLASS

Cherry Creek Enterprises, Inc.
937 Santa Fe Drive
Denver, CO 80204

Columbia Glass and Plate
Works
329 North Pulaski Road
Chicago, IL 60624

Dureco Corp.
204 Commercial Street
Boston, MA 02109

International Glass Creations,
Inc.
425 Shatto Place
Los Angeles, CA 90020

Johns-Manville Corp.
Ken-Caryl Ranch
Denver, CO 80217

Libbey-Owens-Ford Co.
811 Madison Avenue
Toledo, OH 43695

Owens-Corning Fiberglas Corp.
Fiberglas Tower
Toledo, OH 43659

PPG Industries, Inc.
One Gateway Center
Pittsburgh, PA 15222

Western Insulated Glass Co.
1021 North Black Canyon
Phoenix, AZ 85009

GYPSUM BOARD

American Gypsum Co.
Box 6345 Station B
Albuquerque, NM 87101

Flintkote Co.
480 Central Avenue
East Rutherford, NJ 07073

Georgia-Pacific Corp.
900 S.W. Fifth Avenue
Portland, OR 97204

Kaiser Cement and Gypsum Co.
300 Lakeside Drive
Oakland, CA 94666

National Gypsum Co.
Gold Bond Building
2001 Rexford Road
Charlotte, NC 28211

U.S. Gypsum Co.
101 South Wacker Drive
Chicago, IL 60606

C. A. Wagner Co., Inc.
4459 North Sixth Street
Philadelphia, PA 19140

HARDBOARD

Conwed Corp.
332 Minnesota Street
Box 43237
St. Paul, MN 55113

Georgia-Pacific Corp.
900 S.W. Fifth Avenue
Portland, OR 97204

Kaiser Cement and Gypsum Co.
300 Lakeside Drive
Oakland, CA 94666

Bill Koehler Co.
Box 95
Hanover, PA 17331

Masonite Corp.
80 Newfield Avenue
Raritan Center
Edison, NJ 08817

Monoco Corp.
1517 College Avenue S.E.
Grand Rapids, MI 49507

New England Hardboard Co.
83 Fremont Street
Worcester, MA 01603

N.Y. Hardboard and Plywood
  Corp.
129-30 Street
Brooklyn, NY 11232

HARDWARE

Albert Constantine and Son
2050 Eastchester Road
Bronx, NY 10461

Builders Hardware
  Manufacturers Association
60 East 42nd Street
New York, NY 10017

Door and Hardware Institute
1815 North Fort Myer Drive
Arlington, VA 22209

Ferum Hardware, Inc.
53 Stiles Lane
P.O. Box 698
Pine Brook, NJ 07050

Ideal Security Hardware Corp.
215 E. North Street
St. Paul, MN 55101

Stanley Hardware
New Britain, CT 06050

INSULATION

Dow Chemical Co.
2020 Dow Center
Midland, MI 48640

Electra Manufacturing Corp.
1133 S. McCord Road
P.O. Box 306
Holland, OH 43528

Frelen Corp.
74 Salem Road
North Billerica, MA 01862

Georgia-Pacific Corp.
900 S.W. Fifth Avenue
Portland, OR 97204

Johns-Manville
Ken-Caryl Ranch
Denver, CO 80217

Pittsburgh Corning
800 Presque Isle Drive
Pittsburgh, PA 15239

LAMINATES

Capital Industrial Fabricators

5331 South Danisher Road
Countryside, IL 60653

Chicago Hardboard Supply Co.,
  Inc.
3131 West 36th Street
Chicago, IL 60632

Chicago Steel Rule, Die
  and Fabricator Co.
6228 West Wrightwood Avenue
Chicago, IL 60635

Design Products Fabricators,
  Inc.
Box 265 D
Clymer, PA 15728

Mallyclad Corp.
31303 Mally Road
Madison Heights, MI 48071

Westvaco Corp.
502 Valley View Blvd.
Altoona, PA 16602

LEADERS & GUTTERS

Alcan Building Products
Box 511
Warren, OH 44481

Ball Metal and Chemical
  Division Ball Corp.
Greenville, TN 37743

Bendix Corp.
300 South Clausen Bldg.
16000 West Nine Mile Road
Southfield, MI 48075

Capital Industrial Fabricators
5331 South Danisher Road
Countryside, IL 60652

Guttermakers, Inc.
444 West Laskey Road
Toledo, OH 43612

Howmet Aluminum Co.
Box 4515
Lancaster, PA 17604

Kaiser Building Products Co.
5119 Enterprise Blvd.
Toledo, OH 43612

Lifeguard Industries
4460 West Mitchell Avenue
Cincinnati, OH 45232

Revere Aluminum Building
Products
45 Gilpin Avenue
Hauppauge, NY 11787

LOCKS

All-Lock Co., Inc.
460 Barell Avenue
Carlstadt, NJ 07072

Best Lock Corp.
P.O. Box 103
Indianapolis, IN 46206

Chicago Lock Co.
4269 West Belmont Street
Chicago, IL 60641

Corbin Lock Co.
Hardware Division
Emhart Industries
Berlin, CT 06037

Eberhard Manufacturing Co.
21942 Drake Road
Cleveland, OH 44136

Hudson Lock Co.
79 Apsley Street
Hudson, MA 01749

Schlage Lock Co.
2401 Bayside Blvd.
San Francisco, CA 94119

METAL

A B C Metal Supply
7081 Consolidated Way
San Diego, CA 92121

The Aluminum Association
818 Connecticut Avenue, N.W.
Washington, DC 20006

Components and Materials
Division
E. Fagan, Inc.
35 Whitney Road
Mahwah, NJ 07430

Copper Development
Association
405 Lexington Avenue
New York, NY 10017

Jacob Brothers
1240 Seaview Avenue
Bridgeport, CT 06607

National Steel Corp.
2800 Grant Building
Pittsburgh, PA 15219

Pancoast International Corp.
3-5 Park Row
New York, NY 10038

Revere Copper and Brass
605 Third Avenue
New York, NY 10016

MILLWORK

Bogert and Hopper, Inc.
23 West John Street
Hicksville, NY 11801

F. A. Edmunds and Co., Inc.
6109 Sayre Avenue
Chicago, IL 60638

Industrial Wood Products
P.O. Box 907
Elkhart, IN 46515

R. A. Mair and Sons, Inc.
Tomley and Goffle Roads
Wykoff, NJ 07481

H. A. Stiles Co.
150 Jennings Street
Westbrook, MA 04092

Strombeck Manufacturing Co.
51st Street and Fourth Avenue
Moline, IL 61265

R. P. Wakefield
Maple and Pine Streets
Waterloo, IN 46793

MORTAR See CEMENT

PAINT & SHELLAC & VARNISH

Bee Chemical Co.

2701 East 170th Street
Lansing, IL 60438

Coddington Manufacturing Co.
5054 North 37th Street
Milwaukee, WI 53209

Colton Coatings and Chemicals
Corp.
P.O. Box 825
Colton, CA 92324

Crown Industrial Products, Inc.
50 State Line Road
Hebron, IL 60034

Devo & Raynolds Co., Inc.
Louisville, KY 40207

Dutch Boy, Inc.
500-A Central Avenue
Northfield, IL 60093

Glidden Corp.
900 Union Commerce Tower
Cleveland, OH 44115

Guardsman Chemical Co., Inc.
1350 Steel Avenue S.W.
Grand Rapids, MI 49507

Harrison Paint Corp.
1929 Harrison Avenue S.W.
Canton, OH 44708

National Paint and Coatings
Association
1500 Rhode Island Avenue N.W.
Washington, DC 20005

PARTICLE BOARD

Aetna Plywood, Inc.
1733 North Elston Avenue
Chicago, IL 60622

Amer-Ply Corp.
123 Dowd Avenue
Elizabeth, NJ 07206

Artile Industries, Inc.
P.O. Box 160
Monroe, OH 45050

Grand Rapids Fabricators
200 Graham Street S.W. at
Viaduct
Grand Rapids, MI 49503

Louisiana-Pacific Corp.
1300 S.W. Fifth Street
Portland, OR 97201

National Particleboard
Association
2306 Perkins Place
Silver Springs, MD 20910

New York Hardboard and
Plywood Corp.
129-30th Street
Brooklyn, NY 11232

Reo Industries
633-5 Third Street N.W.
Massilon, OH 44646

PLASTICS

American Acrylics
4868 N. Clark Street
Chicago, IL 60640

Brandywine Fiber Products
1465 Poplar Street
Wilmington, DE 19801

Colonial Kolonite Co.
2232 West Armitage Avenue
Chicago, IL 60647

Kaufman Glass Co.
1301-1 Northern Blvd.
Wilmington, DE 19899

Modern Plastics and Glass, Inc.
61-63 Cedar Avenue
East Greenwich, RI 02818

Runnel Filter Co.
82 Progress Street
Union, NJ 07183

The Society of the Plastics
Industry, Inc.
355 Lexington Avenue
New York, NY 10017

USI Chemicals
99 Park Avenue
New York, NY 10016

PLUMBING

American Standard
33 Circle Drive
North Piscataway, NJ 08854

Bradley, Faucet Division
P.O. Box 348
Menomonee Falls, WI 53051

Crane
300 Park Avenue
New York, NY 10022

Fernco
300 South Dayton Street
Davison, MI 48423

L.C.P. Plastics, Inc.
861 North Lishon Street
P.O. Box 217
Carrolton, OH 44515

Mansfield Plumbing Products
Perrysville, OH 44864

Owens-Corning Fiberglas Corp.
Fiberglas Tower
Toledo, OH 43659

The Society of the Plastics
Industry, Inc.
355 Lexington Avenue
New York, NY 10017

PLYWOOD

Aetna Plywood, Inc.
1733 North Elston Avenue
Chicago, IL 60633

Amer-Ply Corp.
123 Dowd Avenue
Elizabeth, NJ 07206

American Plywood Association
P.O. Box 11700
Tacoma, WA 98411

Conwed Corp.
322 Minnesota Street
P.O. Box 43237
St. Paul, MN 55113

Georgia-Pacific Corp.
900 S.W. Fifth Avenue
Portland, OR 97204

Bill Koehler Co.
Box 95
Hanover, PA 17331

Louisiana-Pacific Corp.
1300 S.W. Fifth Street

Portland, OR 97204

N.Y. Hardboard and Plywood
Corp.
129-30th Street
Brooklyn, NY 11232

PUTTY

Atlas Minerals and Chemicals,
Inc.
121 Norman Street
Mertztown, PA 19539

Biggs Co.
612 E. Franklin Street
El Segundo, CA 90245

D. Durham Co.
P.O. Box 804
Des Moines, IA 50304

H. B. Fuller Co.
315 South Hicks Road
Palatine, IL 60067

Johns-Manville
Ken-Caryl Ranch
Denver, CO 80217

Lake Chemical Co.
270 North Washtenaw Avenue
Chicago, IL 60612

Marquette Industrial Materials
Co.
P.O. Box 3421
392 E. Lake Street
Peoria, IL 61614

Mobile Paint Co.
P.O. Box 717
Theodore, AL 36590

United States Plastic Corp.
1384 Neubrecht Avenue
Lima, OH 45801

RE-SIDING

Alcan Building Products
Box 511
Warran, OH 44481

The Aluminum Association
818 Connecticut Avenue, N.W.
Washington, DC 20006

Howmetal Aluminum Co.

P.O. Box 4515
Lancaster, PA 17604

Kaiser Building Products Co.
5119 Enterprise Blvd.
Toledo, OH 43612

Lifeguard Industries
4460 West Mitchell Avenue
Cincinnati, OH 45232

Republic Steel
1441 Republic Steel Building
Cleveland, OH 44101

Revere Aluminum Building
  Products
45 Gilpin Avenue
Hauppauge, NY 11787

The Society of the Plastics
  Industry, Inc.
355 Lexington Avenue
New York, NY 10017

ROOFING

Asphalt Roofing Manufacturers
  Association
750 Third Avenue
New York, NY 10017

GAF Corp.
140-A West 51st Street
New York, NY 10020

Gold Bond Building Products
2001 Rexford Road
Charlotte, NC 28211

Johns-Manville
Ken-Caryl Ranch
Denver, CO 80217

Owens-Corning Fiberglas Corp.
Residential Roof Division
Fiberglas Tower
Toledo, OH 43659

Penn Ventilator Co.
Gantry at Red Lion Roads
Philadelphia, PA 19115

F.A. Wilson Co.
Box 7 LV
27350 Southfield Road
Lathrup Village, MI 48076

SCREENING

Buffalo Wire Works Co., Inc.
P.O. Box 129
Buffalo, NY 14240

I.F.C. Industrial Fabrics Corp.
7208-B Boone Avenue North
Minneapolis, MN 55428

McNichols Wire Cloth Co.
5501 Grey Street
Tampa, FL 33609

Ron-Vik Co.
802 Columbus Avenue South
Minneapolis, MN 55416

Tetko, Inc.
422 Saw Mill River Road
Elmsford, NY 10523

Wire Cloth Manufacturers, Inc.
1330 Kings Road
Madison, NJ 07940

SHAKES & SHINGLES

Alliancewall Corp.
P.O. Box 48545
Atlanta, GA 30362

Celotex Corp.
1500 North Dale Mabry Highway
Tampa, FL 33607

Flintkote Co.
The Washington Plaza Building
1351 Washington Blvd.
Stamford, CT 06904

GAF Corp.
140-A West 51st Street
New York, NY 10020

Georgia-Pacific Corp.
900 S.W. Fifth Avenue
Portland, OR 97204

Gold Bond Building Products
2001 Rexford Road
Charlotte, NC 38311

Johns-Manville Corp.
Ken-Caryl Ranch
Denver, CO 80217

A. Wilbert & Sons Lumber
  and Shingle Co.

Plaquemine, LA 70764

SHEATHING

Blandin Wood Products
Box NR
Grand Rapids, MN 55744

Celotex Corp.
1500 North Dale Mabry Highway
Tampa, FL 33607

Champion Building Products
  Corp.
1 Landmark Square
Stamford, CT 06921

Flintkote Co.
The Washington Plaza Building
1351 Washington Blvd.
Stamford, CT 06904

GAF Corp.
140-A West 51st Street
New York, NY 10020

Georgia-Pacific Corp.
900 S.W. Fifth Avenue
Portland, OR 97204

Johns-Manville
Ken-Caryl Ranch
Denver, CO 80217

Louisiana-Pacific Corp.
1300 S.W. Fifth Street
Portland, OR 97201

SHINGLES—ASBESTOS
  CEMENT

GAF Corp.
140-A West 51st Street
New York, NY 10020

Gold Bond Building Products
2001 Rexford Road
Charlotte, NC 28211

Johns-Manville
Ken-Caryl Ranch
Denver, CO 80217

Lake Asbestos of Quebeck, Ltd.
120 Broadway
New York, NY 10014

Supardo Manufacturing Co., Inc.

122 East 42nd Street
New York, NY 10017

SIDING

Blandin Wood Products
Box 745
Thompson, GA 30824

Flintkote Co.
The Washington Plaza Building
1351 Washington Blvd.
Stamford, CT 06904

Forest Fiber Products Co.
Box 68
Forest Grove, OR 97116

GAF Corp.
140-A West 51st Street
New York, NY 10020

Georgia-Pacific Corp.
900 S.W. Fifth Avenue
Portland, OR 97204

Gold Bond Building Products
  Corp.
2001 Rexford Road
Charlotte, NC 38311

Hoover Universal, Inc.
Box 746
Thompson, GA 30824

STAIN

S. Cabot, Inc.
One Union Street, Dept. 1371
Boston, MA 02108

Cincinnati Varnish Co.
1778 Menter Avenue
Cincinnati, OH 45212

Flecto Co., Inc.
1000-02 45th Street
Oakland, CA 94608

Glidden, General Paint Division
1000 16th Street
San Francisco, CA 94107

Lilly Industrial Coatings, Inc.
666 South California Street
Indianapolis, IN 46225

Preservative Paint Co.

5410 Airport Way
Seattle, WA 98108

STAIRS

Duvinage Co., Inc.
P.O. Box 828
Hagerstown, MD 21740

Equipto Co., Inc.
227 Griffith Avenue
Aurora, IL 60507

Manis Metal Works, Inc.
P.O. Box 6280
Bridgeport, CT 06606

Marwin Co.
P.O. Box 9126
Columbia, SC 29290

Morton Manufacturing Co., Inc.
P.O. Box 640
Libertyville, IL 60048

Quick Flight Stair Co.
2030 Will Ross Court
Chamblee, GA 30341

Stairways, Inc.
4323-A Pinemount
Houston, TX 77018

STONE

Carthage Marble Co.
Box 718
Carthage, MO 64836

Feartherock, Inc.
2890 Empire Street
Burbank, CA 91510

Fond du Lac Stone Co.
Box 148
Fond du Lac, WI 54935

Indiana Limestone Co., Inc.
Box 72
Bedford, IN 47421

Johnston and Rhodes Bluestone
  Co.
East Branch, NY 13756

McCorkle Stone Co.
Route 1
Milroy, IN 46156

Stone Institute
420 Lexington Avenue
New York, NY 10017

Whiterock Quarries, Inc.
10 Noll Street
Bellefonte, PA 16823

TILE—CEILING

Armstrong World Industries, Inc.
P.O. Box 3001
Lancaster, PA 17604

Celotex Corp.
1500 North Dale Mabry Highway
Tampa, FL 33607

Cid Associates, Inc.
Box 10, Dept. 6
Allisan Park, PA 15101

Conwed Corp.
322 Minnesota Street
St. Paul, MN 55164

Flintkote Co.
The Washington Plaza Building
1351 Washington Blvd.
Stamford, CT 06904

Gold Bond Building Products
  Corp.
2001 Rexford Road
Charlotte, NC 38311

Johns-Manville
Ken-Caryl Ranch
Denver, CO 80217

Kaiser Cement and Gypsum Co.
300 Lakeside Drive
Oakland, CA 94666

TILE—CERAMIC

American Olean Tile Co.
Lansdale, PA 19446

Atlas Mineral and Chemical Co.
121 Norman Street
Mertztown, PA 19539

Erie Ceramic Arts Co.
Homer and 22nd Streets
Erie, PA 16505

Forms and Surfaces

Box 5215
Santa Barbara, CA 93108

Frame Brick and Tile Co.
705 Qunitard Avenue
Anniston, AL 36202

Monarch Tile Manufacturing Co.
Box 2041
San Angelo, TX 76901

Vikon Tile Corp.
130 North Taylor Street
Washington, NJ 07882

VENTILATION

Airmaster Fan Co.
150 West North Street
Jackson, MI 49202

Burt Manufacturing Co.
940 South Broadway Street
Akron, OH 44311

Cincinnati Fan and Ventilation
Co.
5317 Creek Road
Cincinnati, OH 45242

Franklin-Morgan Co.
P.O. Box 3992
Charlotte, NC 28203

Leslie-Locke Building Products
11550 West King Street
Franklin Park, IL 60131

Lomanco, Inc.
2101 West Main Street
Jacksonville, AR 72076

Moffitt Co., Inc.
P.O. Box 158
Zelienople, PA 16063

Penn Ventilation Co., Inc.
Gantry and Red Lion Roads
Philadelphia, PA 19115

Philip Industries, Inc.
843 Indianapolis Avenue
Lebanon, IN 46052

WINDOWS

Amerlite Aluminum Co.
Suite 1511-A
230 Park Avenue
New York, NY 10017

Andersen Corp.
Bayport, MN 55003

Bliss Steel Products
1948 Bliss Street
East Syracuse, NY 13057

Elgar Products, Inc.
P.O. Box 22348
Cleveland, OH 44122

Fiberlux Products, Inc.
59 South Terrance Avenue
Mount Vernon, NY 10550

C. E. Morgan
523 Oregon Street
Oshkosh, WI 50903

National Woodwork
Manufacturers Association
400 West Madison Street

Chicago, IL 60606

Pella Windows and Doors
100 Main Street
Pella, IA 50219

WOOD

American Forest Institute
1619 Massachusetts Avenue,
N.W.
Washington, DC 20036

N. Cohen Co.
1519 North 21st Street
Philadelphia, PA 19121

Constantine and Son
2500 Park Avenue
Bronx, NY 10451

Georgia-Pacific Corp.
900 S.W. Fifth Avenue
Portland, OR 97204

Germain Timber Co.
304 Center Avenue
Pittsburgh, PA 15215

Monteath Co.
2500 Park Avenue
Bronx, NY 10451

Potomack Supply Corp.
Box 800
Kinsale, VA 22488

R. P. Wakefield Co., Inc.
Maple and Pine Streets
Warerloos, IN 46793

INDEX